Refractions of Reality

Refractions of Reality

Philosophy and the Moving Image

John Mullarkey
University of Dundee

palgrave
macmillan

First published 2009 by
PALGRAVE MACMILLAN

Palgrave Macmillan in the UK is an imprint of Macmillan Publishers Limited, registered in England, company number 785998, of Houndmills, Basingstoke, Hampshire RG21 6XS.

Palgrave Macmillan in the US is a division of St Martin's Press LLC, 175 Fifth Avenue, New York, NY 10010.

Palgrave Macmillan is the global academic imprint of the above companies and has companies and representatives throughout the world.

Palgrave® and Macmillan® are registered trademarks in the United States, the United Kingdom, Europe and other countries.

ISBN-13: 978–0–230–00247–0
ISBN-10: 0–230–00247–1

This book is printed on paper suitable for recycling and made from fully managed and sustained forest sources. Logging, pulping and manufacturing processes are expected to conform to the environmental regulations of the country of origin.

A catalogue record for this book is available from the British Library.

Library of Congress Cataloging-in-Publication Data

Mullarkey, John.
Refractions of reality : philosophy and the moving image / John Mullarkey.
p. cm.
Includes bibliographical references (p.) and index.
ISBN 978–0–230–00247–0
1. Motion pictures – Philosophy. I. Title.

PN1995.M73 2009
791.4301—dc22 2008035183

10 9 8 7 6 5 4 3 2 1
18 17 16 15 14 13 12 11 10 09

Printed and bound in Great Britain by
CPI Antony Rowe, Chippenham and Eastbourne

Contents

Acknowledgements

This book is the fruition of two lives that have coexisted over the last seven years, one actual and philosophical, the other virtual and cinematic. Its philosophical gestation owes a vote of thanks to many, but especially to my colleagues at the University of Dundee (Beth Lord in particular). Its cinematic life was born when I had the privilege to be taught by my colleagues in film theory at the University of Sunderland, either when taking their classes or teaching alongside them: they include Susan Smith, Trish Winter, Sue Thornham, Deborah Thomas and Steve Cannon. I also want to acknowledge the film philosophers and theorists who have helped this book see the light of day: Andrew Benjamin, Paul Douglass, Daniel Frampton, Mark Bould, Mark Richardson, Nicole Hewitt, Jennifer Parker-Starbuck, Stephen Zepke, Miriam Baldwin, Suzanne Guerlac, Will Large, Anna Powell, David Deamer, David Martin-Jones as well as everyone at film-philosophy.com. Without the advice of Elie During and Barbara Muriel Kennedy, this would have been far lesser work. It is especially Edward Branigan's sage counsel that has had the largest impact, however, and as such I am truly grateful to him. In addition, I would like to thank those at Palgrave Macmillan who have helped this project along – Dan Bunyard and Priyanka Pathak, in particular, deserve my appreciation. The copy-editing and proofreading skills of Keith Povey and Nick Fox have improved the book greatly. Finally, any sophistication this text has when discussing anything contemporary in the arts is due to long conversations with Laura Cull, to whom I am always indebted, both for her tolerance and scholarship.

Earlier versions of some of the material from the Introduction, Chapter 4 and Chapter 7 appeared, respectively, in Mullarkey 2008a, 2008b, 2007a. I gratefully acknowledge permission to use this material. This project was supported by a research leave grant from the Arts and Humanities Research Council.

Preface: The Film-envy of Philosophy

> World is crazier and more of it than we think,
> Incorrigibly plural. I peel and portion
> A tangerine and spit the pips and feel
> The drunkenness of things being various.[1]

Who wants to be a philosopher anyway?

In the introduction to his own work on film and philosophy, *Reel Arguments*, Andrew Light makes an interesting confession: there have been times in his career when he wished he was a film-maker rather than a philosopher.[2] Let me also come out of this same closet with an even stronger declaration – I have always believed that it would be much more rewarding to make films than practise philosophy. Indeed, I have written philosophy books mostly in order to compensate for the fact that nobody would let me make films (I won't bore you with the details). Yet, my retreat to philosophy was not on account of some vague likeness with cinematic storytelling, but because both film and philosophy share a relation with something far grander: reality itself. On the one hand, film, like philosophy, has its double in reality: both can (though don't always) give us powerful depictions of reality, the one primarily through the use of words, the other principally through the visual medium. On the other hand, writing philosophy, especially philosophy with leanings towards metaphysics, is a bit like being a film director. Before the blank screen of the word processor, one has the power to create a reality of one's own, designating what goes where, which piece of information is relevant and which irrelevant, what will count as truth and what as mere appearance. Both practices involve god-like constructions, ones where a reality is constructed through artistic means; others where a world, though perhaps no less fictional, is constructed through thought. The obvious difference between these two activities, of course, is that, these days at least, few people are interested in the realities that philosophers create, whilst seemingly everyone is interested in those displayed through film.

It is a commonplace to say that each century has had its distinguishing art form, that it was poetry in the eighteenth century, the novel in the nineteenth and cinema in the twentieth. This poses the question as to which art form will be the one for our twenty-first century, and whether or not it will remain cinema, or at least some form of cinema. Before exploring this question, it is worth noting that the French philosopher Alain Badiou has typified both the art and philosophy of the twentieth century as propounding a 'passion for the Real'.[3] Certainly, what Allan Kaprow has described as twentieth-century art's 'fevered search for essences' (modernism's 'pure' forms of literature, sculpture and painting) evinced a passion that stands out as peculiarly philosophical for its era. Surely, however, it has always been philosophy's passion to have the power to capture reality in its thought: with a few (disingenuous) exceptions, its pleasure principle has constantly been reality and nothing less – even if only to say, from on-high, that we cannot know reality at all.[4] And in this ongoing obsession, philosophy found a strange rival in the one art form that, from the twentieth century onwards, struck it as singularly capable of such a power – film.

From such early theorists as André Bazin, who argued in the 1940s that cinema is the art of reality that captures 'the object itself... freed from the conditions of time and space that govern it', through to Siegfried Kracauer in the 1960s, who thought that film could redeem our impoverished perception of physical reality, or Gene Youngblood in 1970, who saw in cinema the possibility of an 'expanded consciousness' that would save our beleaguered world, right up to contemporary philosophers like Stanley Cavell, Jean-Luc Nancy and Colin McGinn, who recognize in the movies an 'indisputable' power over our understanding of reality, a 'ubiquitous' power to 'take in everything' – there have always been thinkers whose overtures to film have been avowedly *metaphysical*.[5] And now, moreover, this passion is being regenerated in the plethora of books and courses currently appearing on film and philosophy (many of which use cinema as a new means of teaching the oldest discipline). In the last hundred years or so, evidently, philosophy's perennial passion for the real has transformed into a film-envy in many quarters.

And yet this envy, as is often the case with such emotions, is not unambivalent. If we 'armchair' philosophers are compelled to consume films from the cinema seat rather than create them from the director's chair, then we can at least cast aspersions on the mode in which film captures reality. When Colin McGinn, for instance, investigates film's ability to create worlds that engage our mind 'so naturally, so smoothly, and overwhelmingly' – a power he dubs the 'mind–movie problem' by analogy with the 'mind–body problem' in philosophy – he still believes that it remains *philosophy*'s preserve to articulate this problem:[6]

> Movies have never been, with rare exceptions, a highbrow medium. They rejoice in the visceral, the gaudy, and the vulgar... There is nothing better after a hard day of philosophical thinking and writing than a 'mindless' movie; I can almost feel my brain shifting its chemical balance, the neurons rearranging themselves.[7]

Films, for McGinn, cannot comprehend their own profound power, for they are primarily a medium for 'sensation and feeling' rather than 'abstract thought'.[8] What the philosopher giveth with one hand...

Such emotional conflicts may well harbour other anxieties, ones that go far back into the history of philosophy and its quarrel with the poets, back to the conflict between word and image. Plato banished the poets, yet he wrote like a poet (notwithstanding its dramatic quality, the similarity between his allegory of the cave and the experience of watching a film in a darkened theatre has not been lost on film theorists either).[9] However, the desire to keep concept and image separate has not been the philosopher's sole prerogative. André Malraux famously said that what is important in the artwork is precisely what cannot be said, whilst Jean Cocteau proclaimed that 'an artist cannot speak about his art any more than a plant can discuss horticulture'.

Nonetheless, this romantic view of the ineffability of art comes in various forms, Theodor Adorno writing that philosophy 'says what art cannot say, but it is art alone which is able to say it: by not saying it'.[10] This seems like a backhanded compliment all the same (Adorno never stopped philosophizing about art in deference to art's non-saying). Ultimately, for most Hegelians like Adorno, art only *becomes* philosophical when a philosopher brings out its inner voice through translation and clarification. The Truth has a sensuous embodiment in art that needs to be told in words by philosophy. Abstractionism, for example, is one obvious way in which the thoughts of art can be expressed.[11] This is an idea that comes to us from Hegel, travelling down through Walter Benjamin to contemporary aestheticians like Arthur Danto. As Daniel Herwitz observes:

> Combining Hegel's view that the point of history is self-knowledge, and the actualization of self-knowledge in the institutions of society, with Clement Greenberg's formalist criticism that abstract art has been about philosophically establishing the underlying possibilities and nature of the medium per se, Danto thus reads avant-garde art history as the search for a philosophical self-definition of what makes art, art.[12]

Only through philosophy does art come into complete self-knowledge. When it comes to modernist aesthetics at least, art needs philosophy more than philosophy needs art.

Philosophical cinema or cinematic philosophy?

In contrast to this chauvinism, however, a hallmark of the most recent philosophy of film is a new-found democracy concerning the origins of thought. On this view, films *can* think for themselves. It is an increasingly popular claim amongst newer film-philosophers that film is no mere handmaiden to philosophy, that it does more than merely make its audience feel or, at best, make philosophers think: rather, it too can think *in its own affective way.* Affect and thought are not separate faculties. A recent case in point would be Daniel Frampton's *Filmosophy*, which claims for film the faculty of a new kind of thought all its own – the 'affective thinking of film'. Similar claims have been made by those inspired by Stanley Cavell's approach to film: one that lets us appreciate how 'films can philosophize'. For the Cavellian, cinematic thinking is shown in the details of *how* things appear on screen, a specificity which indicates the presence of mind.[13] Each of these positions, and others, will be examined in the pages that follow.

A word of caution, though. In March 1945, at the launch of France's first official film school, the Institut des hautes études cinématographiques, the phenomenologist Maurice Merleau-Ponty proclaimed that 'if philosophy is in harmony with the cinema, if thought and technical effort are heading in the same direction, it is because the philosopher and the moviemaker share a certain way of being, a certain view of the world which belongs to a generation'. Here philosophy and film 'share' the same world, without need for any mastery of the one over the other. Yet, we should be careful about this new rapprochement between word and image, for Merleau-Ponty makes it clear from the outset of his talk that he understands film in a singular fashion, that is, according to his phenomenological views of philosophy. Film is a 'temporal gestalt', he says, and with that he gives the game away, given the centrality of gestalt psychology to his own philosophy and, now, his concept of film as well. If the 'philosopher and the moviemaker' share a reality, it is one already made in the philosopher's image. Similarly, when Jean-François Lyotard writes in his essay, 'Acinema', of film either being caught in or escaping the movements of capitalist production and Freudian return, we realize at once that he is giving us a 'libidinal economy of the cinema' wholly fashioned after his own peculiar philosophical approach in the mid-1970s.[14] In both this case and Merleau-Ponty's, we have examples of thinkers who do purport to find *indigenous* philosophical value in film, but only on account of refracting it through their own thought. Film is seen to be philosophical because philosophy's light has already been shone on film.

The circularity evident when philosophers do extol the thinking of film (or art in general) is not an easy obstacle to avoid, though. For even the most attentive to cinema's native powers, like Gilles Deleuze or Jacques Rancière, can be found wanting in this regard (as we'll see). So is it possible to avoid such prejudice at all? Not for so long as we remain philosophers, according to François Laruelle. For him, there is an 'idealism at the heart itself of thought' such that philosophical representation inevitably colours its object with extrinsic conceptual schema. What philosophy calls 'reality' is first and foremost a *concept of* the world. Every philosophy is a '*mixte*' of reality with a predecided interpretative schema, be it phenomenon and noumenon, gestalt and non-gestalt, or excessive and non-excessive expenditure within a libidinal economy, and so on. A philosopher's reality can never capture (and exhaust) what Laruelle calls the 'Real' itself, be it the Real of film or anything else. Nonetheless, we will still attempt to look at both sides of the film–philosophy relationship without favouritism, such that we might, in Laruelle's own words, 'pas de penser sans philosophie mais de penser sans l'autorité de la philosophie'.[15] This thinking 'without the authority of philosophy' may not be possible, but we'll only know for sure by trying.

How should we begin? Without wishing to rehearse any further the debates concerning whether or not philosophy itself is more beholden to the image than it would like to acknowledge, it remains important – contra Colin McGinn – to address what W. J. T. Mitchell terms the 'pictorial turn' vis-à-vis the relative power of philosophy to film. Mitchell describes this turn as 'the widely shared notion that visual images have replaced words as the dominant mode of expression in our time'.[16] The general scopic regime of modernity is such that philosophers must choose between the role of idolater or iconoclast. Like Mitchell, I am an idolater. By this I mean that I see the power of film as simultaneously perceptual *and* conceptual. The 'pictorial turn' enunciates the heterogeneous materiality of thought, and it is this embodied heterogeneity that allows film to think as a material medium.

What does this mean exactly? Boris Pasternak famously described art as 'Philosophy in a State of Ecstasy'. But such an affective state should not be regarded as mere dumb feeling: if the art of film can be said to be conceptual *on its own terms* (rather than those set for it by loquacious philosophers), then it must be on account of an ecstatic naturalism of thought rather than a mediation that supposedly dumbs thought down. This is our true starting point. Instead of reducing thought to 'mere' images (through a purported imperialism of 'visual culture'), the turn to pictures inflates material images into thinking processes. Yet again, however, this idea is not new. No less a figure than Leonardo da Vinci argued that painting was philosophical on account of its treatment of bodies in motion: the painter is a philosopher using algorithms for the visible (a position that Félix Ravaisson and Henri Bergson later took up in the idea of a 'figured metaphysics').[17] But note the conjuring trick involved in this bringing together of art and philosophy (this time by an artist). A third, mediating term has been introduced, the equation being facilitated by importing *mathesis* into art *and* philosophy. Da Vinci must presuppose that it is the algorithm that thinks, as well as positing that philosophy and art are *essentially* algorithmic. As already mentioned, biases like this are evident in much contemporary discourse surrounding philosophy and film too. In other words, if it is to be shown that film can think *for itself*, that it too philosophizes, then it cannot be on account of reducing one to the other, nor of introducing an extraneous third term. Avoiding such presuppositions (of either reduction to one term or mediation through a third) will be a constant hurdle for the philosophies examined in this study, as well as for any alternative we might forward ourselves.

Convergence on the film process: the *élan cinématique*

Yet, we are moving too quickly. Before examining the possible obstacles to any convergence between film and philosophy we should look more closely at what brings them together in the first place, to wit, their shared passion for the real. On the film side, there is a notable convergence peculiar to cinematic form and technology. Its power to capture reality is based on both its synthetic function in art – the fact that it captures aspects of every other art form (literature, poetry, theatre, music, painting, photography, sculptural form, and even dance) – as well as its ever-enlarging incorporation of more and more of our sensory powers across its historical development, from the silents to the talkies, black-and-white to colour, normal to panoramic vision, two-dimensions to three-dimensions, low-definition to high-definition. With regard to its synthetic function in art, such power affords the philosopher an opportunity to think of film as the art form par excellence, the one that captures the essence of all the other arts. Alain Badiou, for example, describes cinema as the point of intersection of all the arts – having no essence of its own precisely because it subtracts the minimal essences from each of the others. Likewise for Jacques Rancière, cinema is the name of an art whose 'meaning cuts across the borders between the arts', just as Roman Ingarden described it as 'on the borderline between the arts'.[18] For these philosophers, film's status as the 'seventh art' reveals more than just a numerical position: it is also a convergent one, one that condenses all the arts into one Art.

But it is the technological convergences of film which have always been most attractive to both philosophers and film theorists. Film's power resides in its multisensory orbit, one that seems to come closest to our own perceptual 'mechanism', even to the extent of making vision its dominant mode, just as our bodies do. André Bazin was much taken by this, noting that cinema, even in its feeble birth in the nineteenth century – immobile, deaf and barely able to see – always promised to be much more, and continues to do so even today: 'Every new development added to the cinema must, paradoxically, take it nearer and nearer to its origins. In short cinema has not yet been invented!' Indeed, today's technological convergences with television, the computer, the Internet, video games and other digital media need not be taken as a sign of the dissolution of film's own identity so much as the revelation of its transformative essence. As Stephen Keane notes, 'convergence can be said to represent either a dissipation of the particular qualities of film and cinema or a challenging reconfiguration of filmmaking, film viewing and the business of film'. For Keane, film has always been at the nexus of new perceptual technologies, 'developing, adapting and converging, leading and following, always familiar but constantly renewed'.[19]

Within such optimism there is a philosophical point to be made, namely that cinema's technological convergence was and is always *asymptotic*, not only on account of old media being perpetually supplanted by the emergence of new media, but also in virtue of the moving target at which its convergence aims. The reality that film is supposed to capture is itself always in motion, such that film must miss its putative target, must converge on something that is itself divergent. In fact, this will be the hypothesis we will begin with, that reality itself is processual or divergent. As such, film's power is always based on a missed encounter, a convergence with divergence. Moving pictures move us because movement is what is Real. Commensurately, there is no essential or 'Ideal' film wherein either a particular technology or aesthetic form would render it absolutely Real ('great or true' film art). Rather, at any one time, there is only a provisional selection of film examples (and film scenes) that converge on one point – what film 'really is' – *from a certain frame of reference*. This point of convergence is only virtual, however, being visible to the pertinent frame of reference alone (with its selection of films and mode of consumption). The *actual* movement of filmic convergence is asymptotic, an 'indefinite' progress that we will later call the *'élan cinématique'*. Movies have an *élan* rather than an essence – a divergent form of movement that participates in (rather than 'captures') processual reality in myriad ways; indeed, it can only so participate when it is myriad. The convergence of cinema is virtual as it tends towards a single point, and actual as it diverges away from one.[20] If that single point is an essence of cinema forwarded by philosophers, then the *élan cinématique* comprises whatever resists it with its own countermovements – whatever resists their 'theory of film'.

This is why the Structuralist film movement of the 1960s and 1970s misconstrues the power of cinema. It sought the essence of film in a minimalist use of its various devices; for example, the zoom shot in Michael Snow's *Wavelength* (1967).[21] Its interest in purity followed a rather philosophical, not to say Platonic, movement of escape from the world into its own reality of eternal, cinematic essences.[22] Rather than transforming film (with new technologies), this Structuralist approach aped the subtractive gestures of modernism in painting, literature and theatre, in the hope that this would somehow reveal the essence of cinema lying beneath. What lies beneath, however, is not a fixed essence but a shifting process. What film converges on, with its various inheritances from the other arts and its increasingly convoluted technology, is not a singular reality but diverging, plural realities.

To make the point clearer, we can take things from another direction. Allan Kaprow, for instance, thinks of art as that minimal event that can shift a reality into artfulness. In a 'Happening', as he would call it, it is the smallest gesture that transforms an everyday action such as shaking hands or speaking on the telephone into art. And it is only the 'conceptual decision' that transforms our awareness of or attention to *anything* ordinary from life into art. Rather than seek the essence of theatrical art, say, in modernist strategies (from Beckett to Grotowski) that strip away the fourth wall, costume, script, set, audience, and so on, Kaprow aimed to unhinge the very notion of art (including the performance arts) by blurring its distinctiveness from life, by un-arting it, de-essentializing it. This is not art as addition to or subtraction from reality, but as part of reality: 'the circle closes: as art is bent on imitating life, life imitates art'. To enable this blurred participation in the Real, there must be an unarting of 'Art' as simulacrum, a withdrawal of the conventions that make art 'Art'.[23] Art is not simply the mirror of life, for *both* are 'made up', as he put it.[24] This 'making up' is not a voluntary, imaginative construction, however, but art *and* reality's own self-construction, each of which are processes in the making. Cinema, by contrast, uses the maximum biotechnological synergies available to maximize artfully what appears as a 'simulation' of reality. Yet, in both the case of Kaprow's minimal artistic gesture and cinema's maximal synergy, the reality that is supposedly simulated is not a difference in kind to be represented, but a likeness of process. 'Reality' too is a process to participate in. Once we have accepted this, we can forego the myth of a pure cinema that would correspond with, capture or reflect a fixed reality. There are only impure realities that participate with each other in refractive processes.

Philosophy's perpetual identity crisis

Turning back to philosophy then, it is now possible to see its own transformations in a new light. When Jacques Derrida proposed that the 'death of philosophy' is the sole question 'capable of founding the community... of those who are still called philosophers', he was nearly right. No less than film's convergence with other media can be taken as either the sign of its dissolution or its ongoing movement, so the death of philosophy may well mark nothing more than its latest transformation, its latest diffusion. As Derrida himself put it more positively: 'I must honestly say that now, less than ever, do I know what philosophy is... It is as impossible to say what philosophy is *not* as it is to say what it is. In all the other disciplines... there is philosophy.'[25] Nonetheless, that philosophy might have lost its way only recalls us to the fact that it has *never* had an essence (though many have tried and continue to try to give it one: in the a priori, or logical analysis, or concept creation, or intention, or fundamental questioning, or simply in being 'Heideggerian', 'Husserlian', 'Hegelian'). Like film, philosophy too has a borderline personality, for it is the discipline that perpetually becomes 'other' through the various non-philosophies with which it engages. The extension, or diffusion, of philosophy into other fields has always been there in the various 'philosophies of' – 'of history', 'of science', 'of art', and so on, from its very beginning. More contemporary refractions, through 'theory' within the humanities, or so-called 'applied' philosophy within bioethics, business ethics, and medical ethics, are simply the same process of extension occurring at a more fine-grained level. According to Derrida, indeed, it is actually false to speak of philosophy spreading into 'other fields', given that philosophy is already ubiquitous. But the question remains as to how philosophy comes to be amongst these other disciplines, by application from without or creation from within.

What worries some philosophers, moreover, is that this process of diffusion is proliferating at an alarming rate in what is an apparent philosophization of everything, one that threatens to leave philosophy nowhere precisely *because* it is everywhere. Philosophy will have lost its own identity. The various texts on philosophy and particular films like *The Matrix* began this trend (as we'll examine in Chapter 1), but now it has reached epidemic proportions with 'philosophy and anything' being possible – baseball, the Atkins Diet, hip hop, Bob Dylan, Harley-Davidson, poker, basketball, football, beer and wine, being only a selection of the recent studies. (It is ironic that amongst these new works there are actually two publications dedicated to philosophy and bullshit, even though one could clearly argue that philosophy has always been about pointing out (others') bullshit.)[26] Yet, in most cases, pure philosophers need fear not, for these studies are nearly all merely illustrative: they do not find any new philosophy in these fields but simply new modes through which to express the old ideas of Plato, Descartes, Hume, et al. The far greater threat to purity comes not from the ignoble fields of 'popular philosophy' but from the discovery that a non-philosophical realm might be able to think *without* being reduced to illustrative mode. That would challenge what we mean by philosophy and thought itself; in our case, not only might film be philosophical but, even worse, philosophy might be filmic.

Our opening hypothesis, we said, was that reality itself is mutable. This is not to deny the very real appearance of fixity around *us* or the contrast between mobiles and immobiles. It is only to say that there is never anything *absolutely* static, for there is always some kind of movement even where we can see none, being too slow (or too quick) for us to notice it. Movement, in other words, is always complex. Indeed, the numerous different kinds of movement in film that I'll show through the course of this study will be evidence in favour of this hypothesis. There is a 'drunkenness of things being various', consequently, that allows us to find something *valuable* both in cinema's convergence on a diverging reality *and in philosophy's lack of essence* as it refracts itself through new non-philosophies. The world is 'incorrigibly plural', and if film has a power, if it 'captures' reality, it is not by mirroring something static, but by being a part of something moving. Indeed, replacing the optics of static reflection with an alternative optics, that of mobile refraction, we'll find, will be one way of depicting this convergence on reality-as-process. The great Soviet film-maker Sergei Eisenstein once told his students that they should always 'think in stages of a process'.[27] It remains a challenge to see how thoroughly we, *as philosophers*, can live up to this maxim to its fullest extent, that is, to think of thought as stages of a process too.

Some of the philosophers of film we'll encounter think less in terms of processes and more in terms of essences, be they natural ones or metaphysical ones; others, by contrast, think in terms of cultural constructions. Contrary to this dichotomy, we will posit throughout numerous processes at various speeds, some slow and some fast, others too slow and others too fast. Neither the frozen essentialism of physics or (Platonist) metaphysics, nor the liquid relativism of culturalists; neither zero velocity nor the infinitely fast – only and always the particular speeds of biology, affect, technology and embodied culture. Whether this hypothesis of process is itself a philosophical posit too far, one more question begging presupposition, must remain to be seen. Critical theories are inevitably self-confirming, of course, but we also hope to mount a large array of evidence in support of our hypothesis that it is process alone that can unite philosophical thought to cinema. This will prove nothing absolutely to be sure, yet it might all the same suggest a type of truth, a growing truth, that the reader can complete in his or her own mind as he or she wishes. Moreover, it might also suggest this: that the failures of theorists to exhaust film in any one philosophy is itself a process that makes *us* think – and that it is always worth thinking about who, or what, is actually doing the thinking when we are made to think something new in this way. So Gilles Deleuze is surely right in saying, at the conclusion of his *Cinema* books, that the question 'what is cinema?' must lead us to the question 'what is philosophy?', for philosophy's film-envy was bound to turn back on itself eventually.[28]

Introduction: Nobody Knows Anything!

> To know that one does not know, is the gift of a superior spirit. Not to know and to think that one does know, is a mistake. To know that this is a mistake, keeps one from making it. I have the knowledge here.[1]

Oh, they both make such good arguments![2]

The fourth chapter of Mario Perniola's book, *Art and Its Shadow*, is entitled 'Towards a Philosophical Cinema'. In it he asks after this possibility, of whether cinema can 'espouse philosophical experience' or, more strongly again, whether cinema might even generate a 'relatively autonomous philosophical work'.[3] Showing clear signs of film-envy, Perniola outlines the powerful links between film and philosophy with respect to 'the relation between reality and its reproduction' while at the same time noting that it is only *documentary* cinema (as seen in his chosen examples of Wim Wenders's *Lisbon Story* (1994) and Derek Jarman's *Blue* (1993)) that can actualize the philosophical potential of film. The philosopher is clear and has his reasons (which are 'hardly challengeable' he says) on where philosophy is to be found in film.

Both the intensity and the range of interest philosophers have shown towards cinema of late – as a teaching tool, as an object of philosophy, and even as a subject that might philosophize – invite an important set of questions: How is philosophy actually taught through film in the current film-philosophy literature? What is the specific value of the cinematic illustration of philosophical concepts? Is its effectiveness due to the immersive nature of film viewing, the psychological trickery of the cinematic apparatus, the hallucinatory effects of story narrative, or the affective manipulations of the audio-visual image? What are the links between cinema, ontology and representation: is film-making an intrinsically hermeneutical, informational or material practice? And what purchase do terms like 'ontology' or 'representation' have on such an industrial and mixed art form? Each of these questions will be addressed here, but the abiding concern throughout will remain whether film can ever reach the holy grail that philosophers frequently speak of when discussing the relationship between film and philosophy – that of a true 'philosophical cinema'.

Of course, what makes it a 'holy grail' at all – that is, something difficult and perhaps even impossible to attain – is partly explained by the conflict of interpretations generated by philosophers and film theorists alike concerning *what film is*. Such hermeneutical problems pertain not only to what particular films are 'about' in their storytelling but also the ontology of film, given that what one looks for in a film must be partly determined by what one thinks film is as such. If one thinks that film, at base, relays our libidinal conflicts in an external medium, then one is naturally more prone to seeing the stories it tells in terms of the figures that populate such accounts (be they Freudian, Jungian or Lacanian). If one believes that film fundamentally reproduces the male gaze that objectifies women, then this aspect of the visual narrative will be foregrounded in one's representation. When Gilles Deleuze comes to analyse Fritz Lang's *M* (1931), for example, it is within a naturalistic discourse of 'milieu', 'lines of action' and the 'strongly structural character of organic representation'; whereas Jacques Rancière looks to its narrative function, how it relates Hans Beckert's account of how he became a child murderer, as well as the stories told by the mothers who have lost their children at his hands. It is no surprise to be told, then, that Deleuze believes that pre-war films are essentially about spatial movement rather than narrative, while Rancière regards the fable as essential to all cinema. Likewise, Deleuze's descriptions of *The Birds* (1963) will contrast strongly with any account we might get from Slavoj Žižek's Lacanian rendering of Hitchcock's film (which goes so far as to say that 'we must imagine *The Birds* as a film *without birds*') or Stanley Cavell's humanistic view of it as an examination of 'cosmic love'.[4] Such a variety of interpretation can even circulate within the same theorist, as William Connolly describes with respect to another Hitchcock classic:

> Consider, by way of a first example, *Vertigo*, a film I have seen three times over a span of twenty-five years. It can be engaged in several ways, and my engagement has shifted each time I have viewed it. Laura Mulvey, for instance, examines how the gaze that governs the film is male. Tania Modleski contends that the male gaze is both there and 'severely disturbed' as the film carries the characters through a series of dizzying experiences. Another interpretation, taking off from Modleski's account, might ask how fantasy, illusion, and disturbance circulate between male and female characters as the film advances.[5]

A cacophony of readings. But does this mean that nobody is wrong and everybody is right, that we can all make 'good arguments' when necessary out of the same raw material? Not exactly. In fact, it is quite the reverse of such an epistemic relativism that I will espouse here.

In 1983 the screenwriter William Goldman famously claimed that the secret behind Hollywood's commercial success could be reduced to one golden rule: 'Nobody Knows Anything'. When it comes to the reasons why one film succeeds at the box office and another fails, there is no secret knowledge at all (other than Hollywood's own ignorance of why it works when it does). In what follows, I am going to argue that the same is true of the philosophy of film. When it comes to what film fundamentally is, and also thereby what any one film essentially means, Nobody Knows Anything, or rather Nobody Knows Everything. This might sound like simply another form of (nihilistic) relativism, but it is actually a claim for something positive, for its corollary is not that *everybody knows nothing* (an obviously self-contradictory position), but that there is more to film than any one transcendent theory (one telling us what film is) can exhaust. This not-knowing is not only an epistemic stance but also an aspect of the ontology of film, perhaps the only thing about it that we can know for sure. It is this inexhaustibility of film, this *more*, this *élan*, that is philosophically interesting and thoughtful, for it is the one *absolute* that resists relativism. Each theory is partially right. There are more effects in film than can ever be captured by textual 'philosophy' (so-called), for more is produced on screen and in the audience than simply representations of stories, of gender, or even of philosophy.

The circular logic of paradigms and examples

In the Preface I remarked on recent arguments from philosophers like Daniel Frampton and Stanley Cavell that film can philosophize in its own way. The argument of our study is that, given the transcendent, all-encompassing nature of most philosophies of film – ones which tell us 'what film is' – even those who seemingly allow film its own mind and thought cannot avoid reducing it to illustrations of extant philosophy. If film thinks, it is *not* in its own way but in philosophy's way. Even Frampton – who is highly sensitive to the abuse of film by theory – begins with a definition of thinking, in terms of 'problems and ideas' and what 'creates pure concepts', that is already reliant upon a pre-existing philosophical model, in this case Gilles Deleuze's. Similarly, it is Cavell's use of Wittgenstein which is said to 'clear the way' for seeing film as philosophy because he forwards a therapeutic model of philosophizing that can be likened to the experience of watching a film.[6] So far, so illustrative. Film philosophizes here because it accords with a favoured kind of philosophy. What begins as an attempt at seeing film *as* (its own) model of philosophy and thought finds itself closer than anticipated to the *explicit* use of films to teach and illustrate philosophy (cases of which we'll examine in the next chapter).

It is consequently arguable that film-philosophy has always been a mix of film hermeneutics *and* some or other philosophical theory. Though many would hope to go beyond this illustrative style, it is extremely hard – perhaps impossible – to explore the way in which film itself might think without simultaneously reducing its non-linguistic dimensions to some or other existing textual philosophy. I will not insist here on the question of the language barrier per se, however (on whether the word is intrinsic to philosophy). In fact, the issue of defining philosophy and thought in terms of language rests on the larger issue of having *any* definition of philosophy and thought malleable enough to accommodate radically new forms of thinking from non-philosophical sources (visual film being just one candidate). Hence, the matter of a definition for thought and philosophy will be addressed in the final chapter.

In any case, the thesis of this book for now is as follows: what frequently claim to be 'open' readings of film *as* philosophy still remain prefigured philosophical interpretations. Consequently, the aim of seeing film as philosophy is more often than not reduced to 'film as text as philosophy' inasmuch as the film's audio-visual properties, no less than its cultural, technological and/or commercial dimensions, are interpreted from a ready-made philosophical vantage point. In Deleuze's own case, very particular films (*Ladri di Biciclette* (1948), *L'Année dernière à Marienbad* (1961)) and film-makers (Vittorio de Sica, Alain Resnais) become examples of material forces (that play a role in Deleuze's larger metaphysical scheme), and as such work to illustrate his philosophy (of film) simply because it focuses on one aspect of cinema rather than any of the others. In fact, the distinction between exemplary and non-exemplary films becomes problematic at this point for any 'philosophy-of-film-as-philosophy', for why should a philosopher making a transcendent, ontological claim about film – that all (proper) films are (essentially) *x* – have favourites at all (that quite conveniently show this trait explicitly)? Wouldn't it prove one's case better to use less obvious examples? In other words, if *film* can think, then *all* films can think: one doesn't prove the claim that all humans can do mathematics just by studying the minds of Fermat and Poincaré.[7]

Of course, one might propose that Richard Curtis's *Love Actually* (2003), for instance – not a favourite amongst film-philosophers – is not a proper film, or at least not a true, real or great example of cinematic thinking. But this clear case of the 'no true Scotsman' fallacy – permitting ad hoc redefinitions whenever required to preserve one's position – may leave one's prescriptions seemingly unmotivated. Unless, of course, one's reason for instancing Michael Haneke's *Caché* (2005) say, as a true, real or great example of cinematic thinking is because *it accords with the philosophy of Emmanuel Levinas*. Typologies within film theory itself have always prescribed various types of film for us. Bazin's realism or Eisenstein's formalism, for instance, furnish us with aesthetic and theoretical preferences for certain films over others. Yet, a transcendent (philosophical) typology ought to accommodate *all* films descriptively rather than prescriptively. And, indeed, Deleuze gives us just that, hoping to accommodate all film within a typology of two: the pre-war 'movement-image' and the post-war 'time-image'. Yet, within such philosophical typologies there still lurk ontological preferences, nonetheless. For instance, to show that all cinema pertains to the Deleuzian body with illustrations taken from the work of David Cronenberg, George Romero and Jerry Lewis (as Steven Shaviro does), is hardly astounding.[8]

There is always what one might call the 'transcendental choice of film' at work in film-philosophy: by this I mean those (inadvertently) illustrative approaches that use particular films to establish a theoretical paradigm of what film is and how it works.[9] Yet, such approaches already make their selections of particular films or film elements (of plot over sound, or framing over genre, and so on) in the light of the theory of film in question, and are therefore circular. The transcendental choice or selection already forms the filmic materials so as to legitimate the theory *ab initio*. Such pre-emptiveness is double-edged, however. Theory must be selective in how it makes film illustrate itself (and its theory of film), but, precisely on that account, it always leaves remainders – other films or filmic properties that it must marginalize in order to save its own integrity (hence, Deleuze must disregard narrative and Žižek must downplay the materiality of the image, for instance).

All-encompassing paradigms can also be critiqued for the totalizing nature of their relationship with film. Ironically, it is precisely because they are totalizing that they lack the complete explanatory power they claim for themselves. In claiming that film as such is representational or non-representational, a function of unconscious desire or a form of existential therapy, a material presentation of time or an ontological world-view (or whatever else), they lose the ability to account for alternative points of view (and alternative films or film elements), *even as derivative illusions or errors*. And this is their Achilles heel. The primacy of any new all-encompassing paradigm inevitably enters it into a relationship with its rivals of reduction, elimination or even just separation; textual hermeneutics, for example, becoming an illusion *derived* from the material sensation of the film-image – that itself remains unexplained. *How* can it be legitimate to marginalize the textuality of cinema or, conversely, the sensation of the film-image? In each case, what does not support and illustrate one philosophical paradigm is ignored in an ad hoc fashion.

Certainly, this logical point is not unique to film-philosophy, but pertains to any ontological monism – 'all (proper) *y* are (essentially) *x*' – be it applied or 'pure'. What is at issue here is the self-sufficiency or identity of any paradigm. In each case, it can be asked whether there is some remainder left of the rival paradigm and, if so, of what type. Though there are always correlations between any two paradigms – at a minimum, that of 'true theory' somehow coinciding with 'false theory' – there are never any complete reductions (even in terms of illusion), and what is left unreduced is always worthy of attention.[10] Film is simply too resistant to one theory alone. Which is basically to say that film-philosophy should be catholic rather than puritan, a messy mix of methodologies and eclectic, random examples, rather than exemplars that illustrate one's point perfectly.[11] What remains to be seen, however, is whether even a philosophical pluralism can avoid reductionism when it comes to positing film as a philosophical medium in its own right. In other words: can even an ecumenical philosophy avoid the illustrative mode? Or is the creep of descriptive typology towards prescriptive ontology necessary and unavoidable?

There is a further, ensuing set of questions for this study that will run as follows: must philosophy always render film per se (or particular films) as pretexts for illustrating philosophy? What logic lies behind this use of examples – is it to prove a theory or to explain it? If the former, how are the genera being abstracted from the exemplary films, and with what success vis-à-vis this explanation? Conversely, what would it take to imagine how film might itself philosophize without reducing it to orthodox forms of philosophy? Finally, and fundamentally, must we change or at least extend our definition of philosophy and/or thinking in order to accommodate the specificities that come with the claim that film can philosophize?

Between theory and post-theory

As a consequence of its infancy no doubt, film-philosophy has been unable to avoid being highly partisan thus far: cognitivist *or* culturalist, Deleuzian *or* Cavellian, pedagogical tool *or* creative medium. Furthermore, the type of dialogue engaged in between philosophy and film has often been reductive. In the search for interdisciplinarity, cooperation has been replaced with co-option, film being understood entirely through one paradigm, cognitive science, cultural studies, Freudian psychodynamics, rhizomatic materialism, and so on.

Perhaps because cinema itself is such a mixed art, any kind of theorizing on film has always had to foster diverse connections with other disciplines. Whether it be an empirical study of film (its national, industrial and technological histories; its genres, audiences and economics), or an avowedly theoretical approach (aesthetic or anti-aesthetic, formalist or realist, culturalist or cognitivist), we are faced with the question of which inter-theoretical paradigm to choose.[12] But which other disciplines are deemed cognate has often seemed axiomatic only to the particular brand of film theory pursued. Hence, the various agendas set for the study of film by each new theory have also sounded like dogmatic manifestos – 'film as film', 'film as art', 'film as language', 'film as psychoanalysis', 'film as cognition' – each one shouting to be heard above the cacophony of counterclaims over the nature of film comprehension. Each claimant is actually asserting an interdisciplinary link, offering us *the* key to understanding how film works.

Throughout this process of forming new alliances, moreover, there has been one constant association: for if film theory from the 1960s to the 1980s was routinely interdisciplinary at all, it was with philosophy. Indeed, it is worth reminding film-philosophers just how philosophical film theory already was (and remains) before they ever entered into the fray. No less than philosophy's aptitude for using films to illustrate itself, conversely, film theory has never been reticent about citing a philosopher or two to prove a point in its own field. Indeed, this latter mode of enquiry has been the norm until quite recently, with versions of structuralism and Marxist critical theory often being the preferred partners. Various 'isms' and schools of thought (sometimes incompatible) such as structuralism, post-structuralism, postmodernism, Freudianism, the ideas of Adorno, Barthes, Althusser, Bourdieu and numerous other *philosophes*, have marked film theory's trajectory for forty years.

The first set of these theories, following the so-called 'subject-position' paradigm, was most popular in the 1960s and 1970s, taking on a mixture of psychoanalytic, Althusserian and semiotic methodologies of reading film as text. The names of Christian Metz, Jean-Louis Baudry and Stephen Heath are closely associated with this movement. And, of course, there are good reasons for this approach. Films are often pleasurable objects, and so the connection with Freudianism, for instance (which focuses on the *travails* of desire), comes easily. Alternatively, given the signifying nature of film, linguistics has had a strong attraction for film theory, though mostly when Saussurean in origin (rarely has Chomskyan linguistics been utilized – though this is now changing). And, in addition, political ideology has never been far from the mix; Peter Wollen reminds us that the 'film apparatus', as it came to be called, is 'the product of a variety of historical determinations, at the interface where the economies of capital and libido interlock'.[13]

Yet, these ideas became increasingly outmoded in the 1980s once academic interest shifted from film as a discrete textual object to the social and cultural contexts of its production and consumption. 'Intertextuality' in the broadest terms (TV, cinema and multimedia; interrupted, reordered and fragmented viewing; gendered and ethnic reception; genre studies and audience studies) gradually supplanted various kinds of *'l'explication de texte'*. As such, the culturalist paradigm was also more historical, on the one hand, as well as more sociologically nuanced, on the other, looking to the everyday *uses* made of texts in diverse situations. This culturalism was, accordingly, more egalitarian and inclusive in its definition of culture, the question of cultural taste (knowing a 'good' film from a 'bad' one) being removed from the domain of aesthetics and placed squarely in socio-politics. Following the ideas of Pierre Bourdieu, taste became bound up with questions of class. Henceforth, we were told, we must cultivate an interest

> in the ways in which issues of taste produce not only different readings of a text within a given historical period, but conflicts between the proponents of these different readings... Articles and reviews can most usefully be understood as one of the ways in which people learn to position themselves within hierarchies of taste.[14]

While some argued (and still do) that we should be wary of the dangers of 'producing a celebratory and uncritical account of popular culture and pleasure', those voices became increasingly rare in the 1990s, with the culturalist position continuing to gain ground rapidly.[15] Toby Miller was one of the loudest arguing for the elimination of classical film theory in favour of this culturalist paradigm:

> policy analysis, political economy, ethnography, movement activism, and use of the social science archive should matter to cinema studies. Because they don't, cinema studies is largely irrelevant outside of its tiny cloister of academic parthenogenesis. In short, it doesn't matter.[16]

Empirical research – backed up by an antitheory theory – was, and in places remains, in the ascendant. And with this proclamation that 'Theory is Dead', we arrive at the contemporary scene and the end of this sketch of forty years of film theory.

Continental or analytic? Once more unto the breach

So what price now a philosophy – theory *in extremis* – of film? Though there had been some serious philosophical and psychological studies of cinema from very early on (Hugo Münsterberg's *The Photoplay* being published in 1916), it wasn't until the late 1980s that the discipline of film-philosophy became established. Yet, almost from the start, the field was divided. Broadly speaking, its current situation can be characterized in terms of two rival paradigms.

On the one side, Euro-culturalism, which term I will use to cover the varied range of culture- *and* text-based approaches to the technology, ideology and materiality of cinematic production, distribution and consumption. Unsurprisingly, it is influenced by philosophies coming from the Continental schools of philosophy – psychodynamics, critical theory, historicism and Deleuzian naturalism. Euro-culturalism is avowedly more historical, more focused on the political dimensions of film, and, in places, more relativistic. It also has a new metaphysical dimension, however (rarely seen in the culturalism of 1980s film theory), that is drawn especially from the work of Deleuze on time and movement, though with closely allied ideas stemming from Henri Bergson, Alain Badiou, Jacques Rancière and Giorgio Agamben.[17]

On the other side is Anglo-cognitivism. This paradigm takes empirical psychology as its modus operandi and is also often close to Anglo-American analytical philosophy in outlook. Anglo-cognitivism sees film-meaning primarily in terms of representation, and tends to be empiricist, apolitical (in aspiration), naturalistic and objectivist. Such cognitivism, in the broader, representationalist sense of the term, is also the hallmark of the conceptual analyses found in much analytical film-philosophy, irrespective of whether or not it explicitly supports a naturalistic agenda. The work of Noël Carroll and David Bordwell is characteristic here. To quote from the Introduction to Bordwell and Carroll's collection of essays, *Post-Theory*: 'a cognitivist analysis or explanation seeks to understand human thought, emotion, and action by appeal to processes of mental representation, naturalistic processes, and (some sense of) rational agency.'[18] And it is this kind of analysis that cognitivists wish to extend to film.

With regard to the circular logic of film ontologies, Bordwell's version of cognitivism is particularly instructive. He arrives at his theory of cinema as information processing by focusing on the individual's experience of certain elements of film (narrative in particular) that both illustrates and confirms his cognitivist paradigm in one fell swoop. In his employment of cognitivist philosophy, what Bordwell calls 'classical Hollywood narrative' (as opposed to avant-garde 'art cinema'), is a case in point. We are given a definition of the former involving seamless, centred, closed and linear narrative that also naturalizes such formal conventions as *cognitively optimal*. Hollywood's abiding style of storytelling gives the brain just what it needs to keep us entertained and coming back for more. Against cultural constructivism, Bordwell posits a psycho-filmic raw material that must be precultural. Hence, a film's avant-garde or classical status is independent of its audience's culture, the exhibition context or physical nature of the medium: it is essentially an informational process. And Hollywood's cross-cultural success reflects its ability to make films *that capture that essence of film*. Without a doubt, David Bordwell's work has been central to the formation of the Anglo-cognitive approach since it first appeared in the mid-1980s, and for that reason Chapter Two will look at it very closely.

Oddly enough, however, Gilles Deleuze's alternative and highly influential dualism of 'movement-image' and 'time-image' makes the same essentialist gesture for the Continental side, only now in metaphysical garb (time presents a break with movement). Indeed, we could say that Deleuze and Bordwell are the flip-sides (metaphysical and cognitive) of the one, essentialist coin: film must fit into two general categories of norm and transgression. Against this, however, I will argue that there is nothing cognitively or metaphysically fixed about the conventions of either Bordwell's classical mode or Deleuze's movement-image, for the properties they ascribe to film are all processual (though at different speeds to be sure). That is, they are elements of a becoming-reality that ensures that no one film property (masquerading as 'Film' per se) is ever isolable from its broader, shifting context. Deleuze's time-image can also *become* a movement-image, art cinema can *become* classical cinema (and vice versa).[19] And this becoming of film – its processual complexity – is its only essence (which is only to say that it has no essence). To posit the one or other property as the essence of film at the outset – using either cognitivism or metaphysics to do this – is to refuse to see how film's complexity resists one's theory.

Rapprochement or impasse? Film as relational process

Given its adoption of a putatively 'scientific' paradigm, Anglo-cognitivism appears to follow a more coherent research programme than that of European theory, which has as many approaches as it has figures – Rancière on film differs from Badiou on film to the same extent that Rancière differs from Badiou. In this respect, two of the most distinguishing characteristics of Continental and Anglo-American philosophy in general (personalism on the one hand, scientism on the other) have been inherited by their progeny in film-philosophy. Anglo-cognitivists accuse Euro-culturalists and other so-called 'grand theorists' of scientific ignorance, poor argumentation and theoretical irrelevance. Culturalists, in their turn, accuse cognitivists of political naivety, existential complacency and, worst of all, inadvertent collaboration with forces of ideological repression. Attempts at ecumenical rapprochement tend to end in failure, but one thing held in common by both sides of this impasse concerns the relationship between film understanding and their preferred form of philosophy: in each case it is an exclusive, illustrative and totalizing one. In each, as we will also argue, there is the presupposition (conscious or unconscious) that film is a fixed object to which theory relates itself transcendentally (as from an outside), whether that object be deemed a genuine artwork or 'mere' cultural produce, social artefact or neurological datum, readable text or material image.

In place of such a selective, essentialist view, I will propose that film be seen instead as an immanent set of processes, specifically as a series of relational processes and hybrid contexts comprising the artists' and audience's psychologies, the cinematic 'raw data', the physical media of the film, the varied forms of its exhibition, *as well as all the theories relating themselves to these dimensions*. This is a stratified approach to film as textual *and* material artefact, visual cognition *and* ontological world-view. As such, each partial view will also be partially accepted and incorporated into the meaning of film (without exhausting it, however), but each one's own partiality for its own view – in other words, each theory's attempt to totalize and reduce film entirely to itself as its illustration – will be deemed illegitimate.

This is not a new idea. Such a wide-ranging and multi-theoretical standpoint can also be found in an older, now neglected paradigm. The post-war French theorists of the 'filmology' movement described their work as a scientific approach to film, but they hoped to include aesthetics, psychology, sociology, anthropology, philosophy, physiology, biology and even ethology into the scope of this science.[20] In other words, their science was madly democratic. Because film is a hybrid technology and art form, its study must also be wildly and eclectically interdisciplinary. They regarded film to be as wide and as hybrid as reality itself, and so concluded that it *must* be approached in a truly multi-theoretical fashion, taking methods and data from both the human and the natural sciences. In the Conclusion we will look in more detail at the filmologists as a way forward for both film-philosophy and film theory in general.

For our part, it is the messiness of film, its resistance to singular theory, that makes it theoretically interesting. Moreover, by making ourselves aware of how the multilayered, contextual and processual nature of film resists any one reductive thought, we might even see how film itself can genuinely think rather than merely illustrate thought. To demonstrate this view, we must firstly show that film is indeed a relational process, one that enfolds within its moments a multiplicity of properties that cannot be set into any preformed philosophical hierarchy (of artist over audience, of author's intention over material medium, of audience reception over genre convention, and so on). Understood through a theory of cinematic process, film encompasses aspects from *every* paradigm of film-philosophy rather than being reducible to any one (as its illustration). In place of philosophical illustration *by* film, then, there is the becoming philosophical *of* film itself, that which resists any singular, reductive theorization of its processual being: the *élan cinématique*. This is a double-sided argument, however. On the one side, film can make us think by refusing to allow us to enforce our thoughts (of what it is) on it. On the other side, this recalcitrance to our thought may well be *its* form of thought too, so that what we are made to think is not our thought alone, but something *co-engendered* between us and film. In addition, finally, this *thoughtful* resistance of film to (any one) philosophy may not only force us to rethink our ontology of film, but equally what we mean by philosophy as well.

Towards a non-philosophical cinema

Film doesn't reflect (illustrate, illuminate or represent) our philosophy – it refracts it, it distorts it with its own thinking. The resistance of film to singular philosophies is a kind of thinking, or metathinking, all its own, precisely because it does not allow us to begin with a definition of thought and philosophy; or rather, it forces us to change our theory of what theory (thinking, philosophy) is. Film refracts the very idea of what thinking and philosophy are.

As a rule, we too often think of art, history, politics, or any other non-philosophy, only becoming 'philosophical' when there is a particular subject that thinks about it in a particular way (its conceptual foundations, presuppositions or contradictions, for instance); that is, when *we* apply ready-made concepts to *it*. If, alternatively, we refuse to go along with this prejudice, if we want to give non-philosophy its due, then at least two consequences follow. At a minimum, if film is going to be 'autonomously' philosophical, it must firstly be so without being *textually* philosophical. Hence, exemplary highbrow films, like Michael Haneke's *Caché*, or Wim Wenders's *Lisbon Story*, or Derek Jarman's *Blue*, must no longer be held up as the only ideal. Because such films wear their philosophical hearts on their sleeves (most often because they can be simply reduced to dialogue and plot that are recognizable to philosophers as 'conceptual'), it is all too easy to think of them as great, 'thoughtful' films. Secondly, it must not be deemed 'philosophical' in view of an implied subject who thinks in a particular way, resulting in findings similar to those in established positions. In other words, it must not be because the film (or film-maker) is a philosopher manqué, that it is doing philosophy.

Yet, to argue as much is hardly controversial. It is the additional consequences of upholding this view that would be immense for philosophy. It would amount to accepting the possibility of 'mediated philosophy', the possibility of theory becoming an a posteriori activity: no longer an a priori defined theory that is applied to subject matter, but a subject matter that is becoming-philosophical in its own immanent process, and on which extant philosophy cannot judge. Before any conceptual expression by the subject, before the expression of traditional theory in other words, there is the becoming of the subject matter itself. As such, the focus moves to the performative dimension of philosophy – philosophy being that which one does, that which one names 'philosophy' after the event. This would be a 'bottom-up', extensional characterization, one that is empirically based on the actuality of experiences that only nominate themselves 'philosophical' a posteriori.

If film is to think, if film is to philosophize, then we must get away from *any* definition of film, as well as any definition of thinking and philosophy. Calling film multiple or processual or relational is *not* a definition: these terms are place-holders marking an openness to every definition, in part. 'Process' here signifies a quasi-concept at best: it marks the lack of an essence to film rather a positive definition of one. This is what the non-philosophy of François Laruelle calls a 'democracy of thought' – what allows every theory to be partially right in as much as each is only partial, but absolutely wrong in as much as each tries to be absolute or transcendent.[21] The theories of film are *a part of* the process of film: they relate to it mereologically rather than representationally. This is what I would call a metaphilosophical thesis, one open to the becoming-philosophical of filmic subject matter. It is a science of film (filmology) with complete openness to the meaning of this science or 'knowing'.

A word of caution before we commence down this path, however. The reader may feel justified in making a *tu quoquo* response to what has been argued here thus far, for haven't I too forwarded a philosophy of film predicated on a given a priori essence of 'multiplicity', 'process', 'resistance' and 'relationality'? Haven't I been equally selective, as one must be, in my examples, be it of films or film-philosophers? And, after all, doesn't my terminology of process and multiplicity, of science and hypothesis, also come from the work of philosophers (Bergson and Laruelle)? I will argue, however, that what I am forwarding here is, nevertheless, *not* one more philosophy of film, but a true non-philosophy of film, a thinking 'according to' the Real, which, in this context, means a passivity towards film as thinking in its resistance to extant philosophy and theory. Film here *is* the Real. What is offered is not the proof of a theory but the suggestion of a way of looking at films that is up to the reader to complete with his or her own examples. It is the suggestion of a new relationship between the thinking subject and the subject of thought that blurs the distinction between the two (for thought is co-engendered alongside the two).

Nobody knows everything: knowing, being and process

In this book I will examine the three basic modes in which film and philosophy can form a more or less productive relationship – philosophy *through* film, philosophy *of* film, and philosophy *as* film: 'through' (where film illustrates philosophy as a pedagogical tool); 'of' (where philosophy offers an ontology for film); and 'as' (where film offers us its own philosophy). In what follows, it may well be that the middle relation will be the crucial one, for it frequently provides us not only with an ontology of film but something more as well: a reason why film can also think for itself, a 'philosophical cinema'. Yet, in going beyond its remit so as also to attain the holy grail of the third relation, it often collapses into the illustrative mode of the first, using film to demonstrate nothing more than itself. Chapters 2 to 5 of this book, covering a range of positions as to the ontology of film, are therefore the most substantial. Perversely, though, the first set of these positions present themselves as solely epistemological. Film *is*, for them, a form of representation, be it conscious information processing (Bordwell's cognitivism) or the conscious representation (or 'traversing') of unconscious processes in the Symbolic and the Imaginary (Žižek's Lacanianism). Their ontology is that *film is* epistemological. The second group are more overtly ontological about their ontology, be it through Deleuze's vitalism, Badiou's substractionism or Cavell's Heideggerian world-views. Where the first emphasize cinema as a Knowing, the second see it directly as Being. Ironically, however, their positions still move in a circular logic of their own, implicating their opposites as an irreducible remainder. This seemingly inescapable conundrum of Knowing and Being is something that Ian Jarvie pointed out in his pioneering book of 1987, *Philosophy of the Film*:

> It can be argued that before we can answer the question of what exists, we have to solve the problem of what we know. Since knowledge is what we know of what exists, it is what we know about what we know that allows us to move towards articulating what we know of what exists...
>
> By parallel reasoning it can also be argued that before we can solve the problem of what we know we must first solve the problem of what exists, because when we ask what we know, what we mean is what do we know of what exists, and how can we assess any claim to know something or other if we have not solved the problem of what exists and hence can adjudicate our claims to know that it does?[22]

In giving us the essence of film as either Knowing or Being alone, each of the transcendent philosophies examined here disregard the other facets of film in order to reduce it to their own theory (of film). Yet, they do so while implicating the alternatives (the irreducible remainders of other philosophies of film) and exposing their circular logic (in the selective choices they make of exemplary films). And this is as true of each individual theory as it is of the groups of theories that oppose epistemology to ontology in general.

So how do we go beyond the dichotomy of either Knowing or Being? If we return to what Allan Kaprow said in the Preface concerning 'Unarting', then it might be through a process of 'Unknowing'. Instead of thinking that somebody must one day learn the secret of film, at least in principle, why not experiment with an alternative, with what follows from relinquishing this ontological desire? Everybody knows *something*, but nobody knows *everything*. This 'Unknowing' itself would be a process immanent to the film and viewer in relation, one that thinks alongside rather than about film as an Unknowing that acknowledges (in its passivity) the resistance of film to totalizing theory. Such a process of Unknowing goes beyond Being and Knowing because it is not something the philosopher gives to film, but what emerges in a new relation between the thinking subject alongside the becoming-philosophical of film. In the process of Unknowing, 'philosophy' too must become, at least temporarily, 'unphilosophical'.

1
Illustrating Manuscripts

For our purposes, the storyline does not quite work.[1]

The *meta-en-scène*

Giorgio Agamben and the films of Tony Scott; Emmanuel Levinas and the films of Michael Haneke; Jean-Luc Nancy and Claire Denis; Žižek and Kieslowski; Deleuze and Godard (or Badiou and Godard, Derrida and Godard, Lyotard and Godard...). Linkages come readily to mind for a philosophically inclined viewer (indeed, I will make one myself between Deleuze and Julio Medem's *Lovers of the Arctic Circle* (1998) later). When Haneke's *Caché*, for example, finally reveals who is the blackmailer, who is filming the guilty, with the answer 'no one', some cannot help but think of Levinas. His idea of a universal responsibility before the Other that comes with human existence as such seems to chime with *Caché*'s refusal to apportion the usual roles of good and bad, yet without at the same time denying that a terrible wrong has occurred. To exist before another is to be guilty, to be responsible for that Other's life. The point-of-view shots in *Caché*, therefore, operate differently from any subjective camerawork precisely because what we thought was the point of view of the blackmailer *was never that.* It was a moral imperative, the camera as accusatory – not towards the one it shoots, the Other, but to all of us who live and see. There is no blackmailer, there is no blackmail, there is only responsibility, and *all of us* are always already responsible before the details of any innocence or blame can be attributed.[2] The camera in *Caché* becomes a moral argument. In fact, the same might be said for Haneke's camera in general, his *Code Unknown* (2001) also betraying this collective responsibility we have for others. The scene comes quickly to mind when Juliette Binoche's character, Anne, is threatened by thugs on the Paris underground: throughout the ordeal, the camera refuses to turn aside, to let the viewer off the hook even for a momentary cut-away, implicating us visually as another fellow passenger who does not come to her aid.

Yet, we still have to ask: does this analogy with Levinas consequently make Haneke a philosopher in film and his films philosophical? Or should we first verify whether that 'camera' was actually Haneke's in any case, rather than that of his cinematographers (Jürgen Jürges for *Code Unknown*, Christian Berger for *Caché*)? Or will extra-filmic details (interviews, reviews and biographical information) establish the fact that Haneke has indeed been influenced by Levinas? And, even if he has not, so what? Perhaps he has invented this philosophical idea independently (great moralists often think alike). But, if this last option were the case, *how* is Haneke's idea philosophical, or philosophically interesting, then, if not on account of its similarity to Levinas's (or some other philosopher's) thought? Or, to invert things a little, could there be a patently philosophical idea coming from a film that has absolutely no analogue in any extant philosophy? I suspect not. The whole compare-and-contrast industry between philosophy and film is a one-way street for a simple reason: there has yet to be an idea identified as philosophical in film which bears no resemblance with any current *written* philosophy.

We can put this in anti-Levinasian terms: philosophy is not responsible for what it does to film, but only its own survival. The model for comparison is not just writing, however, but perceptibly philosophical writing – it has to belong to a certain genre, be it as a problem in philosophy or an idea of a philosopher. Having said that, such asymmetrical uses of film come in different strengths, the following being a less than subtle comparison of Lars von Trier's *Dogville* (2003) with Alain Badiou's notion of grace ('Grace' also being the name of Nicole Kidman's character in the film):

> In a 1997 interview with Peter Hallward, Alain Badiou defines 'laicised grace' as that which raises man above his animality... He further specifies that grace is 'an evental giving, based absolutely on chance, and beyond any principle of the management or calculation of existence'. Grace offers us a 'chance of truth, a chance of being a little bit more than living individuals'... Adopting Badiou's own terminology, we could thus further suggest that if Dogvillians reduce themselves and Grace-Kidman to animality in the name of the 'principle of management', this happens because they are not 'faithful' to her evental giving, or, in the narrator's own words, they are not able 'to look ahead'. (Let us leave aside here the fact that, as I have repeatedly pointed out, the unconditional giving of Christian Grace is itself problematic; let us suppose for a moment that Grace-Kidman is right from the beginning, a laicised gift of grace, what Badiou names an 'event'...).[3]

It is not that this passage misrepresents Badiou. Nor is it wrong to base its analogy on homonymy (no doubt von Trier too had something more in mind with 'Grace' than just a name). It is simply that what philosophy there might be in *Dogville* is apportioned in virtue of its correspondence with Badiou's categories rather than those of its own (irrespective of them being 'cinematic' or not).

Of course, there are other ways in which a film might be categorized as philosophical beyond mere analogy: Christopher Falzon sets out a typology that includes films that are explicitly works on philosophers, like Derek Jarman's *Wittgenstein* (1993), films inspired by philosophers' works (Jean-Jacques Annaud's adaptation of Umberto Eco's *The Name of the Rose* (1986) being a renowned example), films inspired by philosophical ideas (Woody Allen's *Love and Death* (1975)), as well as films with philosophical potential, such as Sidney Lumet's *Twelve Angry Men* (1957).[4] Falzon's own study, which we will turn to shortly, primarily addresses the last two types given that the work of philosophical unearthing has been done in the first pair by the films themselves.

Falzon, like the two others under examination in this chapter (Mary Litch and Mark Rowlands), is unapologetic in his use of film as a pedagogical tool: film is a rich medium for communicating ideas, for what it adds is a new form of embodied expression for philosophy – it stages its abstractions, putting the 'meta' *en-scène*, so to speak. But whether it offers us any new philosophy as such remains moot. Certainly, writings like his form part of a burgeoning subgenre of introductory literature for philosophy undergraduates. Yet, they have their own distinctiveness. Other texts in the field turn their philosophical investigations towards either individual film-makers – *The Philosophy of Stanley Kubrick* and *The Philosophy of Martin Scorsese* being two we can add to our opening list – or individual films – *The Lord of the Rings, Harry Potter, Star Wars, The Chronicles of Narnia* and *James Bond* being recent entries. By contrast, Falzon, like Litch and Rowlands, takes the 'classic' problems of philosophy as his point of departure.[5] Hence, it will be the plot of *The Matrix* that is compared with problems in epistemology; *Star Wars* (1977) or *Crimes and Misdemeanors* (1989) with problems in ethics; *Being John Malkovich* (1999), *Total Recall* (1990) or *The Sixth Day* (2000) with the question of personal identity; *Gattaca* (1997) or *Minority Report* (2002) with freewill; *Artificial Intelligence: AI* (2001) or *Terminator* (1984) with the mind–body problem; *The Seventh Seal* (1957) with existentialism; and so on.

Nonetheless, even these three are not homogeneous in their treatment of film as a teaching tool, there being different degrees of cinematic exploitation evident amongst them that ranges from the thoroughly non-filmic at one end (Rowlands) through to some obvious interest in film as film at the other (Falzon). Indeed, once we have looked at these three (most of whom are analytical philosophers), we can then tackle an example of the single-work genre, the paradigmatic case being *The Matrix and Philosophy*, which was the first entry in Open Court's ubiquitous 'Popular Culture and Philosophy' series edited by William Irwin. In this text we have a singular instance of philosophical pedagogy that, all the same, is still able to attend to the importance of cinematic aesthetics in a manner that proves impossible for Rowlands and the others.

The advent of high-concept cinema: 'once upon a premise ...'

Philosophers write, or rather, people who call themselves philosophers, write. They write lectures, conference papers, essays and books. They also write reviews of other philosophers' writings. In the absence of any visible groundswell against this fact, one must also presume that philosophers like to write. However, we are looking at the possibility that philosophy and writing are *not* eternally betrothed, forsaking all others, or, indeed, that thinking and human language (be it written *or* verbal, for philosophers also like to talk) are *not* exclusive to each other. The first way to answer the question as to why philosophers ignore the image for the word comes easily then: because they are in the word business, they are word processors. Why do they mostly reduce film to text? Why do they focus on dialogue and plot? Why do they generally use narrative film in their examples? Because this allows them to focus on the human language used in the stories told through film.

For a certain kind of philosopher, moreover, narrative film has an even stronger relation to language than simply a shared means of expression: they also share *argument* as an important formal feature. Because narrative film is most often plotted, with a beginning, middle and end, many philosophers from the analytical tradition – which puts much store on the value of argument in philosophy – equate the story with syllogistic reasoning.[6] There is a major premise (beginning), a minor premise (middle) and a conclusion (end). In narratology, the tripartite plot is most often understood in terms of an equilibrium at the start, a disequilibrium somewhere towards the middle and either a restored or new equilibrium at the end. Take *Minority Report*, for instance. The plot opens in 2054 when it appears possible to predict major crimes before they actually occur. Then, a crime (murder) is predicted that will be committed by the head of the 'pre-crime police force', John Anderton (played by Tom Cruise). After much adventure involving Anderton's attempt to avoid capture while also trying to prove that he could never commit murder (mostly by just not committing it, despite the prediction of the 'pre-cogs'), the story concludes with the realization that infallible crime prediction is flawed and unworkable. After having been falsely arrested and incarcerated, John Anderton regains his liberty and good reputation. Equilibrium, disequilibrium and restored equilibrium. But this is also a major premise (there is a world where crime can be predicted), a minor premise (it is predicted that one of the predictors will commit a crime) and a conclusion (reflexive prediction has too many inherent paradoxes to make sense).[7]

Obviously, there is some slippage here between plot and argument and any neat, one-to-one mapping between the two would be impossible. The dramaturgy involves too many extraneous elements that make the film more than a simple thought experiment, elements that will get in the way and even contradict any translation of the story into pure syllogistic argument. What still makes the syllogistic view inviting, however, is the fact that some film plots are *highly conceptual*, and so do lend themselves to such a reduction to three parts. Indeed, though philosophers have found philosophical interest in all sorts of films – be it existentialist themes in the films of Ingmar Bergman in the 1950s or ethical ones in Woody Allen's work in the 1980s – it is the rise of the 'high-concept' film from the 1980s onwards that has really made this possibility evident to academics.[8] And philosophers (continental *and* analytic) love concepts even more than they love arguments.

A high-concept film is a movie with a simple but enthralling idea, often one that can be 'pitched' to the producers (and so also marketed to audiences) in a few words: a cyborg from the future travels back to the present in order to kill the mother of the future anti-cyborg rebel leader (*Terminator*); future machines with artificial intelligence control humans (whose body heat is needed as their energy supply) by keeping them in an artificial dream sleep (*The Matrix*); *Jaws* in space (*Alien, Aliens, Alien 3, Alien Resurrection*).[9] Such films are predicated on the entertainment value of their simple, but often very exotic, major premises. It is unsurprising, therefore, that they are most often in the science-fiction genre. Unlike the more pedestrian concepts behind films in the romantic genre, for example (boy meets girl, loses same, finds same again), where the star actors, or performances, or dialogue, or photography, or direction, must raise the film above its humdrum storyline, a high-concept science-fiction film can prove inadequate on all these other fronts while still remaining of interest to its audience. To be sure, there had better be excellent special effects and plenty of excitement in the film as well if it is to be a commercial success, but, for the philosophers in the audience at least, it wouldn't matter too much if there weren't – it is the extraordinary ideas behind the films that interest them.

As a genre of literature, of course, science fiction has always been concerned with abstract ideas, and many of the most successful high-concept films of late have been adaptations of books by authors like Philip K. Dick (*Blade Runner* (1982), *Minority Report, Total Recall*), Brian Aldiss (*Artificial Intelligence: AI* (2001)), Isaac Asimov (*I, Robot* (2004)) and Arthur C. Clarke (*2001: A Space Odyssey* (1968)). Without wishing to downplay entirely the aesthetic dimensions of science-fiction writing, it wouldn't be going too far to say that it is the ideas it contains more than their form of expression that marks out the genre as a whole (with some notable exceptions, of course).[10] Indeed, with respect to philosophers who do focus on science-fiction cinema, one can always ask whether or not any difference would have been made to their discussions if they *had* kept to the original literary source of their chosen works rather than their film adaptation. Conversely, some of the thought experiments produced by philosophers themselves, from Descartes's malign genie through to Robert Nozick's 'experience machine' or Derek Parfit's 'teletransporter', do sound like part of the major premises lying behind much recent science-fiction literature and film. Nonetheless, neither medium, literature nor film, presents its ideas directly, so there will always be some reduction of the *mise-en-scène* when a set of propositions are extracted from it to prove a point in philosophy.

Extreme pretexts

The subtitle of Mark Rowlands's *The Philosopher at the End of the Universe* encapsulates much of what we've discussed so far, namely philosophy explained through science-fiction films. Science fiction also dominates the choices of film in Litch and Falzon, but only Rowlands restricts his range entirely to this genre. He does so, he says, because it lends itself extremely well to explaining philosophy (in a new literary genre that Rowlands baptizes 'sci-phi'). Rowlands is upfront about his approach throughout. His text is clearly introductory, both in terms of philosophical content and mode of address. His interest in science fiction, literary and cinematic, stems from its engagement with abstract ideas rather than any attraction to its artistic merits or demerits: science fiction simply provides 'a vast store of information relevant to the study of philosophy'. In *cinematic* form, however, we have a medium that makes the difficult ideas of philosophy more accessible because they are less abstract: cinema concretizes, it is the 'external embodiment... of philosophical thought'. Cinema is also said to be particularly good at reflecting human mores on-screen, placing our more dubious moral traits in stark, perspicuous form.[11]

Rowlands has, he admits, 'lowbrow' tastes in cinema, but given that it is the ideas embodied in film that make it valuable for his purposes, the aesthetic qualities of each example used become irrelevant. Philosophy is a doing, not a knowing – the teaching of philosophy is less about the exposition of facts than the induction of thought about problems – and in Rowlands's mind the visualization of a problem readies it all the more for such inducement. The question of whether or not there might be better or worse visualizations is not broached, for Rowlands is only interested in extracting the problem or argument from each film. And here is where the tension lies in his approach. Given that he spends little to no time on the cinematic qualities of the films under discussion, nor much time on their plots even when reduced to text, it is obvious that each movie acts as a pretext for a philosophical analysis in abstraction from its filmic 'embodiment'. Hence, the point of that embodiment is soon lost since the content of each film is, to all intents and purposes, reduced to a chapter heading. The films selected generally act as a structuring influence for discussions that could have taken place just as well in a non-cinematic context.

This pretextualism reaches its near zenith when Rowlands deliberates on whether to use Paul Verhoeven's *Starship Troopers* (1997) or Roland Emmerich's *Independence Day* (1996) as the film through which to discuss the issue of animal rights and the scope of morality. His final choice of the latter, it turns out, has nothing to do with the films themselves; rather, because Rowlands had already discussed two other Verhoeven films (*Total Recall* and *Hollow Man* (2000)), to treat a third would imbalance his book.[12] For a substitute, all he needs is another alien invader film, and *Independence Day* will do nicely. Moreover, almost *any* film with aliens treated as inimical would have sufficed. Indeed, this indifference is born out in the actual 13 pages of the discussion, which refers vaguely to the (admittedly woeful) plot of *Independence Day* in just four short paragraphs. Each film is truly reduced to its (high) concept, as premise and pretext, and little more.

Rowlands's motives become even more obvious, however, during a discussion of *The Sixth Day* and personal identity, when it is said that 'for our purposes the storyline does not quite work'.[13] The film is about cloning, but the story has one character, Adam Gibson (played by Arnold Schwarzenegger), who exists at the outset of the story before he is cloned, and then coexists subsequently alongside his clone. The problem is that this makes it clear to the audience which Gibson was the original and which the copy, so Rowlands is unhappy with the set-up. Reduced to an illustration, the film doesn't adequately fulfil its role of explaining the basis of identity in memory. Consequently, Rowlands responds to the film's recalcitrance by amending the story 'slightly'. In order to pursue the philosophical puzzles of personal identity all the better, he assumes that the original Gibson is 'destroyed, and his memories are implanted into a custom-made clone'. Now, at last, we can ask the 'philosophical' question of whether or not Adam Gibson has survived, that is, whether one's identity is the same as one's memories.

Admittedly, Rowlands is clearly not interested in any dramatic reasons why the film might have deviated from its exemplary role. But we are. So, why is the original Gibson kept? Here is one possibility: it might have something to do with a different kind of 'identification' altogether – that of the audience with the main *character*. The first Gibson is not simply 'the first Gibson', but the character who receives most of the audience's empathy. Perhaps Rowlands would acknowledge this, only then to deny that there is any philosophical interest in this extraneous fact. Yet, here is the rub, for cinematic science fiction is supposed to work because it makes ideas stark, because it concretizes them. Surely, though, part of what makes a film perspicuous *is* its emotional engagement of the audience. *Character* identification, therefore, should not be irrelevant, even when the film is reduced to teaching purposes. Moreover, emotional engagement with the particular (the original Adam Gibson) that cinema evinces may actually tell us something about personal identity that is philosophically important as well: namely, that a substitute is never the same as an original *when we know it is a substitute*, no matter how identical they may be in their properties. Hence, it is not only memory but also amnesia or at least ignorance that should be part of the question. And this lesson, though not original to the film, still comes through it in the most perspicuous manner, that is, through one of its cinematic functions.

This criticism of Rowlands is not to say that *The Philosopher at the End of the Universe* is a poor work; far from it. It is an entertaining book that does exactly what it promises to do. It contains many interesting discussions of classic philosophical problems. It does not, however, contain any interesting discussions about *whether or how* film is a good medium for discussing these problems – it simply asserts that it is and then goes on to ignore any possible filmic contribution to the debates. For instance, one leitmotif that runs through Rowlands's treatment is that of the inside/outside gap in understanding, between how it feels to be a subject inside (as free, immaterial and significant) and how we appear as an object to the outside (as determined, material and absurd), be it to others in our everyday experience or to scientific theory as physical beings. In this vein, near the book's conclusion there is a specific discussion of inside and outside in terms of an analogy between a life with no 'horizon' in it (a deathless life in other words) and a limitless visual field (which Rowlands says would be 'almost impossible to imagine').[14] The moral of the analogy is that finitude is a good thing. Astoundingly, however, there is one particular visual field that is never mentioned by Rowlands: *the cinema frame*. Not only would this throw a very interesting light onto this question, but it is also a topic that has consistently occupied film theorists for decades. Yet, neither of these matters can be found in Rowlands's analysis of inside and outside, presumably because it would take the discussion off on a tangent into the nature of film (which, for Rowlands, is not philosophically interesting).

Philosophies through films

In contrast to Rowlands's more blasé approach, Mary Litch and Christopher Falzon do make an earnest effort at integrating the films they use into their philosophical discussions. In *Philosophy through Film*, for instance, Litch gives full storylines for each of the films she uses and also asks the reader to watch them all before reading her work. There is, in addition, a much smoother integration of cinematic and philosophical material, with a good deal of switching back and forth between the two media, rather than what we get in Rowlands – a quick, isolated outline of each film, followed by the real business of doing philosophy. Like Rowlands, though, Litch comes from the analytic tradition. What they consequently share, therefore, is a structure that progresses along traditional lines, starting with metaphilosophical questions and proceeding from metaphysics and epistemology, through philosophy of mind to ethics and social philosophy.

After such an auspicious start, however, some reticence quickly appears. Litch claims, for instance, that any intentions the film-makers (writers, directors or whoever else) might have for their films are irrelevant for her discussion. Though such avoidance of the cult of the auteur is no doubt noble, one suspects nonetheless that it may mask her omission of any discussion of film aesthetics as well. Certainly, her treatment of each film – with one exception – reflects an aversion to what film can achieve when it is doing *more* than simply delivering plotlines and dialogue.[15] Two examples will suffice to show this.

Firstly, Litch's analysis of *Artificial Intelligence: AI* involves a number of abstract discussions of Turing, Searle and the nature of consciousness, but wholly avoids analysing the film itself. Admittedly, the director Steven Spielberg does transform the original story by Brian Aldiss into a morality tale more like Pinocchio and, with that, loses a good deal of its conceptual narrative. But because Litch is so reliant on narrative content for her philosophical ruminations, she is mostly left with little more than the film's title and object (an artificial boy) as a pretext for discussing the merits of Searle et al. Once again, film is primarily acting as a chapter heading.

Litch's treatment of Woody Allen's *Crimes and Misdemeanors* begins with more promise, however, making good observations of how the different characters' positions can be related to various 'isms' in moral philosophy – relativism, subjectivism, egoism, utilitarianism, Kantianism, and so on. Moreover, she uses scare quotes fittingly when she says that the main characters in the film each 'represent' a moral viewpoint.[16] Clearly, then, Litch knows that there's a lot more to this film than the set of mouthpieces for various ethical stances that it can appear to be (an easy temptation too, given that Woody Allen has a well-known interest in philosophy). But this is where the nuances of filmic storytelling end for Litch. Though movies are said to turn theories into 'flesh', the precise manner by which they do this is never broached.

Crimes and Misdemeanors makes many references to light and vision, both in the dialogue *and* visually. The lead character, Judah, who commissions a murder, is an ophthalmologist; his patient, Ben, is a rabbi who is going blind. There is a strong connection between losing one's sight and one's moral vision throughout the film, the great irony being that the rabbi keeps his faith in an absolute moral order while his ophthalmologist ends up a relativist (having escaped punishment for his crime). The subplot's lead character Cliff (played by Allen himself) is a film-maker who spends much of his life in darkened cinemas; but he is also a good man who receives little reward in our seemingly unjust society (at the end of the film he loses both his film project and 'the girl'). That Plato famously compares knowledge, especially knowledge of the good, to the light of the sun, while also likening ignorance to dwelling in a dark cave, would be of interest here, one would think. That *Crimes and Misdemeanors* itself is so focused on images of vision, of light and dark, and all the shades of grey between them, would surely be of interest too. Yet, Litch avoids these matters entirely, and continues to talk about the film only in terms of the argument it supposedly puts forward through its plot and dialogue.

The one exception to this avoidance of aesthetics and what is peculiar to film comes when Litch turns to Anand Tucker's *Hilary and Jackie* (1998). The film tells the story of the cellist Jacqueline du Pré and her sister Hilary. Its narrative structure is slightly peculiar in having the same events shown and then reshown from the very different perspectives of each sister (a device that goes back to Kurosawa's *Rashômon* (1950) and Welles's *Citizen Kane* (1941)). As Litch turns to the film when introducing arguments for 'cognitive relativism', she sets out what is unusual about it:

> *Hilary and Jackie* differs from most of the other films presented in this book, in that its philosophical import is not to be found in its story or in bits of dialogue, but in the structure of the film. In the film's various retellings the viewer is made aware of the markedly different interpretations each of the characters puts on the 'same' set of events.[17]

The film's structure *enacts,* rather than *relates,* the philosophical point. In fact, Litch admits that philosophical arguments often treat relativism too abstractly, whereas film makes concrete and comprehensible what a 'different perspective' might actually mean.[18] This concession to the power of film form, however, only highlights Litch's avoidance of aesthetics in every other film she tackles. That she does find philosophical content in their stories and 'bits of dialogue' does not obviate the fact that their structure, or cinematography, or *mise-en-scène,* or acting performances, may have contained more than was apparent at first glance. They too may have been philosophical. In other words, *Hilary and Jackie* is not unique at all.

Gone to the movies

Christopher Falzon's *Philosophy Goes to the Movies* is the exception that proves the rule in this genre. Though he constructs his book along analytic lines (moving from epistemology through mind to ethics), he also incorporates ideas from continental thought (such as Foucault's social philosophy), and is unique in having a section on 'critical thinking'. Topics such as political hierarchy, dystopia and science versus antiscience are broached through films like *Antz* (1998), *1984* (1984), *Brazil* (1985), *Things to Come* (1936) and *The Name of the Rose* (1986). The final chapter on critical thinking uses *Monty Python and The Holy Grail* (1974), amongst many others, to elucidate logical fallacies like 'affirming the consequent' and 'denying the antecedent', as well as ad hominem arguments, closed thinking, deduction and induction.

He begins, as we did earlier, with an excursus on the conflict between word and image in the history of philosophy, from Plato to Michèle Le Doeuff on the power of images in structuring philosophical thought. Out of this comes a promise from Falzon that imagery will do more than merely illustrate ideas in his analyses: films are not 'mere examples', he says, but are 'rich texts' that can actually act as a 'corrective' to philosophy. Certainly, Falzon begins to make good on his promise by looking at the importance of the cinematic images in his chosen works. When discussing Bernardo Bertolucci's *The Conformist* (1970), for instance, due attention is paid to the film's use of light (for which it is renowned in film studies) in the scene when would-be assassin Marcello Clerici confronts his old university professor, Luca Quadri. In the professor's study, Clerici (now a fascist collaborator) reminds him of his old lectures on Plato's allegory of the cave and, while doing so, closes the shutters on the window to plunge the room into almost complete darkness.[19] Such an obvious clue from the dialogue will ensure that even a philosopher cannot avoid the *mise-en-scène* here, yet, nevertheless, Falzon is still making a giant leap by including this observation into his use of film for teaching philosophy (one that proved impossible for Litch when discussing *Crimes and Misdemeanors*).

Furthermore, Falzon is clearly familiar with some of the debates in film theory, citing when necessary major figures in the field like George Wilson and Victor Perkins on the question of visual narrative.[20] Falzon also works with a much wider and more nuanced selection of examples than usual, and integrates them into his expositions in fairly seamless fashion. When making his own way through *Crimes and Misdemeanors*, for instance, he quickly introduces *Casablanca*, *On the Waterfront* and *Wall Street* when their relevance arises. Though his chosen themes are fairly standard, he fleshes them out through many different films, not just the one or two that headline each chapter. Falzon is obviously someone who has accrued a knowledge of film as an end in itself, rather than a narrow selection of films gathered as a means to an external end.

With such praise, one might think that *Philosophy Goes to the Movies* has found the perfect formula for linking film to philosophy. Certainly, this is the most sophisticated entry in a market necessarily restricted by its self-imposed remit of introducing philosophy through film: given the task to teach one discipline, he still does remarkably well in alerting the student reader to issues in another discipline, film theory. But whether he also reaches his own declared holy grail of using films as more than 'mere examples' and even as 'correctives' to philosophy, remains debatable. Indeed, this idea of correction implies no more than film's facility to 'address philosophical issues in a concrete way' wherever philosophy, by contrast, 'has lost itself in abstraction and universalization and has forgotten its connection to concrete existence'.[21] Yet again, the *mode* of film's concretization is left aside, that is, how film *as film* actually might correct philosophical ideas.

What we get instead, on the one hand, is how film *as text* (that is, as reduced to plot and dialogue) might possibly supplement certain extant philosophical thoughts, or, on the other hand, how some film images might give those ideas greater impact through visualization. But how visuals might themselves philosophize, might not merely illustrate but actually think for themselves while still being visual – *this* possibility is not entertained.

And perhaps it never could. The difficulties that would arise in any attempt to construct an audio-visual model of philosophical thinking are probably too challenging for entry-level texts such as Falzon's (or Litch's or Rowlands's). In this connection, it is surely not insignificant that not one of the three works examined here has a chapter on philosophical aesthetics amongst all the others on epistemology, metaphysics, mind, logic, ethics and politics. To bring in aesthetics would be to open the way to discussing cinematic aesthetics, which would finally necessitate providing some details as regards how philosophy can be communicated through what is *specific* to the medium of film. In other words, we would have to learn more about how film concretizes philosophy, about how a thought can be visual.

Which brings us to our fourth, and slightly different, example of philosophy through film, William Irwin's collection, *The Matrix and Philosophy*.[22] Apart from the fact that this is a collection of 20 different authors writing on *The Matrix*, its other distinction from the monographs we've already looked at is that it does tackle film aesthetics alongside the usual suspects of epistemology, metaphysics and mind, ethics and religion, and socio-cultural issues. The final essay in the section on aesthetics, for example, brings in research from genre studies, arguing that *The Matrix* is a *mixed* genre film, at times promoting action and suspense at the expense of reflection (so it is not purely a film of ideas), while also stimulating the audience to reflection during the moments in-between (so it is not a pure action film either). And it is not insignificant that this essay was co-authored by George McKnight, a film-studies specialist. In addition, the collection also includes an essay by Cynthia Freeland, an established philosopher of film rather than an enthusiastic amateur, that critiques *The Matrix*'s antibiologism and masculinist bias, contrasting it unfavourably with David Cronenberg's *eXistenZ* (1999) on both accounts. Freeland also does something that remains rare for this genre of philosophical literature: she allows the theme of *The Matrix* to emerge through the nature of the cinematic 'illusion' *per se* – the form itself of film teaching us something about appearance and reality.[23]

Conclusion

Though in this chapter I have struck a generally negative, critical tone throughout, this was an unfortunate inevitability given, on the one hand, my own undertaking to discover the most productive encounters between film and philosophy and, on the other, the fairly limited ambitions of most contemporary works that try to teach introductory philosophy through film. In my own defence, however, the chapter has been mercifully short. And in defence of the works dealt with, it must be said again that they mostly achieve what they set out to achieve, and follow a very clear pedagogical agenda – to educate in philosophy using cinematic illustrations.[24] It is only that the ambition of that agenda falls well short of what film and philosophy can do together.

So, what more can they do? To be specific, what more would the proper incorporation of film aesthetics bring to these studies? In fact, we've already encountered some possibilities. For instance, some engagement with character identification, which we saw lacking in Rowlands's treatment of *The Sixth Day*, would be one area where a broader knowledge of the filmic would serve philosophical ends. In particular, the difference between optical 'alignment' and affective 'allegiance' would be of great use, given that we are not necessarily allied with the characters that we are aligned with optically. When Mary Litch analyses *Total Recall*, for example, she simply takes it for granted that '*the viewer* is in exactly the same position as the character'.[25] Though the film uses 'restricted narrative' – putting us in a similar (though not identical) epistemic position as the hero of the film, Doug Quaid – this is not the same as being in the same affective situation as him, for our attitude as viewer is a product of numerous forces other than just knowledge. Yet, it is the affects produced in the audience that give films their 'force', according to Litch, so surely some more reflection is warranted on how they are produced *aesthetically*. One has only to think of how such a naivety towards camera and point of view would reduce the philosophical possibilities of *Caché*, to realize how important it is to incorporate aesthetics.

To get us started, therefore, here is a short list of some of the aesthetical properties that give film its full force: the elements of *mise-en-scène* (setting, lighting, costume and make-up, figure and camera movement, acting performance, props, and colour, as well as the broader elements of camera framing and composition, angle, distance, and focus); *editing* (cuts, dissolves and fades, establishing shots and close-up shots, 'continuity' versus 'dynamic' editing, 'montage sequences', elliptical editing, and expanded editing); and *narrative* (narration versus narrative, restricted and unrestricted narration, cause and effect plotting, linear and non-linear chronology, reflexivity, multiple narratives, and unreliable narration). And this is still not to mention the importance of sound, music, acting or the difference between realist and anti-realist film aesthetics in general. Beyond aesthetics *simpliciter*, there are many other non-textual issues in film apt for philosophical reflection, including whether the psychological experience of seeing a film can be restricted to the film object at all, for example; or whether the means of distribution and consumption (that is, exhibition and viewing) are not also implicated in the 'meaning' of any film. Of course, moving like this, firstly beyond the text to the aesthetical, and then beyond that to the non-aesthetical, inevitably opens up a Pandora's box of other knowledges, be they from the cognitive sciences, psychoanalysis, cultural studies or even metaphysics. Yet, the complexity of the task should be no excuse for not pursuing it. Hence, many of these features will be discussed in the following pages.

The theorists who follow in the rest of this study are well aware of this complexity, yet they remain resolute that the richness of film has philosophical import that goes well beyond the illustrative model. The question remains, however, whether or not these theorists, in their own way, inadvertently reduce cinema to certain exemplary choices that, in subtle and intricate fashion, still serve to illustrate their philosophy of what film is and what film can do.

2

Bordwell and Other Cogitators

> The idea of cinema's history as an unfolding potential treats the medium as holding at the outset the seeds of future growth. Yet the later developments to which the historian points are always a mere sampling of the uses that have been made of the medium; if the historian picked different instances, she might be forced to posit a different essence *ab initio*.[1]

Introduction: going back to the future

The 'sampling' we have already seen in the illustrative mode of film-philosophy throughout the work of Rowlands, Litch and Falzon was never disavowed: only certain films, or film scenes, or aspects of film scenes, would do to teach philosophy, namely those ones whose text was judged to be philosophical according to extant, non-filmic, philosophical standards. The part of the film-philosophical landscape we are heading into presently has much greater ambitions as regards its interdisciplinarity: here the theory will endeavour to prove itself worthy of film itself, by *showing us what film really is*, be it in metaphysical essence or in our psychological experience of it. The explicitly ontological approach (the *being* of film) will be tackled in Chapters 4 and 5 where Deleuze, Cavell and Badiou are engaged; whereas the psycho-epistemological aspect (film-viewing as a form of cognitive process, be it conscious or unconscious) is the object of our enquiry in this chapter and the following one. But we shouldn't underestimate the moment of this latter engagement. Though it would seem to bear more on empirical method than metaphysical doctrine, on *how* film ought to be viewed rather than on what film is, the choice of method, as we will see, reflects a theory, more or less explicit, of what film (viewing) *really is*.

With David Bordwell's work within the cognitivist paradigm, which is our subject here, the philosophical comportment is, admittedly, quite nuanced. At certain points, in fact, it even takes on the mantle of an anti-philosophy, rejecting 'theory' in preference of an empirical *science* of cinema. There are various facets to this enterprise that will have to be explored, both in what this cognitivism affirms and in what it rejects. For the former, the questions of its own computational (or informationalist) perspective, its normativity, biologism and universalism, will all be addressed in turn. And as to the latter, what it rejects most adamantly is an excess of *hermeneutics*, what Bordwell calls 'making meaning' out of film. The illustrative mode of film-philosophy discussed in the last chapter would certainly prove guilty of this sin when it reads perfectly legitimate yet still ultimately arbitrary (philosophical) meanings into various films. Meaning is always a subjective sample. Though philosophers and other theorists (historians, psychoanalysts, culturalists) can take what they want out of film, it will only be on account of the aforementioned sampling process that Bordwell condemns.

It is the ontological vice that is most often to blame for this tendency according to Bordwell, the notion that there is an 'essence of cinema', such as 'pure movement' for example, that is projected 'back onto cinema's origins, treating the most significant changes in style as developing toward that goal'. Following Ernst Gombrich's ideas on visual art, Bordwell labels this a 'Hegelianism without metaphysics', the treatment of film history as the 'exfoliation of the *a priori* categories of an aesthetic system'. In actuality, cinema is too 'variegated a medium' to lend itself to any such 'medium-specificity'. The key problem with this approach is that it proffers a false, retrospective purity that takes the contemporary moment as the 'ideal vantage point'. Jean Renoir's work, for instance, only achieved its pre-eminence after its marginal place in the canon was re-evaluated in the light of André Bazin's reading of cinema history in terms of a new, realist ontology of film. The essentialist view also focuses too much on selected individuals instead of 'collective norms'.

Such approaches, says Bordwell, are incapable of any 'systematic explanation of how innovations were encouraged, blocked, spread, or sustained'. They remain personal impressions based on selective readings of small numbers of films. A *science* of cinema, on the other hand, would be suitably empirical, basing itself on the latest models of human perception, the most rigorous and widespread historical research, and the closest examination of films from the best archives. And, thereby, it would be a truly explanatory science, looking at the recurrent 'patterns of stylistic continuity and change' that comprise film history (and indeed, that give it its history) with a view to explaining them through cognitive psychology.[2]

Certainly, even opponents of this new empiricism cannot but admire Bordwell's tenacity, both as the leading cognitivist in contemporary film studies and for the consistency of his approach. From his early 1985 work, *Narration in the Fiction Film*, through to the more recent *The Way Hollywood Tells It* (2006), Bordwell has argued, constantly, for one filmic constant (albeit with some variation): that there is an enduring style of 'classical narration' created and subsequently sustained to this day through Hollywood film-making. It is a narrative style composed of individualized character-psychology, local agency as primary plot motivator, cause and effect logic, and canonical storytelling (moving from an initial situation, through its complication, to an eventual resolution). *It's a Wonderful Life* (1946) has it, *On the Water Front* (1954) has it, *Jaws* (1975) has it. This consistent style can even be found in contemporary Hollywood concept films and blockbusters, despite their increasingly exotic plotting, cinematography, acting and editing. Moreover, other modes of narrative, especially those of the international 'art film' and Hollywood independent film, are no less defined and characterized by Bordwell in relation to this enduring Hollywood norm. It is this norm that predetermines the pattern of continuity *and* change within film history, one that Bordwell exposes and explains through close empirical observation.

The reason why this norm endures is not a fundamentally cultural one, however, for its ultimate origins are psychological. Incorporating the work of Gombrich as well as R. L. Gregory and Julian Hochberg on the psychology of perception, Bordwell sees film narrative as a 'dynamic process' that involves the film-maker in the selection, arrangement and rendering of 'story material', as well as the active participation of the viewer, who responds to this input by constructing 'a perceptual judgment on the basis of nonconscious *inferences*'. In this, Bordwell shows himself to be partly *constructivist*, allowing the viewer an active role in composing the film story or *fabula* (to use the term Bordwell inherits from the Russian Formalists) from the partial information provided by the film (or *syuzhet*) itself.[3] Where Vladimir Propp's morphology of folk tales analysed them into such common structural features as seven character functions and 31 narrative units, Bordwell outlines classical cinema in terms of 'devices' (such as the dissolve, the pan or the shot/reverse shot – to name but three), 'systems' (time, space, and narrative causation), and the relations between these systems. It is these that provide the viewer with the raw material out of which he or she will construct a film. As such, Bordwell's is a perceptual–cognitive model of film comprehension, a 'problem/solution model... [that] invites us to reconstruct decisions made by active agents, and it treats persons as concrete forces for stability and change (or both)'.[4] In other words, the story of film spectatorship told by Bordwell is quite like the stories told in certain movies themselves, with a central plot composed of questions and an agent who propels it in search of answers.

Without a doubt, the research paradigm of Bordwell and his associates – Noël Carroll, Charles Eidsvik, Torben Grodal, Paisley Livingston, Joseph Anderson, Wayne Munson, Carl Plantinga, Stephen Prince and Murray Smith – has been extremely influential from the 1980s onwards, playing no small role in the decline of 'Grand Theory' (for the most part, the Freudian and Althusserian subject-position approaches of the 1970s). Indeed, with the increasingly empirical bent of the post-Bordwellian era, it is arguable that film *theory* has been transformed back into the film *studies* from which it once emerged.[5] Bordwell has brought us back to the future.

Alongside this neutering of 'Theory' also comes a naturalization of film aesthetics, with evaluation being dropped in favour of a purely descriptive approach. Admittedly, some might accuse such a purportedly scientific stance of both naive empiricism and teleological formalism (the better a film suits the scientific ideal, the better it is), but Bordwell always defends his paradigm swiftly against such charges. Looking to styles of narrative implies neither a priori normativity nor a teleology of form, nor does it indicate a dogmatic, *scientistic* position – it is 'empirical without being empiricist' he says.[6] Yet, as we'll see, to avoid the more nuanced charge of verificationism (over scientism), Bordwell will have to broaden his empirical point of view to include numerous kinds of film experience, not only the putatively quantifiable (or 'naturalistic') ones. If this is not granted, then Bordwell too will have fallen foul of the same retroactive selectivity with which he charges Grand Theory, only one that samples according to a dogmatic cognitivism, reducing film to certain psychological aspects of its consumption.

Though he never claims his approach to be free of all 'theoretical assumptions' – for 'all knowledge involves the subsumption of a phenomenon to a conceptual frame of reference' – Bordwell will still assert that 'some frameworks are more complex, precise, and nuanced than others' without substantiating any standards for such complexity, precision or nuance.[7] And it is *this* presupposition that is Bordwell's first manifestly philosophical stance. Hence, despite his denial of any 'univocal metaphysical or epistemological or political presumption' latent within the cognitivist programme, the suspicion remains that Bordwell's work does have a particular vision – a philosophy even – of what film and film viewing mostly entails; that is, what it really is. Indeed, both Bordwell *and* Slavoj Žižek, as we'll learn in the following chapter, share a *representationalist* platform to the extent that there is a *qualitative* difference between physical reality and conception or perception for Bordwell, just as there is also a qualitative difference between the Real and the Symbolic or the Imaginary for Žižek. Yet, neither believe that physical reality and the Real are absolutely unknowable – there are optimal situations when we are in touch with, or represent, the world veridically. Moreover, it is because thought and perception (or the Symbolic and Imaginary) *can* refer veridically beyond themselves in the form of immaterial information or knowledge (the optimal cases for Bordwell and Žižek being science and 'traversing' our fantasies respectively), that both can allow themselves a normative selection of films. A question mark remains hanging, however, over how and why it is that certain representations (be they films, philosophies or sciences) can pierce through the veil set by both between mind and world.

Classical and art-house: hurray for Hollywood

Within Bordwell's approach, the principle tenet is the endurance and universality of the classical Hollywood style of narration, one that demands a naturalistic justification. The clear use of events and actors; individuated characters who are psychologically rather than socially motivated; linear chains of cause and effect; the division between main and secondary plots; the use of mostly unrestricted narration, itself structured with a beginning, middle and end; the provision of a proper (often happy) resolution at the end; and the use of continuity editing – all of these principles are firmly rooted in the Hollywood mode of film-making, such that even the more experimental strategies of plot and style found in recent Hollywood output, actually only deviate from the norm at their margins. Indeed, even their deviations have precedents in the Hollywood norm, the peculiar use of extended travelling shots in Gus Van Sant's *Elephant* (2003), for example, being already prefigured in films by 'Max Ophuls, Stanley Kubrick, or the Alfred Hitchcock of *Rope* (1948) and *Under Capricorn* (1949)'.[8]

The Hollywood style of telling stories with 'classical continuity' is the rule against which other kinds of cinema, like the 1960s art film, for instance, characterized themselves: 'art-cinema narration has become a coherent mode partly by defining itself as a deviation from classical narrative'. Jean-Luc Godard's adage that 'films should have a beginning, a middle and an end, but not necessarily in that order' gives some indication as to how that artful margin deviates from the norm for Bordwell too. If one transgresses the well-established laws for creating a 'fabula world' – by flouting 'the most common assumptions, the most valid inferences, the most provable hypotheses, and the most appropriate schemas' – then one is in the realm of self-conscious art. All the same, even art has its norms, be they extrinsic to the particular film (as part of the art genre), or intrinsic to it (as a pattern built up gradually during its own development). In other words, a norm-breaking film can't break *every norm* – the art film too must abide by some standards: if 'every card is wild you can't play cards at all'.[9]

A specific example of Bordwell's approach to art cinema can be seen in his analysis of Godard's *Tout va bien* (1972), though he might easily have chosen *Contempt* (1963), *Le Chinoise* (1967) or any other of Godard's works. He alights immediately on the Brechtian elements of the film, especially with regard to its dilemma of a left-wing film-maker (Jacques) and his lover (Susan, a radio journalist) having to work within capitalist society.[10] In particular, Godard uses the Brechtian 'principles of separation' to describe how the audience of *Tout va bien* is prevented 'from being wholly absorbed in the illusionary aspects of the action'. These principles heighten the viewers' awareness of the artificiality of the film that they are watching (having characters speak to camera, exposing the film sets, disrupting the editing, and so on), and so block any tendency they may have to naturalize its depictions as genuine realities. In this reflexivity, therefore, it is a typical art film. It is a film about watching (a) film. Seeing that the reality depicted in a movie is an effect allows us also to imagine alternative realities. It awakens in us the possibility of thinking about ourselves historically, the contingency of the status quo (the 'everything's fine' that is just a surface effect), and so the possibility of change.[11]

In all, *Tout va bien* uses three principles of separation in its narrative – interruption, contradiction and refraction. Here is what they mean, according to Bordwell. In a classical (Hollywood) film, the cause and effect chain of narrative links scene to scene, 'thoroughly' motivating each event: if a character buys a gun in one scene, one can be sure it will reappear in another. *Interrupting* this cause and effect series functions to confuse us as to the relation between one event and another. Yet, such interruptions are common in *Tout va bien*, as in Susan's interview with striking workers at a meat factory, which is stalled by another worker breaking into song; or when Susan confronts Jacques concerning her dissatisfaction with their relationship, which is interrupted with scenes from their working lives.[12] We soon lose the plot or 'narrative causality' on account of these interruptions. Secondly, *contradictions* arise when discontinuous editing is used to create spatial and temporal ambiguity, as when Susan sits down twice to begin her confrontation with Jacques at breakfast. Mismatches between visuals and soundtrack (often we hear a voice but don't see the character's mouth move) have a similar effect. But of the various modes of separation, it is the third, *refraction*, that both stands apart and subsumes the other two. It is defined as what

> draws our attention to media that stand between the depicted events and our perception of those events. We do not seem to see a series of 'natural' events, as we might in a Hollywood style film. Rather, *Tout va bien* takes the media as part of its topic.[13]

This process of refraction works explicitly on various levels: in terms of plot (Susan and Jacques both work in the media industries of film and radio); in terms of narration (some of the film's voice-over narration is provided by factory workers, some by a broadcaster, rendering the narration 'arbitrarily selective, even capricious'); and in terms of symbolism (the mode of production of the media is clearly compared with that of a meat factory). Yet, refraction can also be said to subsume contradiction and interruption given that these two phenomena, in their own way, alert us to the artificiality of the medium by breaking with its conventions of seamless editing, synchronous sound and cause-effect plotting. As Bordwell puts it: 'the emphasis on *Tout va bien* as a "film about cinema" makes refraction an overriding principle'.[14] And, commensurately, this use of refraction is what makes Godard *the* 'art-cinema' film-maker – his 'authorial presence hovering over the text', the '*superauteur*' playing cinema.[15]

As a refractive film, *Tout va bien* breaks the rules of Hollywood cinema in a self-conscious fashion. This is a very *knowing* transgression of the norm, one that marks it out as 'art-house'. As such, Hollywood (the norm) remains as powerful as ever, despite Godard's insubordination. Admittedly, there is one point when Bordwell seems to be on the verge of conceding something more intrinsic to the art film, when he discusses Roland Barthes's idea of a 'third meaning'. This is what Bordwell's colleague, Kristin Thompson, calls 'excess' material, forms of meaning beyond denotation and connotation, comprised of 'casual lines, colors, expressions, and textures'. Art here equals excess. Yet Bordwell, by his own acknowledgment, is not interested in such excess, but only in the central 'process of narration'. Of course, there will be those who argue that the division of filmic material into norm and transgression or excess is illegitimate, for no such norm, or central process, can be isolated. From this perspective, the art of film saturates *every* part of it. The inherent aspects of an 'art film' *really are inherent* and are not just relative to classical standards.[16] And the 'excess' of an art film is not gratuitously exotic either, but must be understood as *a different form of realism*.

Yet, the taming of the aesthetic dimension of cinema, be it in terms of transgression *or* excess, is absolutely necessary for Bordwell when isolating narration *as a cognitive process*. As Daniel Frampton notes:

> In analysing typical art-cinema or parametric narratives Bordwell only seems to want to *rationalise* them. Radical cinema is reduced to *principles*, *systems*, all towards trying to bring artistic cinema into the *rational* fold of classic cinema.[17]

These are not thoughts that Bordwell could ever support, however. Claims by avant-garde film-makers themselves, for instance, that new forms of realism are being innovated through film, are dismissed by him as merely attempts to 'justify novelty' and cultivate ambiguity. The real offering of the art film is to *inform* the spectator of its reflexivity – it is a metalevel communication only: 'put crudely, the procedural slogan of art-cinema narration might be: "interpret this film, and interpret it so as to maximize ambiguity"'. For a science of film such as Bordwell's, therefore, ambiguity in film cannot be realistic because reality really is clear cut. If there is any ambiguity in the film, it must be because the film is saying something about itself.[18]

Messages are for Western Union

> Contrary to what many believe, a study of United Artists' business practices or the standardization of continuity editing or the activities of women in early film audiences need carry *no* determining philosophical assumptions about subjectivity and culture, *no* univocal metaphysical or

> epistemological or political presumption – in short, *no* commitment to a Grand Theory.[19]

What Bordwell and his allies mean by 'Theory' (capital 'T'), is described as 'an abstract body of thought which came into prominence in Anglo-American film studies during the 1970s'.[20] It is not that Bordwell is against theorizing per se, he claims, but rather its abusive Grandeur, its non-empirical basis.[21] The proponents of Theory share many tenets: that 'human practices and institutions are in all significant respects socially constructed'; that 'verbal language supplies an appropriate and adequate analogue for film'; that one must follow a 'top-down inquiry'; a taste for 'argument as bricolage' and 'associational reasoning'; 'the hermeneutic impulse'; and a penchant for 'expressing their disdain for "empiricism"'. Yet, despite these and many other distancing references to Theory, Bordwell actually employs some of its most important principles.[22] He too adopts a tempered conventionalism, for instance, arguing that much of what we do when watching a film is learnt, even though certain conventions are so strong and cross-cultural (as in the shot/reverse shot, for example) that we must have inborn dispositions to acquire them. And Bordwell even admits that the breadth of the cognitivist perspective in film studies might remind some of a 'Theory of Everything'. All the same, he quickly adds that it is not another Grand Theory or ideology, being neither metaphysical nor pseudoscientific, but concentrating instead on observation as part of an empirical research programme.[23]

Indeed, Bordwell's anti-ideological stance is crucial to his overall position. He believes, in particular, that perception must be understood primarily as psychological and biological rather than ideological. He has no time for the idea that each epoch has its own 'way of seeing' that is socially constructed. This notion, says Bordwell, is another 'deeply Hegelian idea' that has come down to contemporary cultural studies (the last incarnation of Theory), via Walter Benjamin, John Berger, Tom Gunning and others.[24] In fact, Bordwell's major objection to this culturalism (a supposed inability to justify its characteristic constructivism and conventionalism) also acts as evidence in favour of his own position that there are innate cognitive processes at work when watching a film:

> contemporary theoretical work...has been both strongly *constructivist* and strongly *conventionalist*. In the first place, the spectator-as-subject is assumed to partly collude in his subjection by contributing expectations, inferences, and desires that the text requires in order to work its effects...The problem with this view is that without *a priori* factors, construction – under the very terms of the metaphor – is impossible. Construction can't occur without a purpose, without principles, and without materials. To deny such *a priori* factors is to render the concept of construction inappropriate.[25]

In other words, constructivism cannot operate *ex nihilo* – it needs some given material to construct with, and this material, though not necessarily raw or unmediated entirely, must be *precultural*. Given this conclusion, Bordwell can then make the case for a new position: when we watch a movie (or anything else for that matter), our brain – which is a type of computer – operates in calculative mode, making inferences from the information delivered by the filmic text. For him, 'perceiving anything involves description, problem-solving, and inference – all constructive processes we would normally associate with higher-level activities'.[26] Be it a classical Hollywood narrative where the problem is to solve the obstacles in the path of the protagonist, or an avant-garde art film, where the difficulty is to solve just what this movie is about (in a typically 'reflexive' fashion), the film-experience is all about encountering problems, generating solutions, testing them and finally having our expectations fulfilled or not.

Alongside the end of this constructivism in film theory comes the demise of 'interpretation' as well. When any theory, like Freud's or Marx's, is applied to a film, the result is a specific 'Meaning', such that the purpose of the film analysis is revealed as hermeneutics: 'to interpret a film is to ascribe implicit or symptomatic meanings to it'. Yet, for Bordwell such meanings are always false, subjective ascriptions based on sampling. Too often the 1960s and 1970s film critics of the *Cahiers du cinema* or *Screen* journal reduced the films they were addressing in order to sustain an ideological position, an interpretation. This reduction process always involved the same a priori, outside and transcendental meaning being forced upon the film, 'sometimes in pseudophilosophical or pseudoreligious terms'.[27]

Against this, Bordwell sees it as his task to reveal the filmic and perceptual mechanisms that generate meaning *immanently* (including the false meanings of the ideologues). In essence, Bordwell follows Samuel Goldwyn's famous dictum that 'messages are for Western Union': films should be analysed for what they do, not what they mean – even when a part of what they do is facilitate the making of meaning.[28] The objective, scientific approach must relinquish any a priori ascriptions and focus only on what film *does* empirically, how its formal devices interact with the viewer's perceptual-cognitive mechanisms to create a story. Film provides information (the *syuzhet*), be it in the dialogue, the cinematography, the *mise-en-scène*, the editing or whatever else. The viewer receives this information in the form of 'cues' (input) that stimulates a set of inferences (output) regarding the story (the *fabula*) of the film: 'film presents cues, patterns, and gaps that shape the viewer's application of schemata and the testing of hypotheses'. The brain, in this cognitivist paradigm, must be seen as an 'inferring machine' that works with its own dynamic set of internalized 'story schemata' (clusters of knowledge that guide our 'hypothesis making'), utilizing them in its 'algorithmic processing' of the cinematic information it receives.[29]

In the course of his argument, Bordwell uses the work of Geoffrey Nowell-Smith, a well-known theorist of the 1970s and 1980s, as a typical example of the hermeneutical trend he wishes to depose. In reply, however, Nowell-Smith raises some interesting points of his own regarding Bordwell's approach. The first concerns whether the mind can be usefully described as an 'inferring machine' at all, as Bordwell asserts. Is he not over-intellectualizing the process, assuming an ideal rational agent as spectator? Bordwell says that he is not (though we will return to this issue later). Nowell-Smith also raises the classic weakness of much cognitivist theory (be it in film studies or elsewhere): it seems impossible for computers to make the leap from syntax to semantics. They may manipulate symbols, but they cannot understand their meaning. Hence, when *we* think, judge, compare or watch films we are not information-processing machines, for these activities *do* involve meaning or semantics rather than mere mechanical syntax.[30]

In more depth, the argument here goes something like this: given that computers do not have minds (to assume otherwise would beg the question), how can the computational analogy explain anything mindful, such as understanding the meaning of films? How can a film property, such as an on-screen colour for instance, 'cue' any meaningful understanding *in the informational brain*? It is arguable that this is, firstly, a retrospective projection, a segmentation of a process (of viewing) into two artificial parts, with one supposed posterior part (understanding information) mysteriously located in the brain under the (correlated) causal influence of the supposed first part, the stimuli of the film data (the anterior part).[31] As such, it is an example of 'reverse engineering' that correlates putative brain states with known perceptual phenomenology.

Secondly, how is the brain capable of being 'cued' at all? Doesn't this already assume a power of comprehension within the brain? It seems highly contestable that a part of the brain-computer could be able to understand at all, when (film) understanding is exactly *what we are trying to explain*. In other words, in the cognitivist scheme, we are led to a regress, with a little, comprehending film-viewer (or '*homunculus*') imbedded in the brain in order to explain the abilities of real-world film viewers. Clearly, what cognitivists like Bordwell have found when collecting research on the brain and visual perception are revealing correlations between cerebral events and perceptual states. But to argue from this that it is a part of the brain that is producing the film comprehension is both an unwarranted leap (from correlation to cause and even to identity) as well as a fallacy (leading to regress). Apropos of hermeneutics, Bordwell himself states that 'to give every film a narrator or implied author is to indulge in an *anthropomorphic fiction*'. But doesn't the cognitivist paradigm also repeat this same fiction by incorporating a miniaturized film-narrative viewer in the brain?[32]

On the other hand, according to Nowell-Smith, another aspect of Bordwell's reformist ambition involves *semantics or meaning itself*: he does not wish to talk about meaning per se, but instead about information and causal effects, and this is part and parcel of his antihermeneutical enterprise. The information provided by a film 'cues' the meaning we make of it. Bordwell doesn't discriminate between interpretations (of the 'implicit' or 'symptomatic' meaning of a film) as better or worse because he regards all such interpretation as 'allegorical': each of them are equally fanciful inasmuch as what is 'covert' within the text is only a meaning that has been *projected* there. Hence, by ignoring interpretations (of covert meaning) he can look instead at what is overtly stated in the dialogue, the film's formal elements and their impact on cognition. According to Victor Perkins, however, this division of the film's 'message' into overt and covert elements 'requires an imperviousness to the complexity of cinematic expression'. Bordwell, he argues, is wrong to think of explicit and implicit levels in film (the latter projected by fanciful interpreters) for this distinction is 'patently vacuous': there are simply readings which pay attention to the complexity of the film's *mise-en-scène* and those which do not (hence, Perkins believes that there definitely are examples of good and bad interpretation).[33] Bordwell is too simplistic, claims Perkins, in taking every movie to propound a 'literal' meaning (information) on its surface. It is wrong to think that there is firstly the objective information and then a merely figurative meaning (either originally lying *or* placed beneath). Every meaning (and that includes 'information') is more or less complex, and found through attentive *reading*, not just looking. Meanings are not necessarily stated explicitly or implied; rather, they are *filmed*: this 'means that they are not hidden in or behind the movie, and that my interpretation is not an attempt to clarify what the picture has obscured. I've written about things that I believe to be in the film for all to see, and to see the sense of'.[34] And such complex, recursive interpretations can neither be reduced to 'units of meaning' in the film (or information cues), nor eliminated as fanciful projections.

The meanings garnered through a critical reading of a film are not offered as proven syllogisms, according to Perkins, but as *suggestions* to the viewer on how to 'renew' (or 'enrich') his or her experience of the film. Such suggestions may require metaphorical description, but they are, nonetheless, *accurate elaborations built upon shared life experiences*, rather than objective, discrete cues: 'intra-textual understanding depends on extra-textual understanding not only about facts but also values'.[35] Perkins's assumption, then, is that (good) films deserve more than one viewing, as further significance can often be found on repeated exposures (either alone or with another viewer). Though they may be subtle, such readings remain with what is perceptible in the film itself: they are not 'implicit' but *attentive* to *film's own way of making meaning*, to filmed-meaning, which cannot be equated with an isolated, literal or propositional meaning ('information'). They are part of the film's form – its *how* is its *what*. Here is an example of Perkins's approach when reading a scene from Max Ophuls's *Caught* (1948):

> No neat disjunction can be drawn between the meanings that Leonora offers to Smith Ohlrig, that Barbara Bel Geddes offers to the camera and that the film offers to its audience. An appreciation of this sequence should encompass all three. The aptness of the writer's invention in having Leonora include 'how to listen to music' in her catalogue of social usage; the skill of Bel Geddes in enacting, via a tiny beat after each 'how to', the split second of recall that betrays Leonora's gestures as unspontaneous and insecurely learned; the precisely graded camera position that gives prominence to the listening gesture while allowing us to see enough of the tea pouring (partially obscured by the steering wheel in the foreground) to supply the informing context: these are all achievements in the construction of meaning.[36]

If such a complex reading as this doesn't gain universal assent immediately it is not because it is ideological, but because it takes time to see it, for we don't all have the same acuity of perception. Like tasting wine, or hearing music, the senses are plastic and sometimes need to be educated to appreciate what is before them. Bordwell, however, would regard this kind of description as belletristic, the product of a meaning-maker whose well-wrought language (or 'rhetoric') ascribes something subjective and speculative to the film, rather than something scientific and publicly verifiable.

Science, empiricism, culture

The new science of film, Bordwell hopes, will produce knowledge of a calibre approaching that of 'the natural and the social sciences'. But this will not be through any crude reductionism: Bordwell's is a project for a 'good naturalization' he says, that is, one that doesn't disguise a particular culture as given nature, but that is 'nibbling at the edges of philosophical doctrine with teeth sharpened by empirical inquiry.'[37] In this endeavour, Bordwell regards himself as a Kantian, taking into account 'the findings of empirical sciences' investigation of the mind and brain' when discussing matters of the mind. Prior to the cognitivist revolution in film studies, on the other hand, too much argument was based on ornate descriptions, 'incomplete syllogisms' and appeals to authority, when what was needed was 'rigorous logic and systematic knowledge' based on sound inductive reasoning: 'a *description*, even a moving or pyrotechnic one, is not an *explanation*. It does not show that the particular case manifests a general tendency'.[38]

Of course, what counts as an empirical study is frequently a movable feast. Bordwell is constantly on his guard to refute charges of reductionism being placed at his door. On the contrary, he claims that he is a methodological pluralist. Responding to a charge of scientism from Dudley Andrew, for example, he asserts that only if *one* kind of evidence, experimental evidence, were admissible to this paradigm, would he then be open to this accusation. So, good, detailed descriptions can also count as empirical, the close analyses of André Bazin and Noël Burch (though presumably not Perkins's) being exemplary in this regard.[39] Moreover, Bordwell even extends this ecumenism to Freud himself, whose ideas were based on, and constantly revised on account of, his original empirical practice as a therapist. This contrasts all the more, therefore, with the contemporary Freudian film theorist who treats Freud's ideas as an immutable authority, no longer adapting them to data from further therapeutic practice. And on this last point Bordwell is surely right.[40] Nonetheless, if he is to avoid accusations of scientism, Bordwell will have to show us that there is nothing totalizing about the claim that cognitivist explanations are superior to psychoanalytical ones *de jure* (as Peter Lehman, for one, has asserted).[41]

In fact, Bordwell sees himself as trying to go beyond the dichotomy of nature and culture when he talks of 'contingent universals' in film comprehension (where Bordwell is once again following Ernst Gombrich). Such phenomena are 'contingent because they did not, for any metaphysical reasons, have to be the way they are; and they are universal insofar as we can find them to be widely present in human societies'. Non-cinematic examples include language use and our ability to distinguish the living from the non-living. But being conventional does *not* mean being arbitrary and lacking norms: it is not arbitrary, for instance, that the 'right rear turn signal on an automobile announces that the driver intends to turn right, not left'. When it comes to films, we can see that a movie is a 'bundle of appeals, some narrow, some fairly broad, and some universal'.[42] There exist visual effects that lie on a continuum: highly specific at one end, but '*cross-cultural, even universal*' at the other.[43]

Culture does indeed have a large part to play in comprehension, for it is doubtless that 'cinematic style is not a closed world of films and technical devices'; but, nonetheless, 'some stylistic factors will be *cross*-cultural, trading on the biological or psychological or social factors shared among filmmakers and their audiences'. There are 'nodal passages' in any film, things that we all commonly comprehend when viewing – where it begins and ends, where its plot develops and twists, what the characters do, what props appear, and so on. These nodes remain constant amongst the various interpretations attributed to them – what the gun *means*, *why* the cowboy stands in the doorway, and so on. Indeed, they form the raw material for those interpretations: 'comprehension, it seems, can often get along without interpretation, but interpretation must appeal to comprehension, especially when it hopes to surpass it'.[44] So much for ecumenism.

The crucial point for us to understand for now is that, for Bordwell, this cultural universality *follows* biology: 'the most comprehensive and powerful explanations of conventions in any art would seem to be those which show them to be functional transformations of other representations or practices, some of which may be biological predispositions or contingent universals'. The exemplary case proposed by Bordwell of a contingent universal in film is the 'shot/reverse shot'. It is its psycho-biological underpinning that explains why the shot/reverse shot is 'instantly recognizable across cultures and time periods'. If the shot/reverse shot treatment of cinematic dialogue has perennially won the approval of film-makers, it is on account of being one of those schemas with psycho-biological efficacy.[45] It exploits our hard-wired disposition to look at faces for information.

Closely observed frames

At this level at least, biology rules our film cognition. And yet there is something already cognitive about this biological level that facilitates the supervenience of the former on the latter. Indeed, it is here where Bordwell's ecumenical claims start to wear particularly thin. We have already heard Geoffrey Nowell-Smith and Victor Perkins criticize Bordwell for his informationalist and computationalist approach to film-meaning. What is now to be said about this biologism? The first point Bordwell can argue for the inherent cognitivity of *every* aspect of mind, irrespective of being more or less biologically 'primitive', is that:

> even the simplest perceptual activity resembles higher-level cognitive activity. Perception has built-in assumptions and hypotheses, it fills in missing information, and it draws a conclusion based on but not reducible to incoming data.[46]

For instance, the phenomena of 'flicker fusion' and 'apparent motion', basic essentials to the perception of film, are regarded as instances of (bottom-up) 'processing'. This much can be conceded no doubt, but it is highly contentious whether such concessions also license a hard-wired cognitivism over what are arguably much more culturally specific and affective traits, such as viewer attention, or what counts as plot points and character action.[47]

This is the recurring weakness of Bordwell's argument here: he constantly cites evidence for the universality of basic psycho-biological mechanisms on the one hand, as well as high-level narrative conventions on the other. But he is less convincing when it comes to those phenomena strung between these two levels, especially the sophisticated audiovisuals pertinent to film experience. Indeed, he tends to conflate what lies between the levels with what lies below and above in the name of a supposed 'panhuman nature' or 'metaculture'.[48] Yet, the former are too primitive and the latter too textual to have the purchase on film viewing that Bordwell ascribes to them.

Hence, Slavoj Žižek is partly right when he queries whether one can say, as Bordwell does, that there is 'a neutral, global notion of what is "comprehensible"'. Even the idea of 'directing [the viewer's] attention' – a *basic* role for the Bordwellian film-maker – is culturally relative: the fact that non-Western painting can often seem confusing to Western eyes shows how even this supposedly transcultural basic is mutable.[49] Indeed, Žižek, in his inimitable way, brings the idea of the 'universal' itself to its limit, asking whether '*the very notion of a trans-cultural universal means different things in different cultures.*' What can seem universal is often itself culturally prepared, so when one looks for common traits amongst films from around the world, one must also be aware of how the ground for each national cinema has been prepared by other, older forces such as European cultural propagation. The flashback in Emily Bronte, for instance, or cross-cutting and close-ups in Dickens, or off-space in *Madame Bovary* – all these were in place before their explicit visualization by cinema.[50]

In addition, one should be no less cautious before accepting the idea that bottom-up processes are themselves cognitive (irrespective of whether they are universal and psycho-biological). Bordwell certainly thinks that they are: 'bottom-up perceptual processes, such as seeing a moving object, operate in a fast involuntary way, but they remain similar to other inferential processes'. There are better arguments, however, from both the 'embodied cognition' theorists like Francisco Varela and 'external mind' theorists like Andy Clark, that show how these functions cannot be seen as inferential, information processing phenomena.[51] They make the case for an embodied and dynamic cognitivism, one that would give requisite space to affectivity and cultural specificity in the film process, while also 'smearing' the distinction between subject and object that is so central to Bordwell's representational approach:

> In fact an important and pervasive shift is beginning to take place in cognitive science under the very influence of its own research. This shift requires that we move away from the idea of the world as independent and extrinsic to the idea of a world as inseparable from the structure of these processes of self-modification ... The key point is that such systems do not operate by representation. Instead of representing an independent world, they enact a world as a domain of distinctions that is inseparable from the structure embodied by the cognitive system.[52]

Clearly, this would not fit Bordwell's brand of cognitivism. This is because he employs a methodological individualism that assumes a strict separation between the representing subject and the represented art object. Be the role of the spectator conscious and active or non-conscious and passive ('involuntary'), it is always a form of knowing, of information processing, because perception itself is 'a process of active hypothesis-testing' for

Bordwell. And perception is 'like thought' because it works with 'assumptions, expectations, probabilistic inferences from data, etc'. Indeed, though Bordwell knows well that there are 'body-centred' forms of cognitivism, and though he rejects a purely 'quantitative' approach to information in favour of retaining, *pace* Nowell-Smith, 'semantic content, grasped in relation to intentions [or] propositional attitudes', nonetheless, the experience of film viewing is always a cognition of information, a computation of data, a representation of 'cues'.[53]

What facilitates this representationalist stance greatly is Bordwell's isolation of the film's *fabula* from its style and *syuzhet*, a binary of cinema's two sides – input (style and *syuzhet*) and output (*fabula*).[54] The *fabula* is always portrayed as a static, separate entity – dynamically produced to be sure, but always at any one time the fixed *product* of other processes. This renders the *fabula* more prone to an analogy with information and Bordwell's judgement that 'an ideal syuzhet supplies information in the "correct" amount to permit coherent and steady construction of the fabula'. Given this view, Bordwell can consequently say that Antonioni's *Blow Up* (1966), for instance, 'fails as a detective story: it presents too few pieces of information to enable the protagonist, or us, to solve the crime'. Or, when discussing Godard's *Vivre sa vie* (1962) he says that Nana's conversation with Paul in the first scene 'could be staged, shot, and cut in many ways and still convey the fabula information about their separation'. Time and again, Bordwell objectifies both the *fabula* as proposition and the film-object as autonomous dataset: 'the same information could be extracted from a film', be it staged and cut in a traditional or experimental fashion. As Victor Perkins put it, Bordwell believes that each film's meaning boils down to the 'literal meaning of any statement spoken in it, or the conventional meaning of any stereotyped visual image shown'. Indeed, though following a different agenda to Rowlands, Litch and Falzon, like them, Bordwell thinks that films contain propositions, so that in each film scene there is some isolable information being communicated to us.[55]

Another aspect of this methodological individualism is Bordwell's psychologism. As the experience of film is psychological through and through for Bordwell (rather than ontological, as we will see Deleuze advocate in Chapter 4), then its *fabula* must be constructed within psychological parameters. For example, flashbacks and flashforwards – which are given metaphysical functions in Deleuze's ontological approach (time itself underlying memory and anticipation) – can only make sense to Bordwell if they are psychologically explicable.[56] An illustration of this comes to hand when Bordwell discusses Nicholas Roeg's *Don't Look Now* (1973):

> One might argue that a film could plausibly motivate a flashforward as subjectivity by making the character prophetic, as in *Don't Look Now.* But this is still not a parallel to a psychological flashback, since we can never

> be as sure of a character's premonitions as we can be of a character's powers of memory. The forward movement of the *syuzhet* will inevitably involve the question 'Will X be right about the future?'[57]

Likewise, Bordwell cannot determine whether the flashbacks in Bertolucci's *The Spider's Stratagem* (1970) are subjective – belonging to the characters – or objective – belonging to the commentary. Subject and object, once again. As Daniel Frampton bemoans, Bordwell's dilemma only arises, however, because his 'schemata are mutually exclusive'.[58]

The other side of the static binary, of course, is the film as object, as dataset, information and objectified artwork. His approach must focus, Bordwell says, 'on the *work* – the film as an object, but also the regulated effort that produces and uses it'. Hence, with rigorous, empirical observation, Bordwell is able to discover barely discernible things, such as the serialism in Robert Bresson's *Pickpocket* (1959), only 'by close viewing'.[59] In other words, his objectification of the film-object itself depends *on an objectified set of viewing contexts*: one only sees *the* film through repeated close observations.[60] Following Noël Burch, Bordwell's empiricism leads to the inevitable conclusion, viz. an elitism of viewing that discovers the real film-object:

> we define 'elite' as those people willing to take the trouble to see and resee films (many films), as one must listen and relisten to a lot of music in order to appreciate the last quartets of Beethoven or the work of Webern.[61]

Such elitism is not unique to Bordwell, of course, but what is of interest for us is how it methodologically motivates an image of what film and film-experience *fundamentally* are.

In sum, what weakens Bordwell's cognitivist paradigm most is that, despite certain nuances, it remains an input/output model. It posits fragmented percepts or images as input (albeit ones that are actively selected), that are then supplemented by associated thoughts (schemata) leading to an output (the inferred *fabula*).[62] What is at issue here, then, is whether Bordwell has artificially isolated and over-intellectualized the film process. Daniel Frampton certainly thinks so, charging Bordwell with an 'over-rational reductivism' when he proposes that 'filmgoing is simply cognitive processing, and that filmgoers should always initially go for the most rational interpretation of a film'. Films in his hands become 'jigsaw puzzles of narrative styles, which we are now tempted to "work out"'.[63] What film is, is cognitive, it is essentially information, and what the viewer does with this information is cognitive too – the construction and representation of a story, the *fabula*. In Chapters 6–8 I will myself query whether the *fabula* is an autonomous, thing-like product at all. I will propose the alternative image of *fabulation*: as an ongoing story-event created by various processes, all of them constructed differently (cognitively, affectively, materially, culturally). This would make the *fabula* less a representation than a process, or the process of many processes, for which neither narrative nor psychological norms can provide a static foundation.[64]

From reflection to refraction

Let us consider a little further the relative stabilities and changes within the film process by returning to the concepts of reflexivity and refraction that Bordwell exposed as the essence of the art film when examining Godard's *Tout va bien*. The very opening of *Tout va bien* enters us straight away into a realm of reflexivity: we hear the title of the film repeatedly announced over images of endless cheques being written to cover the movie's production expenses. The 'diegesis', or story-world, immediately reflects on itself non-diegetically by showing us an important aspect of how this movie was made. Yet, at another level, one can also see that there is a *new* diegetic content or world created once the audience is inured to this repetitive effect (which doesn't take very long): this film becomes a film about making *other* films. After all, who believes that the actual cheques for the film were signed *in just this manner*, when it is obvious that the signatory *already* has a film camera hovering over his shoulder? These signatures become a performance, no matter how subtle, and so a sign of *another* reality (how films are made) rather than *that* reality itself – the actual film being made.

In other words, this film's attempt to reflect on itself is refracted such that it remains outside of its own reflection and misses its original target (itself): what we see is a film that is *really about* making (political) films. The 'really about' or referentiality of the film is not a failing on Godard's part, but stems from the tendency of any audience *to naturalize what it sees over time* – to create a new world. Presumably Godard did hope to highlight the artificial, constructed and economic nature of his own creation, and yet, in doing so, he, *or the film and audience together* (once the latter gets used to the former's contrivance), do eventually refer to something real, viz. the alienating effects of either film-making in general or other particular films. Alternatively, perhaps this is all that Godard wanted – to say something about the malign political effects of *other* films. If that is the case, though, then perhaps we should also rethink Bordwell's depiction of self-reference in the realm of avant-garde film and, with that, the classical realism in Hollywood's output.

There is actually a name for this creation of reality by an audience – 'Branigan's Paradox'. According to Edward Branigan, disrupting the story-world (by revealing the artist's devices) does not expose the cinematic illusion for what it is, but only creates a new world within the film. As Joseph Anderson explains it:

> Even if you break the diegesis, you do not thereby gain a glimpse of reality. You simply create another formal element in the narrative (of lights, camera, cables, and microphones) or another embedded 'world' within the film. It is all occurring inside the framed event, which we already know is of a different order than the reality outside the frame.[65]

When looking at Bordwell's analysis of Japanese art films from the 1930s, for example, Branigan puts the case plainly: materials and metaphors 'wear out' – 'what was once bright and arresting – an expressive flourish – becomes merely a conventional denotation when its underlying metaphor is short-circuited'. Hence, what Bordwell marginalizes as 'decorative' in these Japanese films is no mere excess, for, 'from the standpoint of a spectator ... these decorative moments do in fact have a meaning'.[66] Contra Bordwell, Branigan even argues for the diegetic quality of intertitles within silent films:

> To take another of Bordwell's examples, an intertitle which goes out of focus and which contains the words of a woman who is crying. The words of the title refer to grief which is also the label we metaphorically connect to the blurring of the lines which constitute the material, written lines of the words. The intertitle represents a massive condensation whereby we are to understand that the spoken words of grief are like the choking sobs which blur the sound of the speech and like the tears which cloud the vision of the speaker. One could imagine this dialogue title being unwound into a series of shots including perhaps an out-of-focus, point-of-view shot. For the character, words, choking and tears go together in a causal fashion, but for the spectator the connections are mediated through a network of cues ... It is almost as if we see the words themselves cry out in anguish and perhaps then one would not be far from the logic that motivates [Noël] Burch when he asserts that spectators at the Bunraku theater are crying over the wooden dolls themselves and not crying because of the story or character.[67]

Excess, transgression or decoration become, with time, part of a new story-world, part of a new reality. The supposed transgression actually bears within itself a cinematic realism of its own kind. Metaphors wear out.

Indeed, Branigan's Paradox has another name when set in the more general context of philosophy: Henri Bergson's concept of refraction. This makes Bordwell's own use of the term 'refraction' with respect to Godard all the more ironic (given his representationalist credentials), because Bergson is anything but a representationalist. For him, images are immanent to the world, a part of it rather than a representation about it. Indeed, despite appearances to the contrary – that Bergsonism has no time for vision or space – there is another side to Bergson beyond the usual stereotype. In him, we find a well-thought-out theory of mediation that unfolds alongside the better known philosophy of radical novelty, which is why 'refraction' is one of the most common and important terms in Bergson's work. Neither *durée* nor the *élan vital* are ever pure, but exist in perpetual tension with their internal other (space and matter). They are not opposites within a fixed dualism but mutually refractive tendencies within a constant process of dualization.[68]

Every representation is actually what Bergson calls an 'impeded refraction', wherein new content is formed through a refraction (rather than reflection) passing through an older form.[69] We could see this partly as a logical point concerning the limits of reflexivity: complete self-consciousness is impossible to the extent that we cannot incorporate the actual act of self-consciousness into what we are conscious of; we cannot say that this film *truly* portrays the *falsity* of *all* film (a variation on the Liar's Paradox, 'this statement is false'). In other words, the performance of *X* cannot be included in *X* (without some magical bootstrapping). The 'of' or 'aboutness' refracts its supposed content to make itself (as form) into a new content. As such, no film, no matter how reflexive, can ever be about itself: it cannot see itself reflected in the mirror, for, in trying to do so, it will always miss or refract the act of seeing itself in the mirror.

Of course, the possibility that art films are not about themselves (and thus, by proxy, about Hollywood or classicism) but about other *realities*, cannot be countenanced by Bordwell. He dismisses their redefinition of the real with scare quotes and condescension: their 'new aesthetic conventions claim to seize other "realities": the aleatoric world of "objective" reality and the fleeting states that characterize "subjective" reality'. Claims for a new realism on the part of artistic film-makers, like Alain Resnais, are subverted by having *their* 'realism' (in scare quotes again) downgraded as 'wholly arbitrary'.[70] Yet, as Stanley Cavell for one notes, Godard's strange camera movements in *Contempt*, while making 'an original and deep statement of the camera's presence', are also 'about its subjects, about their simultaneous distance and connection, about the sweeping desert of weary familiarity'.[71] These films are not essentially rebuffs to Hollywood's realism – they have their own realities to contend with.

Play time

These realities are not localizable, however, either in some subjective world (where Bordwell places art) or in an objective world (where he places the hard-wired cerebral dispositions that underwrite Hollywood's realism).[72] It is in the temporal relationship between *all* sides of the film process (subjective and objective) that they each can become real. The question of time is a matter for Chapters 6 and 7 of this study, but for now we should remind ourselves that the conventions of producing, distributing and consuming films are ones that we have mostly become inured to over time, that we have forgotten are conventions, symbols or metaphors. As Paul Douglass notes, everything about cinema was once an 'oddity' that has now lost its strangeness with repeated exposure, from the two degrees of vision that it presents us (compared to our normal 200 degrees of vision), to all the other perspectivist conventions that we have internalized through repeated exposure.[73] Likewise, the interruptions and contradictions that Bordwell's own work analyses in Godard are only a *more recent* set of distortions of time and space. But such distortions are not new, as Bordwell knows perfectly well: cinema has always played with time.[74] It is a peculiar irony that Andy Warhol's supposed real-time films, like *Empire* from 1964 (composed of a single eight-hour shot of the Empire State Building), were actually taken to be avant-garde works on account of their ultra-realism, that is, their *continuity* regarding time. Indeed, the consequent question arises automatically: when has a film ever represented 'real', continuous time when it has involved more than one continuous shot?

The answer, of course, is 'never', but not because film lacks the ability to capture real time, so much as film itself being just *one instance* of the myriad forms of time. There is no pure, single, continuous time to capture; or rather, real time just is the host of *different kinds of* time being made continuously. Continuity versus discontinuity or ellipsis is a false opposition when time actually comes in different varieties, when there is no one 'objective' time that can be taken as bedrock. The ellipsis is there in every film, only in some it has been normalized to seem real and continuous on account of the conventions of cutting internalized by the spectator. Most classical films are incredibly elliptical in their treatment of time – abbreviating conversations, actions, travel times and so on. They also lengthen time when necessary (think only of any action sequence where we count down to the bomb's explosion in 60 seconds, in an interval much longer than that). Films also shorten and lengthen spaces through the intercutting of long, medium and close-up shots, shot/reverse shots, and so on. But the supposed seamlessness of such editing is an acquired, learnt convention that has become the sign of reality. Similarly, so-called 'matches' on action (cuts that connect two different views of the same action, at the same moment, in a movement, such as getting into a chair from long shot to close-up) are only ever approximate because movement is, by definition, a mismatch of sorts. Movement is the ellipsis *in*, and so the elision *of*, every being that changes. Such changes occur at different speeds of course, and they are normalized by both our cultural and embodied dispositions. But because they are changes all the same, they can never be framed in an *essential* form: the slippery thing about letting any change in is that it opens up the permanent possibility of further change.[75]

Though Bordwell obviously knows that the classical norms of editing are not *actually* continuous (whatever that might mean), his treatment of their transgression by art films belies the presupposition that they are. I quote:

> These three factors [use of informative technique, spatio-temporal coherence and stylistically stable devices] go some way to explaining why the classical Hollywood style passes relatively unnoticed. Each film will recombine familiar devices within fairly predictable patterns and according to the demands of the syuzhet. The spectator will almost never be at a loss to grasp a stylistic feature because *he or she is oriented in time and space* and because stylistic figures will be interpretable in the light of a paradigm.[76]

But how does this orientation in 'time and space' succeed? Is it because it conforms to the (seemingly) natural, Euclidean space of our everyday surroundings, or because it conforms to *habituated forms of space and time* that were once, nonetheless, inventions? Bordwell opts for the former view, taking realism to be some variant of the neoclassical unities of space, time and action (with distinct cause and effect).[77] When it comes to Godard's famous discontinuities, for example, they yield 'the impression that footage has been excised from within a shot…[but] the device signals one thing unequivocally: the intervention of the filmmaker at the editing stage'.[78] Art as reflexive again.

Yet, many supposedly conventional action films today use both elliptical and overlapping editing (repeating part or all of an event, like an explosion, by showing it multiple times from different angles – an especially popular Hollywood import from Hong Kong cinema). But does the target audience of these films – adolescent American males – believe that there were multiple events instead of one when exposed to overlapping cuts? Of course not. Do the film-makers worry that this recurrent editing will jar with the serial editing of the rest of their films? Obviously not. For what were once the hallmarks of experimental or avant-garde cinema have been domesticated, despite their huge deviations from previous versions of 'real' or 'continuous' editing. These devices no longer serve supposedly reflexive ends, but now, even in adult cinema, are there to forward the diegesis. The jump cuts used throughout Danny Boyle's *28 Days Later* (2002) and Thomas Vinterberg's *Festen* (1998), or sporadically in Martin Scorsese's *Taxi Driver* (1976), for example, neither impede the narrative nor signal the author's presence: in both cases they propel the story forward and possess huge expressive powers. The fact that *Festen* can 'get away' with so much discontinuity is because the jump cuts express the highly strung, enervated and neurotic nature of the characters and situations, *as well as* how much we have been inured to their oddity. Or think of the jump-cuts that Steven Spielberg places throughout *E.T.*, a film which even as early as 1982 caused no confusion at all amongst its audiences.[79] Indeed, the commercial success and normality of the 'independent' films of the 1990s, which appropriated everything they could from European art-house cinema of the 1960s and 1970s (Tarantino's work being the most famous example), is a testament to how well popular audiences have internalized and naturalized the artistic style as a new realism.

Even causal logic is a mutable category that resists any essential hierarchies of representation. According to Bordwell, however, logic is the preserve of classicism. Hence, by contrast, the causal chain is typically *broken* in art films. One example Bordwell provides is Michelangelo Antonioni's *L'Avventura* (1960), in which the crucial search for a lost woman eventually drops out of the plot as the story meanders to an inconclusive finale: when 'the recovery of Anna is no longer the causal nexus of the action', we have a 'loosening of causal relations'.[80] Yet, even if we leave aside the fact that 'what happens next' in most Hollywood 'quest' films rarely follows a linear mode, in terms of strict cause and effect, these searches are always pretexts for other adventures. Or rather, what counts as a linear pursuit is always an *acquired* taste depending on the film and its audience. Films like Roman Polanski's *Frantic* (1988) and Paul Schrader's *Hardcore* (1979) are both classical in many ways, yet they also renege on their ostensible search in favour of other narrative pleasures. The search-object is a pretext for journey-entertainments (*Frantic*) and/or education (*Hardcore*). Like *L'Avventura*, both films involve a man and a woman searching together for another missing woman, a man's wife and daughter respectively. The major difference is that in *L'Avventura* the search is seemingly aborted while in the others it is completed (indeed, they are ultimately successful). Yet, the non-search pleasures, as we know from the genre conventions of this kind of film, are central (these are films about what happens when one *doesn't* find what one is looking for). In *Frantic*, for instance, the sexual frisson between Richard and Michelle (especially during their dance at the club), the physical comedy of Richard (knocking his head twice in the interior of the barge), and the situation comedy created by Michelle (whose inopportune avarice leads to further capers and danger) – all these joys are narratively motivated by the genre (the search that is *not* a search). By the end, one wonders whether the pair really ought to find his wife Sondra (and whether the fact that he does find her is indeed an *inconclusive* ending for the film). It is not so much that cause and effect are absent (or 'loosened'), but that there is a different type of genre causality evident here, one often motivated by a regular, rather lifeless, man encountering either a femme fatale or muse that inspires him into a new life of adventure: Peter Bogdanovich's *What's Up Doc?* (1972) and Jonathan Demme's *Something Wild* (1986) evince this type of causality too, but so does, in its own way, *L'Avventura*.

The fact that Antonioni's film is serious and European does not render it any less 'realistic' than Hollywood's output. The meanderings in these films are examples of what Jacques Rancière describes as movements 'deflected by the imposition of another movement' (rather than movements brought to a 'fictional end').[81] There is always movement, only sometimes of a different, more adventurous kind. Conversely, it is interesting that Michael Curtiz, whilst directing *the* Hollywood classic, *Casablanca* (1942), reassured those with doubts as regards the film's *illogical* storyline with the following promise: 'don't worry what's logical. I make it so fast no one notices'.[82] Curtiz knew how important time is to belief, not simply as regards masking an illogic with speed, so much as creating a new logic with time. Paraphrasing Nietzsche (and Branigan) on truth and metaphor, we might say that continuity (like space, time and causality) is a worn out, forgotten ellipse.[83] Or as Christian Metz writes: 'what is experienced as a simple figure of speech today was quite frequently, for the first spectators of the cinematograph, a magic "trick", a small miracle both futile and astonishing'.[84]

Counter-arguments against Bordwell's universalism often focus on the particular (in opposition to his predilection for the general), on *how* certain films implement genera, such as the shot/reverse shot or cause and effect. Slavoj Žižek, for instance, points out four different examples of cross-cutting that can be seen beneath its abstract conceptualization.[85] Victor Perkins, meanwhile, emphasizes the variability of Hollywood's 'happy endings', even so far as to show how classical conclusions, as in *The Wizard of Oz*, are anything but cheerful, or even conclusive, resolutions. And Gilles Deleuze, as we'll see later, alerts us to the different forms of action in the supposedly classic action films of Hollywood in the 1930s, 1940s and 1950s, through what he calls its 'large' and 'small' forms. Of course, Bordwell would defend his position by saying that all of this is to ignore the real continuities in Hollywood's output over the last 60 to 80 years in favour of the exceptions to its rule.[86] However, perhaps this tension between change and stability is less about accepting or denying absolute *differentia* so much as nuancing the *genera*: there are indeed continuities at one level, but it also remains true that, at another level of observation (and so remaining within the empirical rather than transporting ourselves out of it into 'Theory'), those continuities are each very different, given the other *relata* they connect with in any specific viewing. *How* has eye-line matching, for example, been implemented *and* received across classical Hollywood cinema from the 1920s to the 1960s? Is 'it' the same, and do *we* see it the same, for each era? And – a different question – *did we see it the same in each era*? How do we remember seeing it? (This last is a question that we will see Cavell ask. For isn't our more or less flawed memory of film also an important part of its experience?)

Moving the continuum

Yet, despite such evidence for the mutability and porosity between nature and culture *in both directions*, Bordwell insists on a *fixed* continuum with easily learnt, hardwired and disposition-friendly effects at one end ('dissolves or fades; most acting styles; and most stylistic innovations such as cross-cutting'); and culture-specific acquisitions at the other end that need more exposure to acquire (such as the artful playing with narrative time). We would not dispute that there is, at any one time, a continuum. But what is on the continuum itself is not fixed; rather, it is always itself moving (and, as we'll see, resting on another, equally mobile, continuum). What orients and fixes Bordwell's continuum is the hard-wiring that makes some conventions (like the shot/reverse shot emphasis on the face) less conventional than others. He takes the human face in 'close-up' to emphasize a character's intentions and reactions; consequently, to have the audience notice an actor's expression, a close-up of the face is non-arbitrary.[87] But, notwithstanding the fact that human brains are obviously evolved to see details in human faces better than in, say, animal display rituals, the question remains moot as to whether this is the non-arbitrary *cinematic* place to look in order to learn about a character (unless one simply begs the question and defines the actor's facial expression *as* the character's expression).

Why should the human face be *the* place to look to learn about a character in a film? The way he or she stands, the movement of a hand, or the spatial configuration of bodies might be far more telling: think only of the shots of Marlon Brando with his back to camera in *On the Waterfront* (1954), or Spencer Tracey in *Bad Day at Black Rock* (1955), or Daniel Day-Lewis at the conclusion of *There Will be Blood* (2007). And where else might one discover character? Might it not also be in the costume design, lighting, tone of voice, sound effects, music, the number and place of the cuts, what has happened before in the film, my knowledge or ignorance of what will happen next (is this my first viewing or my tenth?), my memory of the other roles played by that actor or actors in this scene, my knowledge of the genre constraints for this scene and this film, the size of the cinema (or living room), the brilliance of the screen, the time of my viewing (as one continuous 120-minute spectacle in a large theatre, or through closely observed five-minute segments watched repeatedly on a TV monitor), the number of people in the cinema, the person I am with in the cinema, my position in the cinema, my own mood at that viewing, my psychological disposition that day (week, month ...), the previous film I just viewed (*Life is Beautiful* (1997) seen after a diet of Italian neo-realism is not the same when seen after a diet of Spaghetti Westerns), my cultural expectations ... ? All of these elements, and more, *together*, might also be the 'place' to look, which is to say, no place at all, but rather the time of the 'viewing' *per se*.[88]

And where should the list end when talking of the effects a moment of film has on, or with, me? Nowhere. No one place can prevail. We cannot situate any one variable in ascendancy over any other, whether it be psycho-biological (following Bordwell) or cultural.[89] The naturalization of 'convention' occurs through the refractive agency of time itself (rather than the self-awareness of the auteur that Bordwell latches on to). Familiarity breeds belief in a reality, or, as Bergson put it, 'the paradox of today is often only the truth of tomorrow'.[90] What starts out as a 'refractory' representation can become a commonplace truth simply in virtue of our manipulation of the concept. And this reality can belong to Hollywood (or to the myriad differences that are crudely aggregated together as 'Hollywood'), as well as to a host of other bearers. Only each time this reality will be slightly different (and a slight difference is all it takes to counter any essentialism).

In truth, I cannot think of any contravention of a so-called norm of film-making that cannot itself become a sign of new reality. To make the point more striking, lens-flare – an *artefact* of 'conventional' film-making that was once avoided but eventually became a stylistic cliché of the 1960s and 1970s – is these days reproduced artificially in animation (using both computer-generated and optical imagery) and computer software games. It has become a token of realism. It is now what Jean Baudrillard would call a sign of the hyper-real, an artifice of media that also 'eclipses the real', that is even better than the real thing.[91] So what Branigan's Paradox names is less an aporia for reflection than the creativity of film, or rather, the temporal productions of the film and audience together. The formalistic transgressions of *Tout va bien*, then, far from only and ever alienating us from an identification with its ostensible characters' and narrative's motivations (by short-circuiting any reality-effects), have become, *now, for us*, but one other set of conventions for creating a message or depicting a reality (however strange it might have been at *first* glance). Any one convention can *come to mean*, because form refracts through its associated content to create a different, though affiliated, content. And this 'coming to mean' is processual, because the relation between form and content is not a fixed duality but a dynamic tension of entities in continual exchange. In other words, we must not forget to think of the viewing context when assessing any film. By that, I don't simply mean the audience in isolation from the film (and embedded instead within its own separate social and economic sphere), but the audience in relation to the concrete context of the *viewing process*. The viewing process mutates with time and must be thought 'historically' (as Godard would say): we learn to read some of the formal incongruities encountered in avant-garde cinema as expressive of content, and we can immerse ourselves in a film (no matter how abstract), because the 'reality-effect' is not the sadistic power of a film over us, but an exchange, refraction or mixture within a process involving viewer and film. In other words, no method of separation or distancing is guaranteed its effect for long, because, with time, its novelty dissipates. It will be the purpose of the final chapters of this work to substantiate what I have said here about the viewing process.

The representationalist axiom of analytic film-philosophy

Bordwell does not work in a philosophy department and would not categorize himself as a philosopher. Yet, were it not specifically for his work on the cognitivist approach to film, what has come to be known as analytic film-philosophy would be a much lesser force than it is. Early advocates of a non-continental approach, like Ian Jarvie, Gregory Currie and Noël Carroll (the last acting as both philosopher and film theorist) have made important contributions, of course. But it was Bordwell, by bringing a film theory previously fashioned by continental philosophy across to an empiricist paradigm of film studies (via cognitivism), who thoroughly promoted the new approach adopted by so many.[92] That so many voices have maintained a similar position (despite certain, relatively small, internal differences) is a testament to the scientific method advocated for it by all. Hence, it is no exaggeration when the editors of a recent study on Lacanian film theory can say that 'theory as such has given way almost completely to historicism and empirical research. The discipline has become, as David Bordwell and Noël Carroll prophesied in 1996, post-theoretical'.[93]

The analytical approach to film-philosophy presents itself as theoretical with a small 't' inasmuch as it claims to avoid the metaphysical tendencies found in continental film philosophy.[94] Instead, it takes pride in following a critical approach grounded in the traditional philosophical virtues of rigorous argument, logical clarity, conceptual analysis, communal debate and a good acquaintance with scientific knowledge when relevant. (Of course, what terms like 'clarity' or 'rigour' mean is left unclear: one must suppose an implied collective understanding by members of the paradigm that certain kinds of method simply are clear and rigorous, on pain of regress.) Books and essays by Richard Allen, Murray Smith, Gregory Currie, Carl Plantinga, Dirk Eitzen and Joseph Anderson tend to follow in the style of analytical aesthetics, focusing on specific problems concerning specific properties of cinema such as authorship, pictoriality and the paradox of fiction, or elucidating the differences between film and theatre, or photography, or literature (Ian Jarvie's *Philosophy of the Film* being a good example of this). Whether or not a point in the argument is explicitly made in favour of cognitivism is less relevant than the fact – and this is crucial – that nearly all analytics presuppose a *representationalist axiom*: filmic features operate on us as representations of reality. Here is Noël Carroll, for instance, showing us what is wrong with Bazin's analysis of representation and fiction:

> The problem with the issue of fiction is a function of Bazin's implicit assumption that there is only one form of cinematic representation. But as in other media, artistic and otherwise, there is more than one mode of representation in cinema. In fact, we can adopt some of Monroe Beardsley's terminology (without necessarily endorsing his resemblance

> theory of representation) to show that there are at least three types of representation in cinema that we must distinguish before we can appreciate the representational range of the medium.[95]

Carroll then goes on to analyse the differences between 'physical portrayal', 'depiction' and 'nominal portrayal' (the details of which need not detain us here). But whatever the particular representational scheme employed – reference, intentionality, languages games, cognitive maps or projected illusion – it is always tied to an approach that sees film viewing as representational, as information *about* the world rather than a direct and worldly connection (which is, as we'll see, professed by Deleuze and Cavell).

This is not to say that the analytical approach totally ignores the seemingly non-representational elements of cinema, such as the emotions that a film can arouse in its audience. While Bordwell does clearly marginalize affectivity in his version of cognitivism, Carroll (who is also Bordwell's close colleague) has argued that 'affect is the glue that holds the audience's attention to the screen on a moment-to-moment basis'.[96] And, in fact, a number of analytical volumes have been dedicated to the matter of film and emotion.[97] All the same, we should note that the embrace of affect within the analytico-cognitivist paradigm comes mostly by way of cognitivizing affectivity as a well-structured, problem-solving and object-related mode of mentation, as the title of the prominent collection of essays, *Passionate Views: Film, Cognition, and Emotion*, clearly attests.[98] Emotion becomes a form of representation about the film-object or world. Hence, it is arguable that what is precisely affective about affect – the subjective *qualia* themselves – has been lost.[99]

An example of this comes in the work of Torben Grodal, for it contains a cognitivist account of the 'paradox of fiction' that tackles this strange affective state (where we are really moved by things we know to be illusions). Grodal's idea is that cinematic fiction directly stimulates physiological and cognitive responses hardwired into us by our evolutionary history.[100] While these responses are often subconscious, they are certainly 'innate and universal', and it is these that generate the 'reality effect'. For instance, the narrative of near disaster ('Indiana Jones is about to be crushed by a huge rolling boulder') becomes a 'push-pull' machine, mobilizing 'powerful mental motivational mechanisms [based in our 'special frontal brain modules'] used by humans to perform complex tasks'.[101] The reality status of an image is analysed on the basis of various physical parameters – the intensity of the image, its temporality, and so on – which constitute a dataset that is processed within the brain. Film conveys a feeling of reality that is cognitive, representational. Affectivity is reduced to the brain's information processing.

Also indicative of Grodal's approach is the 'reverse engineering' evident throughout: his explanations – like so many in cognitivism, including

Bordwell's, as we saw – are retrodictive rather than predictive. Moreover, we are given little indication by Grodal as to *why* we are so susceptible to the reality effect, *why* we have this faculty for proto-empathy. A related problem is *how* we are able to see these images as real, or even quasireal, for it remains a mystery how a two-dimensional image depicting a pretence of reality can convey, however fleetingly, the impression of reality. One might answer the second question, a biological issue, with biology – our brains just are able to tell the pictorial apart from the real (though Grodal denies this); but the first issue of why we have this faculty in the first place requires a more *psychological* answer, however rooted in biology it may also be. In other words, Grodal conflates levels (also like Bordwell), answering a psychological question with a biological mechanism rather than a psychological one.

Grodal's cognitivism is clear. What is left unannounced, however, is the representationalism that lies at its core. And in this he is typical of the analytical approach as well. Indeed, given that many of the analytical film theorists give piecemeal accounts of particular films and filmic features, and so eschew any explicit theorizing on film per se as representation, I will engage with them mostly in the later parts of this study when I too take a piecemeal and problem-driven approach with regard to cinematic 'representation' and reality. For now, though, I will progress to a position that does purport to go beyond seeing films (or film viewing) as a reproduction of the world, as pictures of reality.

Slavoj Žižek believes that his Lacanian approach to film can do precisely this by decentring the subject as a figment of the Real's imagination. We do not represent the Real; rather, through cinema, the Real imagines us. In addition, Žižek's method is strongly motivated by psychological and philosophical concerns. His own peculiar return to (Lacan's) Freud is mediated through German Idealism (Kant, Schelling, Hegel), while his psychoanalytic approach (already well-worn by the 1970s) is mostly novel on account of the philosophical bearing it attributes to cinema – that film tells us something fundamental about 'the Real'. Whether or not this idea remains faithful to what is unique to film, or whether it reinstalls representation at another level, remains to be seen.

3
Žižek and the Cinema of Perversion

We must imagine *The Birds* as a film *without birds*.[1]

Good theorist, bad theorist: Bordwell contra Žižek

David Bordwell's confidence in the prevalence of continuity, not just within cinema but also amongst good cineastes, stems from a belief that, beneath the multiple interpretations of theory, there lie formal aspects, 'nodal passages', that all will commonly comprehend (beginnings and endings, plot points, what characters do, and so on). There is a lowest common denominator, so to speak, 'structural and substantive aspects' upon which critics 'have reached consensus and from which they launch their various interpretations', and it is this that will form the bedrock for any proper empirical study. Moreover, these commonalities can even stretch to the interpretations themselves in terms of their shared values of 'plausibility', or 'notions of comprehension that members of all critical schools share'.[2] These mutual values allow Bordwell to think of his approach as a research programme, a communal and scientific project open to debate and refutation, and built upon close observation of films and dialogue between film theorists.

Grand Theorists, we learnt, are not like this. Their starting points in Freud, Lacan or Althusser are axiomatic, and each film is simply an exemplification of the truth of the theory rather than a test that might refute it. The film must fit the theory rather than the other way around. They do not like counter-examples, falsification or any other of the hallmarks of genuine, dialogical research. Indeed, Bordwell's cognitivism is itself portrayed by him as dialogical on two levels. Firstly, the spectator is said to enter into a dialogue with film through a visual form of question-and-answer: What is the hero to do next? Answer: reach for his gun. Will his opponent now make his escape? Answer: no, he too pulls out a gun, and so on. At a second metalevel, however, the film critic is also building up interpretations dialogically by ascribing certain meanings to certain cues.[3] And here is where we find the source of the failings of Grand Theory as a type of film analysis. The film critic following this path can only see one kind of response to the ascriptions he or she has applied to the film – the one desired from the outset. *Everything confirms the theory.* Any falsifying replies are filtered out. And for Bordwell, one of the clearest exponents of this practice of one-way viewing and non-dialogical enquiry, is Slavoj Žižek.

Indeed, Žižek is a very bad film theorist, according to Bordwell. His film theory is derived entirely from 'axioms or first principles'. He only uses films exploitatively to illustrate his master theory, 'with each film playing out allegories of theoretical doctrines. And he never doubts his masters Hegel and Lacan'. In addition, Žižek's chief strategy against *other* theories (such as Bordwell's), consists of 'invective and rhetorical questions' with no place for reasoned argument. He ignores the intersubjective dimension of (good) theorizing, the need to engage with 'a community committed to both rational and empirical investigation'. The good theorist seeks to advance any argument through dialogue and, in this way, to *'cast out error'*. Yet, this is something Žižek cannot ascribe to because, as an *'insistent monologist'*, he doesn't believe in theory 'as a conversation within a community, a process of question and answer and rebuttal'.[4]

In Žižek's defence, admittedly, there *is* a very large community of Lacanian film theorists – especially those influenced by Žižek's approach – who do converse with each other no less than Bordwell dialogues with (cognitivist) minds like his own. And here is the rub: Žižek has actually engaged with cognitivist science in his own work, not only indirectly through his critique of Bordwell's post-theoretical views, but directly too. He has written positively, for instance, on Catherine Malabou's 'Hegelian reading of the brain sciences' (the idea that people 'make their own brain'). He has also made connections between Antonio Damasio's work and German Idealism, looking especially at the notion that 'the I is not an agent who acts, but an agent who has no substantial identity outside its acting' as a 'fundamental Fichtean theme'.[5] Indeed, the radical overhaul that cognitivism is capable of making to our concept of the self is not lost on Žižek:

> Is not the *frisson* of cognitivism precisely in its radical notion that consciousness is in effect a 'user illusion' behind which (just as behind a PC screen) there are just blind asubjective neuronal processes, and, consequently, that there is absolutely no theoretical need to posit some psychic global Entity, something 'in me more than me' which is the true agent of my acts? Paradoxically, it is thus precisely as true Freudians that we should reject the notion of 'Me' as the substantial background of the ego.[6]

Of course, Bordwell might now intercede that what is on show here is not an example of *good* cognitivism (because Žižek is merging quite distinct levels of discourse, German Idealism and contemporary psychology in particular), and that Žižek is only exploiting cognitive theory for ulterior ends, as with his abuse of film. All the same, Žižek's engagement with cognitivism contrasts starkly with Bordwell's dismissal of Grand Theory from film studies, which he accomplishes mostly through the assumption that Freudianism has been superceded by cognitivism as the best psychology of perception now available. For Bordwell too can fall foul of that most common idol of the cave, the appeal to authority (nearly always to the 'scientific view' of the mind).[7] Bordwell never actually engages with Lacanianism as a psychology, only with its rhetoric.[8] So when he does look to Žižek's actual counter-arguments (against himself in particular), it is only to rebuff them as 'vague, digressive, equivocal, contradictory, and either obviously inaccurate or merely banal'. Clearly, Bordwell is coming from a position that *sees itself* as so different from Žižek that even where a dialogue of sorts might begin, it amounts to nothing.[9]

Is this a question, therefore, of different, incommensurable axioms, of a 'differend' in Lyotard's sense – adversaries using language rules from one 'phrase regimen' and applying them to another? Certainly, Bordwell does define good theory as dialogical in a specific sense of the term. And it is a fact that Žižek does write seriously about cognitivism, whereas Bordwell simply dismisses Žižek's Freudianism with little discussion (though, again, their standards of what might count as 'serious' writing might lead to another differend). Sometimes, however, Bordwell hints at a realization that Žižek may have more than just prejudice on his side, but also a different idea of *what dialogue is* – as when he shares his 'hunch' that Žižek sees 'intellectual work as a struggle for power'. This is presumably an insult, but Žižek does indeed have a theory of dialogue, and of alterity, that is pertinent here. It is not a Foucauldian one concerning power, though.

According to Žižek, the fantasy of a 'Big Other' (which we will soon see is his key to understanding film meaning) has a dialogical component: 'the world out there, inclusive of all the catastrophes that may befall me, is not a blind meaningless automaton, *but a partner in a possible dialogue* so that even a catastrophic outcome is to be read as a meaningful response, not as a realm of blind chance'. Meaning-making for Žižek, just as for Bordwell, is an effect, the product of other, more fundamental processes. Where these are inferential forms of computation for Bordwell, they are forms of unconscious projection and conscious interpretation for Žižek. *But they are both cognitive, both forms of representational knowing.* For both of them, as we'll also see, still believe in representation. For Bordwell, the viewer is a set of representational capacities within the brain, a narrative- or *fabula*-making faculty.[10] And Žižek, in his own way, has also prioritized representation, only now within the familial romance of the unconscious mind and its errant representations of the Real, as well as the conscious effort to represent those representations (what Žižek calls 'traversing the fantasy').

The irony is that the scope of Žižek's paradigm involves a view of dialogue and film criticism as well (which might be one reason for the dialogical impasse with Bordwell). And yet the fact remains that it is Žižek who appears most open to having a dialogue with this Big Other – in this case, cognitivism. As a consequence, we have the curious situation that Bordwell *says* that he believes in the (benign) face value of dialogue, *and in so doing demands it of others*, while Žižek, who doesn't believe in the natural integrity of dialogue, nonetheless engages in a form of it with cognitivism. Their impasse can thus be put down to both of them ignoring the performative aspects of their non-dialogical dialogue in favour of its *representational* element.

All in all, one might say that Bordwell is being monological in his own dialogism, starting, as he does, with a different and contrasting axiom as to the meaning of dialogue, otherness and cognition.[11] There are other questions to ask in what follows between them, of course, such as whether there are also different metaphysics of the subject at work here: Bordwell is, after all, a methodological individualist, whereas Žižek's subject is a decentred one. It is these matters that will be tackled next.

Freudianism for beginners

> Psychoanalytic film theory has taken on all the attributes of a religious cult, complete with rites and sacred texts. Twenty years of obsessive invocations of 'lack', 'castration', and 'the phallus' have left us with a stultifying orthodoxy that makes any fresh discussion impossible. It is time to recognise that not all problems can be resolved by repeated references to, and ever-more-subtle close readings of, the same few articles by Freud and Lacan.[12]

This quotation has harsh words for the Freudian approach to cineanalysis. Yet, it comes not from David Bordwell but the Deleuzian film theorist Steven Shaviro. 'Freud bashing' has been in intellectual vogue for over 20 years now, and it has come from all quarters – phenomenological, Deleuzian, culturalist and cognitivist. How droll, then, that just when many theorists thought that they had seen the back of the last Freudian film analysis, suddenly, and seemingly from nowhere, its most ardent and prolific champion appeared in the figure of Žižek. Yet, even then his employment of Freud is far from orthodox, coming via Lacan, with large doses of German Idealist philosophy, and the overall ambition to extend psychoanalysis into a form of cultural critique.

Stanley Cavell once asserted that 'psychoanalytic interpretations of the arts in American culture have ... been content to permit the text under analysis not to challenge the concepts of analysis being applied to them ... as if each psychoanalytic reading were charged with rediscovering the reality of psychoanalysis'. Against this well-worn complaint, Cavell believes that psychoanalysis should allow the resistance of the text to help it think and evolve. In doing so, it would remain faithful to both its own past and its development as a species of philosophy born from the ideas of Kant (despite Freud's own protestations to the contrary). Taking 'Freud as philosopher' may be one way in which Freud can be resurrected, especially given his death in so many other circles.[13] And this is precisely what Žižek does with both Freud and Lacan. But whether Žižek is also able to let psychoanalysis respond philosophically to the resistance of film, as Cavell directs, or even whether his approach can help us see film philosophize for itself, are the fundamental questions for this chapter.

It is undoubtedly true that, in their heyday, Freudian and Lacanian film theories were strikingly prevalent. As Todd McGowan and Sheila Kunkle remark: 'Lacan dominated film studies so thoroughly that Lacanian psychoanalysis dictated the very terms of debate within the field. Theoretical innovations, when they occurred, arose as counterpoints to a Lacanian understanding'. And with such a powerful standing, its markedly dogmatic nature is not surprising. Echoing Bordwell's critique of that hegemony, Cynthia Freeland explains how 'typically in film studies, psychoanalytic interpretations are advanced *a priori*, rather than in an open-minded spirit of testing how well they actually work'. Psychoanalytic tropes, it is also claimed, were mostly applied on the unquestioned assumption of their cinematic probity and socio-ideological relevance, irrespective of the criticisms of Freudianism from Hans Eysenck and Adolf Grünbaum (on its status as a science), Marie Balmary and Jeffrey Masson (on its medical abuse of patients, especially women and children), or Deleuze and Guattari (on its reactionary ideological effects).[14]

Eysenck once wrote that where Freudian theory was true, it was not new, but that where it was new, it was not true. Certainly the notion of the unconscious was not new even in 1900: though Freud certainly shocked the intellectual world with the idea of repressed childhood eroticism, the unconscious has origins going back through Bergson, Nietzsche, Schopenhauer, Kant, Leibniz and Plato.[15] Yet, it was Freud's implementation of the unconscious that made the concept all-pervasive, and, emerging as it did at the same time as cinema, it was inevitable that the two would become closely linked.

Christian Metz has suggested that our fascination with film is so out of line with reasonable behaviour that it can only be explained as an unconscious operation.[16] It is on this basis that one can build up a set of parallels between reading a film and Freud's reading of the mind. Film works at an unconscious level. Of course, the other advantage of Freud's model (and possibly the source of its popularity in the arts in general) is its general *melodramatic* structure: for it is not simply an abstract theory of undischarged (sexual) energy, but a personalized family romance, with apparently good and bad characters, mythical underpinnings and a strong plot (with a three-act structure complete with suspense, complications and a 'happily ever after' if everything goes right during development, or subsequently during analysis). The Freudian dreamwork of visualization, displacement, condensation and secondary elaboration is also pertinent to such an obviously visual medium as cinema, especially one so commercially devoted to visual fantasy as Hollywood cinema (the perennial 'dream factory').

It is no wonder, then, that a dramatic art like film should lend itself to Freudian analysis to such a degree. Nor is the success of the psychoanalytic paradigm surprising when it comes to reading Hollywood films produced in the heyday of professional Freudian practice in the US, from the 1940s to the 1980s. When the writer or director of a film is so *au fait* with Freudian theory – as Alfred Hitchcock was for instance – the degree of hermeneutical perspicuity rises several notches. Indeed, the theory becomes a self-fulfilling prophesy. In Hitchcock's *Strangers on a Train* (1951), for instance, Bruno can and has been seen as the unrepressed alter ego of Guy; or, in John Ford's *The Searchers* (1956), Scar is easily interpreted as an expression of the unconscious libido of Ethan. The list of perfect examples goes on and on, right up to contemporary films by Martin Scorsese, Brian de Palma and David Lynch, none of whose work would be the same without Freud's ideas.

Of the elements from Freudianism that were embraced by film theory, Sue Thornham cites the 'Oedipus complex' as the central one. This famous syndrome names the process whereby the male child, threatened by what he sees as the rival affections of his father for his own love object, his mother, switches allegiance from mother to father. This is achieved by dint of fear (of castration by the father), repression and the creation of unconscious thoughts and feelings. In all, we have a three-act drama of situation, complication and resolution. Lacan's notion of the 'mirror stage' encapsulates the visuality of the early stages of this process, while also describing the formation of a (false) identity through the child's identification with his mirror image – a recognition which is a misrecognition.[17] Who we think we are, as unitary subjects, is a construct of reflections, the way that things *look (at me)* – mirrors initially, but then by imaginary extension, everything in the world that affirms me as One. The two primary hangovers from this procedure are scopophilia (due to a residual fascination of the boy with seeing bodily sexual differences) and fetishism (a retained belief in the woman's phallus, despite a knowledge of its absence). Ergo, the flood of film analyses from *Gilda* (1946) to *Blue Velvet* (1986) concerning the family romance (mommy, daddy, me), involving festishistic images (mostly of women), phallic objects, symbolic castrations, and so on. What happens to the little girl in all of this, of course, is problematic, with Freud infamously laying the blame for his omission at women's own door ('you are yourselves the problem').[18]

Central though it is, Oedipus is not the only way of connecting Freud to film. For instance, Jean-Louis Baudry, who with Christian Metz was the first to introduce the Lacanian approach into film theory, looked at the *technology* of film consumption – the 'cinematic apparatus' – in order to argue for a different psychoanalytic analogue. In the darkened cinema we regress to a primitive, suggestible state of awareness. He writes:

> dream and hallucination are already states of simulation (something passing itself off as something else, representation for perception)...While in dreams and hallucinations representations appear in the guise of perceived reality, a real perception takes place in cinema, if not an ordinary perception of reality. It would appear that it is this slight displacement which has misled the theoreticians of cinema, when analyzing the impression of reality. In dream and hallucination, representations are taken as reality in the absence of perception; in cinema, images are taken for reality but require the mediation of perception.[19]

According to Baudry, cinema is a 'simulation apparatus' directed at the viewer or audience in order to generate an impression of reality like that of a dream state. We dream when we go to the movies.

Another Freudian incursion into film theory came from feminist psychoanalysts who pushed the potential for such analyses of cinema even further. Their work on visualization, sadism and the abject subject introduced revisionist readings of Freud and Lacan that subverted and overthrew the masculinist prejudice of their work. The ideas of Laura Mulvey, Linda Williams, Kaja Silverman, Barbara Creed and many others cannot, of course, be simplistically reduced to a common set of principles. Creed is even further from Freudian orthodoxy than Mulvey, for instance – but they did all remain psychoanalytic throughout their approach.[20]

The return of the Real[21]

In all of this, we should note, the emphasis on images, mirrors and the illusory is evident everywhere, no matter which type of Lacanian theory is in question. This is due to the fact that Lacan's conceptual triad of 'Imaginary, Symbolic and Real' – the three forces operating behind every mental state – has been traditionally employed by Lacanians with a focus on the relationship between the Symbolic and the *Imaginary*, as would seem fitting for discourse on an audio-visual medium like film. When Kaja Silverman, for example, writes on Michael Powell's *Peeping Tom* (1960), she interprets the various strategems of the murderer Mark as ones working 'to conceal male rather than female lack, and to promote the imaginary coherence of the male rather than the female subject'.[22]

But Žižek is different. His use of Lacan shifts the discourse away from the Symbolic–Imaginary relation over to the Symbolic–Real. And the Real, which should not be confused with 'reality', is primary. Despite the Imaginary appearing to be the most appropriate category for cinema studies, Žižek justifies his move with reference to the fact that in the last years of Lacan's teaching he began to place most emphasis upon 'the barrier separating the real from (symbolically structured) reality'.[23] Whereas the old Lacanian orthodoxy in film theory suffered from what has been described as a 'near-total exclusion of the Real', the return to Lacan by Žižek and his followers revises his reception through this new emphasis.[24] In a sense, then, it is in virtue of a greater *fidelity* to Lacan that Žižek treats film in this surprising fashion.[25] It is also noteworthy for us, moreover, that 'the Real' is a predominantly *philosophical* term that Lacan inherited from Emile Meyerson (who took it from Bergson before him). Indeed, contrary to Lacan's own avowedly *anti*-philosophical stance, Žižek not only operates as a philosopher *simpliciter*, but as one endeavouring to connect Lacan's ideas with their philosophical forebears. The 'impossible Real', for instance, is linked to the Kantian *Ding an sich* that generates the antinomies of misplaced reason, while Žižek's methodological embrace of contradiction (that are the signs of this Real) comes from both Hegelian and Marxist dialectics (Hegel overcoming Kant by placing the 'abyss' between the phenomenal and the noumenal '*into the thing itself*').[26]

This Real and the 'little bits of the Real' (or '*objets a*') come in many forms: both in things such as 'the voice, the breast, the feces, and the phallus', and in processes like the primal scene, disaster, perverse sexuality, near-death and any other traumatic or extreme event.[27] The *cogito* too is a piece of the Real for Žižek, being in truth an empty space. The subject is a void. In fact, the whole Symbolic Order is only the retreat from this void, 'the void of subjectivity (the Lacanian "barred subject")'.[28] The Real emerges most conspicuously through contradiction. Some of these sources of the Real work together: contradiction, for instance, can also be traumatic. Most significantly, as we'll see, the Real also comes through the representation of these '*objets*' in films, in the 'excremental objects, mutilated corpses, shit, and so forth' depicted through film.[29] Nonetheless, the Real in itself is not representation; indeed, it cannot be known at all as it is only in itself *before* language cuts into it. The Real simply persists, undifferentiated, while language and imagination try to capture and categorize it. Against the panlinguistic prism used by structuralism and post-structuralism to mediate every reality, the undeniably direct experiences of trauma, especially transgressive sexuality and near-death, allow Žižek to re-establish a place for the Real: 'such is the fate of all of us, the bullet with our name on it is already shot... At the end of the imaginary as well as the symbolic itinerary, we encounter the Real'.[30] (And who, save for a spiritualist, would argue that death is merely *our* construction?)

The Real is described as 'impossible' because it is impossible both to imagine it or to integrate it within the Symbolic Order. Here we see more evidence of Žižek's German philosophical heritage – in this specific case,

Kant. For the Real *in itself*, though never known directly, is, nevertheless, *inferred* as the source of the impossibilities, contradictions and inconsistencies generated whenever we do try to represent it (through language or imagination). Indeed, these aporia are its representatives. The Real is the noumenal that resists our phenomenal categorization through the antinomies of reason, a confluence of contractions. Consequently, when analysing a film such as *The Matrix*, for instance, Žižek counts up the number of inconsistencies in the film's depiction of what 'reality' really is (a world entirely controlled by machines that generate the illusion of a world (the Matrix) where humans are free): why, then, must we die in the real world when we die in the virtual one? Why does the Matrix need *human* energy in particular? Why is there only one Matrix rather than one for each of us? Each of these inconsistencies, says Žižek, 'are the film's moment of truth'. They are the signs of the Real.[31]

Yet, we should not push this affinity with Kantian thoughts too far. The Real is neither a metaphysical support nor a transcendental condition, both of which rest on a logic of presence. It belongs in the illogic of what is both present and absent and so punches a hole in reason. It is not some kind of virtual or ulterior world (*Hinterwelt*): it is only the void that makes our 'reality' incomplete or inconsistent on any further examination: 'the Real is not the "true reality" behind the virtual simulation, but the void which makes reality incomplete or inconsistent'.[32] This notion of 'void' – a variant of Lacan's conception of desire as *lack* – will return later as a target for Deleuze's criticism in favour of his productive theory of desire (given that it seems inconsistent to say that the void is beyond the logic of both presence *and* absence).

For now, however, it is important to see how the void of and in the Real leads to a perpetual alienation. We can never capture the Real: inconsistencies, and ultimately traumatic near-death, keep interposing themselves as gaps in our supposedly seamless interpretations of what goes on around us and inside us. This failure, however, only encourages us further to create ever more symbolic fantasies to fill the gap. We create fantasy explanations for our, literally, vacuous lives: Christian Heaven, All-knowing Science, Heideggerian Being, and so on. Each of them is a 'Meaning', a 'Big Other' that explains (away) the trauma, the disaster, the misfit. The Big Other is the 'subject supposed to know', who both protects us and explains the disaster. The Father in Roberto Benigni's *Life is Beautiful* is one such Big Other, providing 'the symbolic function that renders this reality bearable'. The father explains away the horrors of the Holocaust happening around him and his son. Other explanations, though more abstract and seemingly mature (as provided by psychology, philosophy or history) are no less a cover-up for the inexplicable nature of the Holocaust. It is a piece of the Real, and, as such, a brute fact that will always resist our disavowals in images and narrative. The desire for meaning is a paranoid one, seeking a conspiratorial agency behind the inherently meaningless mess of brute facts that we encounter.[33]

One symptom of this repulsion from the Real of near-death and trauma is the *construction* of substitute realities, seen most obviously in those fantastical worlds created through perversion, but no less applicable to those mutually sustaining fantasy-realities held together by whole communities as 'common sense' or the 'real world'.[34] This construction or constitution of external reality must be understood, however, 'in the precise meaning this term acquired in German idealism', according to Žižek. This is no voluntary, subjective idealism, but a necessary symptom of the psychic system being put under stress by intolerable truths. Scottie's fantasy of Judy *as* Madeleine, for instance (in Hitchcock's *Vertigo* (1958)), is what lets him avoid looking into the abyssal Real (at least until the end of the film). In this case, the Real is 'the hole in the Other (the symbolic order) concealed by the fascinating presence of the fantasy object', that is, the inescapable fact that the other's desire is void (Madeleine was never Madeleine either). Likewise, it is only at the end of Kieslowski's *Three Colours: Blue* (1993) that Julie is able to mourn the death of her husband and daughter because she has finally learnt how to reconstruct 'the fantasy frame which allows her to "tame" this raw Real'.[35]

The film gaze

In all of this, Žižek often assumes some prior knowledge of the ideas of Lacan, Kant and Hegel (as well as his own variations on their ideas), even as he makes certain introductory gestures (as when he repeatedly says 'what Lacan calls the *object a*'). Indeed, Žižek is a great teacher of Lacan by use of film as well as popular culture in general. The readings of films themselves often start from orthodox Lacanian positions such as the reversal of subject and object, where the object (the film) now gazes at us, and in doing so creates us in *its* image: 'the Gaze is on the side of the object, it stands for the blind spot in the field of the visible from which the picture itself photo-graphs the spectator'.[36] It is another kind of mirror. And, in Žižek's readings, Oedipus is never far away either. Mothers and fathers appear frequently, be they literal character roles in the film or symbolic ones:

> The enigma, of course, is the enigma of the (m)other's desire (what does she really want, above and beyond *me*, since I am obviously not enough for her): and 'father' is the *answer* to this enigma, the symbolization of this deadlock [not its creation through intrusion]. In this precise sense, 'father' is for Lacan a translation and/or symptom: a compromise solution that alleviates the unbearable anxiety of directly confronting the Void of the Other's desire.[37]

In fact, the Freudian element of Žižek's readings can at times appear a little crude and passé, as when Bobby Peru, from David Lynch's *Wild at Heart* (1990), is described as a 'gigantic phallus', or when it is pointed out that the first name of the character Dick Laurent (in *Lost Highway* (1997)) 'is also a common term for phallus', and so supports reading the line of dialogue, 'Dick Laurent is dead', as an assertion of 'castration', and so on.[38] What remains fundamentally impressive about Žižek, however, is his consistent ability to find Lacanian potential in even the least promising raw material. Hence, in one of his most popular works, *Enjoy Your Symptom!*, he examines arcane concepts like the Symbolic and the Real, Sexuation, Repetition, the Phallus, the Father and the Multiple almost entirely through the works of Chaplin, Rosselini and Hitchcock. And, of course, there is also the philosophical dimension to expose in these works, as when Hitchcock's *Rope*, for instance, is described as 'an inherently Hegelian film', and this too Žižek does with flourish.[39]

Sometimes this interpretative activity takes Žižek away from the audiovisuals of the film to focus almost entirely on the plot and dialogue, for example when he discusses the key scene at the party between Fred and the Mystery Man in *Lost Highway* without any reference to its extremely complex, multilayered soundtrack (also 'designed' by Lynch). Indeed, his book devoted to Lynch, *The Ridiculous Sublime*, makes little of Lynch's famed iconography of flickering fluorescent lights, smoke, fire, red curtains, cigarettes and ominous industrial background noises in favour of the symbolism of the characters (as femme fatales), the dialogue and the plot. Admittedly, psychoanalysis is the *talking* cure, and though Lacan's visualization of Freudian structures – especially in the Imaginary – was obviously attractive to early Lacanian cineanalysts (who always looked closely at the visuals), Žižek's emphasis on the Real sometimes takes him away from tackling sound and vision directly and towards a narrow focus on *how* those elements symbolize the interruptions of the Real instead. Žižek's performance on this front is uneven, however, ranging from the textual to the filmic and back again, depending on the film under analysis. His monograph on Krzysztof Kieslowski, *The Fright of Real Tears*, is replete with the non-verbal details of his films, whilst *Enjoy Your Symptom!*, though still emphasizing plot and dialogue in its analyses of Rossellini's *Germany, Year Zero* (1948) or Hitchcock's *Rope*, also has close filmic readings of Chaplin's *City Lights* (1931). In any case, Žižek is unapologetic when the 'interpretive effort' demands that we resist letting ourselves be immersed in the 'full ambiguity and richness of the film's audio and visual texture' – an orientation that he believes smacks of a 'leftist, anarchic-obscurantist, anti-theoretical insistence'.[40]

Representationalism again: Žižek and the pre-cogs

When Žižek does concentrate on the verbal, moreover, he has a twofold motivation. On a very general level, with the emergence of humans from the animal state there is, according to Žižek, 'a qualitative leap marked by the emergence of the symbolic order'. He also elucidates this shift as a 'passage to language, *the* medium of communication'. So far, so uncinematic. On another, more specific level, if Freudianism is the talking cure, it is because it involves speech *acts*. This was true even for Lacan, says Žižek, when he forwarded a 'theory of the speech act (performative) *avant la lettre*'.[41] Once again, there is a philosophical aspect to Žižek's use of Lacan, only here again stemming from Hegel more than John Austin's ordinary language philosophy. The abyssal Real, Hegel's rendering of Kant's *Ding an sich*, can only be seen for what it is if words are taken as acts (rather than as external and unified signifiers representing the 'I'). Only when words are viewed in their 'violent and contingent "becoming"', do we look into the abyss.[42] Moreover, performative utterances such as these gain their purchase, their power, because they are reflexive, because they re-present (rather than simply act out). The canonical Freudian example from *The Interpretation of Dreams*, Irma's 'injection' dream, is, claims Žižek, '*the* dream, the inaugural dream, because of its reflexivity'.[43] It is reflexivity, qua representation, awareness or consciousness, that sets us free.

All of this is pretty standard stuff from the Freudian perspective – after all, where Id was, representational Ego is meant to be. But Žižek gives these ideas new mileage through the films with which he illustrates them. The question of freedom is the central 'high concept' of Spielberg's *Minority Report*, for example, and it is a freedom born from a consciousness of one's situation. Because John Anderton is aware of, and can represent, his supposed fate (that he would commit murder), he can also thwart this fate with an alternative future (where he does not kill). And this is even true of the original 'pre-cogs' who predicted his crime: 'insofar as the three "pre-cogs" are a direct medium of the "big Other", their discord [that leads to the 'minority report'] is not simply subjective, an erroneous cognition of the future, but a direct expression of the inconsistency of, inherent cracks in, the "big Other" itself'. The crack in reality, the inconsistency, *is the awareness or representation* that the subject brings to the situation.

The subject, remember, is a piece of the Real, a void, and so it must void whatever it is conscious of: 'the alternate path of future reality, is, rather, generated when the agent whose future acts are foretold gets to know about them; that is to say, its source is the self-referentiality of knowledge'. And it is this consistent representationalism – reflected in both the form and content of Žižek's film interpretations – that also leads him to explore the possibility of a 'Cognitivist Hegel' and a 'Cognitivism with Freud'; research which would, incidentally, bring together the core element of Bordwell's cognitivism with a central strand of Žižek's own 'Grand Theory' (Freud meets Hegel).[44] Indeed, Žižek's recent embrace of cognitivism is a clear testament to the representationalism at the heart of his approach: 'phenomenal selfhood results from autoepistemic closure in a self-representing system ... What exists are information-processing systems engaged in the transparent process of phenomenal self-modeling'.[45] The Real equals Self equals Void equals Representation.

Traversing the fantasy or transcending the Real?

An unavoidable question arises in the face of this double-sided approach. On the one side, there is an integral place for representation in Žižek's method. On the other, representation, qua the Imaginary or Symbolic (and there are no other media than these for Žižek), is always in error, it always misses its target, for the target was never really there. Explanatory meaning is a Big Other. So what, then, of Žižek's own explanations, and what of the explanations of psychoanalysis, or cognitive science, or even certain films – these other representations and images that do somehow touch the Real? In other words (in any words), how is Žižek able to enunciate his own interpretations? If Žižek is right, then all meaning is a Big Other – including his own. But, of course, this problem, or inconsistency for Žižek, only emerges if his account is otherwise correct. If he's right, he's wrong. This is a self-referential paradox that Žižek himself will be familiar with: what makes his dialectics different from cognitivism per se, he says, is the way that 'the subject's position of enunciation is included, inscribed, into the process'.[46] And the solution to it will be familiar also: by multiplying the kinds of meaning, none being totally inadequate, all being variable in scale and alterity (there never was *one* 'Big Other'), we can attempt to transcend the aporia of self-reference.

Lacan himself was well aware of the philosophical problem of having to clear a space for the probity of his own representations, given all that he had to say against the Symbolic. In his *Four Fundamental Concepts of Psycho-analysis*, he writes: 'the fact that I have said that the effect of interpretation is to isolate in the subject a kernel ... of *non-sense*, does not mean that interpretation is in itself nonsense'. This is what allows Lacanian film analysis to posit itself as touching the Real. Contemporary Lacanians, especially those following Žižek, take psychoanalytic interpretation to involve 'isolating the traumatic Real through its effects within the text'. Their analyses interpret films like Scorsese's *Cape Fear*, 'in order to illustrate our close proximity to the Real', elaborating 'the contours of the Real'. This image of 'contours' is significant: Žižek writes in *The Ridiculous Sublime* that the 'contours' of the Real 'can only be discerned as the absent cause of the distortions/displacements of symbolic space'.[47] His representations of the Real, therefore, are neither full images nor captures (we only 'touch', never seize, the Real): they are its merest outline. In Kantian parlance, we only ever infer the *Ding an sich* indirectly through the antinomies of reason (the inconsistencies – 'distortions/displacements' – of the Imaginary and Symbolic), but the noumenal itself, by definition, never appears.

If one subsequently asks *how* Žižek can support a distinction between an interpretation that outlines the Real and another that only reflects fantastical impostures for it, then the answer must be that the distinction *itself* is axiomatic. This basically means that the distinction between reality (the Real) and ideology (fantasy) is taken as given (indeed, that is how dialectics must work – through a constitutive antagonism).[48] And the sign of the non-ideological or non-symptomatic is, again, *consciousness*.[49] What Žižek calls 'traversing' the fantasy (which marks the point of cure in Lacanian analysis) is a form of awareness of one's own fantastical strategies. As John Anderton learnt, it is self-knowledge alone that liberates us. To traverse the fantasy is to transcend the fantasy: it is the 'subject's most profound form of self-recognition'.[50] *Γν θι Σεαυτόν* – 'know thyself'. This traversal comes with the knowledge that there is nothing behind the fantasy, for the idea that there is something, there is a Big Other, precisely marks the persistence of the fantasy – acting out rather than representation. Once cured of this idea, one no longer posits the Other as a lost object of desire, for this Other, which is ultimately the desire of the mother (in all its myriad guises), does not exist – it is voided and void. Significantly for us, analogues of such cures can also be seen in film, for instance as Žižek discerns in David Lynch's *Lost Highway*. Lynch, he writes,

> 'traverses' the fantasmatic universe of *noir*... by staging its fantasies *openly, more directly*, i.e., without the 'secondary perlaboration' which masks their inconsistencies. The final conclusion to be drawn is that 'reality', and the experience of its density, is sustained not simply by A/ONE fantasy, but by an INCONSISTENT MULTITUDE of fantasies.[51]

In being open, direct or unconcealed, Lynch transcends the image and symbol qua fantastical symptom (the classical film *noirs*, with all their fetishes, knowing femme fatales, and so on) in favour of an *intentionally* inconsistent plurality of images and symbols that, thereby, touches the Real. Nobody knows anything, the charade hides nothing – though only Lynch and us, Socrates-like, know this.

The return of the Real to reality

Another axiom is needed, therefore, to facilitate Žižek's evaluative judgements: an axiom of the Real and the unReal, so that one can say 'this touches the Real, that distorts it'; 'this is a true (open, direct) representation, that is a fantasy', and so on. There must be an inaugural and generative dualism that allows Žižek to say why one film is good (emancipatory) and another is bad (ideological). Pared down to just this bare-bones dualism, it would be hard to say anything against such a minor presupposition: that there is some kind of duality, if only one of tendency, would seem to be the minimal condition of any possible judgement ('this is this, that is that'). But, of course, the superstructure of Žižek's thought is much more fleshed out than this: along with German Idealism and cognitive science, its architectonic is composed of Freudian elements, a universe of familial eroticism – mommy, daddy and me. What remains contentious, therefore, is which parts of this universe we choose to ascribe to the Real and which to the unReal, even as tendency or necessary distortion (in the Symbolic and Imaginary).

Despite his overall constructivism ('reality' is something we make), Lacan himself allowed science, especially mathematics, to 'touch the Real'. Though not a meta*language* (any form of which Lacanianism is loath to admit, given its necessarily Symbolic nature), mathematics is nonetheless a fundamental ingress *of*, and so contact *with*, the Real.[52] And Žižek, in his turn, extends that allowance to the cognitive sciences (sometimes even to quantum science).[53] So what else can be allowed in? The paradigm case is near-death – it is the quintessential piece of empirical reality, a brute fact that touches the Real in what is often described as a 'missed encounter' (a full encounter would be death itself). Its promised void (of our life) is unassailable (on pain of being called a spiritualist). The traumas of disaster, transgressive sexuality and contradiction are also counted as faithful to the 'contours' of the Real, even though these are much more open to counter-arguments from the social-constructivist perspective as unreal. The final irony, though, is that it is the *sexual* Real – which makes up the Freudian kernel in particular – that would seem especially prone to such counter-argument.

The issue is this: it is possible that Freud's own metapsychology is itself a construction built in response to the trauma of too much reality. It has been argued, for example, that his theory of the Oedipus complex should be seen as his own fantastical response to the traumas of incestuous rape (or family 'seduction') recorded during his clinical practice. The historical cornerstone of Freud's metapsychology is his abandonment of the 'Seduction Theory' in favour of Fantasy Theory (Oedipus). Freud originally found that a large number of his patients recounted childhood sexual abuse. He documented some of these case histories in his *Studies in Hysteria* (1895), particularly in 'The Aetiology of Hysteria'. By 1900, however, what were originally deemed by him to be real episodes of child abuse within families came to be understood as cases of mere childhood fantasy. From some historians, therefore, comes the argument that, faced with this horror that childhood abuse might be endemic in Viennese society, Freud had to reinterpret these histories as fantasies of desire rather than records of abuse.

In following this line, the argument continues, Freud made a twofold error: first, he ignored ('repressed') the possibility that his patients *had* been abused (or 'seduced') as children by their parents (this is the view taken by writers like Marie Balmary, Alice Miller and Jeffrey Masson); second, he refused to see amongst 'normal children' (that is, ones without ostensible symptoms of neurosis/abuse), the self-sufficiency of their desires, childhood desire being seen as a lack (this is the critique of Deleuze and Guattari).[54] From these perspectives, Freud's Fantasy Theory is itself an adult fantasy about children. But without *this* fantasy, Freud could have no Oedipal complex and, without Oedipus, there would be little left of the Freudian underpinning to psychoanalytic film theory, old or new (and this includes Žižek).[55]

In this context, the constant use by film theorists of Freud's 1919 essay, 'A Child is Being Beaten', is extremely enlightening. This is the *Urtext* in much psychoanalytically informed theory, being utilized by Mary Ann Doane, Kaja Silverman and Barbara Creed for articulating the nature of fantasy in their work. In particular, its emphasis on shifting, multiple fantasy identifications seems to offer an escape route from the rigid and unilinear structures of sexual identification found in earlier versions of psychoanalytic film theory. And it is also especially important to Žižek. He cites 'A Child is Being Beaten' as the 'fundamental fantasy', one that is 'a pure retroactive construction, since it was never present to the consciousness and then repressed'.[56] Yet, in all of this, the emphasis has always been on the alleged *fantasy* of the child being beaten, the lesson learnt being that the production of sexuality and sexual identity is a work of fantasy through and through. But what about the beatings themselves – didn't they touch the abyss, weren't those physical assaults ever a part of the traumatic Real? Alice Miller et al. would take the realist line when it comes to child abuse. And, in similar vein, Deleuze (with Guattari) remarks that in 'A Child is Being Beaten' 'never was the paternal theme less visible, and yet never was it affirmed with as much passion and resolution. The imperialism of Oedipus is founded here on an absence'.[57]

We'll return to Deleuze's critique in the next chapter. For now, though, we should only mark how orthodox Žižek remains in his alignment of what counts as fantasy and what as Real; the double child rape in Vinterberg's *Festen*, for example, being read as a fantasy and not 'the Real of a trauma'. Žižek even brings popular accounts of False Memory Syndrome into his reading in opposition to the distressing facts presented by the film: 'it is, on the contrary, this horrible secret of a brutal father behind the polite mask which is itself a fantasmatic construction'. Instead of fantasy being erected as a shield against the traumatic Real, now it is *this* trauma that is itself fantasized as a shield against the even more distressing reality of the void of the Other.[58] As a good Freudian, Žižek tells us that there are no monsters, no real ones anyway – but how is he able to judge? Of course, sometimes a cigar is indeed just a cigar (traumas needn't all signify equally), but, given that Žižek is here allowing that some images of catastrophe, 'far from giving access to the Real, can function as a protective shield AGAINST the Real', the question must be asked – what has become of our means, through trauma, of discerning the Real from fantasy?

Films, time and time again

What this means for Žižek's approach to film is that, like so many others, his theory must make certain transcendental choices in order to support itself, and this includes his choices of good films over bad. Žižek believes that he only truly understands his Lacanian concepts after he has thought of examples in film and popular culture that bear out their truth: 'I am convinced of my proper grasp of some Lacanian concept only when I can translate it successfully into the inherent imbecility of popular culture'.[59] The illustrative mode is at work here once more, albeit in a more sophisticated view of film than that of simple pedagogy. But it still remains *a* view of film. We asked at the outset whether Žižek would let psychoanalysis respond philosophically to the resistance of film, and even whether he might help us see film philosophize for itself. The answer has been disappointing. It is not a revelation, of course, to learn that Žižek harks back, de facto, to favourite examples like Hitchcock and Lynch again and again in his work of eking out the psychoanalytic message in their films (and any others he comes across). And that message is certainly there in them, *de jure*, just as Bordwell's informationalist reading can be – if one looks hard and long enough. But both these protagonists see film *according* to a theoretical model, in this case, the model of representation, be it as the processing of knowledge (information) in itself, or as the psychoanalytic dyad of unconscious and conscious knowledge (or traversal) of the Real. Neither of them see film *in itself* as philosophical. Neither do Bordwell or Žižek see film as Real, that is, as ontological (a position we'll soon see articulated by Deleuze and Cavell). Because they take the view that film represents, it can do so for better or for worse, and hence there can be selective norms: in that some films are deemed superior to others, they can be chosen to illustrate what film per se is best at doing (for their respective positions). The suggestion that I will ultimately put forward, on the contrary, is that the processes of film viewing (rather than 'films') *make themselves* good at what they do: they can transform any theory into an illustrated theory, if they are looked at hard and long enough. Or rather, these processes already involve this long and hard look. Their 'superiority', or illustrative power, lies not in *how* they represent nor in *what* they represent, but in what they are, which must involve how they are viewed, in all their relational properties.

In a revealing remark from *Enjoy Your Symptom!*, Žižek relates an episode when he was thinking of a particular philosophical idea (concerning why reality is always multiple) 'while watching *Psycho* for the twentieth time'. This over-exposure can be contrasted with a more recent anecdote that relates a visit made by Žižek to a local cinema in Slovenia to see *The Matrix*. During this viewing, he reports, he had the 'unique opportunity of sitting close to the ideal spectator of the film – namely an idiot'.

Žižek adds that he actually preferred the 'naïve immersion' of this idiot to the 'pseudosophisticated intellectualist readings' that project philosophical and psychoanalytic meanings onto the film (which people are all too prone to do). Žižek sounds here like Bordwell, of course, only now turning the hermeneutical tables in favour of his own proper readings rather than no readings whatsoever. And, evidently, those readings of his require, amongst other things, multiple viewings. What I am going to propose is that it is with those viewings that the isolation of a filmic text emerges, a lowest common denominator generated through close and repeated observation (rather than naive immersion). There is indeed an 'ideal spectator' to ground Žižek's ideal reading – but it is Žižek himself and all those who see films as he does. It is not a meaning 'intrinsic to the filmic text' as some Žižekians put it, for it is founded on the plural processes of viewing themselves.[60]

In his valorization of the repeated viewing, it is noteworthy that Žižek echoes Bordwell perfectly. At the end of his *Figures Traced in Light* (2005a), Bordwell cites Jean-Marie Straub calling for 'a certain block of time' to be given to film viewing 'for the audience just to see'.[61] Great films require more time, and close and frequent inspection. *My* argument, by extension, will be that the apparent greatness and autonomy of the artwork is not only what stands the 'test of time' but what also *emerges with* the test, or experience, of time by being presented and re-presented over and over again to a certain point of view. The process of viewing is generative of both spectator and film, subject and object, alike. In this respect, re-presentation lies even more at the heart of Bordwell and Žižek's knowledge of film than we first suspected. (We could think of the alternative in these terms: is it possible to imagine *not* wanting to watch a film again *because* it was so good, because whatever artistic power it had would diminish with repeated exposure and the alteration that foreknowledge inevitably brings? Some films are best only when remembered; or as Andy Warhol said, 'if you look at a thing long enough, it loses all of its meaning'.)

Conclusion

In the next two chapters we will look at approaches to film that claim to forego treating it as textual, or even as representational, in favour of analysing it, in one phrase, as 'experience, as sensation, as a perception-consciousness formation'. Cinematic images cannot be representations because sensation and affect are not intrinsically cognitive. Another version of this paradigm claims that cinematic images are worldly on account of their singularity, film having the power to call our attention 'wholly for *that* thing *now*, in the frame of nature, the world moving in the branch'. Such singularity even has a spiritual dimension, with the view that movies arise 'out of magic, from *below* the world'.[62]

Of course, ontological approaches, like the Deleuzian or Cavellian ones just cited, can also be represented as a type of representation (or cognitive process), be it conscious or unconscious. Sensation and singularity must be representable after all (otherwise Deleuze and Cavell literally do not know what they are talking about). Conversely, any representation can also be given an ontological rendering – information as immanent process. Here we have the old circle of Being and Knowledge again. Let us remind ourselves of what Ian Jarvie said the last time we encountered it:

> It can be argued that before we can answer the question of what exists, we have to solve the problem of what we know. Since knowledge is what we know of what exists, it is what we know about what we know that allows us to move towards articulating what we know of what exists... By parallel reasoning it can also be argued that before we can solve the problem of what we know we must first solve the problem of what exists, because when we ask what we know, what we mean is what do we know of what exists, and how can we assess any claim to know something or other if we have not solved the problem of what exists and hence can adjudicate our claims to know that it does?[63]

My own ongoing hypothesis, alternatively, is that film is the Real-as-process, or process reality: it is that which engenders this very circular movement between subjective, epistemic viewing (along with all the theories that it 'inspires'), and the artwork viewed. Film-subject and film-object are co-engendered. And, in fact, after introducing the circle of Knowledge and Being, Jarvie goes on to articulate it in terms of subject–object relations:

> The problem of knowledge seems to be about 'us', since it queries what 'we' know. The problem of ontology, though, in asking what there is, leaves out any reference to us and appears only to speak about 'the world'. The question arises of the relation between 'us' and the world, whether knowledge is a state of 'us' or some other sort of thing and if that, what sort of thing?

The answer, I'll suggest, is that we too are not any sort of thing at all, but a relational process. We are neither an informed brain nor a formless void: we are a mutating connection. The relation of world to subject, or film to spectator (and critic), is indeed central. But I will claim that it is also multiple, that there is not one film-text but many, and that many of these are not even textual. Likewise, there is not one (kind of) spectator but many, many of whom are not even human.

Before I make any further contributions to this thesis, however, I must set out in the next two chapters the best possible cases for an ontology of film that can bypass the epistemic dimension of film viewing in favour of a direct relation between viewer and the film-world. Where Žižek and Bordwell might be said to contrast with each other as subjective (culturalist) and objective (cognitivist) vis-à-vis epistemology, Cavell and Deleuze can be seen to set up a similar contrast vis-à-vis ontology – as a phenomenologist and naturalist respectively. Hence, we will see what Roland Barthes described in *Camera Lucida* as the 'ontological desire' being consummated in two fundamentally different ways.

4
Deleuze's Kinematic Philosophy

> The relationship which holds in the application of a theory is never one of resemblance... Practice is a set of relays from one theoretical point to another, and theory is a relay from one practice to another.[1]

Deleuze's ambivalence: *philosophia sive cinema?*

It would not be an exaggeration to say, that of all the philosophers this study tackles, it is Gilles Deleuze who suffers most from film-envy. Though it is perhaps insensitive to attribute such a Freudian cliché to Deleuze of all people – for we will see that the Freudian approach to film is all too 'puerile' for his taste – it is nonetheless striking how closely Deleuze watches the films of his choice with an eye to recreating his own philosophy in their image. The magnanimity he shows to film's conceptual power is seen most clearly at the very end of his two-volume work on film, *Cinema 1: The Movement-Image* and *Cinema 2: The Time-Image*, when he writes that 'cinema's concepts are not given in cinema. And yet they are cinema's concepts, not theories about cinema'. Yet, at every point and turn of the preceding 500 pages of text, films and their makers are continually compared with philosophical thinkers, only ones that 'think with movement-images and time-images instead of concepts'.[2]

Nonetheless, it would be plain 'stupid', as Deleuze remarked in one interview, 'to want to create a philosophy of cinema': he is not trying to apply philosophy to cinema, but move directly from philosophy to cinema *and* from cinema to philosophy. Indeed, this two-way movement is based upon shared problems, such that the philosopher turns to cinema only because he or she is 'compelled... to look for answers in the cinema', answers that respond to problems belonging to both disciplines. And the crucial problem for Deleuze, as we will see, is that of 'abberant movement' – a problem that is as much cinematographical as it is philosophical.[3]

Deleuze's democracy of thought, concept and problem is crystalized well in what he says about Alain Resnais – for him, one of cinema's most reflective film-makers:

> When we say that Resnais' characters are philosophers, we are certainly not saying that these characters talk about philosophy, or that Resnais 'applies' philosophical ideas to a cinema, but that he invents a cinema of philosophy, a cinema of thought, which is totally new in the history of cinema, and totally alive in the history of philosophy, creating, with his unique collaborators, a rare marriage between philosophy and cinema.[4]

This employment of artistic work as valid philosophical matter – the movement from cinema to philosophy mentioned above – is symptomatic of Deleuze's broader strategy to incorporate art into a field of problems shared with other forms of thought, including science as well. As Jean-Clet Martin puts it, 'philosophy, art and science comprise a multilinear ensemble formed from relations of resonance between melodic curves [*courbes*] alien to each other. Leibniz *and* Rembrandt, philosophers and architects'. This 'resonance', however, is not a reduction, for though Deleuze himself might write of an 'identity of concept and image' in *Cinema 2*, this identity is of movements, of proximate becomings. Hence, it is also crucial when Philippe Mengue writes of Deleuze's approach, that Spinoza *neighbours* Lawrence, Kant *neighbours* Artaud, and Heidegger *neighbours* Jarry according to specific differential relations. A neighbour lives beside you, not inside you, which is why the relationship between theory and practice is 'never one of resemblance' but 'relay', as the quotation at the head of this chapter declares.[5]

Yet, an ambivalence remains all the same, one that is marked by Deleuze's own philosophical development subsequent to writing the *Cinema* books. What was nascent in the stance that there are 'concepts specific to cinema, but which can only be formed philosophically' becomes altogether more evident by the time Deleuze co-authors *What is Philosophy?* with Felix Guattari in 1991. Now there is a clear specialization of roles, with 'the exclusive right of concept creation secur[ing] a function for philosophy'. While philosophy, alone, creates concepts, the role of art now is to extract *'percepts and affects'*.[6] For *What is Philosophy?*, the aim of art, and so cinema (though film is mentioned only rarely), is 'to wrest the percept from perceptions of objects and the states of a perceiving subject, to wrest the affect from affections as the transition from one state to another: to extract a bloc of sensations, a pure being of sensations'. Art is altogether more material than mental, more sensational than conceptual, a *'composition* of sensation through matter'. For, while there is a 'concept of sensation' and even a 'sensation of concept', according to Deleuze there is no sensation *as* concept. Any apparent identity between the two is actually only an 'indiscernibility' on account of art and philosophy each (with science too) having a virtual origin in chaos, being 'daughters' of chaos. This indiscernibility only exists, however, in a zone of proximity, it is not an actual identity.[7] *'East is East...'*

Hence, it is no surprise that Ronald Bogue, for instance, can write that 'Deleuze's proposal... is to complete what Bergson started and give cinema the corresponding metaphysics *that it lacks*'. It seems as if, now, because the artist for Deleuze 'is a seer, a becomer', it is only to be expected that 'he' cannot 'recount what happened to him, or what he imagines' since he is no more than 'a shadow'.[8] And, of course, it is only to be welcomed, consequently, that philosophy should lend a hand in conceptualizing what the artist can only sense and feel – to give every art the metaphysics it lacks (even though Deleuze elsewhere decries 'the indignity of speaking for others'). 'Conceptual Art', therefore, is a misnomer, if this means bringing art and philosophy together: the concept cannot be substituted for sensation, for art creates 'sensations and not concepts'. There can be intertwinings between philosophy and art, but no synthesis.[9] Neighbours, not lovers. *'And West is West...'*

This (for some) undoubtedly romantic view of the ineffability of art is not, again, without some subtlety in Deleuze's case. For he does not equate the concept with thought *per se*, and even goes so far as to nominate philosophy, science and art as the 'three great forms' of thought: thinking can be done through concepts, or functions, or sensations, 'and no one of these thoughts is better than another, or more fully, completely, or synthetically "thought"'. So we must distinguish concept from thought and note that *What is Philosophy?* can thereby allow art to be thoughtful without being conceptual. Nonetheless, the focus for our enquiry, Deleuze's *Cinema* books, seem more radical again, allowing even a conceptual power to film and so a philosophical function to the film-maker, such that Deleuze could write that the director Werner Herzog 'is a metaphysician. He is the most metaphysical of cinema directors'.[10]

Cinema's concepts

But rather than wrestle any more with Deleuze's ambivalent movement from cinema to philosophy, what requires our attention now is his movement in the opposite direction, from philosophy to cinema. In Deleuze's case, it is patently obvious that this could not be a stupid application of philosophy to film through some kind of one-to-one reduction. Rather, it is a true makeover of philosophy within cinematic thinking, the expression of a common problematic field through a different medium. Indeed, the renowned exclusion of any film-stills from the *Cinema* books is not only because Deleuze holds that a still cannot illustrate what moves, what is temporal, but also because, as he says, 'it is in fact our text alone which aspires to be an illustration of the great films'.[11] In the *Cinema* books,

Deleuze's philosophy becomes a movie remake, a remake of the history of film. This illustration, though, is not in pictures but through common, resonant problems. Between Dreyer and Kierkegaard on the problem of choice; Hitchcock and Hume on the externality of relations; Pasolini and Kant on the conditions of reality (or Gance and Kant on the mathematical sublime); as well as Robbe-Grillet and Augustine on the simultaneity of past, present and future – Deleuze fills his pages with as many philosophical problems as there are films.[12]

Every theorist must be allowed his or her own characteristic approach to a topic, and the conjoined materialism, vitalism, processualism, immanentism and anti-representationalism that typifies the Deleuzian way is clearly evident in the two *Cinema* volumes. But there is much more specificity than just a list of 'isms' in Deleuze's rewriting of film history. Aside from the overt use of Henri Bergson and C. S. Peirce in his approach, his treatment of cinema's auteurs and their artworks echoes many of the themes from Deleuze's own *oeuvre* between 1962 and 1983. We can list them as follows:

- The discussions of 'the truthful man' who must judge life as evil, the power of the false to free itself from 'appearances as well as truth', the artist as '*creator of truth*, because truth ... has to be created', and life as the relation of qualitative forces – all derive from Deleuze's work, *Nietzsche and Philosophy*;[13]
- Hitchcock's mental image as 'the perfection of all the other images', the essence of cinema having 'nothing but thought and its functioning' for its higher purpose, and the mathematical rigour of Pasolini's cinema, which no longer concerns the image 'but the thought of the image, the thought in the image?' – all bear the mark of Deleuze's reading of the infinite mode of thought in *Expressionism in Philosophy: Spinoza*;[14]
- The affection-image belonging to seemingly inanimate bodies like the edge, blade or point of a knife, each being 'bearers of ideal events' – this comes directly from the Stoic philosophy of incorporeal events in *The Logic of Sense*;[15]
- The eternal return, good and bad repetition in Buñuel, the power of cinema to shock the brain into thinking (*Difference and Repetition*);[16]
- The cinema of minorities and missing people (*Kafka: Towards a Minor Literature*);
- The types of perception (liquid, gaseous, molecular) and superhuman eye, the molecular woman and molecular child, deterritorialization and the plane of immanence, the individuating function of the face and facialization (*A Thousand Plateaus*).[17]

More generally still, the depiction of the pre-war French school of Epstein, L'Herbier and Grémilon as a 'sort of Cartesianism', with Abel Gance adding spiritualism and dualism to the French cinema; or the great, omnipotent naturalisms of Stroheim and Buñuel (which aren't opposed to realism); or the shift in film history from the movement-image, through its crisis, and then onto the time-image, which matches the Nietzschean diagnosis from theism, through the death of God, to the birth of the Overman; or, finally, the bare fact that cinema (like metaphysics) is not dead but 'still at the beginning of its investigations' – all of these parallels convey the strong impression that Deleuze is reliving both the history of post-Kantian thought as well as his own philosophical development through the eyes of films and their makers.[18]

Overarching all these correspondences, of course, is the emulation in cinematic thought of the huge philosophical shift that came with Kant's work. In particular, and what gives the *Cinema* volumes their twin titles, is the change in attitude towards time from the Greek view to the Kantian one, from time being subordinated to movement to movement being subordinated to time. Art, and in particular cinema, emulates this shift according to Deleuze, and so has a 'role to play in the birth and formation of this new thought, this new way of thinking'. Cinema repeats 'the same experience' as philosophy. Naturally, we might be wondering whether Deleuze's proposition here is a historical thesis or a philosophical one (by his own definition), or both. At one level, it is a metatheoretical one. Deleuze is happy to admit that he has given us, amongst other things, a 'natural history' (not to be confused with a chronological history) and a 'taxonomy' of cinema, and these remarks have important metaphilosophical implications.[19] Deleuze, of course, is famous for his classifications: the tables, lists and dualisms operative across all his work. And that he uses this approach with almost baroque intensity when analysing film is one of the most obvious traits of the *Cinema* books. Within the simple dyad of movement-image and time-image there are the subdivisions (which we will explore) of perception-image, affection-image, impulse-image, action-image and mental-image; opsign, sonsign, lectosign, noosign, mnemosign, chronosign and crystal-image, and even more at a still finer level of analysis. But why this plethora of images and signs, this glossomania of divisions and distinctions?

The first reason goes back to Deleuze's Bergsonian inheritance, for Bergson was fond of citing Plato's adage that the good philosopher must, like the good cook, cut nature at its joints when employing universals. As Bergson interpreted this idea, we must create concepts adequate for each object of enquiry. It is not that reality must be made to fit the concept (that would be pure butchery, pure vivisection, the killing cut), but rather that the concept must be cut (created) to fit the object, to become the thing. And Deleuze's excess of tables and classes are just such an invention: 'it is necessary to create more precise concepts to identify the unities of movement and duration'.[20] Hence, all his classifications are

> mobile, modifiable, retroactive, boundless, and their criteria vary from instance to instance. Some instances are full, others empty. A classification

> always involves bringing together things with very different appearances and separating those that are very similar. That is the beginning of the formation of concepts.[21]

Classifications are part of the conceptual work of philosophical engagement, but they must trace 'singular symptoms or signs rather than general forms'. This is why the concepts *belong to cinema*. Even if it is philosophy that brings them forth, philosophy must mould itself to the contours of cinematic practice (rather than vice versa), such that the different types of space discussed in the *Cinema* books, for instance, only reflect the fact that 'there are as many spaces as there are inventors'. Likewise, for colour, there is a specificity to Antonioni's use of colour, to take just one case, such that 'Antonioni's formula is valid for him only, it is he who invents it'.

Yet, Deleuze also cautions us that the work of individual auteurs must be grafted onto 'differentiations, specific determinations, and reorganizations of concepts' that will allow one to consider cinema as a whole. Indeed, consideration of the whole demands some generalization, as when Deleuze asks, for instance, 'what are the laws of the action-image across all genres?'.[22] Otherwise, we would literally be left with as many concepts as there are films.

Two processes are involved in this taxonomy, therefore – differentiation *and* integration: cutting concepts to fit the specific films (differentiation), as well as generalizing film to fit all of these concepts together (integration). In the face of not *actually* having one concept per shot, or per film, or even per auteur (though Deleuze can sometimes approach that last situation), therefore, the question must remain as to whether the goodness of fit overall (which might for some indicate the transcendental applicability of Deleuze's philosophy to film) is actually made by butchering the object to fit the theory. Alternatively, the good intention to avoid butchery, to avoid recutting the films to fit the philosophy, might come at the cost of ramifying that philosophy ad infinitum, and consequently making it all the more scholastic and non-explanatory. The more the theory matches the films, the more it simply repeats cinematic history with a new jargon, and the less it tells us about cinema as a whole. The *perfect* fit indicates fidelity – the concepts are cinema's after all; but also sterility – they tell us nothing that film hasn't already 'told' us. Indeed, we might even ask whether what is at work in Deleuze is not another kind of reverse engineering, one that follows the lineaments of film history and then essentializes them within a set of concepts. Hence, it would appear that the concept must be allowed to generalize if it is to have any function or, indeed, if it is to avoid the charge of retrospective logic. It will be these questions to which we will return once we have completed the exposition of the basics of Deleuze's film-philosophy.

A non-reductive materialism

The most striking thing for a reader in 1983, when *Cinema 1* first appeared, is that the general approach of the book, its overarching concept, looks to a microbiology of the brain in place of psychoanalysis or linguistics, which were still the prevailing paradigms in cineanalysis at the time. Indeed, a particularly antipsychoanalytic stance is one of the hallmarks of both *Cinema 1* and *2*. As Deleuze puts it himself, 'I don't believe that linguistics and psychoanalysis offer a great deal to the cinema. On the contrary, the biology of the brain – molecular biology – does. Thought is molecular. Molecular speeds make up the slow beings that we are'. Precisely because films put images in motion, or give them 'self-motion', they also continually trace, and renew, the circuits of the brain, helping it form new synapses, connections, pathways. By contrast, psychoanalysing Carl Dreyer, for example, tells us very little about anything other than psychoanalysis; but comparing him with Kierkegaard (on the problem of choice) can tell us a good deal more. The psychoanalytic treatment of the images of the creamer and spurting milk in Aleksandrov and Eisenstein's *The General Line* (1929), for instance, is typically 'puerile'.[23]

Once again, though, there is a history to Deleuze's position, in this case an antipathy towards psychoanalysis that goes back to his first collaborations with Félix Guattari, especially in the *Anti-Oedipus*. And not without motive. We noted in Chapter 3 that the Oedipus complex was the key element of Freudianism borrowed by film theory. For Deleuze, psychoanalyses of film have 'only ever given cinema one sole object, one single refrain, the so-called primitive scene'. In Deleuze (and Guattari's) understanding, by positing the primacy of the Oedipus complex, Freud and Lacan confused consequences (symptoms) for causes. Deleuze does not say that the Oedipus complex and castration anxiety do not exist – 'we are oedipalised, we are castrated' – but that psychoanalysis takes as constitutive what are actually derived from other forces.[24] It is these other forces that Freud and Lacan omit by making their theory a determining ideology (biologically determining in Freud, culturally determining in Lacan), that is, a constitutive necessity for being a subject.[25]

So what are these 'other forces'? They are forms of material becoming, real processes. Hence, when looking at Freud's case study of 'The Wolfman', for example, Deleuze takes an antirepresentational and anti-oedipal standpoint: the aetiology of the case does not involve a wolf *standing for* a father, it involves a wolf or, rather, a man *becoming* a wolf. The image, for Deleuze, is not a metaphor for something else, it does not represent: it is its own thing, a real process. Metaphors are metamorphoses. Yet, Freud never lets the positivity of the image of the wolf stand out:

> it was already decided from the very beginning that animals could serve only to represent coitus between parents, or, conversely, be represented

> by coitus between the parents. Freud obviously knows nothing about the fascination exerted by wolves and the meaning of their silent call, the call to become wolf... The trap was set from the start: never will the Wolf-man speak. Talk as he might about wolves, howl as he might like a wolf, Freud does not even listen; he glances at his dog and answers, 'It's Daddy.'[26]

Behind this difference of approach towards the positivity of the image also lie different conceptions of desire. Deleuze and Guattari happily maintain, along with other psychodynamic theorists, that the unconscious is a site of desire, of libidinal forces. But, for them, these forces are a plenum, not a vacuum: they lack nothing and are wholly productive. Once again we are on philosophical territory. One tradition, from Plato through Hegel, to Sartre, Lacan and Žižek, has always seen desire as a *lack*, as a teleological need: desire aims at a transcendent object, the possession of which alone will satiate the desire.[27] 'Desire as lack' renders any perception of the object specular and representational, a permitted or defeated access to reality:

> To a certain degree, the traditional logic of desire is all wrong from the very outset: from the very first step that the platonic logic of desire forces us to take, making us choose between *production* and *acquisition*. From the moment that we placed desire on the side of acquisition, we make desire an idealistic (dialectical, nihilistic) conception, which causes us to look upon it as primarily a lack: a lack of an object, a lack of the real object.[28]

Deleuze, on the other hand, sees desire in the tradition of Nietzsche and Bergson: it is material and 'immanent' to the world – it has no transcendent object constituting it. Nor is it teleological, for it wants for nothing.

The consequences of these different notions of desire are fundamental to both the Freudian and the Deleuzian conception of the cinematic image. For those in the Freudian tradition, the film image is a representation that we lack. Combined with our negative desire for plenitude, filmic representations are able to position us as masochists, sadists, scopophiliacs or fetishists – a whole panoply of neurotics and perverts. For Deleuze, however, the cinematic image is an object (a physical process) itself, not just a *transparent sign of* a missing object. As the Deleuzian film analyst Steven Shaviro writes:

> the fundamental characteristic of the cinematic image is therefore said to be the one of *lack*... But is it really *lack* that makes images so dangerous and disturbing? What these [psychoanalytic] theorists [of film] fear is not the emptiness of the image, but its weird fullness; not its impotence so much as its power.[29]

The power of cinema's images stems from their *not* lacking anything (as a supposed representative of an absent Real), from their own plenitude as material and real in themselves, and as all too present and affective to the viewer. Where, for example, we sympathize with events on-screen that we would normally represent as morally reprehensible – as in Hitchcock's *Psycho* (1960) when we want Norman Bates to succeed in clearing up the bloody mess after the first murder committed by 'mother', and then later again in his attempt to sink Marion Crane's car – it is the processes, physical and minute, that gain our empathy *directly as processes impinging upon our senses*, not the representation of any 'wicked' character (that we might like or loathe). It is Norman's movements, as well as the car's and that of the changing perspective (due to the camera's own movement), that directly affect us (a process that I will explain further in Chapter 7 using Henri Bergson's concept of 'fabulation').

This direct presence of the image does not only preclude the Freudian symbolic approach, though, but any *linguistic* one too; that is, any approach that makes the film image a representation or symbol. Instead, cinema for Deleuze 'is a plastic mass, an a-signifying and a-syntaxic material, a material not formed linguistically even though it is not amorphous and is formed semiotically, aesthetically, and pragmatically'. He wants to replace the linguistically dominated semiological approach with a 'semiotics' – a 'system of images and signs independent of language in general'. Any language system only exists in its reaction to a *non-language material* that it transforms. This is why Deleuze is 'rigorously antilinguistic', as Marie-Claire Ropars-Wuilleumier puts it. Film's supposedly poor powers of expression are only apparent when it is erroneously compared to a verbal utterance: it does seem then to have no power of metaphor, for example (as Roman Jakobsen argued). But, when taken in itself as a *movement*-image, it has its own set of connective powers, being able to '*dissolve* movement by connecting with the whole that it expresses'. Cinematic dream-images, for instance, where one image becomes another, are not metaphors at all but a 'becoming which can by right continue to infinity'. Material metamorphosis over linguistic metaphor.[30]

This non-linguistic or 'signaletic' material has direct, sensory affects on the brain, not the symbolic imagination. But we must understand the brain in the *Cinema* books non-reductively, in a non-objective manner quite opposed to the one lying behind the cognitivist approach to film. It is in *What is Philosophy?* that Deleuze elucidates this notion of a non-objective brain:

> If the mental objects of philosophy, art, and science (that is to say, vital ideas) have a place, it will be in the deepest of the synaptic fissures, in the hiatuses, intervals, and meantimes of a *nonobjectifiable* brain...That is to say, thought...does not depend upon a brain made up of organic

> connections and integrations: according to phenomenology, thought depends on man's relations with the world...but this ascent of phenomenology beyond the brain toward a Being in the world...hardly gets us out of the sphere of opinions... Will the turning point not be elsewhere, in the place where the brain is 'subject', where it becomes subject? It is the brain that thinks and not man... Philosophy, art, and science are not the mental objects of an objectifiable brain but the three aspects under which the brain becomes subject, Thought-brain... At the same time that the brain becomes subject...the concept becomes object as created, as event or creation itself; and philosophy becomes the plane of immanence that supports the concepts and that the brain lays out.[31]

With respect to film, *Cinema 2* doesn't locate this brain in a separate organic cerebrum but in a relation with the *cinema screen itself*: 'the brain itself has become conscious... The screen itself is the cerebral membrane where immediate and direct confrontations take place between the past and the future, the inside and outside, at a distance impossible to determine, independent of any fixed point'. Deleuze is influenced by the ideas of Antonin Artaud here: his view of cinema as neuro-physiological vibration and his argument that 'the image must produce a shock' in order to create thought (it must make us jump, as if every cut were a jump cut). Cinema makes us think by working on our senses, by shocking them – in horrific, sublime excess – and in so doing it creates new brain circuits.[32] It is this ability to communicate vibrations to the cortex automatically, to touch the brain and nervous system 'directly', that gives film its power. Genuine thought can only be born when an outside encounters the unthought, the automatic, within the thinking brain.[33] What counts as a genuine, shocking thought, however, and whether such a thought can also be philosophical, will be a matter for further consideration later.

From movement to time: images and signs

The story arc of *Cinema 1* and *Cinema 2* is as dramatic as it is (narratively) classical. It begins with a state of nature, followed by its fall and subsequent redemption: there was once a cinematic image adequate for expression (movements that mattered), that then fell into crisis (the shattering of the movement-image), before its resurrection as a time-image, an image adequate for its time, even when it is a time of loss and decay. First act (*Cinema 1*), last act (*Cinema 2*), with the middle act coming in the transition between the two volumes.

Time in modern cinema, Deleuze tells us, 'is no longer empirical, nor metaphysical; it is "transcendental" in the sense that Kant gives this word: time is out of joint and presents itself in the pure state'.[34] Once again, we are seeing film repeat the history of philosophy. In a sense though, it is only the same thing that is being said in different ways, and this is in-line with Deleuze's theory of univocity (that Being is said in the same way of, and by, every different thing). There is but one Being, with many languages through which it may express itself. *Philosophia sive cinema*. This is an inclusive disjunction: not a choice within a hierarchy of discourses, but different modes of expression. Nonetheless, the signs of hierarchy still remain, for Deleuze's cinema manages to express itself adequately only in so far as it reflects a specific philosophy of cinema, namely Bergson's (as interpreted by Deleuze). As we will see, it is by using Bergson's philosophy (and, to a lesser extent, C. S. Peirce's) that we are able to understand cinema's achievement in expressing a time that is out of joint, when the time-image finally provides us with a *direct* presentation of time.

The time-image in *Cinema 2* indicates the possibility of new images, new signs, a future art of cinema. But before we get to this, it is the task of *Cinema 1* to tell the story of the rise and fall of the movement-image – its various incarnations as perception-image, affection-image, impulse-image, action-image and mental-image – as well as the various signs related to them. We should firstly note that it is *images* that Deleuze writes about and not the *imaginary* – there is no gaze or 'look' at work in Deleuze's approach, be it male or female, sadistic or masochistic. The image is for itself and not *for* a consciousness (as both phenomenology and Freud would have it). For, if Husserl claimed that consciousness is *of* the image (and the image is for consciousness), then Deleuze follows Bergson's alternative view in *Matter and Memory* that consciousness already *is* the image. There is an 'eye' already 'in things, in luminous images in themselves', for it is not consciousness which illumines (as phenomenology believes), but the images, or light, that already are a consciousness 'immanent to matter'.[35]

Image as already consciousness, consciousness as already image. Reiterated here is the materialist identity of brain and screen that we looked at above.[36] It is a new form of material monism, going beyond phenomenology. The very notion that 'the brain is the screen' stems from Bergson's understanding of the material universe as an '*aggregate of images*' (which, in the modern parlance of philosophy of mind, makes him a 'radical externalist'): 'an image may *be* without *being perceived* – it may be present without being represented – and the distance between these two terms, presence and representation, seems just to measure the interval between matter itself and our conscious perception of matter'.[37] Yet, despite the centrality of the Bergsonian image in his theory (one which would strike many as already veering back towards a phenomenology of appearances), Deleuze does not regard his approach as subjectivist; rather, it is that image equals consciousness equals matter in an *objective* phenomenology (the flip-side of the 'brain as subject'). It is a phenomenology that transcends 'normal', anthropomorphic perception, showing us how things see themselves (and us), rather than how we (normally) see them. Whereas Lacanian theory proposes that we see the mirror *as if* it sees us, in Deleuze's world, the mirror, or the processes that comprise a mirror, *really do* see, and touch, us.

Nonetheless, Deleuzian images do have subjective and objective poles or profiles, which are themselves related to each other in different ways. Indeed, these varied relations are what Deleuze means by the perception-image, affection-image, action-image, and so on. And how those different relations are generated is given to us in the story of images that Bergson provides in Chapter 1 of *Matter and Memory*. This imagology sets the script for Deleuze's work too: from the movement-image, that gives us only an indirect representation of time (in so far as it depends on montage), to the time-image, that provides us with a clear view of time in 'false movements' that shatter our 'sensory-motor schema'.[38] Also in the script are all the permutations by which subject and object might connect with each other in between this alpha and omega. Cinematic images come with varying degrees of bias, sometimes leaning more to the object-side (in the static frames of early cinema), sometimes more to the subject-side (in the mental images of Hitchcock that bring movement-image cinema to its completion), though they are never one or the other *entirely*. The image is always a becoming between these poles.

Two things must be said here. Firstly, if there is no independent reality to subject and object – they are merely the poles of the image – then there is nothing to stop us saying that cinema, with *its* images, gives us reality rather than some pale imitation of it. *Image is every thing*. The two ways it does this are through time and movement, the latter being the indirect representation of the former.[39] But irrespective of being direct or indirect, the movements shown in cinema are all real. And this is so not only on account of everything being an image. Hence, there is a second point to be made, that compounds the first: *every thing is in motion*. In a universe where only 'duration' (change) is real, the moving images of film have an equal claim on reality – films give us immediately self-moving images. That is why *Cinema 1* begins its study with real movement, understanding by this something totally unlike any subjective *impression* of movement. For this, says Deleuze, is exactly how Bergson understood images, as 'mobile sections of duration', duration itself being the Real.[40] In fact, it is due to the ontological priority of change that the image is adumbrated as a set of relations between subjective and objective poles (in the perception-image, affection-image, and so on), *as well as* being unopposed to reality (in virtue of the latter's own mobility). Mobility makes the image real (for the Real is change); and the mobility between subject and object makes the image real as well (for their variable relations are embodied in its various types).

These various types of image (perception-image, affection-image) do not, therefore, *represent* the relations between subject and object; rather, they instantiate or exemplify them. This is seen vividly (though also rather abstractly) at the beginning of *Cinema 1* in the relation between one or more images and the set of all images surrounding it (the 'Whole', which is itself incomplete or 'Open'). Even in the relatively static framings of early cinema – that were often quite geometrical, with the use of golden sections (in Eisenstein), horizontals and verticals (in Dreyer) and diagonals (in German Expressionism) – there is a relation with an out-of-field that is always *qualitative*. Alluding to Bergson's famous simile in *Creative Evolution* of sugar dissolving in water, Deleuze talks of a variable thread linking the particular to the whole, a thread made manifest in the duration of this event.[41] We have to *wait* for the sugar to dissolve. The local is never closed off: there is always a bidirectional movement that extends the *quantitative* change in the part to the *qualitative* state of the whole. And this is plain to see in cinema, where the moving images on-screen (a quantity) extend to an off-screen set of images (a quality). Indeed, in the simple shot we see 'the essence' of the cinematic movement-image: it lies in the extraction from 'moving bodies' the 'movement which is their common substance, or extracting from [quantitative, partial] movements the [qualitative, holistic] mobility which is their essence'.[42] There is a 'pure movement' extracted from 'moving bodies', or, if you prefer, a qualitative feeling, a whole world, created from just the way in which an actor might silently raise a hand during an otherwise static shot, or, in a modern movie, when a camera cranes high into the sky above its subject.

This thread or relation between part and whole is expressed even more clearly with the use of editing or 'montage', be it in the American, 'organic' style of editing, Soviet 'dialectical' montage, the 'quantitative' style of pre-war French film-makers, or the 'intensive' cutting of the German Expressionists. Montage – a new, abberant connection between images – releases even more the qualitative, holistic movement from the local (on-screen) movement-images in an indirect 'image *of* time'. But we must remember that this extension of the local to the whole is bidirectional, or reciprocally determining. The pure or qualitative movement also rebounds on the on-screen images before us. And it does so in different ways according to the kinds of gap or 'interval' expressed on-screen between the actions and reactions displayed between images. This interval belongs to the interrelationship between the images as they frame each other: one shot calls for another kind of shot, one cut leads to another – actions and reactions – according to the interests of the film, in particular its directorial style. Crucially, these 'interests' or selections are defined by Deleuze (after Bergson) *as forms of perception*.[43] In other words, perception itself is an infra-imagistic delimitation, a further selection or filtering of images from the whole, though nonetheless still linked to the whole. Its link to the whole, therefore – that is, what it expresses of the whole by its infra-imagistic selection – itself constitutes a kind of (qualitative) image that Deleuze calls the 'perception-image'.

Like the movement-images, of which they are a subspecies, perception-images have their own variable characteristics as well, namely a bias towards passive *perception* at one limit, *action* at another, and the *affect* that occupies (without filling) the gap in between.[44] The perception-image, however, should not be regarded as subjective, but rather as an objective subjectivity (it is formed from the *real* autodelimitation of images). With the perception-image, Deleuze tells us, 'we are no longer faced with subjective *or* objective images; we are caught in a correlation between a perception-image and a camera-consciousness which transforms it'.[45]

The action-image, on the other hand, expresses the well-organized, sensory-motor relationship between characters and the story-worlds that they inhabit. It is typified best by classical Hollywood narrative and the acting methods accompanying it (though, for Deleuze, narrative is derived from the images, not the other way around). Indeed, this organicism is said to culminate in the acting 'Method' itself, whose rules apply not only to the actor but to 'the conception and unfolding of the film, its framings, its cutting, its montage'.[46] Here the sensory-motor schema takes 'possession of the image' in two basic ways. Deleuze calls the first of these the 'large form' (following Noël Burch's nomenclature), wherein situations lead to actions that then lead to altered situations, as seen in Westerns and action films in particular. Things happen for a reason – framings and cuts expressing either the challenges an agent meets with or how he or she responds to them. Deleuze gives this large form the term SAS' (situation–action–new situation). Conversely, the other action-image follows the small form of ASA' (action–situation–new action) where small shifts in an agent's activity hugely alter the situation and so also the agent's next action. The small form is typically seen, according to Deleuze, in melodrama and burlesque.[47]

Finally, the affection-image – the in-between of perception and action – must not be understood as subjective any more than the perception-image. Deleuze explains it as an affective inside made outside, expressed par excellence in the close-up of the face. Indeed, it is the face in close-up that is *the* model for all affection-images, even if comprised of close-ups of hands, knives or guns. In each case, there is a facialization of the object, the face/close-up always being a disclosure of qualities or, rather, the passage from one quality to another in pathetic states such as wonder, anger or fear.[48]

These different types of image, with their salient features (emphasizing agency or affect or situation) also encompass, and are intimately tied to, their own respective forms of space and time, each of which possesses the same emphases.[49] Variously active, reactive, affective, antagonistic, melodramatic or comedic, such spaces nevertheless remain fairly complicit with the well-determined space–times of the movement-image, whose coordinates come from a sensory-motor organization. The history of cinema in the first half of the twentieth century is comprised of all the various permutations that these images and their space–times can take on, the purpose of Deleuze's *Cinema 1* being to chart each and every one of them. Daunting though this objective is, it is not an infinite task, for after 50 years or so, Deleuze finds that cinema had exhausted all the variants of actual movement possible in the image. Indeed, the culmination of *Cinema 1* tells us that it was Alfred Hitchcock who brought these relations amongst images to their completion, directing the movement-image to its 'logical perfection'.[50] In his works, every variation of the movement-image, with biases towards one pole or the other, towards perception or action, is brought together and mentalized, represented through the pole of intellect. Every permutation in plot and agency is explored and exhausted *in cerebro*. Hitchcock makes film think or, rather, he shows the calculative intellection involved in plotting a murder, an escape, a capture, a concealment, an evasion or a blackmail. He gives us the mental-images (of movement) rather than the action-images themselves, virtual movement over actual movement. Characters and actions become specular, quasimeditative – processed for their spectrality to create suspense or unease.

Time regained

However, with this completion came the inevitable re-examination of the 'nature and status' of the movement-images by theorists and film-makers alike. No less than the apparent completion of philosophy by Hegel brought about a crisis in Western thought, so the completion of the first phase of cinema by Hitchcock occasioned new levels of critical re-examination. This second crisis, still current today according to Deleuze, concerns the uncreative, cliché-ridden nature of movement-image cinema (that is, Hollywood and its imitators). Even more, it concerns the stalled nature of movement in the world beyond cinema. Cliché is everywhere. The inability to move convincingly is no less true of our own lives, there being no qualitative difference between image and reality. Physical, optical and auditory clichés surround us, they are inside and outside us, thinking for us, turning us into a cliché, a bad film, an 'urban cancer'. Movements become false, hackneyed, cynical, as unbelievable as they are unbelieved. The question set at the end of *Cinema 1*, portentous though it may seem, is whether cinema can 'attack the dark organization of clichés'. Can cinema extract a new image from our clichéd world at the end of the movement-image? For the cliché is not just bare repetition, it also marks out our 'mental deficiency', 'organized mindlessness' and 'cretinization'.[51] The crisis for cinema, then, is also one for our culture and philosophy, for our ability, fundamentally, to think anew.

In *What is Philosophy?* Deleuze makes it the artist's task to struggle against the clichés and repetitions of opinion.[52] And, after Hitchcock, after 1945, cinema certainly seemed in need of a new artistic image. Would one emerge to save it? Would film survive to fight the good fight against cliché? *Cinema 1* asks us to wait and see. We anticipate that it will survive, of course, as heroes always do. Yet, the crisis of the image that Deleuze sets up between the last chapter of *Cinema 1* and the first chapter of its sequel, *Cinema 2*, does mark a crucial fissure, a genuine intermission or gap in Deleuze's own thought as well. Into the gap comes many things: a real sense of anticipation (for the advent of the time-image), of suspense (over the life or death of cinema) and of suspendedness (how long before the sequel, '*Cinema 2: The Time-Image*', would come out?). And alongside the cliff-hanger ending and curtain-fall (in true film-envy fashion), there also comes a real crisis in Deleuze's film-philosophy, though we will have to wait until we have seen what the time-image does before we can tackle that.[53]

So what does it do? In a reflexive move typical of modernism, the time-image *thematizes* the lack of creativity in the movement-image, the historical exhaustion of the movement-image. The cliché is embraced in order to be resisted, by taking a failure of form as new content. The five characteristics of the new image, then, are '*the dispersive situation, the deliberatively weak links, the voyage form, the consciousness of clichés, the condemnation of plot*'.[54] Together, they transform a vice into a virtue, wresting a new image from the bare repetitions of Hollywood. It can do this because, by thematizing a failure, the time-image gives us a *direct* representation of what reality is like itself: time as breakage, as wound, as fissure, as crack, as differential – all the features that Deleuze's process philosophy explores across its corpus. Time out of joint is true time, for time really is what puts things out of joint, what dismembers any organized situation. Deleuze is saying no more than what Nietzsche, James, Bergson and Heidegger said before him: when something breaks, when a habitual act fails to find its target, it emerges (as it really is) into consciousness. When vision fails, we see (the truth of) vision, we see the searches in *L'Avventura* or *Ladri di biciclette*. We don't see the thing, but what it is to see (or not see) the thing. We see the *process* of seeing.

In one respect, *all* the movement-images, or set of action-reaction images, can be thought of as clichés because, following Bergson, Deleuze sees any perceived image as a selection and deletion of reality in accordance with *preset instrumentalist formulae*.[55] But these clichés become *too* formulaic if they cannot adapt to external changes impinging *on them*. They lose their utility when they cannot respond to the new challenges after 1945 (post-war European anomie and exhaustion, class upheaval, social reorganization, physical and spiritual dislocation, moral re-evaluation, vast economic migrations). This is the moment of transition when anything is possible, when all the normal motor-linkages, motivated actions, logical plots, rational cuts and well-organized spaces find no purchase. What Deleuze calls 'any-space-whatevers' arise ('*espace quelconque*', a concept he takes from the anthropologist Marc Auge).

Consequently, new images of a potentially more 'readable' or 'thinkable' nature can emerge because they are made thematic. Deleuze talks of a new breed of signs, 'opsigns' and 'sonsigns', where optical and sound images are directly apprehended: we *see* the actor seeing his seeing, hearing his hearing – it is an image *of* an image, a thematized image.[56] In the comedies of Jacques Tati, for instance, we see (and read) what it is to be a sound (as when the sound of a swinging door becomes boredom itself in *Les Vacances de Monsieur Hulot* (1953)), or in the numerous false fidelities between sound and image (a car horn that is also a duck's quack, a door hinge that is a plucked cello) that make us hear and so think about sound as sound. What it is to be a place is also thematized when set-descriptions replace the 'situation'; or what it is to act, when a farcical 'to-and-fro' replaces proper action. Tati's Hulot is not an example of a true agent, then, but one who is 'always ready to be carried away by the movements of world to which he gives rise or rather which themselves wait for him to be born'. Time, space and even thought itself are made perceptible in such time-images: they are made visible and audible by being thematized in the breakdown of 'natural' sights, sounds and actions.[57] Direct time is the 'out of joint' of perception, action and affect, therefore, of all the dimensions of movement.

The new time-image was needed to meet the challenge of the cliché. It was born to restore our belief in the world, to awaken us from our cynical, hackneyed lives. Where the movement-image weakened itself in formulaic, 'false' movements, it is superseded by and subordinated to the time-image. This is the power of the 'false' as such; the power to create untruths, the power *not* to correspond (with the old 'truth', the formulaic truth), but *to* respond to the world of change by instantiating it anew.[58] Cinema tries to restore our belief in the world by creating reasons to believe in this world: 'we need an ethic or a faith…a need to believe in this world'. How is this done? By inventing new relationships between sound and vision, new types of space, and even new kinds of body (that correspond to a 'genesis of bodies' rather than fixed organic coordinates). The power of the false is the power of creation, invention or novelty. New kinds of actor will also have to emerge: amateurs, 'professional non-actors' or 'actor-mediums', capable of 'seeing and showing rather than acting'. The French new wave gave us an instance of this with its 'cinema of attitudes and postures', going so far as to make even the scenery accord to the 'attitudes of the body' (Deleuze is thinking of Jean-Pierre Léaud here, François Truffaut's cinematic alter ego). A cinema of the body emerges in contrast to the old cinema of action, with a body that is caught up in 'a quite different space': 'this is a space before action, always haunted by a child, or by a clown, or by both at once'. This is a cinema of bodies that is not sensory-motor, but 'action being replaced by attitude'. It creates a 'pre-hodological space', pointing to an 'undecidability of the body', where any obstacle is dispersed 'in a plurality of ways of being present in the world'.[59]

In all of this, time is weighty. Opsigns and sonsigns, being breaks with the sensory-motor, are glimpses of real time, the time that lies virtual behind all actual (movement) images. We find their 'true genetic element when the actual optical image crystallizes with *its own* virtual image'. Indeed, Deleuze explains virtual ontology plainly: 'for the time-image to be born…the actual image must enter into relation with its *own* virtual image as such'. And this virtual, real time, which cannot occupy any actual present, must therefore occupy the past or 'past in general' (a past that has no actual date). In the cinematic time-image, past and present or virtual and actual become indiscernible. The films of the Italian *neo*-realists, the French *New* Wave, *New* German Cinema and the *New* Hollywood of the 1970s only give us glimpses of this virtuality, but they are direct glimpses all the same.[60] These 'news', evidently, bring the virtual with them.

The cinematic glimpses of real time also come in various guises, some more and some less obviously temporal. With the work of Alain Resnais, for instance (*Je t'aime, je t'aime* (1968), *Hiroshima mon amour* (1959)), we 'plunge into memory': but it is not a present memory or psychological recollection so much as a direct exploration of time: 'memory is not in us; it is we who move in Being-memory, a world-memory'.

The locus of the indiscernibility of the virtual and actual is named (after Guattari) the 'crystal-image' by Deleuze. But its ontology comes directly from Bergson's philosophy of time in *Matter and Memory* as well as his essay on déjà vu, 'Memory of the Present and False Recognition'.[61] Deleuze articulates it as follows:

> What constitutes the crystal-image is the most fundamental operation of time: since the past is constituted not after the present that it was but at the same time, time has to split itself in two at each moment as present and past, which differ from each other in nature, or, what amounts to the same thing, it has to split the present into two heterogeneous directions, one of which is launched towards the future while the other falls towards the past ... Time consists of this split, and it is this, it is time, that we *see in the crystal*.[62]

Because cinema is time itself in direct presentation, its time-images are glimmering instantiations of the 'most fundamental operation of time'. The past persists in the present, though we are never aware of this save for those rare moments of temporal paradox such as déjà vu.[63] But its persistence is what allows for change, the past being what makes each present *pass on*.[64] Once again, because the time-image (like every other image) is also a relation between subjective and objective tendencies or poles, it can present itself in two possible forms: one grounded in the past, the other in the present.[65]

Film can explore Being-memory across a varied landscape formed with what Deleuze calls 'peaks' and 'plains' (or 'sheets') of the past. Welles's *Citizen Kane* is a case in point of the copresence of past and present, the famed depth of field photography expressing 'regions of past as such ... The hero acts, walks and moves: but it is the past that he plunges himself into and moves in: time is no longer subordinated to movement, but movement to time'. When Greg Toland's camera bears down on Susan at the club, for example, there is a 'contraction of the actual present' in its 'invitation to recollect'. Or, to take an example of our own, Jaco van Dormael's *Toto le héros* (1991) tells a story concerning the profound effects of an old man's past on his and others' present. This is a common storyline for many films, but *Toto le héros* realizes it as much with typical scenes of a man recollecting *his* past as by *showing* a continuity of past and present *in general* with resonating cuts, graphic matches and matches on action between different events. The 'past in general' is here in the present *on-screen* or, rather, we are directly in the presence of the past on-screen through the manner in which bodily gestures, camera movements and story motifs resonate across different eras. From the Deleuzian position, therefore, it is a mistake to think that the film image is 'by nature in the present'. Or if it is, then at least it is not within a *simple* present, as *L'Année dernière à Marienbad* demonstrates when its events derive from three types of present, that of the past, of the present and of the future.[66]

Amongst the different kinds of time-image, the crystal-image itself maintains the closest link to the virtual. It is described as a kind of 'expression' (Deleuze here shifting to his own Spinozist language), be it the expression seen in the relation between past and present (or the virtual and the actual), or in other more oblique relations.[67] Various films provide examples of the different forms of the crystal's expression: some of them perfect (Ophuls's *La Ronde* (1950)), some flawed (Renoir's *La Règle du jeu* (1939)), some in the process of its composition (Fellini's *Amarcord* (1973)), some in the process of its decay (Visconti's *The Leopard* (1963)). The curious fact about *Cinema 2*, however, is that the most powerful embodiment of the time-image throughout the book is not an image at all but the lack of one: the irrational cut. Indeed, the irrational cut is the paradigm case for Deleuze. It is more than just false continuity, though, for such cuts come in diverse forms, be it

> the steady form of a sequence of unusual, 'anomalous' images, which come and interrupt the normal linkage of the two sequences; or in the enlarged form of the black screen, or the white screen, and their derivatives.[68]

What matters in each case is that the cut now exists for itself, no longer for what it conjoins, but for its own disjunctive value. The cut, being itself now cut through and broken (irrational), gives us a vision of real time. It captures the essence of how the movement-image differs from the time-image, the disjointedness of the latter being rendered fully in a mutilated joint.

Any further analysis of the distinction between the time-image and the movement-image will therefore need to tackle the essential nature of this irrational cut, not only to keep Deleuze's dualism of movement and time under investigation, but also in order to see the value of the cut in his own thought between *Cinema 1* and *2*. Is this cut in his work itself rational or irrational, consistent or inconsistent? To begin to examine this, though, we must look firstly to the philosophical roots of Deleuze's cinetheory, to Bergson and to Deleuze's reading of Bergson. To do this entails examining the theory of the image in *Matter and Memory* and also Bergson's attack on cinema in *Creative Evolution*, the one that Deleuze so skillfully turns to his own purpose so that he can proclaim the peculiar truth that, despite everything, 'cinema is Bergsonian'.[69]

Is cinema Bergsonian?

The unbiased answer to the question of Bergsonian cinema must be equivocal, at least initially. Certainly, Deleuze is not alone in his high estimation of Bergson's value for film theory, with Dominique Chateau writing recently on Bergson being one of the first philosophers to adopt cinema as a model for philosophy.[70] This may again seem improbable given Bergson's famed antipathy to 'the cinematographic mechanism'. But Bergson's cinephobia is more analogous to Nietzsche's misogyny than to an elitist dismissal of a toy for mass entertainment, for it is philosophically principled: 'When I first saw the cinematograph I realized it could offer something new to philosophy. Indeed we could almost say that cinema is a model of consciousness itself. Going to the cinema turns out to be a philosophical experience'. So it is unfair to think that cinema is a bête noire for Bergson, for it actually models the activity of mind, and thereby depicts a fundamental part of reality:

> As a witness to its beginnings, I realised [cinema] could suggest new things to a philosopher. It might be able to assist in the synthesis of memory, or even of the thinking process. If the circumference [of a circle] is composed of a series of points, memory is, like the cinema, composed of a series of images. Immobile, it is in a neutral state; in movement, it is life itself.[71]

Perception, intellect and language are said to proceed like cinema, for the '*mechanism of our ordinary knowledge is of a cinematographical kind*'. Here is where the real irony lies, for Bergson has used film to model the ordinary mind even though he is interested in transcending the ordinary in inhuman forms of consciousness. In other words, cinema is important as the model of how we normally *misunderstand* reality, how we see it as quantitatively changing, when in fact it is qualitatively mobile. Cinema recomposes movement from immobile celluloid frames, and this con-fusion of stasis with and for process is metaphysically interesting, even as it is metaphysically confused.

> This is what the cinematograph does. With photographs ... it reconstitutes the mobility ... It is true that if we had to do with photographs alone,

> however much we might look at them, we should never see them animated: with immobility set beside immobility, even endlessly, we could never make movement. In order that the pictures may be animated, there must be movement somewhere. *The movement does indeed exist here; it is in the apparatus.*[72]

Note how Bergson insists on looking at the apparatus *here*, at cinema's origins in photography and optical projection. He does not look at the *projected* film images, as Deleuze does, because he is interested in a different phase of the film process. By contrast, Deleuze takes a stand elsewhere at the phenomenal end of the process (where the projected images appear to the viewer), albeit with the intention of making those images real (by turning to Bergson's ontology of the image in *Matter and Memory*) – the universe itself becoming a 'metacinema'.[73] Paul Douglass is right, then, to declare that, while Deleuze may be justified in identifying Bergson as 'a philosopher of the cinema', *we* must nonetheless retain 'Bergson's distrust of the camera, despite what Deleuze has said'. It remains our task, therefore, to explain in detail how Deleuze uses and misuses Bergson's positive conception of time and the image, without which, Ronald Bogue warns us, 'much of *Cinema 1* and *Cinema 2* is obscure'.[74]

There are three parts to Deleuze's reading of Bergson, each of which is contentious. The first move is to ensure that Bergson's critique of cinema is neutralized. The cinematic illusion, for Bergson, exposes the *normal* perception of change for what it is: apparent movement composed from immobile, spatialized sections. Hence, cinema captures the metaphysical essence of perception as *suppression* – what suppresses movement *here* in favour of seeing apparent movement *elsewhere*. The actual movement of the apparatus is suppressed in favour of the virtual movement of the image. But, according to Deleuze, this artful reproduction of perception by cinema is also its 'correction'. For while the cinematic apparatus does involve static frames being given their mobility by proxy of another's, what it *gives us* via the mediating screen is still real movement, *immediately* self-moving images!

What is given is movement: the very movement that exists 'above' perception in the realm of pure images in *Matter and Memory*. Consequently, while the frame does give us a section, it is a section which is mobile, not an immobile section plus abstract movement. Furthermore, cinema eventually conquered its own limitations through the development of montage, and montage is crucial to cinema as its temporalizing force. But note the sleight of hand here where Deleuze shifts the discussion from the *celluloid frame as part of the cinematic apparatus* (Bergson's sense) to the *camera's framing as the seen cut in the viewed image* (Deleuze's). As Douglass notes in bemusement, 'Deleuze has done something wonderfully perverse here, as he admits. Bergson never was ambiguous about "cuttings". For him, these always referred to film's individual frames, never to an editor's "cuts" (or montage)'.[75]

The reason underlying Deleuze's need to shift attention away from the apparatus to the film image is because he wants to show cinema transcending its representationalist limitations through its imagery rather than through its physical technology. The fundamental time-image goes 'beyond movement', and therewith emulates post-Kantian philosophy's escape from Aristotle, when time was liberated in the direct 'time-image'. Movement now follows from time rather than vice versa. The physical apparatus is all too mortal, too organized and too bodily: only through a new type of image can time avoid spatialization and measurement. But there is a second slippage in Deleuze's reading here. Deleuze neglects to tell us that it is the subordination of time to the *measure of* movement (Aristotle's definition of time) that is the major philosophical error in Bergson's eyes.[76] Indeed, for Bergson, far from liberating time, Kant only *inverted* the old binary opposition of time and space by making *measured* (spatially quantified) movement subordinate to the *measure of* (spatially quantified) time.[77] Bergson's thesis is not about the movement–time binary in fact (which he wouldn't recognize at all), but one concerning measure and immeasure, or quantity and quality. Kant simply internalized space and called it time. Bergson instead wants time to be understood as *qualitative movement, that is, to have its qualitative actuality restored.* Movement is not a mere 'actual' to time's 'virtual' – it *is* the time of the living world. Movement *is* Time. So Deleuze is incorrect to say that 'movement is a translation in space' for Bergson; rather Bergson argues that *the* illusion is that movement is translation in space when, in fact, it is transformation in itself (qualitative change), that is, movement is the same as real time.[78]

The final abuse of Bergson concerns the positive theory of the image in *Matter and Memory*, at least as regards Deleuze's demotion of the apparatus in favour of the image. In the Bergsonian image, Deleuze tells us, the 'identity of the image and movement stems from the identity of matter and light. The image is movement, just as matter is light'. Further, Dziga Vertov's work in the Soviet school is said to realize 'the materialist programme of the first chapter of *Matter and Memory* through the cinema, the in-itself of the image'. Or finally, 'the movement-image is matter itself, as Bergson showed'. On the contrary, however, Bergson nowhere showed that the image was material, in fact it is absolutely clear in the first chapter of *Matter and Memory* that an ontology of the image is offered in place of both materialism or idealism. The image is a between: *neither idea nor matter*, neither representation nor thing. As Bogue acknowledges, 'Bergson nowhere explicitly equates matter and light'.[79] This final infidelity allows Deleuze to turn to *Matter and Memory* and identify its images as material parts of the real world.[80] It is a sleight of hand that shifts the reader's attention from actual celluloid, projection rates and their effects on perception, to directorial cuts, viewed images and their effects on brain.[81]

It is sobering to realize that Bergson once admitted to regretting his choice of the term 'image' as an attempted, neutral starting point in *Matter and Memory*. Far from thereby avoiding the arguments between materialists and idealists, the representational connotations of 'image' laid him open to the charge of begging the question in favour of idealism. Of course, by 'image' we are meant to understand a percept without a perceiver (and hence not a kind of Berkeleyean 'idea'). But even admitting the percept as a necessary methodological starting point can appear to load the dice against materialism. Yet, this very same bias, purporting to be simultaneously neutral, offers Deleuze a powerful categorial term, one that belongs to cinema while also pertaining to a metaphysical reality. As Deleuze puts it, 'there's no difference at all between *images, things,* and *motion*'.[82] And it is this lack of difference in the matter of motion that is essential.[83]

Movement-image and time-image: *when* is a cut irrational?

Having gone over Deleuze's remake of Bergson's thought, we are now in a better position to examine the crucial binary opposition that it sets up between the movement-image and the time-image: in particular, its locus in the cut, rational on the one side, irrational on the other. Firstly, it is notable that the irrational cut has a long history, according to Deleuze, having 'always been there' like a

> phantom which has always haunted the cinema, but it took modern cinema to give a body to this phantom. This image is virtual, in opposition to the actuality of the movement-image.[84]

With its ascendency in post-war cinematic modernism, however, the cut appears for itself 'in its own right, as the black screen, the white screen and their derivatives and combinations', and no longer merely to link or mark beginnings or endings.[85]

There is some amount of debate amongst Deleuze's commentators as to the historical legitimacy of the time- and movement-image periodization, and, in part, this stems from Deleuze's own equivocation in places.[86] Clearly, the two *Cinema* books are historically oriented, beginning with 'primitive' cinema and ending with contemporary works from the mid-1980s. Yet, Deleuze can at times talk of using only 'a rough periodization', foiling any simple developmental account (with harbingers of the time-image also to be found in the works of Welles, Dreyer, Renoir and Ozu).[87] Moreover, Deleuze is careful to state that no film is ever made up of just one kind of image: rather, there are always mixtures of the two, albeit with 'one type of image which is dominant'.[88] Thus, if false continuity was prefigured in classical cinema, it was as an exception to the rule, a 'mere anomaly of movement'. And yet, wasn't the emergence of montage in the movement-image already the release of a new, *aberrant*, connection between images, albeit in a putatively indirect 'image *of* time'? Why isn't this aberrance not also a direct presentation in virtue of its own irrationality?

Nonetheless, irrespective of ambiguities over the purity or specificity of each image's historical locale, where Deleuze is always consistent is with regards to their qualitative distinction: these are two different kinds of image, 'fundamentally distinct', indirect and direct presentations of time, with 'irreducible differences'. Admittedly, he also adds that this distinction is not hierarchical, the time-image not being 'something more beautiful, more profound, or more true' but simply 'something different'. However, Deleuze doesn't practice what he preaches, on this score at least, for too often it is also said that the time-image is closest to 'the soul of cinema', a necessary step 'beyond movement', less 'simplistic' and 'much more subtle and differentiated' in its cinematography, a 'great' achievement in fact.[89] Indeed, there is a teleology towards the time-image that is unavoidable given the evolutionist nature of Deleuze's story. This is something that David Bordwell takes him to task over, seeing in it a naivety typical of certain philosophical appoaches to film. Deleuze's idea of the two types of image in cinema is also lazy, because it

> echoes Burch, Ropars, and the *Cahiers* writers, who claimed that the classical cinema was succeeded by a modern one that manipulated time in such ways. Deleuze's unquestioning reliance upon our research tradition is further revealed in his belief that a cinematic essence unfolds across history...
>
> This philosopher's foray into film theory illustrates how uncritical adherence to historiographic tradition can disable contemporary work.[90]

Given Bordwell's own penchant for dualism, this might seem a bit unfair, to say the least. In any case, the real problem for Deleuze's story as we see it, however, is the relativity (or relationality) of the time and movement *function* in the film image. Deleuze's essential dualism of the two, born from his non-Bergsonian disassociation of time from movement, can be easily relativized, only less by history than through its own functional essentialism. We are told that with the time-image, for instance, 'the sensory-motor action or situation has been replaced by the stroll, the voyage, and the continual return journey'. Action has been replaced with seen-action, the act with the pose, the quick, rational cut with the long take and fade to black (irrational cut).[91] And yet, as already discussed with respect to Bordwell's *own* dualism of classical and art cinema, the irrational cut has been incorporated into Hollywood's film genres with perfect ease (in *E.T.* or *28 Days Later*, for example), and elliptical editing has been used for wholly narrative purposes, expressing characters' story-world emotions (*Festen*) with clear narrative force. Think of the numerous ways that a film like *Shrek* (2001) subverts the movement-image through distanciation and reflexivity, and not only in terms of narrative (upending the classic fairytale), but also through its manipulation of sound and vision (intertextuality, revealing the device, hyper-realism). And as regards the direct exploration of time or memory, aren't supposedly movement-image films like *Labyrinth* (1986), *Total Recall* or *Titanic* (1997) doing exactly this as well, merging past and present, both in narrative and audio-vision?[92] Even further, weren't the first cuts already aberrant movements, the first close-ups of the face not being an image of wonder or fear (affection-images), but shocking images of a giant dismembered head (that audiences later *learnt* to reconnect to the body as a face)? Finally (and to go back to the most primitive cinema), the very first camera shots were arguably the most deviant too, the shock of a train looming towards one in two huge dimensions, being an unnatural movement par excellence.

Conversely, the action-image genre can *already* be seen in possession of many of the features of the time-image. John Ford's *The Searchers*, for example, is extremely ambivalent about action: what Deleuze would read as an epic, cosmic cycle of action in the large form (ASA') can also be seen as a form of aimless repetition, aberrant and perverted movement (and not simply on account of the psychoanalytic interchangeability of Ethan and Scar).[93] Both in the famous last scene (at the doorway) and throughout *The Searchers*, the hero Ethan is a spectator of actions that are not of his own making, but that of the story-world as such (dances and homecomings). There is a stillness to Wayne's body-movements that are not at all the well-organized, sensory-motor linkages that Deleuze purports them to be.[94] Indeed, Deleuze's more general comments on The Actors' Studio's Method only essentialize as sensory-motor what are now regarded as highly stylized interpretations of the natural and naturalistic performance (as I will explain further in Chapter 8).

All concepts of 'action', in other words, can be relativized (through culture, psychology, technology): 'action films' themselves can appear to some as uneventful, with nothing happening except for more explosions, more gun-fights and more car chases in acts of pure repetition. 'Art-house' films that seem wholly uneventful for some, can for others have epic tragedy discernible in the very smallness of their events (as in *Ladri di biciclette* for instance). Qualitative and quantitative change are not intrinsic but relational. And this relationality spills over into questions concerning what events are, how rare they are, whether or not they are heroic (or need to be heroic), and so on (which I will discuss in Chapters 6 and 7). As Jacques Rancière writes: 'movement-image and time-image are by no means two types of images ranged in opposition, but two different points of view on the image'. Even with respect to Deleuze's favourite examples in Robert Bresson's work, it is 'impossible', Rancière says, to isolate any time-images with properties that would distinguish them from movement-images: 'the very same examples ... can be used to illustrate the constitution of the any-space-whatevers of the affection-image [and so the movement-image] and the constitution of the pure optical and sound situations of the time-image'.[95]

Given that the time-image (so-called false continuity) has now itself become both a cliché of bad art films *and* been normalized within neoclassical cinema, we might even speculate on the possibility of a renewed form of movement-image becoming the latest cinematic avante garde, a kind of innovative, but still pre-Kantian, cinema.[96] Yet, such speculation pertains as much to the artwork as it does to its potential audience and the viewing context: with *what* it expects, *when, where* and *how* the film is shown, and so on. If, as Deleuze writes, the art of the work is to 'break through the cliché, to get out of the cliché', then we must open up the location of this eruption beyond the 'artwork', so-called.[97] When it was innovative, the movement-image was artful. Now, for most Western viewers, it is less so. Until a time comes, of course, when, due to new ways of seeing (at home, on a PC, with interrupted viewing, in new social contexts, and so on), it finds a way to be artful again, by finding a time and a place where it is innovative again. Thus, too, only when innovative is the time-image artful, because it also, with repetition, becomes mundane.

If my claim is correct, then the time-image is actually a place-holder for *whatever transgresses*, and in itself it has no cinematographical essence (unless we employ a very broad notion of the film process). Indeed, the timeliness of the time-image is only its novelty. But, then, likewise, the movement-image has no essence either, and it too *can be* connected to time no less than the time-image, that is, when it is innovative. And this innovation is relational.[98] While the time-image is (supposedly) the refraction of the movement-image, it too can be refracted, moved within a meta-time-image, though one that must itself be understood as another kind of movement, without any immobile essence. Certain styles of film – popular Indian cinema, for instance – may well instantiate just such a double refraction *currently, for us*, and therewith prove their resistence to categorization within any fixed binary system.[99]

It is not a matter, then, of action/movement being absent or present (and, therewith, the time-image erupting or not) in the artwork or the artist, but different kinds of actions/movements that are different on account of *their extra-artistic relations with the art* (which is not reducible only to its audience). Nor is it that we should believe in artists more than art (as Marcel Duchamp claimed), or in the 'total social fact' more than either of these, but in the varying combinations of all three. Indeed, it will be argued in subsequent chapters that many of the properties of film that Deleuze rejects – story, representation, action, movement, actuality – can be shown to be more complex and multiple than he gives them credit to be, on account of their relationality with audience, culture and technology.

What it is that makes a film 'new' or 'artful' cannot be a content of the artwork alone, then, whether or not by proxy of the film-maker's intention. Indeed, what better way is there to de-authorize the director's intention than to say that a bad, cliché-ridden and unoriginal film can, to a certain set of eyes, be a work of art nonetheless? But what work is it doing when we say this? Of course, these are questions in aesthetics that concern more than just cinema. What is of interest is not only when or where time- or movement-images are to be found, but also what they do there. My purpose in later chapters, then, will not be to show that there *were* pre-war time-images, but to expose the movement-*function* of the time-image when it happens.

Films and their makers: from the automatic art to the autonomy of art

In his emphasis on art cinema as a unique medium, his historical essentialism regarding the types of cinema-image prevalent at any one time, and his evolutionist approach that culminates in images that either exhaust what cinema was hitherto capable of, or take as their theme (visually and audibly) the conditions of possibility for the film medium, Deleuze betrays his modernist credentials throughout. Certainly, there is no doubting the fact that he is modernist as regards the autonomy of art: 'a work of art is a new syntax, one that is much more important than vocabulary and that excavates a foreign language in language'. The 'work of art' has a 'necessity of its own'. The distinction between true, creative art and the commercial artwork (so-called) must be maintained. Indeed, any attempt at deconstructing it only plays into the hands of capitalism and its requirement for rapid turnover (as opposed to art's essential need for different, lengthier durations).[100]

Clearly, Deleuze has followed the position of the *Cahiers* writers who politicized their view of Hollywood following the events of May 1968 in France. While not disagreeing with the earlier *Cahiers* position that it was *once* possible for artists to survive within the Hollywood system (Hitchcock, Ray, Ford and all the other canonical authors that Deleuze hails), Deleuze argues that was no longer the case after 1968. Hollywood pleasures now entail a state of false consciousness, and the cinematic apparatus has become an apparatus of ideological repression.[101] That is why Deleuze's *Cinema* books do not refer to any popular films made after 1968, and why he states plainly that there can be no commercial art. Art cinema is sovereign, unique (amongst other films) in its power to make us think. And this power invested in the artwork is put there by its author, the director. In commercial film, by contrast, there is mediocrity:

> What becomes of Hitchcock's suspense, Eisenstein's shock and Gance's sublimity when they are taken up by mediocre authors? When the

> violence is no longer that of the image and its vibrations but that of the represented, we move into blood-red arbitrariness. When grandeur is no longer that of the composition, but a pure and simple inflation of the represented, there is no cerebral stimulation or birth of thought... Cinema is dying, then, from its quantitative mediocrity.[102]

This power of the artist-director persists, irrespective of cinema being a collaborative artform heavily reliant on technology and industrial commerce. For, in fact, it is 'cinema's great *auteurs*... [who] call forth new equipment, new instruments. These instruments produce nothing in the hands of second-rate *auteurs*, providing only a substitute for ideas. It's the ideas of great *auteurs*, rather, that call them forth'.[103]

A definite canon exists for Deleuze, then: there are 'masterpieces' that cannot be put into a 'hierarchy' (for such 'cinema is always as perfect as it can be') and there are the masters who made them (especially those who have also written eloquently about their art, such as Eisenstein, Godard, Resnais and Bresson). Deleuze will at times talk of some others in the film-making process, especially actors and musicians, but nearly always by reference to their director (Brando to Mankiewicz, Hepburn to Hawks, Falconetti to Dreyer, Chaney to Browning, and so on; or Zinneman and Tiomkin, Carné and Jaubert, Fellini and Rota, Resnais and Henze, Resnais and Eisler). When he writes about actors it is in terms of how they were filmed by the director, rather than in terms of their own star aura, performance or casting. It is as if the actor's image always varies with reference to one central image, that of the director. And the same is true of all the other images in the film process – cultural, commercial, technological: they all owe their art (if they have any) to the director (the first shocks of sound or CinemaScope, for instance, must have been mere trickery – a passing sensationalism – until director-artists transmuted them into genuine media for art, some time *after* they first appeared). What might count as a non-directorial source that would conflict with the mastery of the director is never mentioned: for example, Greg Toland's brilliant work with Welles on *Citizen Kane*, or Robert Wise's less fortunate but still hugely significant re-editing of Welles's *The Magnificent Ambersons* (1942). Nor does Deleuze mention the possibility that a *collective* subject might be capable of creating artistic films (that the artist in Hollywood's 'golden era' of the 1930s and 1940s might have been the *studio itself*, MGM or Warner, for instance), which is peculiar given Deleuze's usual antipathy towards the molar subject.[104] Such possibilities cannot be entertained seriously, for that would widen the definition of the artist and so also the artwork too greatly. Film itself might be lost in the process.

The few other cultural mediators that Deleuze does employ are pitched at a level that is both extremely broad and very abstract. On the one hand, the importance of the aftermath of the Second World War in Europe, the decline of the American Dream, consciousness of ethnic minorities, the rise of new media culture, and new modes in literature are cited as influences on the emergence of the time-image. But this cultural input is set so wide that no actual particular causes are offered. Indeed, most of the specific influence of national identities on film-making are recounted in *Cinema 1* in the pre-war role of American empiricism, Soviet dialecticism, French quantitative psychologism and German intensive spiritualism. The time-image is much less culturally specific. On the other hand, what social role the time-image itself plays is highly abstract, concerning either the (future) fabulation of minorities in a new cinema of ethnic storytelling, or the (current) cretinization of film-going audiences under the weight of Hollywood commercialism. Other cultural references are sparing at best, and even offensive at worst. There is some discussion of Jean-Luc Godard's use of genres, subgenres and reflexive genres, but still with reference to their *directorial* use (which really concerns tone rather than genre understood culturally); there is a reference to the economics of film-making, though only by way of how its cinematic depiction shows the reflexivity of the crystal-image; and there is an embarrassing remark regarding women actors ('all non-made-up faces look like Falconetti, all made up ones like Garbo').[105]

Deleuze's selective approach is obvious, then, and it leaves behind glaring gaps in the story of film-making in the West. Where, for instance, do the time-image films of Jacques Tati or Jean Cocteau fit into the post-war '*cinéma de papa*' that pre-dated the emergence of the New Wave in the late 1950s?[106] Were they the exceptions to the rule? If so, then we are left with the problem that the French New Wave was *itself* also the exception and remains the exception to the French rule. Even in their heyday, their films were always in a minority for the film-going public in France throughout the 1960s. If the vindication comes back that film art, 'the soul of cinema', must always remain rare and uncommercial, then why can't this same tenet apply to the rarity of Tati or Cocteau (and so back-date the arrival of the time-image)? Conversely, where do Ingmar Bergman and Rainer Werner Fassbinder fit within the time-image epoch, given their strong adherence both to temporal experimentation *and* the primacy of classical narrative?[107] But again, I am not offering a counter-history concerning time- and movement-images, but only some examples of the unavoidable omissions in any Grand Theory such as Deleuze's.[108]

One way of grounding his partiality, of course, would be by recourse to cognitive science (as Bordwell does for his). Deleuze may be non-reductive and non-representationalist in his references to the brain – a cerebrist of the brain–screen interface rather than an informationalist of mind representing 'reality' – yet it nonetheless offers him a possible anchor point. This possibility also has its problems, however. While Deleuze extends out both brain and cinema-screen to touch each other, he still objectifies them in a *static* relation. Rather than each brain being allowed the film it needs to rewire it (*whatever* that film may be), Deleuze argues that only certain kinds of film can rewire *the* brain. But then, taking such a naturalistic line leaves Deleuze bereft of any source of norms (and so any selectivity regarding films) *unless* he also signs up to some kind of representationalism like Bordwell's (*this* rewiring is better *because* it matches 'reality').[109] But we know that Deleuze is a process philosopher who can't accept such notions of an essential reality, and this is what leaves his own cinematic elitism seeming so arbitrary. By the lights of his own theory, there should be a non-hierarchical set of numerous, different brain–screen interfaces because the brain's reception is only a part of *any* film's *whole* process (most of which is filtered out by any one brain). No less than any other philosopher, however, Deleuze's theory remains selective (despite his awareness of how theory should never simply be applied, as we heard at the outset of this chapter). In his case, Deleuze sees only the reflexive 'seeing' of post-war cinema – the signs and images of vision, sound and acting – and such attentiveness keeps him too busy to see the story, genre, production design, acting, audience reception, and all the other dimensions of the whole film process. Indeed, how can anyone avoid perceiving only some aspects, when perceiving itself (as Bergson showed) is *only ever* seeing aspects?

Amongst the Deleuzians: a thousand tiny examples

Of course, the Deleuzian film theorist in need of a concept of viewer reception with at least some cultural specificity might always turn to his collaborative works like *A Thousand Plateaus* or *Kafka: Toward a Minor Literature*. Deleuze and Guattari's discussion of bodies, affects and minor audiences is much more socially particular than anything found in the *Cinema* books, given the latter's greater focus on the author–artwork dyad. Perhaps this explains, in part, why there are (at least) two quite different kinds of post-Deleuzian film theory, depending on which Deleuzian texts are sourced by the theorist. One would imagine that the two cinema books would be central for every Deleuzian cineaste, and yet they are not. While David Rodowick, Ronald Bogue and Laura Marks, for instance, do utilize the semiotics found in them, Barbara Kennedy and Steven Shaviro focus much more on the vitalist metaphysics arising from the two volumes of *Capitalism and Schizophrenia*. So divergences in content and method are bound to be seen, not only as regards artwork and author, versus audience and reception, but also with respect to images, signs and memory, versus vital forces, affects and becoming. Where one approach emphasizes the Proustian experience of the presence of the past, the other focuses on a Heraclitean flux of changing images and Nietzschean forces; where one prioritizes commemorative Being, the other seeks out unreflective Action; where one is 'Virtualist' (to coin a phrase), the other is 'Actualist'.

I believe that it is a significant fact that each post-Deleuzian theorist must select *which* Deleuze to follow when applying his theories to films he did not examine in his own work. This selection is both an after-effect of Deleuze's own choices of film and theory (from philosophy) and independent of it. It is independent because it is unavoidable: no other theoretical reference point could have evaded the reduction of film to certain conceptual presuppositions, either. I have argued that Deleuze's film-philosophy is, like every other theory of its type, a kind of remake, using films as stand-ins for philosophers and philosophical concepts, as the 'new means of philosophical expression' that *Difference and Repetition* called for as early as 1968.[110] But our argument here is not forwarded as a prescription, the exposure of a mistake: in itself, it is only one more redescription, another remake.

One might add that the different kinds of Deleuzian film theorists also remake Deleuze in their own images. Indeed, this too is difficult to avoid. There does appear to be a need not only to choose but also to reinvent one's own 'Deleuzian film-philosophy'. And with good reason. Stepping back a moment, it is remarkable how Deleuze exemplifies each of his various categories with not merely one or two examples, but myriad ones. Most readers of the *Cinema* books are impressed by the knowledge of film that he displays throughout. He has undoubtedly seen an awful lot of films.[111] Indeed, this *awful* lot of films partakes in a logic of illustration unique to Deleuze. Where other philosophers will select one or two examples of films or film scenes to substantiate their argument as a whole or one of its components, Deleuze's method is much more baroque. On the one hand, his argument itself is built from the bottom up through a taxonomy of many parts, the whole of which (that cinema is riven between the movement-image and the time-image) is proven on account of the aggregation of those parts (the time-image exists, for instance, because its components, the opsign, sonsign, crystal-image, and so on, exist). On the other hand, each part has numerous examples provided as evidence for it. And yet not one of these examples amounts to more than a few sentences. Deleuze will cite a phenomenon, like American 'organic' editing, and then illustrate it with snatches from D. W. Griffiths's work, or Soviet 'dialectical' montage with numerous bits of Eisenstein.[112] And that's it. As Rancière puts it, 'an ontology of the cinema [is] argued for with bits and pieces gleaned from the entire *corpus* of the cinematographic art'.[113] Whereas Deleuze's engagements with literature or painting give rise to whole essays dedicated to one novel (Michel Tournier's *Vendredi*), and whole books to one artist (Kafka or Bacon), his film books rarely offer more than half a page to any one film. There are no sustained readings, but simply lists of film scenes or auteurs to correspond with his list of film images and signs. And yet, by sheer dint of the number of films cited, the argument is almost won through attrition. Ascent by a thousand cuts. It is *this* that leaves the commentator in a difficult postion: either he or she can offer the same list as Deleuze does, often with the qualification that Deleuze doesn't adequately explain *why* there is a correspondence between *this* film and *that* image rather than some other pairing (but then why not simply read Deleuze himself rather than a mere commentary); *or* he or she can devise other more detailed examples that attempt to make a more convincing case (as I will myself in Chapter 6), though with the added danger of introducing non-Deleuzian or extraneous ideas when going into such extra depth. And here is where the need to reinvent and remake arises.

Moreover, this reinvention of Deleuze by the Deleuzians is only a part of Deleuze's own reinvention of cinema through his philosophy. *Cinema 1* and *2* are a remake of film as such. A remake is a part of what it does, it is an instantiation or exemplification rather than a representation (that is mistaken or not mistaken) – 'a take' on the reality of film that exemplifies only itself and instantiates only the Real of film (not film itself, but its resistance to theory). What Deleuze writes about *Citizen Kane, L'Année dernière à Marienbad,* and so on, is neither totally right nor totally wrong, for on one level these films clearly are *about* the past, *about* the 'virtual' persistence of the past. And the level where this is true is *at the Deleuzian level,* where it takes what it does from film in its 'take' and uptake. What Deleuze *actually exemplifies* here is nothing other (nothing transcendent/al) than the Deleuzian theory's own mixture or refraction with (or resistance from) the film-Real. The examples do not uncover the pre-existing virtual from film but actually produce something new with film (while virtualizing it). And perhaps Deleuze already knew this when he wrote: 'I don't think cinema can be reduced to the model of an open totality. That was one model, but there are and always will be as many models as cinema manages to invent'.[114] In what follows we will investigate a selection of some of the other possible models that cinema promises to invent.

5
Cavell, Badiou and Other Ontologists

> What broke my natural relation to movies? What was that relation, that its loss seemed to demand repairing, or commemorating, by taking thought?[1]

Cavell and the ontology of ordinary film

Stanley Cavell's *The World Viewed* is for many a founding text in film-philosophy. Despite initially receiving a hostile reception within both film studies (where it was thought obscure and impressionistic) and philosophy (where it was thought vulgar and impressionistic), despite it being, as Cavell's own friends judged, 'a difficult book, sometimes incomprehensible book', it has nonetheless attained a retrospective value as a truly pioneering work.[2] Its attempt to provide a foundation for the study of film by means of an ontology of the medium, though neither unprecedented nor untroubled, has generated an approach to film matched only by Deleuze in its philosophical breadth and specificity. Compared to Deleuze, Cavell's methodology is Heideggerian, Wittgensteinian and Freudian. Yet, regardless of their theoretical differences, both purport to show how important film is for philosophy, and, given that Cavell made his overtures more than a decade earlier than Deleuze, he could be said to have paved the way for every 'philosophical' approach (all the time remembering, however, than film studies itself had been mining philosophical ideas for decades beforehand).

Cavell singles out cinema, in part, for theoretical reasons concerning modernism (alone of the arts, he argues, it has remained both popular with audiences and true to its modernist origins), but also for personal reasons (his own relationship with film having changed in the late 1960s from a 'natural' one of audience member to a theoretical one of enquiring philosopher). For Cavell himself, though, the personal cannot be divorced from the philosophical.[3] Strewn across the pages of *The World Viewed* are intimate accounts of highly popular films, directors and actors, interwoven with references to

Descartes, Kant, Hegel, Marx, Nietzsche, Rousseau and Machiavelli.[4] And yet such belles-lettres are not to be taken as condescending applications of esoteric philosophy to mundane film, but allusions to the philosophical significance of the *very ordinariness of film*. At one level, this adds Cavell to the number of later twentieth-century American philosophers working in the neo-Pragmatist tradition, like Richard Rorty, who have also attempted a transformation of analytic philosophy 'from within', replacing its technical formalism with subtle descriptions of everyday practices, especially linguistic ones.[5]

Ironically, Cavell (like Rorty) was aided greatly in this enterprise by two Europeans, Wittgenstein and Heidegger, the two thinkers who, as Cavell puts it in his later text, *Contesting Tears*, 'opened for me what philosophy in our age may look like, such as it interests me most'.[6] Reading *Being and Time*, for a start, led Cavell to trust in the resources of ordinary language for bearing more than simply personal prejudice. It is instead a crucial opening onto reality. The Heideggerian idea of *Weltanschauung* or world-view, as we will see, is another significant, if unobtrusive, presence behind Cavell's notion of film as a viewed world.

It is Wittgenstein, however, who is the fundamental influence on Cavell, and not only for his take on film. Published just two years after 1969's *Must We Mean What We Say?* (Cavell's first major work), the readings of *The World Viewed* are his own Wittgensteinian attempt to direct any philosophy of film away from metaphysical abstractions and towards an analysis of our everyday experience of going to the 'movies' (to use Cavell's highly motivated preference for its colloquial name).[7] In other words, his philosophy of film *is* an instance of his philosophy of anti-philosophy (or at least of anti-metaphysics). It is an ontology of the filmed ordinariness of the world or, better, a study of the ontology of the world revealed by the ordinariness of film viewing. Film (-going) becomes philosophy. Indeed, beyond even the philosophical importance of film, we can recall that this Wittgensteinian approach is said to show how 'films can philosophize' for themselves, given that Cavell likens the experience of watching a film to a therapeutic model of (anti-metaphysical) philosophy.[8] Of course, in his *Tractatus*, Wittgenstein clearly divided what can be 'shown' from what can be 'said', such that saying anything about aesthetics can only lead to nonsense: art should be left to silence. His later work in the *Philosophical Investigations*, however, proved less rigid when distinguishing different forms of expression, and it is from this other Wittgenstein that Cavell takes his cue. In what follows, then, we will see whether Cavell's attempt to show film philosophizing avoids any nonsense of its own.

The philosophical ordinary

Writing in 1996 about his seminal work on scepticism and morality, *The Claim of Reason*, Cavell makes an important admission concerning what he meant there by the 'ordinary':

> An essential drive of my book *The Claim of Reason* (1979) is to show ... [that] Wittgenstein's teaching is on the contrary that skepticism is (not exactly true, but not exactly false either; it is the name of) a standing threat to, or temptation of, the human mind – that our ordinary language and its representation of the world *can* be philosophically repudiated and that it is essential to our inheritance and mutual possession of language, as well as to what inspires philosophy, that this should be so. But *The Claim of Reason*, for all its length, does not say, any more than Austin and Wittgenstein do very much to say, what the ordinary is, why natural language is ordinary, beyond saying that ordinary or everyday language is exactly not a special philosophical language and that any special philosophical language is answerable to the ordinary, and beyond suggesting that the ordinary is precisely what it is that skepticism attacks – as if the ordinary is best to be discovered, or say that in philosophy it is only discovered, in its loss.[9]

Cavell has what seems at first glance to be a very philosophical view of the ordinary as some kind of undefined place-holder for whatever opposes the excesses of theory. Later on in his work, however, he says that his work on what the Romantics (like Wordsworth) meant by the 'rustic and common' and what Emerson and Thoreau meant by 'the today, the common, the low, the near', is a close approximation to the philosophical concept of the ordinary forwarded by Wittgenstein and Austin. Yet, we should not understand this to mean that one theory of the ordinary has finally been defined in terms of another, but rather that there is something in the works of the Romantics and the Transcendentalists (in whose number we can safely put Cavell as well) that suggests and exemplifies the ordinary in the performance of their works. And this is true also of Cavell's own writing in film theory, where, for example, the discussions of marriage and remarriage in *Pursuits of Happiness* flesh out the meaning of the ordinary even more in terms of 'the domestic', the seemingly trivial film comedies it studies (*Philadelphia Story* (1940), *It Happened One Night* (1934), amongst five others) being in actuality subtle lessons on the sharing of life and love between men and women.

What do I mean by the performance of the ordinary in 'Cavell's own work'? In the first instance, it is his articulation of the ordinary in particular studies, those on the film comedies of remarriage in the studio era of Hollywood (*Pursuits of Happiness*), or the 'women's pictures' of the same period (*Contesting Tears*). But it is equally in what he says about ordinary films in *The World Viewed*, and also how he says it. In a typically understated manner, it is in this text that Cavell makes the startling claim that one can only like and admire the highest or most artistic instances of film if one also likes its typical instances (indeed, knowledge of either is codependent). On the one hand, this gesture against elitism no doubt also safeguards Cavell against both the charge of unreflective popularism (a predictable reaction from many in the philosophical community at the time) and that of hypocrisy (should he suddenly reject the most popular instances of an art that he was commending for being popular). On the other, the problem of establishing how film can be important and artful is more pressing, as Cavell puts it, if one cares about film per se, and not just when 'the only films you care about are carefully chosen masterpieces'. It is quite apt for Cavell, then, that the very first films were the popular *actualités* that showed ordinary people doing ordinary things – using a watering hose, leaving work, travelling by horse-drawn carriage – all transposed onto the magical screen, making ordinary lives extraordinary and making the world, the viewed world, magical too. Hence, Cavell has little time for a canon – the selection of which will often rest on spurious grounds – nor with the auteur theory that often accompanies a theoretical investment in canonical works (great art seemingly needing a great artist): 'a standing discovery of the *auteur* theory was of the need for a canon of movies to which any remarks about "the movie" should hold themselves answerable. Without this, the natural circle of theory and evidence will not inscribe the knowledge we want'.[10] Cavell has discovered the circle of theory and example that also motivates our study; though, as we will see, it is a circle he only partially evades himself with recourse to a notion of the 'ordinary'.

Against such auteurism, Cavell will place more emphasis (much more than Deleuze) on genre ('a movie comes from other movies'), on spectatorship, on actors and acting, and on the cultural reception of film technology (colour in particular) in our 'natural' relationship with cinema.[11] Such a wide scope of investigation is partially facilitated by Cavell staying true to his Wittgensteinian performance, with a focus on description over explanation, and the avoidance of too much 'theory'. It is with what we ordinarily say about actors, genres or colour that Cavell will engage, not with any theories proffered by advanced studies within the field. As William Rothman and Marian Keane put it: 'in pursuing its philosophical investigation of film, *The World Viewed* embraces Ludwig Wittgenstein's methodological principle that we can find out what kind of object a thing is by investigating expressions which show the kinds of things that can be said about it'. And these expressions are our ordinary expressions. Rothman and Keane continue by adding that, if we are alert to the different ways in which a concept is used – both by others and by ourselves – in its different living incarnations, then we will also be aware of the primacy of what Wittgenstein called 'language games'. Or rather, philosophical work *will consist in* rendering these games visible or 'perspicuous'.[12] Moreover, Cavell will argue that the *natural* relation with film does not involve written reflections on film in the abstract, but specific viewings of films. *Our* task, therefore, is to enquire whether *any* natural relation to film can ever exist outside philosophy, and whether the valorization of the ordinary is not already a highly theoretical move, a symptom of what Simon Critchley calls Cavell's 'romanticization of everyday life'.[13]

This philosophical work, or performance, of the ordinary is not without hazard of course, and it is not surprising that the first reception of Cavell's work did emphasize how impressionistic it appeared to be to those readers. The 'ordinary' is not only theoretical but also a matter of personal impressions. The primary reason for this stems from Cavell's wish to reflect on our ordinary experience of film, and our ordinary experience of film (at least up until the advent of domestic video recording in the 1980s) mostly involves one-off viewings of films in a public, social situation. It does not involve multiple, private viewings, for that mostly pertains to the academic context, a metaphysical viewing of cinema, so to speak. Hence, much of what Cavell has to work with in his reflections are *personal* memoirs of *first* viewings, with all the inaccuracy, fragmentation and condensation that must accompany such a biographical method. *The World Viewed* – a work that comes 'out of the memory of films' – is an attempt to be as faithful as possible to our everyday (and so first) 'responses' to movies, not only despite the ensuant errors, but also because of them. What is vital is the *way* that films are remembered, for Cavell is just as interested in the occasions when memories are inaccurate as when they are accurate, such errors often being highly informative.[14]

Cavell's mnemonic approach opens up issues that we will have to tackle in the second half of this study: issues concerning the identity of artworks (and even objects in general), that involve performance – which for film means projection and spectatorship – as well as issues over the relativity of response as both personal and cultural phenomena.[15] More relevant for now is the fact that even this fidelity to ordinary film-experience is not without philosophical mediation, as Cavell acknowledges. There was a time, Cavell tells us, when he didn't think about movies, but simply went to them for enjoyment alone. But this prereflective moment was eventually lost, he adds, and *The World Viewed* is both a product and an investigation of that loss. Indeed, it is also a commemoration of the loss in writing.

Reflections on the ontology of film

The subtitle of *The World Viewed* is 'Reflections on the Ontology of Film'. It begs the question, then, as to what Cavell's ontology is in itself. An obvious starting place for an answer may well be the complex relation Cavell maintains with the film realism of André Bazin, as most famously set out in the latter's essay 'Ontology of the Photographic Image' in his *What is Cinema?* For Bazin, the essence of cinema is as document, as record of a world, a recording facilitated by the analogical photographic technology that lies at the heart of the cinematic apparatus. Films record a world using the light that comes from that world. Given much that Cavell says in *The World Viewed,* it has seemed reasonable to see Cavell as an advocate of Bazinian realism (as, for instance, Noël Carroll does), given statements such as: 'the *a priori* condition [of movie-making is] that its medium is photographic and its subject reality'. Yet, if this is a realism, it is not one founded simply on the analogical basis of photographic technology. Rather, Cavell has something more conceptual in mind when he invokes the realist ontology of photography, namely that, in essence, 'objects participate in the photographic presence of themselves; they participate in the re-creation of themselves on film; they are essential in the making of their appearances'.[16] What is real is not one, simple reality, nor one world, but the presence of a world, the being of a world.[17]

This participation of objects in their own coming to filmic presence, and our witnessing of it in the cinema, is both fascinating and mysterious for Cavell. On the one hand, film lets us be fascinated with objects, with the elements of a world. We can see them as they seemingly are, for themselves: 'film returns to us and extends our first fascination with objects, with their inner and fixed lives'. On the other, this is a mystery, the mystery of film as permanent recording (but of nothing, for it is not a *reproduction* of the world) *as well as* evanescent performance (yet one that is seemingly repeatable). Cavell is fascinated with this mode of presence to and absence from film – 'I am seeing things, things not there, experiencing them as overwhelmingly present'; and it leads him to ask, 'how can one be present at something that has happened, that is over?'. The photographic quality of film is 'unlike anything else on earth', in that it lies in the absence of what it 'causes to appear to us'. It does not bear a relationship to anything present, yet we are still in the presence of things which are not present.[18]

Despite this photo-ontology of cinema, film does not have to be *used* photographically for Cavell (this is why he actually refuses to take sides between Bazin's realism and Eisenstein's formalism), and film certainly does not have to be photographic to be artful.[19] Yet, film is a technology (analogical or otherwise) that is *of* a world.[20] Movies are not 'recordings' (or 'reproductions'), but, nonetheless, reality has a role to play. This reality is not a separable event recorded on film, however, but *whatever it is that is* 'photographed, projected, screened, exhibited, and viewed' in film technology. Manipulations of the *mise-en-scène,* or of the photographic composition, or even of the camera itself (as seen quintessentially in Vertov's *The Man with a Movie Camera* (1929)), only help to underscore this realism rather than undermine it, Cavell argues, for each of these supposedly anti-realist tropes actually 'serve for reality, from the camera's point of view'. And for Cavell, the term 'camera' stands for everything between the *mise-en-scène* and the screened image, that is, 'the camera, plus its lenses and filters, plus its film, plus the light required to expose its film, plus the physical procedures of preparing the film for projection'. Only that which appears within the projected frame counts or exists for film, and yet the frame only *masks* a whole world, it does not exclude it.[21]

What is significant in all of this is that Cavell has revealed our ordinary ('natural') experience of film to be of theoretical interest (and personal fascination) on account of the mystery of our presence to and absence from it, on account of the ontological enchantment of being and non-being when watching a film and the world it views. The language here is, without too much surprise, strikingly Heideggerian, and we should note that, on the page prior to where Cavell talks of the objects of the world participating in their re-creation on film, he quotes Heidegger (from *What is Called Thinking?*) discussing Plato and the relation of beings to Being as one of 'participation'.[22] One might say that the objects (or beings) of the viewed world are *of* that world, not because they represent it, but because they participate in that World (or Being) – *they make World (or Being) appear.* The 'photographic', in that sense, does not mean representation, but participation. And it is a participation that involves us as witnesses (or viewers) of the world photographed (or viewed).

This is not the only Heideggerian influence on *The World Viewed.* Doubtless, the concept of *Weltanschauung* is in the background to the idea of 'world-view' too, and though Cavell cites Heidegger's 'Age of the World View' in this context, he is careful both to link *and* unlink himself to this reference, lest his readers think that everything he writes can be reduced to it.[23] Heideggerian *Gelassenheit,* or 'letting be', is also evident in the foregoing ideas. Film is said to allow us to view the world 'unseen', not with a sadistic gaze that positions that world, but through a view (of the world) without power, beyond power. Yet, such views are not beyond knowledge as well for, according to Cavell, 'to say that we wish to view the world itself is to say that we are wishing for the condition of viewing as such'.[24] Despite his references to magic and mystery, Cavell is still a philosopher seeking a knowledge of conditions and is not a mystic.

Nevertheless, film's condition of possibility is indeed magical. The idea that art has its origins in religion is a well-worn one, with André Bazin being again the film theorist who most obviously anchors the artfulness of cinema to its supreme ability to fulfil the religious desire of recording the world, of making it survive after its passing. Cavell's own thesis is a secular variation on this theme (with Heideggerian undertones): the origin of film lies in magic, in that which arises '*below* the world'. That magical quality is part and parcel of film's ontological mystery of photographic presence and absence, of course, and Cavell is mindful to point out that most of us have forgotten just how mysterious photographs (and so also the photographic nature of film) are.[25]

Automatism of the medium

Cinema's essental link to photography begs the question, for Cavell, as to the distinction between film and photography, and important parts of *The World Viewed* are dedicated to distinguishing the two art forms, as well as explaining why film is essentially different from theatre and painting. A definition of film arrives only towards the end of the first half of the book; but even then in order to keep theoretical reductionism at bay, the build-up to Cavell's position is one based on an openness to the empirical richness of film. In other words, for film (though also for the other arts), it is vital that we do not apply a pre-given essence to it, for, as he puts it, the 'aesthetic possibilities of a medium are not givens'. We can never tell what will give an art medium 'significance'. That, for example, the narrative form would be the major bearer of cinematic art was not deducible from its artistic, technological or sociological origins. The *'creation of a medium'* – what it is, what it is best at – was achieved by the first significant successes in film-making, but what they would be was wholly unpredictable. No variation or combination of 'angle, distance, duration, composition, and motions between' could be ruled out in advance 'as a sign of significance'.[26]

Though Cavell's view here has a streak of American pragmatism running through it (nothing succeeds like success), and therewith all the circular logic that usually accompanies this, we should note the emphasis Cavell places on 'significance'. No one possibility can be an inevitable success for an art medium, Cavell writes, unless its use by the artist in that work 'gives it significance'. The use of slow motion can be the most tiresome of clichés in film, but its use at the end of Arthur Penn's *Bonnie and Clyde* (1967) has a genuine significance concerning the inevitability of one couple's tragedy, the abolition of wanton freedoms in favour of social securities, and the impotence of the camera to intervene in history.[27]

In Cavell's own estimation, it is the *narrative* significance of film that has historically counted most, but, then again, this was not inevitable. Cinema could have gone elsewhere. All the same, cinema is not a wholly plastic medium either, and its range of artistic possibilities is limited by its physical nature at any one time. And this is true of all art according to Cavell. Any emergent significance will have its possibility latent within the physical medium of the particular art in question. There is a set of 'automatisms' that belong to the physical, automated nature of a medium. Hence, the audio-visual nature of film's moving images have technological possibilities – panning, editing, slow motion or freeze frames, for example – that are not inexhaustible.

As said, these automatisms must be discovered and given significance by the artist. Though Cavell at times likens film to a language with its own syntax and lexicon, and even says that these automatisms are 'the bearers' of the film-maker's intentions 'like the syntactical and lexical elements of a language', we should not think that *the significance* of such automatisms is automated and determined, be it physically *or* logically. There is more to an art than its medium. The possibilities of a medium only emerge when someone *creates* them. But their significance is not obvious, and neither is their affect on the medium, for this, again, is what the artist does. Or rather, the artist *creates a new medium* for his or her art – for 'only an art can define its media' – having explored its automatisms. Some possibilities for a medium may come to an end (perhaps then to be reborn later), others may continue to evolve. But the fact remains that 'there are physical limits upon how fast a camera can move or a scene change' (at least, Cavell says, if 'the depiction of human actions and events' is one's goal).[28] As we'll see in Chapter 8, the vices and virtues of computer-generated imagery (CGI) in film both endorse and contest parts of what Cavell has to say here.

Contra Deleuze?

In his progression towards a definition of cinema, it is noteworthy how Cavell brings the restraints and possibilities of its physical medium together with the intentions and creativity of the artist interacting with that matter. Freedom is mixed with necessity. Another essential dimension of cinema are the hopes and expectations of its socially situated audiences: an automatism is a success only if it is significant; if it is created with 'conviction' and integrated meaningfully into the narrative of 'human actions and events'.[29] All three levels must be accommodated in any robust theory, medium, artist and audience. Cavell characterizes film, then, as 'a succession of automatic world projections', a phrase that captures the physical mechanism, ontological bearing and phenomenological reception of any movie.[30] There is both inhuman matter *and* human mind.

At first, Cavell's position would appear to contrast greatly with Deleuze's prioritization of the inhuman eye, of film as a means to transcend human meaning – especially in the epoch of the time-image. But this would be a hasty conclusion. Certainly, Cavell's much greater focus on the human, social dimension to movie-going – its reception by different audiences, the importance of genre for that audience, the companionship involved in collective spectating – puts him at odds with Deleuze's more spartan approach. As mentioned at the outset, Cavell is a humanist: the protagonists in Hitchcock's *Marnie* (1964) are analysed as 'thieves of love', whilst *The Birds* is said to examine the nature of cosmic love, with Tippi Hendren being penetrated by 'all the birds of heaven'. He is also a Freudian in many instances, claiming, for instance, that 'in horror movies, sexuality is not suggested but directly coded onto, or synchronized with, the knives and teeth as they penetrate'. We saw that Deleuze would regard such interpretations as puerile. The hermeneutics of narrative, though somewhat marginal to the central concerns of *The World Viewed*, is also essential to Cavell's work on film overall in a way never seen in Deleuze (save to reduce narrative to cinematography). Indeed, Cavell admits that *The World Viewed* provided a foundation for his later writings on genre film, because 'cinematic narration' can only be properly investigated *after* an investigation 'of the medium of cinema itself'.[31] Hence, the comedies of remarriage in *Pursuits of Happiness* and the melodramas of the 'unknown women' in *Contesting Tears* (which owes a huge, highly un-Deleuzian debt to Freud on topics of forgetfulness, repression, fantasy, repetition, acting-out and scopophilia) are not incidental, but crucial to the way narrative film places society and human relations at its core.[32]

Of particular human interest is the role of acting and the actor, greatly neglected by Deleuze (as we saw) but given a primacy in *The World Viewed*. For Cavell, the screen actor often has a star persona that plays a part in mediating our reception of the film. Film roles are coextensive with an actor's life, be they singular – Clark Gable and Rhet Butler, Sean Connery and James Bond – or multiple (Clint Eastwood brings both the Stranger with No Name and Dirty Harry into every other screen role he plays, be they related or not). Earlier roles are taken into later roles; later roles are seen retroactively acting upon earlier ones. According to Cavell, then, the screen performer is not an actor playing another (fictional) subject alone – he or she *is* the subject, always partly playing him or herself in a role whose meaning keeps evolving. The power of Anthony Perkins's role in *Pretty Poison* (1968) or *The Champagne Murders* (1967), for example, 'depends on his *not* being what his role in *Psycho* showed him to be'.[33] This is just one example of Cavell's dictum that *movies come from other movies*. The understanding of genre would be another. Hence, in Cavell's view, the creation of meaning is not controlled by one individual (the auteur), but is an emergent, social phenomenon involving the multiple talents and contingencies that go into making, marketing and exhibiting a film, as well as the social and personal determinations of the audiences' uptake of that film, all of which are building upon the physical specificities of the medium itself.

The different, and greater, emphasis Cavell puts on acting in particular highlights both a convergence and a divergence with Deleuze concerning action itself, and its purported breakdown into the wandering, gesturing and posturing styles of the time-image. On one front, Cavell differs starkly. Where Deleuze sees the gestural, ironic mimicry of action in the performances of Jean-Paul Belmondo or Jean-Pierre Léaud in European post-war cinema, Cavell sees only a *different kind of acting* instead. He cites Belmondo, as well as Bergman's and Antonioni's leading men, as exemplaries of a 're-birth of unexpressed masculine depth' with 'conviction in their depth' due to an athleticism and a capacity to enter into 'unknown regions of physical articulateness and endurance'. In other words, at least with respect to acting, time-image cinema does not offer images of enfeebled action, with the action-images of John Ford and the sensory-motor acting of John Wayne providing the other side of a supposed binary; rather, they convey *a different kind of action*.[34] This is where Cavell and Deleuze diverge most.

With regards to cinema as a whole, however, Cavell does at first appear to adopt a chronology of premodern and modern akin to Deleuze's one of movement-image and time-image. At times, Cavell sports the idea that modern cinema has undergone a 'loss of connection' with the world, a 'loss of conviction in the film's capacity to carry the world's presence' due to a 'draining from the original myths of film of their power to hold our conviction in film's characters'.[35] This would seem to prefigure greatly the *ennui* of the time-image. To investigate this link with Deleuze more fully, however, we must turn to the question of modernism as such in Cavell's writing, both for its positive and troubling aspects.

Modernism

When *The World Viewed* appeared in 1971, some film journals took Cavell to be advocating the already out-dated form of modernism associated with Clement Greenberg.[36] This has been subsequently contested by Cavell's supporters. But the matter is not at all clear (Cavell does admit to being influenced by the modernist Michael Fried for instance), and most obviously because the meaning of modernism is itself so complex. With respect to Cavell's putative version of modernism, however, there are three issues to deal with, namely film's own essence as self-reflexive, as well as the resultant associations with essentialism and elitism towards the artwork. With respect to the first of these, in the first edition of *The World Viewed* Cavell forwarded the idea that post-war modernist cinema had entered into a new, self-reflexive relationship. Modernist film makes the camera known to the viewer, exposes the apparatus for what it is, and thereby indicates the loss of the medium's belief in its own worlds (which Cavell also sees as a contemporary condition of both art in general and all experience). Films are now concerned less about their subject matter than the powers of the medium itself; they have evolved into films about film, about viewing.[37]

In this respect, Cavell does momentarily prefigure Deleuze's opposition between the movement-image and the time-image. Yet, Cavell subsequently amended his position by extending this reflexivity to all cinema, without any historical breaks. Contra Deleuze's dualism, Cavell contended that either 'movies from their beginning have existed in a state of modernism' – that is, that they have always explored their own ontology (especially in the comedy genre) – or that they always did so in parallel with being traditional. Either way, cinema's facility to explore the powers of its own medium has *always* been there, and is essential to it as an art form: 'pride of place within the canon of serious films will be found occupied by those films that most clearly and most deeply discover the powers of the medium itself'.[38] So far, so modernist.

However, according to Rothman and Keane, the critic Rosalind Krauss went too far when she read the modernism of *The World Viewed* to imply an essentialism towards film. It was erroneous to imply that 'the ontology of film is something that Cavell takes himself to be *constructing* in the pages of *The World Viewed*, as one might construct a *system* of thought'. Likewise, it was erroneous to imply, as she also did, that it was 'the business of *The World Viewed* to "set out", to determine *a priori*, film's "conditions and limits"'. Yet, I'm not so sure that Krauss was wholly wrong. The subtitle of *The World Viewed* is, after all, 'Reflections on the Ontology of the Image', and providing an ontology – a science of the being of the medium itself (that Cavell himself says must precede any study of actual films a posteriori) – would seem to be a move towards an essentialism of some sort, even if it is an ontology of the mystery or underworld magic of film. As Cavell himself put it: 'the better the film, the more it makes contact with this source of its inspiration; it never loses touch with the magic lantern behind it'.[39] This would appear to be a clear prescription of how film should be rather than a description of how films actually are.

The question of modernist essentialism leads us finally, then, to the elitism consequential to this, and which is to be found in Cavell's valorization of certain films over others. It is an elitism quite at odds with Deleuze's more avant-garde tastes, to be sure, for it prioritizes the ordinary over the extraordinary – classical, Hollywood narrative film over more experimental forms: 'it is because movies can still work their original fortune that most good movies are still largely traditional'.[40] If it appeals to the masses; if it gains a response from an audience by touching their everyday lives, *then it is art*. One might call this an inverted snobbery, for this is certainly a highly mediated notion of the 'ordinary', one that creates a set of elite and canonical works for Cavell: the popular comedies and melodramas of Hollywood's 'golden age' of the 1930s and 1940s. After all, Cavell's idea of the ordinary is not very ordinary; likewise, not just *any* popularity will suffice to make a film valuable.

Reflexivity: film's other minds

Irrespective of the associations of essentialism and elitism, though, Cavell explicitly states that the modernism of film lies in its reflexive nature. The objects projected on the screen are inherently self-referential, their presence referring to their absence, their physical origins in an absent object. But this presence/absence dialectic does not exist in the abstract; if it is to work it must be specific and concrete. It is a matter of the *how* of the presence and the *how* of the absence, as Cavell explains:

> What I wanted to capture by saying that film is inherently self-reflexive is simply the significance of the fact that what you're given in film is

> a view of a place or a person or an object that is from one place rather than any other, at this time and not another, for this interval rather than another, in this light and with this texture and not others, and so on. Choice – thought, reflection – is on the surface.[41]

This reflexivity is, therefore, also a *kind of thinking*. The specificity of how things appear indicates the presence of a mind, an intention. There is intention in a film's design, arguments from its design. But it is not necessarily the intention of an artist. The above quotation is from a 2005 interview with Cavell by Andrew Klevan, who also asks Cavell outright what he means when he says that films can think. At first, Cavell retreats from his position by toning down its rhetoric, but what he then adds is worth quoting in full:

> Well, of course, that is to begin with just a somewhat provocative way of saying: Don't ask what the artist is thinking or intending, but ask why the work is as it is, why just this is here in just that way. The implication that the way the work is, is a matter of its own thinking or intention may be brought out by noting that to ask 'Why has the artist done that?' (namely, modulated to the subdominant, held this shot longer than one would have expected, used a canvas whose vertical is many times longer than its horizontal span), and to ask 'Why does the work modulate, prolong the shot, employ this format?' are differently emphasised formulations of the same demand. Intending something (as in Anscombe's book on the subject) is a function of wanting something. My formulation employing the work's thinking or intending or wanting something, is meant to emphasise the sense that the work wants something of us who behold or hear or read it. This is a function of our determining what we want of it, why or how we are present at it – what our relation to it is. It and I (each I present at it) are responsible to each other.[42]

Specificity of appearance (of presence and absence) is a hallmark of design, but it is a design that is intersubjective rather than the token of either a vicarious mind (the artist being assimilated into the artwork) or a solitary mentation (artwork as cognitive processor). Pictures *want* something from us, for their 'thinking' is conative too, affective, demanding a response from and with our lives as spectators. And it is this *relation* which is thoughtful. This is one more near parallel with Deleuze. Deleuze cuts (or creates) his concepts to match each film's particularity in a philosophy that moulds itself to the contours of cinematic practice, rather than vice versa. For Cavell, this responsiveness to filmic individuation simply is what genuine thinking does in any domain: its response is its responsibility *for* and *to* the otherness or specificity of film.

Here we arrive at Cavell's abiding concerns over knowledge and acknowledgement, over the connection between (other) minds and morals, thought and affect. Philosophy, for Cavell, is defined as 'responsiveness, as not speaking first'; it is an *acknowledgement* of limits, of alterity, of other minds. And this is precisely what modernism in film means too: the need to 'acknowledge' its limit as outside the world, for exactly this allows film to fulfil its role in 'letting the world exhibit itself'. The 'significance', discussed earlier, which makes any automatism artful, is due to the care and integrity with which it appears in the film, a care that is itself established intersubjectively, embroiling the camera, the projection and the audience's reception. Referring to the famous 360-degree tracking shot of Scotty and Madeleine in *Vertigo,* Cavell writes that the meaning of this shot applies only 'in this context, in this film'. Tiny, nuanced moments, no matter how trivial, can be productive of meaning if done carefully, responsibly, acknowledging the specificity of the narrative and its audience: 'why did the hand do that? Why did the camera turn just then?'.[43] Similarly, on a more general level, montage or continuity only have a significance 'within an "acknowledgement" of the limits of film as outside the world and so what reveals the world as such'.[44]

Must We Mean What We Say?, which appeared a little before *The World Viewed,* tackled the traditional problem of scepticism towards other minds – another enduring concern of Cavell's – and it responds to the problem with the notion of acknowledgement as 'the mode in which knowledge of mind appears'.[45] Film too is concerned with other minds – not cognitively, not through deduction, not by analogy – but by the affective restraint that comes with acknowledging one's own limits. Indeed, that is one meaning we can ascribe to the Cavellian version of the 'ordinary': the concern to adapt one's view, one's language, in the light of what others ordinarily mean and say.[46] And this concern is precisely what thinking is for Cavell, and a sign of filmic thinking. *Our* acknowledgement of each film's particulars is also a response to *its* careful acknowledgement of the specifics of its world. Its careful details show a mind, an intent, a something that wants something from us.

Other Cavellians

No less than the film-philosophers who, following Deleuze, find it difficult to apply his ideas consistently in actual film analyses (either emphasizing the signs and images of the *Cinema* books or the embodied affectivity of *Capitalism and Schizophrenia*), so too there have been problems for the cinetheorist who wishes to enact a Cavellian response to film thinking. A case in point is a recent collection edited by Rupert Read and Jerry Goodenough entitled *Film as Philosophy.*[47] Despite Cavell's injunction against applying philosophy *to* film, and even their own allusions to this interdiction, time and again the essays gathered here read films by 'adapting' ideas from Cavell and Wittgenstein, with talk of films that are 'like' Wittgenstein's philosophy, films that argue 'in much the same way' as Wittgenstein, 'illuminate' Wittgenstein, and so on.[48] There is knowledge of the sovereignty of film (which is commendable), but a lack of acknowledgement of it inasmuch as the films and film-scenes selected are all there to fulfil a specific task, namely to establish the cogency of applying Cavell and Wittgenstein to cinema.

For instance, in his introduction to the collection, Jerry Goodenough writes that the 1992 'Director's Cut' of *Blade Runner* – where we no longer know clearly whether or not the hero, Deckard, is a robot (or 'replicant') – is a good example of film *as* philosophy because 'the very fact that the film *is* ambiguous about Deckard's humanity is philosophically relevant. Personhood is not an all-or-nothing business'. But note: the idea that 'personhood is not an all-or-nothing business' is itself a common enough philosophical position, one that is here allowing the philosopher to see in one film a mirror of his pre-established position. Indeed, an alternative reading might well say that any ambiguity about personhood in *Blade Runner* is simply there as a narrative device to create suspense (is he or isn't he a human?), and that the film's ultimate philosophical message, at best, is that we are all robots (or robotic), being as cruel and heartless, when required, as the replicants are frequently portrayed to be in the film. Which is still to leave aside a racialist reading (the portrait of Asians in *Blade Runner* is highly problematic), or a feminist reading, and so on. And yet, Goodenough still insists that his position is one that allows films to 'do' philosophy in their own manner of thinking, *without* statements, without explicit, articulated syllogisms. Films are said to show us philosophy through their own serious and systematic thinking 'about philosophical arguments and issues'.[49] Once again, though, even were we to leave aside the philosophically loaded meaning of terms like 'serious', 'systematic' and 'thinking' here, we might still ask how one is to recognize a philosophical argument or issue *when one sees one on screen* without invoking our prejudices of what a philosophical argument or issue looks like.

On the one hand, the answer may be clear. In contrast to the novel on which *Blade Runner* is based (Philip K. Dick's *Do Robots Dream of Electric Sheep?*), which Goodenough describes as forwarding a 'dry and lifeless proposition' concerning the personhood of replicants, the film adaptation lets us *see* the replicants live and breathe, and this 'is to engage in a form of life with them'. It is to 'feel them as part of our lives, as something we cannot avoid thinking of as being like us'. This may sound Cavellian at first (in alluding to the intersubjectivity of film and audience), but because it only outlines a one-way system (a philosophical film 'forces the audience to engage with them') it is actually closer to the approaches of Mark Rowlands and Mary Litch: the 'film-as-more-real/life-like/forceful/concrete' school of film-philosophy. For instance, *L'Année dernière à Marienbad* is said by Goodenough to engage with Cartesian solipsism by turning the film audience into solipsists – 'we inhabit solipsism' while watching it. Or, in another of the essays by Phil Hutchinson and Rupert Read, the film *Memento* is described as setting out 'to induce in us an experience as of the very protagonist whose experience we are seeking to understand'. This position is a first person variation of the 'concrete' school of film-philosophy – in which inhabiting the problem *visually* is said to make us think about it: '*watching* film, engaging both perceptually and intellectually with the cinematic events in front of you, can be another way of doing philosophy'.[50] But what does such 'engagement' entail here? Apart from the conflation of optical alignment with affective allegiance in these arguments (a naive assumption that ignores years of scholarship in film studies), it remains moot whether a point of view shot per se makes us think anything at all, or at least whether it makes us think about philosophical things. Does the point of view shot of a tiger make us think about animal rights, or what it is 'like to be' a tiger? Could watching *Jungle Book* (1967) ever make an untrained audience think Peter Singer-like thoughts about great apes?

The problem is that film has always been a forceful medium *in any case* because of its multisensory and affective form, especially when an audience judges it be a 'good film', finds it pleasurable, entertaining, and so on. So the question remains as to what makes a film *philosophically* forceful, if it is *not* due to its scriptual similarity to written philosophy. If it exists, this force must be something else besides, because terms like 'engaging', or 'watching', or 'inhabiting' are either superfluous or bear too much theoretical burden to be of value to any argument for the philosophical mindfulness of film.

Other Cavellian approaches have proved equally ambivalent in so far as they combine a care for the integrity of film with the need to show its philosophical nature via some already current philosophy. In Stephen Mulhall's admirable study of the *Alien* quartet of films, *On Film*, much is made of the need to show these films doing philosophical work, but there remains an indecision between seeing 'film as philosophizing' and seeing film as 'philosophy in action'. While aiming especially for the former, too often the book succeeds only at the latter, that is, at film being recognized as philosophical because it puts philosophy's problems into action (in this case, the problem being the 'relation of human identity to embodiment' – a well-worn issue long before these films began appearing in 1979).[51] Once again, film illustrates.

Finally, while writing in Cavellian mode, Simon Critchley falls foul of this bivalency in a most startling fashion, for in just a few sentences on Terrence Malick's *Thin Red Line* (1998) he both gives and takes away from film any of its own philosophical resources:

> To read from cinematic language to some philosophical meta-language is both to miss what is specific to the medium of film and usually to engage in some sort of cod-philosophy deliberately designed to intimidate

> the uninitiated. I think this move has to be avoided on philosophical grounds, indeed the very best Heideggerian grounds. Any philosophical reading of film has to be a reading *of* film, of what Heidegger would call *der Sache selbst*, the thing itself. A philosophical reading of film should not be concerned with ideas about the thing, but with the thing itself, the cinematic *Sache*.[52]

We should care for film because Heidegger says so, and in German too! Film thinks, because we philosophers see it thinking. After this self-refuting paragraph, the essay goes on to fulfil its promise by reading *Thin Red Line* in terms of its protagonists' pious questioning, their calm before death, and so on.[53] Pure Heidegger.

The lesson seems to be that Cavell's ideas may work well in theory, but less so in practice, in actual viewing. But we've always known that retaining the particularities of film whilst also fulfilling a philosophical remit would probably be harder than we could ever imagine. At least Cavell himself knows that performance is everything. We must firstly *perform* his idea of film-philosophy before we record it, before we spot it 'in action'. In other words, if film thinks, if we must respond to its alterity before thinking for it, we have to stop recognizing our philosophy in it; we have to find another way of acknowledging the difference between film's philosophizing and our own.

More ontologies: Frampton's affective thinking

To commence the end of this part of our study, however, we need to examine a recent and radical attempt to establish a brand new form of thinking that is wholly peculiar to film, one that combines ideas from Deleuze, Heidegger and Cavell, while introducing a most ambitious neologism, 'filmosophy'. As already mentioned, Daniel Frampton's book *Filmosophy* claims for film the faculty of a new kind of thought all its own – the 'affective thinking of film'.[54] His study aspires to be a new theory of film that incorporates aspects from every dimension of film, its being, its thinking, the audience's reception of it, and even how we should write about it:

> Filmosophy is a study of film as thinking, and contains a theory of both film-being and film form. The 'filmind' is filmosophy's concept of film-being, the theoretical originator of the images and sounds we experience, and 'film-thinking' is its theory of film form, whereby an action of form is seen as the dramatic thinking of the filmind. In a sense filmosophy can therefore be understood as an extension and integration of theories of both para-narrational 'showing' and mise-en-scène aesthetics. *Filmosophy proposes that seeing film form as thoughtful, as the dramatic decision of the film, helps us understand the many ways film can mean and affect.*[55]

The way in which a person is filmed must now be seen as a thinking 'of the film's idea of that person. When a film frames a person that act of framing creates a way of seeing that person (as central or peripheral or close-up)'. Focus, colour, speed, sound, editing, camera movement and framing are all ways of thinking a certain 'relation to the story being told'. These are signs of mind, of choice and decision, in what we are shown or what we see. Similarily, what is kept in focus, or out of focus, in close-up or in the background, what is left audible or made inaudible (and by what other sound), are all modes of thought.[56]

There is clearly a Cavellian dimension to all of this. Frampton talks not only of film thinking and a 'filmind' but also of film being and film worlds. The filmind creates (and re-creates) various film worlds (many of them exotic, using the latest CGI): 'film presents a unique world, almost a future-world (not least because the film's "experience" of its people and objects feels "new"). Film is its own world with its own rules (and philosophy should certainly learn from its fluid re-situating of experience and knowledge)'.[57]

All the same, being sensitive to the abuses of film by theory, Frampton does not write merely as a 'Cavellian'. More often than not, he says, 'philosophers are simply concerned with how some films *contain* stories and characterisations that helpfully *illustrate* well-known philosophical ideas', such that 'much writing within the area of "film and philosophy" simply ignores cinematics and concentrates on stories and character motivations. It only takes one character to say "man is not an island" for somebody to jump up and declare the film philosophical'.[58] Frampton's objective, then, is to find the philosophy peculiar to 'cinematics' and nowhere else.

However, there is ambiguity on a number of fronts regarding what Frampton's theory of a cinematic mind amounts to. On the one hand, it can sound like an instrumental concept, akin to Daniel Dennett's concept of an 'intentional stance', Frampton even using one of Dennett's phrases when he calls cinema a 'kind of mind'.[59] We attribute the word 'mind' to film in order to aid our explanations of what film does. Hence, Frampton writes that '*the concept of filmind is conceptualised in order to assist the film-goer in getting the most out of cinema*'. Frampton adds that we do not need to 'know' about the mind to use it in relation to film for, indeed, we often talk quite normally outside of art about things 'having minds' without this involving any specific knowledge at all. There is no 'external force', or 'mystical being' or 'invisible other', involved in this attribution of thought to cinema, but simply a new way of conceptualizing our encounter with film, albeit one that is 'attempting to see film for the first time'. So now the filmind appears only as a 'rhetorical extension'.[60] Alternatively, one might conjecture that Frampton is also performing a kind of phenomenological reduction on cinema, bracketing both the auteur and the mechanics of film production, and attending only to what we see, the film's own choices, its own on-screen thinking.

On the other hand, though, Frampton also espouses the view that attributing thought to film reveals something real, and that it is a metaphysical insight: 'cinema allows us to re-see reality, expanding our perceptions, and showing us a new reality'. Indeed, in an orgy of dense philosophical references towards the conclusion of the book, this new theory of film reveals cinema as 'a free and open way of apprehending something; a shining-through of non-essential being (*phainestai*); a letting go; a kind of thinking beyond simple representation; a disjunctive kind of judgement (*Gelassenheit*)'.[61]

And these are not the only ambiguities surrounding the idea of filmosophy. It is said to be a sovereign form of thought, disanalogous to human thought. Film thinking is not like human thinking (which is defined in terms of 'planning, meditating, problem-solving, reverie, reasoning, daydreaming, figuring, judging, imagining)'; rather, film is both 'less and more' than human mentation because it *shows* planning, meditating, and so on. In fact, Frampton spends a good part of his book setting out the errors of earlier theories of film thinking that too readily characterized it in terms of a human model of thought, instead of the inhuman one he favours (following Deleuze). Yet, despite this separation between the human mind and the film mind, it is we who are said to 'complete the thoughts of film, who decide, if we so wish, on the ideas to be gained from a film'. The human mind must join with that of the film to reveal its philosophy. But how can two so dissimilar things merge, how can there be this 'encounter between film and filmgoer as a *mix of thinkings*' if they are *not alike* (given that one 'shows' and the other doesn't)? Similarly, it is unclear as to whether cinematic thought is non-linguistic, involving a 'languageless thinking' that operates 'as if our cognitive, linguistic thought had never come'; or whether it must remain linguocentric because language mediates all thought and 'our capacity to receive those affective film-thinkings is somewhat dependent on whether we are "ready" linguistically'.[62]

Certainly, the great value of filmosophy, apart from alerting us to the exploitation of film by philosophers and the numerous ways in which film exceeds our theories of it, comes in its emphasis on enriching our language of cinema, on the need to make our descriptions more baroque. A technical term like 'tracking shot', for example, misses too much of what we actually see on the screen, for there is always a peculiarity to the movement – a kind of movement, a kind of tracking – that is best described in thick descriptions that only fit the scene at hand and its affects on us.

Yet, Frampton's method of thick descriptions to capture the colours, images and sounds of a film, though admirable, takes a step too far when he calls them *the thinking of the film itself.* He forgets thereby how socially mediated his (and all) descriptions are, and that any ascription of beauty, sympathy or horror, say, to an image, sound, movement or composition is already determined by certain presuppositions.[63] Frampton also goes too far when he thinks that he can isolate the ontology of film with his own focus on the artwork as an object of experience. His view that 'we first must study the personal *affects* of film' before we can engage with a 'sociology of the cinema', or that it is possible to reveal 'the pure poetry of cinema, before films are mangled by contextual knowledge', is excessively optimistic, to say the least.[64] His own preferences – for works by Tarr, Haneke and Godard – is typical of the high-brow approach. His choices are those of an intellectual, favouring Godard over Cameron. Doesn't *Titanic* also make 'us' think about history, class, inevitability, chance and necessity? Or is it *just me* who thinks so? (And how many others must I find who think like me before I can conclude that I am not so wrong?)

Ultimately, Frampton is guilty of the charge of presupposition that he lays at the door of other philosophies. He begins with a definition of thinking, in terms of 'problems and ideas', 'becomings' and what 'creates pure concepts', which is already reliant upon a pre-existing philosophical model of thought, in this case Deleuze's. Frampton says that he is seeking a 'post-metaphysical thinking' that creates concepts 'within nonphilosophy'.[65] Yet, the Deleuzian definition of thinking as 'concept creation' is an avowedly metaphysical one. As we stated as the outset, if film can at all be said to think for itself, if film is to philosophize for itself, then we must first of all attempt to get away from *any* prior philosophical definition of thinking and, indeed, of philosophy too.

Badiou's inessential cinema

One approach to film that might be read as making just this kind of attempt can be found in a short essay by Alain Badiou. 'The False Movements of Cinema' is only an outline (when Badiou writes about art, it is more often about literature, theatre and music), yet it is indicative of Badiou's approach to any non-philosophy in that it claims to respect its autonomy. Indeed, for Badiou, philosophy itself is dependent on four other fields, or 'conditions', for its truths – science, politics, art and love. Philosophy itself does not produce truth, but only collects together the truths that are created within these fields in any particular era. Philosophy is radically conditioned by the local truths of these multiple domains, one of which, art, must include film as well. His essay on film appears in a collection on art entitled *Handbook of Inaesthetics*.[66] This neologism of 'inaesthetics' inaugurates a new relationship between philosophy and its non-philosophical conditions, one of submission to their truths and modes of thinking. There is no philosophy *of* art, as the older name of 'aesthetics' implied (nor is there one *of* science, *of* love, or *of* politics). If aesthetics traditionally denoted the philosophical practice that stood in judgement over art, adjudicating what counts as true and false, as worthy for knowledge or not, then inaesthetics reverses the relationship. Film instructs philosophy.

Of course, we've seen similar testimonies to such humility before, but we've always found that they came with a hidden agenda, some kind of ontology of film that presupposed a philosophical position that consequently stopped them following through on their good intentions. With Badiou, though, the situation may be different, not because he does not have an ontology of film, but because of the type of ontology it is. If Frampton says too much about film, and applies too much philosophical baggage to what film is, then Badiou says very little about it, indeed almost nothing (or at least he seems to). For Badiou, most ontologies are 'generative' – they always add their own philosophical history to the object. His own ontology is 'subtractive', it says as little as possible about the object – less rather than more. There are complex reasons for this position which we can't enter into here, but fundamental to Badiou's view is that ontology is a non-philosophical discourse. In fact, ontology, the science of being as such, belongs to mathematics, one of philosophy's conditions.[67] The truth of an object as such, then, is not found in what can be said of its qualities (which are only our subjective impressions of it), but in as little as can be said of it at all, that is, *only* in what can be said of it quantitatively or mathematically. A subtractive ontology strips away our subjective, additive, qualitative impressions of the object to find the thing itself, and though this need not literally entail using mathematical symbolism, the language of an object, even an artwork, must aspire to express as little as possible lest it interfere with it.

With all this in mind, then, the little that Badiou does say about cinema is significant, for it gives cinema an even more subtractive characterization than the other arts. Indeed, cinema is the point of intersection of the other six arts according to Badiou, having no essence of its own save for the barest outline of what minimal essence there is in literature, theatre, music, painting, dance and sculpture. Film cuts out and splices together these minimal essences:

> Cinema is the seventh art in a very particular sense. It does not add itself to the other six while remaining on the same level as them. Rather, it implies them – cinema is the 'plus-one' of the arts. It operates on the other arts, using them as its starting point, in a movement that subtracts them from themselves.[68]

Badiou does admit that there is, in fact, no way of moving from one art to another, 'the arts are closed', and no painting could ever become a piece of music. But, nonetheless, cinema is still the 'organization' of just such an impossible movement amongst the arts. Only it works by subtraction, not addition. This makes cinema *the* impure art. It is 'internally and integrally contaminated by its situation as the "plus-one" of arts'. In Visconti's *Death in Venice* (1971), for example, alongside a script based on the novel by Thomas Mann, we also have the intersection of various other arts: Mahler's music, artistic echoes of Venetian style, pictorial themes from Guardi and Canaletto, literary themes from Rousseau and Proust, and the acting of Dirk Bogart (especially in his face).[69]

However, leaving film with no essence of its own (save as the intersection, the 'plus-one', of the other arts) also leaves us with very little to say about film. Certainly, recounting the qualities of a film will not suffice:

> It is clear that film criticism is forever suspended between the chatter of empathy, on the one hand, and historical technicalities, on the other. Unless it is just a question of recounting the plot (the fatal novelistic impurity) or of singing the actors' praises (the theatrical impurity). Is it really so easy to speak about a film?[70]

Film itself, we are told, 'operates through what it withdraws from the visible', through editing, framing, through holding up or suspending movement, 'the controlled purge of the visible'.[71] But, then, Badiou asks, 'what here is, strictly speaking, the film?':

> After all, cinema is nothing but takes and editing. There is nothing else. What I mean is this: There is nothing else that would constitute 'the film'. It is therefore necessary to argue that, viewed from the vantage point of an axiomatic judgment, a film is what exposes the passage of the idea in accordance with the take and the editing.[72]

Given that there is nothing to film other than a subtraction from the other arts, such that it is subtraction and impurity in person, film can only *do* rather than *be*, it can only be the *passage of ideas* rather than have an idea of itself (an essence). Film *is* simply thought on its way to philosophy (rather than the other way about). Against normative judgements of film ('this is good', 'this is superior'), Badiou proposes an *axiomatic* attitude that enquires into 'the effects for thought' of each particular film. We don't ask what the film is, but rather what it makes us think, how it transports ideas: 'to speak about a film axiomatically comes down to examining the consequences of the proper mode in which an Idea is treated thus by *this* particular film'.[73]

In the Chapters 6–8 we will try to make good on Badiou's proposal that film always moves beyond any positive essential claims for it, that it is a kind of nothingness which, nonetheless, allows for the passage of thought on account of this nothingness. Apart from enquiring into the meaning of this 'passage', we will have one important proviso to add to Badiou. Despite his 'inaesthetical' approach, Badiou still fixes cinema within a strict and traditional aesthetic domain (it is the 'seventh art' after all), and his method is highly orthodox in various ways, choosing very specific films and filmic-features to fit his theory (for the most part, works by the same authors Deleuze favours – Murnau, Welles, Visconti, Tati, Straub, Beckett).

One apparent exception to this comes in an essay by Badiou on three science-fiction films, *Cube, The Matrix* and *eXistenZ,* all of which were released in France in 1999. And here, indeed, Badiou tells us that cinema 'can only put philosophy to the test with some degree of rigour if it demands *a variation in the regime of the sensible*. Basically, we must verify that the cinema enjoys a certain aptitude for the concept, once it has the power to render the certainty of the visible visibly uncertain'.[74] The art of cinema now lies precisely in 'showing that it is only cinema, that its images only testify to the real to the extent that they are *manifestly* images'. This is the reason why Badiou concludes his essay by commending *The Matrix*'s philosophy over that of the other two films, because its challenge to 'the image on the basis of the image itself, in the direction of its foundational beyond, is the very question of cinema'. Or, to be precise, *The Matrix* advances 'the most robust' cinematic inquiry *because* it is 'the Platonist one'. Accordingly, *The Matrix* is philosophical because it repeats Plato's *anti-imagistic*, written thought, and not because it possesses its own cinematic one. For Badiou, the written letter is everything.[75] So, even here, in this momentary embrace of popular film, Badiou remains a modernist (elitist *and auteurist*). He also neglects the other dimensions that film also intersects in its inessential essence – technology, commerce, genre, audience, sociology – that might make it philosophical in its own manner.

For our part, alternatively, we will see that expanding the outlines of cinema outward beyond the aesthetic will not only make it even harder for us to say anything positive about it, it may also allow cinema to say things back to us. It may allow cinema to make us think again about what thinking is and what thinking might become.

6
Extended Cognitions and the Speeds of Cinema

> JOEL: Wait!
> CLEMENTINE: What, Joel? What do you want?
> JOEL: I don't know. Just wait. I just want you to wait for a while.[1]

Anderson's elusive reality

Knowing or Being. The film-philosophies we have looked at so far have aligned themselves with one or the other. Is this division of approach ineluctable? According to Ian Jarvie, of course, the one logically follows from the other, but can their interdependence be recovered in any more material fashion, in a manner going beyond purely logical entailment? The work done by Edward Branigan and Joseph Anderson, that we turn to now, may provide just such a solution, for they do their best to take epistemology out of the mind and place it back in the world. And yet they both work within an analytical and cognitivist paradigm that would, prima facie, retain a bias towards the subject. Whether their pursuit is fruitful, therefore, is still to be seen.

Joseph Anderson's *The Reality of Illusion* begins and ends with two deceptively simple questions: 'why does a movie seem so real? And why do the spokes of a wheel turn backward on screen?'[2] These two questions, together, generate the dilemma that lies at the heart of Anderson's study, the essential question actually being why, despite the artefacts of cinematic illusion being so visible before us, do we persist in thinking that what we see is real. As a cognitivist, his answer concerns the brain's involvement in film-perception. On the one side are the hard-wired, primitively evolved parts of the brain that make the illusion of apparent movement in film possible; on the other are the higher faculties that allow us to reflect on certain anomalies (like reversed wheel rotation, caused by spoked wheels revolving at a rate slightly slower than the camera's frame-rate) and that consequently break the spell of this feigned reality.

As we saw with Torben Grodal's cognitivist explanation of cinematic reality, there can be a confusion in the form that these questions take. The illusion of film *reality* is not solely due to the phenomenon of apparent movement. This is indeed the 'hard-wired' basis for the medium as such, its most fundamental condition of possibility (at least as regards projected film). But the 'reality effect' (why film seems so real) concerns what is moving and how it moves *in* the film on screen rather than the movement *of* the film in the projector (though this is indeed where the former derives its movement). These are two related, but still different, processes: the former depends on the latter as its necessary, but not sufficient, cause. If the story, acting, camerawork, editing or music is *deemed* 'poor' (for any of a multitude of reasons), *this* too will interfere with the reality effect, and even more so *at the level through which we immerse ourselves in a film*. Proper projection, adequate screen size and luminescence, sound audibility, and so on, are all vital, naturally (if the projector breaks down, the film will no longer enthral). Yet, the same would result from the film being stopped and the cinema evacuated for security reasons. To be able to talk about film (and its effects) *in any theory*, it is a *sine qua non* that there must have been, at least sometime, what we agree to call a film that was seen by someone. But the conditions for that possibility should not be built up to explain everything that can be said about film thereafter. Even so, no less than most other cognitivist approaches, Anderson's arguments (concerning narrative, character and diegesis, as well as sound and vision) rely on data from particular levels being directed to phenomena at *all* levels in an *exhaustive* explanation. But this explanation is only ever partial.[3] Indeed, our 'awareness of real-but-not-real that accompanies film viewing', as Anderson describes it, is connected to the 'paradox of fiction', the phenomenon of believing (to a degree) to be real what we know to be unreal.[4] It is something that pertains to literature and theatre as well as film, yet it has little to do *directly* with the technologies of bookbinding and stage-building.

Perhaps I'm being prematurely critical, though, for Anderson does muddy his own waters of explanatory levels (through perceptual brain states) by offering an *ecological* version of cognitivism; and in this view, perception *is also in the world*. Anderson is interested more than most in 'the interface between the film and the viewer', as he puts it, and this interface is vital. He calls his theory 'ecological', firstly, because it 'attempts to place film production and spectatorship in a natural context'. The perception and comprehension of films is a subset of 'perception and comprehension in general' (and the 'context of their evolutionary development'). But the radical aspect of this ecologism is that it is a model of *direct* perception, involving 'neither mediation nor interpretation'. It is inspired by Gregory Bateson's 'ecology of mind' (which we will turn to later), though it is worked out more precisely in terms of J. J. Gibson's theory of ecological perception, which is 'based upon the creature's interaction with an environment'. Gibson was an anti-representationalist in psychology, and as such his ideas were and remain outside of mainstream cognitive science. By bringing his ideas into film theory, however, we can see that our 'visual and auditory systems are directly interfaced with a motion picture'.[5]

Our perception does not represent the world but simply selects from it *directly*. Perceptions are worldly, they are filtered aspects of the environment we inhabit: 'we do not stumble around collecting random information' but rather seek the 'things we need' from the world: 'perception, then, is a matter of selection'. Better: the world we see simply is what we need, what is afforded us at any one moment. Gibson called these perceptions 'affordances', of which there are a multitude for any one object or event. Hence, there is still subjectivity, inasmuch as any one set of affordances is always a subset of another. However, they are not constructions of another *kind*, made by the mind from parts of the world (the Kantian view favoured by Bordwell and most other cognitivists in film theory): what we really see is of the world, only as a part is related to a whole: 'an affordance is a relationship, or potential relationship, between us and our environment'. Thus, an affordance should not be taken as information that is 'in' the world or 'from' the world: an affordance is *world-and-self-in-relation*. It is a kind of (non-Heideggerian) phenomenology of ready-to-handedness: things are *for me* and my needs – the world is perceived in terms of my possible action on it. What we see are 'objects and events with implications': when a fish encounters a projection in the rocks, for example, it can immediately 'perceive the affordance of a ledge to hide under'.[6]

If all of this sounds familiar, it is because Gibson has reinvented Bergson's theories of the image and perception set out in *Matter and Memory*.[7] In his own way, then, Gibson is saying that the brain is in the world, and Anderson, if he follows him astutely, may well be saying what Deleuze concludes from this in his film theory, that the brain is the screen. Yet, Anderson shies away from fulfilling the potential of an ecological theory by once again taking information as a *representation* (despite avoiding all use of the latter term in his writing). Anderson still talks of 'sensory systems that extract information from the environment', or of information as what 'resides in the ambient array of light reflected from objects in the world', and finally that 'through our perceptual systems, we gain the *information* about objects and events'.[8] It is this 'aboutness' that is the give-away here, as reference or representation. What makes the *original* concept of affordance one of *direct* perception, by contrast, is that it is a *relation* of the animal to its environment, as even Torben Grodal (also writing on Gibson) states: '*affordance* is a concept used...in order to describe the functional relations between world, perception, and animal or human action'.[9] Affordance is not present in the object so as to be re-presented in or by the subject – it is the direct relationship of the object to the subject. Nonetheless, Anderson remains ambivalent regarding this direct relationship.

Signs of the representationalism lurking within Anderson's ecologism are evident throughout his work: the film camera is treated as a set of on-looking eyes;[10] the metaphor is used of the brain as computer hardware and the mind as software (a view Gibson himself always resisted);[11] and, perhaps most inappropriately of all, the language of 'erroneous information' and 'illusion' versus '*veridicality*' is ever-present, which makes no sense at all within a materialist and relational view of mind and world (where no percept can fail but be *some* part of the world and none can be a false copy of it).[12] Perception as access to and subsequent re-presentation of world remains the paradigm. Indeed, had Anderson pursued to the end the implications of a mind-world ecologism, then he might have seen the paradox of filmic reality as less a problem of *fiction* (or *false* representation) than a constitutive duplicity. Seeing *x* as *y* in the cinema must always only be partial, given that 'reality' itself is always only partially glimpsed from varying perspectives.[13] Reality is elusive, so it is hardly surprising that cinema is too.

In attempting to incorporate this ecological aspect into film theory, Anderson talks of the film-percept as an environmental selection rather than a representation, yet he also retains an immaterial, internal homunculus (like Bordwell) qua information processor (hard-wired in the brain). For Bergson, on the contrary, selection is never of anything *localized*. It is rather the temporal process that creates types of localization or space. Derrida called it *espacement*; Bergson called it, amongst other things, 'refraction'. But what counts is that it is a process, not a thing (a process-*or*). If we are trying to avoid thinking of representation as localized (Cartesianism, homunculism), then it is never *in* a place (be it a theatre, the mind's eye, the brain and nervous system, or even the external world). The Bergsonian brain is described in *Matter and Memory* in terms of analyses and selections of movements. But the brain too is a movement. So there is only the selection of movements by other movements. Movements *circulate*. And, as we will see, such circulating movements also pertain to explanations and theories, for explanatory circles are movements too. Representation does not reside in any one place (even when dubbed 'the circulation of theory and film') but in the ongoing, open, circulating movements of the indefinite whole (film) and its selective parts (our theories).

Branigan's radial camera

Edward Branigan's *Projecting a Camera* does, on the contrary, propose a theory about film theories that forwards a much wider concept of selection, a theory which he calls 'projecting a camera'. He is also much happier to embrace the epistemic pluralism that goes with an embodied model of cognition; in so doing he broadens the scope of a knowing cinema far beyond Bordwell and Žižek. Using Wittgenstein's language-game approach to film and film theory (though without any of the Heideggerian ontology that Cavell adds to *his* Wittgenstein), Branigan is at once more critical and more metatheoretical in his understanding. His film theory is a theory of theories and where they go wrong in their totalization of cinema:

> A 'theory of film' may be thought of as *the grammar of an ensemble of words*, such as frame, shot, camera, point of view, editing, style, realism, auteur, performance, spectatorship, and medium specificity, accompanied by selected radial extensions of these words. I believe that a film theory is not simply a set of objective propositions about film, because 'film' – that is, the grammar (the vocabulary) of the words that describe film – is not fixed.[14]

By 'radial' Branigan means a category or meaning in which 'ambiguous meanings of a word are linked, creating, as Wittgenstein says, "a continuous transition" from one group of things to another group of things with the same name'. A radial concept is any with polysemous meanings, each one of which relates to another by radiating extension, 'projected from a specific image schema through a series of metaphors and metonymies'. This pluralism of meaning ensures that any fixed extension of a term is merely 'an outline' of the way in which our concept has 'framed' its object, and not the object itself. Theories only see aspects of film, not the whole. It is futile to search for one 'pure' description for 'there is no film theory that is purely objective in its description of film because there are no objective descriptions. There are only moves within a grammar or language-game'.[15]

Branigan is stinging in his rebuke of other theories (without mentioning their authors' names), examples including 'film brings meaning to light', 'film presents absence', 'film is an experience of time' and 'film is an experience'. In true Wittgensteinian spirit, Branigan says that all of these thoughts are 'nearly vacuous':

> They are based on selecting some *fact* about film, positing a causality for the 'fact', overgeneralizing the causality, and finally elaborating the result into an ontology, epistemology, and aesthetics of film where the favored causal principle is scaled to fit assumed modes of film experience.[16]

It is in this process of 'overgeneralizing' where the body enters. From the well-known work of Mark Johnson and George Lakoff on bodily meaning, Branigan takes the idea of 'image schema'. A case in point would be the 'container schema' that is rooted in our awareness of being embodied in space. This awareness is extended radially when we use such metaphors as 'meaning *in* a film', the 'ideas *in* words' or 'a case *in* point'.[17] Branigan in his turn applies this same understanding to various film theories' radial usage of terms like 'camera', 'movement' and 'frame'. It is this extended and diverse use of the selected terms at the heart of each theory that leads to their excessive and vacuous scope. At one point, Branigan goes through 15 related but different meanings of 'frame', running from the real edge of the screen, through to the illusory border of an image, the gestalt of the image, and on to the situation or context, the scene, the narrative structure, the narration, the psychic state undergirding the spectators' emotions, and the world-knowledge presupposed by the story and/or the viewer.[18] Each of these meanings can be latched onto and made the focal point around which the others are oriented. It should be noted that the first meanings listed pertain more to 'bottom-up', objectivist explanations of film, and the latter ones to top-down, culturalist accounts. As such, the former point towards absolutism, the latter towards relativism.[19]

And, of course, 'camera' too is a radial concept, projected by various film theories in their own selective fashion, extending it well beyond 'photographicity, beyond pictured-ness, beyond even the visible and visual'.[20] The camera that views James Bond, for instance, is not the same camera that views Sean Connery or Roger Moore (the former involves 'perceiving fictionally' in contrast to the latter's optical recording). Indeed, there are 'many separate superimposed cameras corresponding to multiple (even incompatible) interpretations that are simultaneously operating during a shot'. More broadly still, when we are alerted to what is called 'Hitchcock's camera', say, and learn to discern it again and again both in his own works and even in those of others (as in Brian de Palma's *Obsession* (1976)), we have extended the image of the camera well beyond its usual remit. It is less a physical object now than a relationship:[21]

> the term 'camera' should be understood against the backdrop of a diversity of bodily processes and judgements ranging from the perceptual to the cognitive, from the emotive to the motive. I believe that when a film critic speaks about a camera, he or she is tacitly invoking some theory of one or more human abilities that a camera is said to mimic, explore, refuse, transcend, and so on.[22]

In all of these radial meanings, Branigan reminds us of another Wittgensteinian precept, namely that the differences and similarities between a plurality of kindred terms is 'indefinite, blurred, or porous'. The boundary between them is 'indefinite', the similarity amongst them more familial than logical.[23] These radial concepts are 'in-between' notions, neither fully in one category nor another, neither fully realist nor constructivist (and neither exclusively in the first half of the list given above, nor the second). And this is where Branigan concludes, with the suggestion that being 'in-between' language games 'may be the best description we have of what a film theory is'.[24]

Unsurprisingly, Branigan is aware of the problems awaiting his own theory of theories and its own meta-use of 'language' and 'meaning'. He is reflective enough to try to avoid the impact that those reflexive terms have for his own concepts (is the meaning of 'meaning' and 'radial' also radial?). Any relational theory such as this is threatened by self-contradiction or regress. Where Anderson extended the cognitive mind outward, even whilst retaining certain tenets of representationalism in order to save his position from relativism, Branigan must, in the end, also cordon off *his* language, lest he follow Wittgenstein all the way into mystical silence (and throw away the linguistic ladder both use). Also like Anderson, Branigan's use of cognitive science is one way in which certain language games, and the forms of life inherent to them, are given special status over others, to wit, the language and life of science. This is certainly how Tomas Kemper sees the matter in his review of Branigan's work: despite the pluralism at the heart of his position, writes Kemper, Branigan steers clear of any attendant relativism by privileging scientific discourse as one that transcends all forms of life.[25] But, as Kemper also admits, this does not rest easily within a position supposedly espousing Wittgensteinian credentials: there is a manifest tension between Branigan's embodied cognitivism and his use of language games.[26]

On the last page of *Projecting a Camera*, Branigan says that 'one must choose a theoretical language-game in which to make moves'. He then adds, 'or, perhaps, the initial question should be, which films are important to us?'[27] And this is indeed the crux of the matter. Which comes first? Are our choices of film based on theory, or are our theories based on the films that we see? Worst of all, perhaps, is the unavoidable circle between film and theory that makes this question unanswerable. The question for us, however, is whether this circle is such a bad thing. After all, what Branigan dubs a 'vacuous theory', that is self-fulfilling on account of the extensive emptiness of its formula, Wittgenstein would simply call the truth of tautology, for all certainly true theories are circular in form, going from axiom to example back to axiom in self-fulfilling vindication. Can't this also be true of a theory of theories like Branigan's?

Of course, the answer to *this* question also invokes a regress (the truth it asks after can only *purport* to be non-circular), but it may be one we can embrace in preference over a self-refuting relativism. The problem with the linguistic approach is that, while it alerts us to the nuances of contextual usage in others, it cannot do so for itself. *Its* context must be objectified. Indeed, it is this objectification or immobilization of context that allows any one theory to represent all the others. But if too much goes through the medium of language in Branigan's approach, then one alternative means of sidestepping relativism (without resorting to scientific authority) would be to anchor our leaky, 'radial' or polysemous descriptions within instances of other larger processes, namely, the very circles that film, along with the words about it, inscribe. In other words, the processes of theory-film infusion, the processes of immobilization (or context 'framing' as Branigan puts it), have a temporality to be explored that is neither objective nor subjective, neither realist nor relativist, and neither epistemological nor ontological. In fact, Branigan himself acknowledges that the one proper question that he has not asked in his study is '*when* does a camera come to exist *under descriptions that we offer* of the functioning of the text?' When undertaking an analysis of time in the cinema, however, the even more fundamental question, according to Branigan, remains this: 'when is time?'[28] It will be with some audacity, then, that the rest of our study will attempt to answer this question of cinematic time, beginning with the concept of the film event itself.

When is a film? The cinematic event

When is a film a film? This could be taken as a question concerning metaphysical identity ('when does A = A?') as well as a question in traditional aesthetics concerning the (post-production) *performance* of film. Of course, film is not one of the performing arts (though it contains aspects of many of them), and so its performative dimension is less obvious. Yet, the mechanical means of cinematic exhibition is, on the one hand, so complex and multifaceted and, on the other, so obviously temporal, that the issue of performance remains a real one for it. Admittedly, there are standards of projection that can be met (by and large) in some circumstances: film is certainly mechanical ('automatic' in Cavell's sense) and so like an artwork whose formal reproduction is somewhat standardized at 'zero degree performance'.[29] Projection is only one part of the story, though. Film is also psychological – at base, a phenomenon of apparent motion – and while this makes it determinable on certain psychological levels (its reception being partly 'hard-wired'), it makes it less so on others. How we consume film mechanically and psychologically is also part of the film's performative identity, be it in the cinema or on television (and whether on a 14-inch portable TV or a 60-inch wide-screen home cinema), alone or in a large group, continuously or interruptedly, and so on. Cinema is also a narrative art and so open to other vagaries of psychological consumption, some more cultural than others (comprehensions of realism, perceptions of progress, and so forth). So the question of film's own identity – 'when is a film *the same* film?' – must be answered with reference to mechanical, psychological and cultural processes that themselves intertwine, possessing only 'indefinite boundaries' between them (as Edward Branigan might say). The performed film is both an objective apparatus, or 'automatic projection', *and* a subjective phenomenon through its appearance to, and interference from, the spectator.

A number of scholars have raised the question of the 'cinema event' with most, though not all, taking a Deleuzian perspective heavily indebted to his concept of the time-image.[30] One of the exceptions is Rick Altman. When introducing his conception, he complains that too often 'critics have fastened on the film itself as cinema's common factor'.[31] By now, this notion will be familiar to us given the number of philosophers we have heard arguing for and against the primacy of 'the film' as (textual) object over the other variables of production, distribution and consumption. In order to show what he means, Altman provides two diagrams, one depicting the film-text as the focal point, the other giving equal space to all its other dimensions (see Figures 6.1 and 6.2).

The description that comes with the diagrams runs as follows:

> In opposition to the notion of film as text, I have found it helpful to conceive of cinema as event. Viewed as a macro-event, cinema is still seen as centered on the individual film, but according to a new type of geometry. Floating in a gravity-free world like doughnut-shaped spaceships, cinema events offer no clean-cut or stable separation between inside and outside or top and bottom. In this three-dimensional Moebius strip world, the textual center is no longer the focal point of a series of concentric rings. Instead, like the pinhole at the center of an hourglass, it serves as a point of interchange between two 'V' shapes, one representing the work of production, the other figuring the process of reception. Beginning as a subset of culture at large, one 'V' progressively narrows as the work of film production runs its course, first broadly, with diverse ideas and

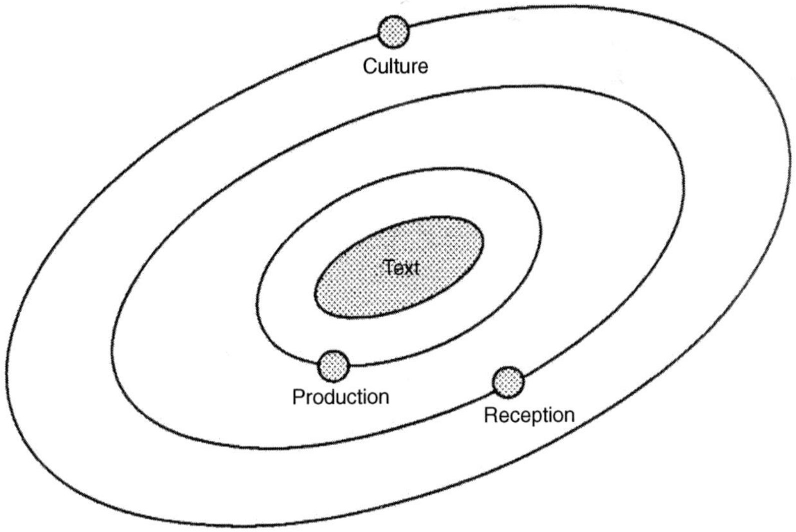

Figure 6.1 The Text-Centered Universe of Traditional Film Studies

Source: Altman 1992.

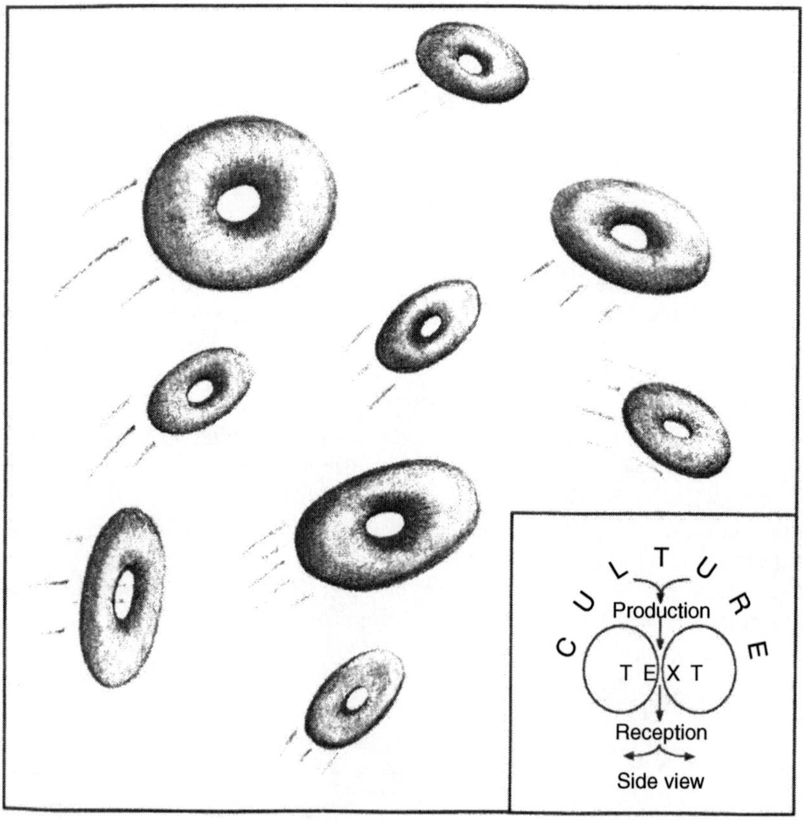

Figure 6.2 The Geometry of Cinema Events
Source: Altman 1992.

> scripts, sets and rushes, technicians and rewrites, until eventually the work of production has been resolved into a single narrow product: the text. The process of reception then broadens out again, eventually reaching the point where it is indistinguishable from culture in general. In a gravity free world, however, this hourglass system is entirely reversible. Just as production flows through the text toward reception, so reception regularly influences production.[32]

In this event-full rendering of cinema, 'the film' is demoted from centre stage to a centre of exchange between cultural reception and material production, less like Branigan's 'indefinite boundary' and more like a black hole: it is insubstantial in itself, but given an observable shape nonetheless on account of how other forces gravitate towards and away from it. *The* film becomes an illusion, but one with real effects on real forces. We will return to Altman's diagrams later, once we have looked some more at what others have to say about films and their events.

This is no easy task, for the philosophy of the Event (or events) has a complex genealogy. Even its name (singular or plural) does not go uncontested for meaning. Its many facets have origins in analytic philosophy (particularly Elizabeth Anscombe's and Donald Davidson's theories of actions and 'events'), in the process philosophies of Bergson, James and Whitehead, and in the ontologies of the 'Event' forwarded, amongst others, by Heidegger, Deleuze, Lyotard and Badiou. Amid the Continental figures cited here, the question of greatest importance is whether or not events are ontologically dependent on substantial beings, or, conversely, whether or not beings are dependent on events. To paraphrase Whitehead, it is a matter of whether we should prioritize the 'being of becoming' or the 'becoming of being'. Also at issue is whether events are objective or subjective, mental or non-mental; are they individuated by their causes, their effects or their spatio-temporal location (past, present or future, here or elsewhere); are they empirical or non-empirical, actual or virtual, singular or plural, historical or natural, perceptible or imperceptible, finite or infinite, pure or impure? Or are they all of these things 'at once'?

One simple way into the discussion is to look at the nature of the (cinematic) event in terms of its speeds and scales (or thresholds). How *fast* is an event anyway? *When* does it occur? The question of speed then leads to another question: are all events perceptible, at least in principle, or is it possible to miss an event? And then comes the deluge: are there any minima and maxima to an event; can some be too fast or too slow to be perceived; have they anything to do with the speeds of history or the even more extreme speeds of nature? In Alain Badiou's case, for example, events are only ever historical, easily missed, and so consequently rare (*nature* has no events). The Badiouian event concerns what he calls 'trans-being', by which he means the radically new and unpredicted moment that ruptures a 'situation' or status quo, be it in art, politics, science or love (the only four realms in which events can occur for him).[33] The 'Event' is change of heroic and historical proportions (revolutions in art, science and politics being his most cited examples). That is why events are rare and frequently overlooked. But they have a peculiar temporality. An event is what will *come to be*, it always exists in the future anterior, never in the present. Oddly enough, then, the event must be atemporal or, rather, it does not *proceed*.[34] If the event did proceed, then it would need another series of meta-events in which to periodize its progress, leading us into a regress. To enquire into the speed of an event is erroneous. The event for Badiou is neither temporal nor atemporal but the 'interruption' of 'a time ... of the situation'.[35]

For Deleuze, on the contrary, events are numerous and natural, yet also imperceptible. In *Cinema 2*, Deleuze cites Nietzsche rejecting the idea of 'great resounding events', for there is something 'peasant in history'.[36] There can be greatness in an unseen moment, neither heroic nor historical per se (both of these simply being the gathering together of moments by biological *and* social captures), but instances of vital change that underlie such 'molar' historical forms. Deleuze's events are ubiquitous in nature, following Cartier-Bresson's adage that there is nothing in this world that does not have a decisive moment. In Deleuze's *The Logic of Sense*, for instance, we get an image of the event as an incorporeal transformation that gathers up everyday objects and individuals for its own purpose:

> It would be necessary for the individual to grasp herself as event; and that she grasp the event actualised within her as another individual grafted onto her. In this case, she would not understand, want, or represent this event without also understanding and wanting all other events as individuals, and without representing all other individuals as events.[37]

A genuine event doesn't happen *to* someone (appearing to come *discretely* to me), but in and through someone (that makes me *part* of the event). Yet, what is the event in itself? Deleuze writes: 'I've tried in all my books to discover the nature of events; it's a philosophical concept, the only one capable of ousting the verb "to be"'. Event as becoming contra being. Yet for Deleuze, the event is understood in terms of multiplicity rather than process: the 'original time' in his *Proust and Signs* (seen in both the involuntary image of eternity and the actual eternity affirmed in art); the 'crystal-image' of time in *Cinema 2*; the 'pure and empty form of time' (*Aion*) or third synthesis of eternal return in *Difference and Repetition*; and the '*eventum tantum*' in *The Logic of Sense* – in each case there is a de-temporalization of time.[38] Why? For the same reason that Badiou gave. Time must be contained in eternity. *Difference and Repetition* talks of the paradox of the present as the need for an atemporal time in which to constitute or synthesize processual time (as the succession of past, present and future): '*there must be another time in which the first synthesis of time can occur*'.[39] And this time cannot be another form of *succession* (lest we instigate a regress) – it must be empty, the time of eternity. Ultimately, it is the Event. So, when does an event occur? Answer, *it* (a static entity) could never *occur* (a process): to change is to stop being:

> The agonizing aspect of the pure event is that it is always and at the same something which has just happened and something about to happen; never something which is happening ... it is the present as being of reason which is subdivided *ad infinitum* into something that has just happened or is going to happen, always flying in both directions at once.[40]

We keep missing the event. Or rather, the event is in this constant missing, about to happen or having happened, but never happening. Take Julio Medem's *Lovers of the Arctic Circle*, a film all about missed identities and encounters. Not only do we have different actors playing the characters of Otto and Ana (a tactic of diffusion already used by Luis Buñuel in *That Obscure Object of Desire* (1977)), but their names are palindromes – moving backwards and forwards, no less than time itself does in this film. The same occurrences are populated by different characters-actors, a case in point being the line 'it's the midnight sun' (above the Arctic Circle), which is spoken twice by different characters in different scenes communicating between two remote points in the film. There are also events – a chase through a forest/park, a fall through trees into snow, near-miss collisions – that repeat across the film, populating themselves with different individuals and settings each time they are 'actualized'. Finally, there are the numerous coincidences throughout that are not psychological premonitions (of the stag, for instance) but actual coexistences of different times gathered together by the same resonating names ('Otto the Piloto') and events (collisions, falls) where things and people don't *co-incide*.

This is the Deleuzian event: above the Arctic Circle the sun never sets – a very Platonic idea evoking both the constancy of the atemporal event as well as the *circulation* of actions and individuals it keeps in play. But, and this is the crucial point, the series of repetitions is kept going by *non-coincidence*. These two lovers keep missing each other, even on their first night of love. At the story's end as well, when Ana does meet her bus in a fatal collision, this one consummated act also stops her from meeting with Otto. Yet, it is such constant errancy and deflection in their lives that sustains their love (and the movie). Their evental difference resonates through all of the other moments, missed encounters, the belated mourning and near-deaths. Perhaps it is too easy to read this film's narrative in terms of Deleuzian events.[41] We have certainly closed off an equally possible Lacanian reading, and others too.[42] For now, though, it can usefully illustrate Deleuze's idea that natural events can be seen in everyday happenings.

Nothing happening: events in the blink of an eye

The disparity between Badiou and Deleuze – events in history versus events in nature – partly explains why film events seem so relative. As we discussed in the last chapter, 'eventhood' in cinema – whether a moment appears event-full or not – is not an intrinsic feature but a relational one. Hence, action films will appear as uneventful to some ('highbrow') tastes, with nothing appearing to happen except for more explosions, more car chases, and so on, while art films will seem wholly uneventful to the average adolescent male viewer (at least according to Hollywood's marketing strategies). Take the following claim from Jacques Rancière:

> Tragedy, Aristotle says, must have a beginning, middle, and an end... Meanwhile, for all those who'd rather have done with anything,

> providence invented television and the serial, both of which can last as long as the world: all they need to do is announce that tomorrow, like today, nothing will happen either.[43]

But when does 'nothing' ever happen (outside of a *ganzfield*, which will only render one unconscious)? The screenwriter and chief theorist behind Italian neo-realism, Cesare Zavattini, once declared that 'the ideal film would be 90 minutes in the life of a man to whom nothing happens'. But nothing *never* does happen, for that is just in the nature of *happening*, or time. Of course, the mostly uneventful life of the old man in Vittoria de Sica's *Umberto D.* (1952), for instance, might *once* have seemed to approach that objective in its everyday ordinariness (and no doubt still attains it for some younger spectators), but its melodrama is consequently to be found in the accumulation of microtragedies over 84 minutes, for those patient enough to await them. The event appears with time. Even less eventful might be Chantal Akerman's *Jeanne Dielman, 23 Quai du Commerce, 1080 Bruxelles* (1976), which has very little on show in its 201 minutes of a woman silently going about her daily tasks (including a five-minute coffee-making scene); or *A Sunday in Hell* (1976), a 110-minute cycling documentary that for many would be the very definition of hell to watch (like watching cycling itself perhaps). To these spectators, nothing seems to happen, or, rather, nothing happens to these spectators.

Why do some people tire more easily than others before some films (or TV serials) and not others? Length does not seem to be important (the most popular films of all time, *Gone with the Wind* (1939) and *Titanic* are both much longer than the average Hollywood fare).[44] It is the units of meaning and so the breadth of perspective that surely counts here. Mere quantitative changes in the parts (daily episodes in a TV serial, the daily routines of an old man or young woman, or in a day-long bike race) can be seen by those who *endure* them as qualitative changes in the whole (even a slight change in the peloton can mean everything). But one must be patient to see the parts accumulate. This is not to say that there is *one* ideal, and very patient, spectator for every film, for it is always possible to watch for longer, watch more often, or watch more closely. *Rather, there are different films that emerge with different types of spectatorship, and different types of spectator that emerge with different films.* And this all happens in the event(s) of viewing.

To turn to the seemingly motionless cinema of Béla Tarr, for a moment, his seven-and-a-half-hour-long *Sátántangó* could well be seen as *the* consummate European art film for its impression of unrelenting slowness. Its 450-minute duration is comprised of prolonged takes (up to 11 minutes long) where no action can be seen as too uneventful to be given a complete rendition (from washing to counting money, from decanting fruit brandy to getting dressed). For the cineaste, naturally, there is a lot to reflect upon here – meditations on the slow zoom, tracking shot, sequence shot or still camera.[45] The less that happens in the 'frame', the more that the camera frames' own movement must portend, in what Bordwell would call our search for meaning (following Godard's cinephilic statement that a tracking shot is a 'moral issue'). Furthermore, at a more basic level than morals, other fine-grained effects of the film slowly dawn on the viewer. Everything does take *its* time – packing to leave, a walk to the bar, an evening of dance, or whatever else. At first, this temporal 'realism' comes across as mannered, artful and sometimes even entertaining for being so *actually* continuous. Eventually, though, this viewer (at least) came to *feel* these prolonged durations less and less. 'We' can get used to the film's time (if we have the patience to wait). Indeed, for a while after watching *Sátántangó*, the world beyond the film seems to move too quickly. So the question of cinematic time, the time of film, may be less about events *simpliciter*, so much as what is happening in us when we *start* to perceive happenings in other things. What we deem to be an event takes its own time to appear to us, so that this question above all remains: why does the event emerge from the imperceptible to the perceptible?

According to Deleuze, the connection between perceptibility and the event is further complicated by the latter's relationship with movement. This is what Deleuze (and Guattari) write in *A Thousand Plateaus*:

> Movement has an essential relation to the imperceptible; it is by nature imperceptible. Perception can grasp movement only as the displacement of a moving body or the development of a form. Movements, becomings, in other words, pure relations of speed and slowness, pure affects, are below and above the threshold of perception. Doubtless, thresholds of perception are *relative*; there is always a threshold capable of grasping what eludes another: the eagle's eye... But the adequate threshold can in turn operate only as a function of a perceptible form and a perceived, discerned subject. So that movement in itself *continues to occur elsewhere*: if we serialize perception, the movement always takes place above the maximum threshold and below the minimum threshold, in expanding or contracting intervals (microintervals). Like the huge Japanese wrestlers whose advance is too slow and whose holds are too fast to see, so that what embraces are less wrestlers than the infinite slowness of the wait (what is going to happen?) and the infinite speed of the result (what happened?). What we must do is reach the photographic or cinematic threshold.[46]

Let's look more closely at this relativism of movement. Deleuze also writes that 'movement also "must" be perceived, it cannot but be perceived, the imperceptible is also the *percipiendum*. There is no contradiction in this. If movement is imperceptible *by nature*, it is so in relation to a given threshold of perception, which is by nature relative'. So, on the one hand, there is the relativity of movement to *perception*; on the other, its 'pure' or absolute relation to an *elsewhere*, the idea that pure movement, an event, 'continues to occur elsewhere'. But why must it be elsewhere? Or rather, if it is always 'elsewhere', how did it get to be there, who put it there, and how is it possible for us, *eventually*, to perceive it there? Deleuze's own answer is to say that it is by 'jumping' or leaping between thresholds of perception, between different planes. By this leaping, he writes, 'what cannot be perceived on one [plane] cannot but be perceived on the other... the imperceptible becomes necessarily perceived'.[47]

I hope that the connection between this notion of threshold and the problem of perceiving film events is evident: what leaps must we make in order to see when a *film itself happens*? What are these thresholds or planes? And what examples can we use to make sense of them? Deleuze mentions the sumo wrestler whose advance is too slow and whose holds are too fast to be perceived. But he also mentions *absolute* movements that can be seen at the cinematic threshold of perception, the central case for our purposes. The question of perceptibility, then, can be posed in terms of speeds and thresholds: *where* do these thresholds of perception themselves come from? Are they natural, cultural or metaphysical in origin?

And here is where we return to Bergson. For him, there can be no atemporal 'pure' event: there are only layers or strata of processes, of other times and the times of others. And these other times are with us right here, though we are often unable to see them. They seem to be 'elsewhere' because they are *suppressed*, bodily and mentally, from our vision. Only some processes are recognized by us, namely the ones we are able to perceive, ones that we subsequently 'fabulate' or narrate as events that have meaning *for us*. Crucial to Bergson's theory of time is the exploitation of others' temporal processes, ones that we must de-temporalize in order to make our lives (and processes) eventful. These others, at base, include the material and natural world. In what is both a metaphysical and a biological act of ostracism, the appearance of our vital, moving freedom is bought at the expense of others being made to seem immobile and determined. In 1922 Bergson wrote that 'all the categories of perception... correspond, on the whole, to the choice of a certain *order of size* for condensation'. A category of perception, or threshold, is an act of 'condensation'. The world we see is the level of existence we choose to condense or contain in an act of perception – a 'choice' that is relatively hard-wired into our species-being. This act of condensation is also an act of containment, where an indeterminate realm is transformed under our gaze into a determinate one: 'the activity of the living being leans upon and is measured by the necessity supporting things, by a condensation of their duration'.[48] We live in an actual multiverse of coexisting, different temporalities, but we can only perceive the one 'block' universe that coincides with our time; indeed, perception just is this selective, narrowing of vision. And only unexpected forces can extend it to offer a glimpse of what lies beyond.

Bergson's point is that each plane of living reality has to treat the other planes of existence surrounding it *as* relatively inert in order to support its own vitality. Our time, our vitality, our events, our history in other words, are formed through an act of exclusion – what produces by contrast the uneventful, the natural, the invisible and the imperceptible. The actuality of others' events is not an 'elsewhere' or 'virtual' awaiting actualization *for them*: they are only virtual *for us* – as the ghosts that appear to us and to whom we appear as ghosts (in Alejandro Amenábar's *The Others* (2001)). In the earlier quotation from *A Thousand Plateaus* Deleuze mentioned the 'cinematic threshold' as a place where we can perceive the imperceptible. Let us remind ourselves what Bergson says of the cinematic apparatus in this regard:

> This is what the cinematograph does. With photographs...it reconstitutes the mobility...It is true that if we had to do with photographs alone, however much we might look at them, we should never see them animated: with immobility set beside immobility, even endlessly, we could never make movement. In order that the pictures may be animated, there must be movement somewhere. *The movement does indeed exist here; it is in the apparatus.*[49]

The cinematic illusion is in truth a variant of normal perception, which also composes apparent movement from immobile sections. But its composition of 'here' is also a suppression of an 'elsewhere'. Cinema thus captures the essence of perception as *suppression* – yet it suppresses movement *here* in favour of seeing apparent movement elsewhere. The actual movement of the apparatus is suppressed in favour of the virtual movement (or event) of the image. The reason why Deleuze ignores the apparatus in favour of the film image, we recall, is because he wants to show cinema transcending its limitations through imagery rather than technology. But Deleuze also renders a certain kind of movement imperceptible by ignoring the apparatus.[50] Of course, this is voluntary on his part; but, nonetheless, it is an extension of the type of suppressions found in cinema and perception. In other words, Deleuze's theory, like cinema itself, is modelled on the essence of perception as suppression. It is this enforced imperceptibility, this economy of attention, that we can demonstrate now with two examples, one taken from film, another from a TV serial. In both their narrative content and their cinematic form, they thematize what may be happening when we look at other films: the ways in which movements and events can often be missed, either by being too slow or too fast. They also show the way in which we can either be sped up or slowed down when patiently watching a film that is initially too slow or too fast for us, or, equally, how we can ignore and suppress that temporality.

Bringing us up and down to speed

Penny Marshall's *Awakenings* (1990) is based on the neurologist Oliver Sacks's memoir of the same name. It tells the story of a doctor (Sacks, fictionalized as 'Malcolm Sayer' and played by Robin Williams) who, in 1969, discovers the beneficial effects of the then new drug L-Dopa. He applies it to a group of catatonic patients who survived the epidemic of *encephalitis lethargica* between 1917 and 1928, though not without some after-effects. For the 40 years since their initial illness, these patients had remained in hospital, mostly abandoned and forgotten about, resting motionless in its most obscure corners. One of the original doctors from the 1920s describes their situation to Sayer thus: 'people who were normal were, now... elsewhere'. After medication with L-Dopa, however, the patients are successfully 'awoken' from decades of being in an immobile, 'ghostly' state, only for Sayer to learn eventually that he cannot stop them from returning once again to that state, no matter how much he increases the dosage. Significantly, Sayer records everything on film throughout the course of these experiments.

The first half of the story shows Sayer trying to read these others, these immobile statues, *without* the intervention of drugs – to become like them, enter into their rhythm, if only by throwing a ball to them, placing a card down on the table before them, playing them music, calling their name, walking with them, or imagining their thoughts. And he puts all of this on film. The second half of the movie, however, concerns making *them* move like Sayer (and 'us') through the use of this drug therapy – accelerating them to our speed. This is their awakening. Yet, we also learn that their supposed near-static lethargy may actually be the product of an even greater speed than ours (Parkinsonian-like shaking so accelerated and condensed that it appears to the less mobile ('us') to be a form of stasis). These people can also be regarded as living motions, therefore, though moving at a rate so fast that they seem statuesque *to us*.

And the imperceptibility to us of these patients' own movements is, in fact, cinematic, one that awaits our patience too. This variability of speed is not just seen in the film's narrative but also in its form. The body language of the actors throughout is notable, especially Williams's physical performance, with numerous tremors and ticks of his own. His star persona also expresses this trembling movement: the limited range of an actor stuck in his socially inept adolescence, in the 1970s, in *Mork and Mindy*, is perfectly appropriate. More broadly still, the film, indeed *film itself*, equally embodies what these so-called statutes really are – movement too fast to be seen in its true light (the flickering celluloid frames of the apparatus).[51] We see the patients objectified (immobilized) in a uniquely cinematic manner, not only through being filmed and projected as spectacles throughout the story, but also by having their own temporality condensed and suppressed by film as such. In a small but interesting scene, we encounter one of the patients staring at a TV set whose image is rolling. This is before the cure has been applied. An orderly appears and fixes the horizontal hold on the TV, slowing it down to a perceptible level. Yet, at this, the patient lowers his eyes in disinterest, only to return them once again after the orderly has restored the TV image to its original, rolling state. The TV serial only interested him at *his* speed.

Where *Awakenings* involves the speeding up of others to match our pace (an acceleration that may actually have been a slowing down), the TV episode from *Star Trek* entitled 'Wink of an Eye' involves our lives being sped up to match a different one alongside us. In this episode from season three (1969), the USS *Enterprise* responds to a distress call from the planet Scalos. The video-call shows several Scalosians asking for assistance. Arriving on Scalos, however, Captain Kirk and his landing party find only an empty city, with no life forms registering on their 'tricorder scans'. And yet the Scalosians really are there, on the planet with them. The truth slowly revealed is that the Scalosians live at a different speed but in the same place: they are visually imperceptible, moving from place to place in the wink of our eye.[52]

Throughout this adventure, Kirk and his crew are challenged by the apparent *illogic* of spatial coexistence – how can they (his landing party and the Scalosians) both be and not be together on the same planet? Kirk constantly demands the 'exact location' of the Scalosians. When the Scalosians finally 'invade' the *Enterprise*, seemingly to take it over, Kirk naturally orders its return, not realizing that 'it', the *Enterprise*, now has at least two lives, one inhabited by Kirk and his crew, the other by the Scalosians. There need be no stand-off, there are no enemies: coexistence in different times is possible. Indeed, Deela, the Queen of the Scalosians, has only come aboard the *Enterprise* in order to seduce Kirk into being her consort.[53] To do this, though, she must accelerate his life to her speed by spiking his coffee. Drugs again.

The accelerated lives shown in *Awakenings* (so fast that they stand still for us) and 'Wink of an Eye' (so fast that they cross the threshold of visibility to us), each pertain to the phenomenon of apparent motion – and so to the cinematic apparatus itself. When movement at 24 frames a second is fast enough to become invisible to us, it also becomes a different movement elsewhere, a solid that moves (bodies across the screen). It is the first movement that Deleuze ignores (and that Bergson prioritizes) in favour of the second moving image. But the lesson we can take from their differences over where true movement takes place remains: cinema, like all perception (and not just 'normal' perception), condenses time, contracts events – others' events. But what is done to the apparatus *can* also be done to the image too, for isn't the slowness (to some) of an 'art-film', or of a TV serial (to others), a product of our impatience, our need to accelerate their lives and introduce into them events we would recognize as such?[54]

Deleuze writes that 'movement always happens behind the thinker's back, or in the moment when he blinks'.[55] This is more true than we might imagine, for there are thresholds crossed even in 'normal' perception where people cannot see or understand motion – they only perceive objects at rest. This is not catatonia they suffer from but akinetopsia (the inability to perceive motion), for it is everything *else* that appears to *them* as catatonic, as immobile. And it is quite a normal pathology: indeed, according to Bergson, vis-à-vis our concentration of the duration of matter into an immobile, it is what we all suffer from selectively – a form of 'change blindness'.[56] Those suffering from akinetopsia, however, are no longer merely selective in where they see change – they cannot see it anywhere. These are individuals who are living the ideas of Parmenides rather than thinking them (as we can only do).[57]

Take the recent *Bourne* (2002–07) series of films. They are widely recognized as having popularized a hyperkinetic form of film-making (involving much hand-held camera work, elliptical editing and extremely rapid narration) that has proven very successful with its target audiences. But some in the audience do not follow them, literally. Here is Richard Corliss on Paul Greengrass's *The Bourne Ultimatum* (2007). Though he admires its 'kinetic perfection', he says,

> it's in those rare moments when the movie slows down, as it does for plot-requisite conversations at the beginning and the end, that *The Bourne Ultimatum* seems empty and ill-used, like an interrogation room after a waterboarding. Greengrass cuts each action scene into agitated bits; but he can't let fast enough alone. Could he please explain why, in the chat scenes, the camera is afflicted with Parkinson's? The film frame trembles, obscures the speaker with the listener's shoulder, annoys viewers and distracts them from the content of the scene. It surely interrupted my enjoyment of the movie; for a minute I wanted to give it a good spanking.[58]

Corliss doesn't follow the film's timing, but, despite his advanced age, I suspect that if he gave the film some time it would dawn on him eventually. Or rather, given enough time, it will change him automatically in any case. When I first saw Lars Von Trier's *Breaking The Waves* (1996), I found its agitated, hand-held camera work distracting from the story. It was too fussy. Now, after more than ten intervening years of pop videos, TV commercials and a host of other films using this technique and others like it (the latest extreme being *Cloverfield* in 2008), I don't notice it at all. Indeed, the technique not only doesn't stop me following a story any more, for me it has actually become a part of it. It almost seems as if something in me has become part of its time, an accelerated viewer, no less than my watching *Sátántangó* drew forth an effort in the reverse direction of slowing down.[59] We may be 'slow beings' as Deleuze said, but our temporality can be altered in many ways.[60]

And this may be where we also find other kinds of art – at thresholds we normally disregard. The art of *Bourne* lies not in its clichéd, patriarchal script, but in *how* it turns that story into a film. As a film of any note to film theorists, it will date very quickly no doubt; but that is because its work, its art, is achieved at a corporeal level. There are short-lived yet artful experiences that rapidly become invisible after their first appearance. They obviously fail the 'test of time' criterion for art, yet this is due to theirs being a different time and a different test: a deep reconfiguration of our viewing thresholds. Their eventhood is short and visceral, but still an event, only one for our bodies as they remould our viewing habits. This is not a cultural thesis concerning 'ways of looking', but an agency at the indefinite boundary between the artificial poles of nature and culture. The orthodox notion of an artful event with content that is discernible, sayable and ultimately intellectual is doubtless all the more 'lasting' as a consequence (though it may have other contents that run quicker, that work bodily and evanescently). But it is only 'lasting' inasmuch as there are other cognitive records to sustain that content (conversations, reviews, interviews, books).[61] In other words, what most *clearly* lasts, exists on a plane of duration close to intellect, indeed that matches the clarity and speed of intellect.[62] Those other, short-lived but deeply felt, non-cognitive events, as found in *Breaking the Waves* or *Bourne*, 'last' in a different way – corporeally and invisibly.

Where Godard is said to have rethought the way conversations can be shot (say, in *Vivre sa vie*), the *Bourne* films can be said to rethink or 'refeel' the way assassinations, pickpocketing, car chases and even shootings can be shot, especially in terms of speed (just as the films of John Woo, Sergio Leone and Albert Broccoli had done before them). As Barry Salt's cinemetric approach to measuring long-term changes in cinema has shown, Hollywood films have become increasingly breathless over time, the average shot length for the *Bourne Supremacy* (2004) being 2.4 seconds, whereas that for the average 1940s film is between 9 and 10 seconds.[63] However, it is a breathlessness that we can eventually get used to, even when it occurs in sudden, large doses.

So far, so Deleuzian, one might say. Granted. Yet, the *Bourne* series introduces its brain-level innovations within traditional story morales that would have been condemned by Deleuze *on that account*. This shows that Deleuze too can be distracted by the script, by the force of 'narrative', and also a certain moralism of his own. That is why he condemns commercial films: not because they cannot innovate (he admits that they can and do), but because they continue to innovate inside the wrong stories, inside 'the demands of capitalism'.[64] But if we don't buy into Deleuze's moral that commercial art is inherently uncreative, then there need be no shame in being 'lowbrow' and ephemeral. *Some things are just not meant to last*, namely the *new*, which can only be consciously experienced fleetingly, but which lasts all the more thereafter. And the new can neither be represented directly nor recalled indirectly, but, as we'll discuss later, only ever felt.

The cultural relativist says that everything can be art, that everything lasts the same or would last the same were it not for power, were it not that some audiences' tastes have more power than others. But it may be truer to say that 'lasting' comes in different types, intellectual and bodily, because time itself is multiple: everything has *its* moment, every dog has *its* day (which need not be 24-hours long). Would this explain why computer-generated imagery (CGI) films, like horror films, like action films, and even like films that attract us with new, corporeal standards of acting 'realism' (from Marlon Brando to Daniel Day-Lewis), only work when *new*, only affect us *as* new? Is this why they can only convince us consciously of their value for a time – the period when they are retuning what 'realities' our perception can see: the truth of dinosaurs, monstrous violence, car chases and 'real' human behaviour? In Chapter 8 I will look at the refractive processes of time that explain why such fast art must also date quickly, coming and going at its own speed.

Bourne is better than its storyline. Yet, films tell stories that can *filmically* exceed and improve on the mediocre conceits of their scripts all the time. Michel Gondry's *Eternal Sunshine of the Spotless Mind* (2004), for example, outruns its own pedestrian concept of eternal return as posited in the original shooting script (whose conclusion has Joel and Clementine repeating their on/off relationship for all eternity). The 'how' of its production, however, subverted the original, simpler 'Idea' by not showing this ending. The 'how' is the real 'what' in film. In script or propositional terms, of course, it makes little difference whether the repetition is shown to be eternal (Joel and Clementine going round and round again) or just a one-off.[65] But it does make a difference that the film doesn't show this eternal repetition; it ends with them choosing just once to try again at having a relationship. And this display, this filmic storytelling, offers a very different affective thinking for the audience, for to *see* this one-off and so poignant choice repeated *ad nauseum* would have rendered it comically mechanical. Implementation – the how, or context, or medium – is *also* a message, because film is more than its Idea. The *'cinéma de papa'* of the 1950s, so despised by the New Wave for its 'quality' (no less than the *'cinéma du look'* of the 1980s was despised for its surface beauty), was trivial in many ways; but for every lazy narrative commonplace it repeated, interesting points of innovation escaped that also gradually rewired our sensibility towards editing, colour, acting style, set design and music. It is as a consequence of *this* that we can see that the French cinema of the 1950s is not like it was in the 1940s, that *something* has happened, even if we cannot clearly say why or point to one film as the source of it all. The absence of an 'auteur's' hand should take away little, unless one is committed to thinking that what wasn't put there intentionally and by one person doesn't count at all.

In his discussion of the cinema event, Rick Altman concludes that it is 'constituted by a continuing interchange, neither beginning nor ending at any specific point', so that 'what we refer to as "the film" is fundamentally unstable in nature'.[66] There is no art object. Film is a set of processes that are multiple and varied, natural and cultural. And these processes must also include our engagement with film (at more than simply an informational level); they must involve the temporalities of our mind and our body, living and concrete processes. From what we have observed so far of this engagement, it would appear that there are movements that we see, the events we recognize, as well as movements that we do not see, the processes to which we are blind. More now needs to said about the nature of this temporal engagement, especially concerning how *it too* changes, how the way we view film changes. If this is a relational phenomena, how can *it itself* form an identity that can change, how do we learn to see films in their own manner of time – or, rather, how do they teach us this time? More importantly still, we might also begin to wonder whether the lessons learnt from film might not be its way of making us think.

7
Fabulation, Process and Event

What century do we ourselves live in to derive so much pleasure – our Deleuzes in our pockets – from the love affair upon a sinking ship between a young woman in first class and a young man in third?[1]

Jacques Rancière's *Film Fables*

Jacques Rancière's *La Fable cinématographique* was published in Paris in 2001 and translated into English as *Film Fables* in 2006. It appeared, therefore, in the century *after* the one that seemed to belong so entirely to cinema. So the time of the question cited in this chapter's epigraph, cinema's time and the cinematic century, would appear to be already over. But the question, taken out of context and placed in another, still persists – what is cinema's time? In this chapter I hope to outline, even further, the temporality of cinema as its most essential, albeit indefinite, feature. For, far from the time of cinema providing us with one more discrete set of properties that might count as an explanation of what cinema is, à la Deleuze's time-image, the meaning of cinematic time is indefinite or differential: cinema has only an inessential essence, an insubstantial substance, and its processes are revealed through the manner in which the various theories of 'what film is' must fail as a result. However, their individual failures do collectively approach something like success by providing an outline of cinema, a moving sketch with no interior volume.

Rancière takes advantage of coming after so many other theorists by being highly aware of the possible pitfalls awaiting any philosophy of film. We must be 'careful to distinguish', he tells us, between what 'someone may tell us about the film and what the film shows', for 'any theory' is first and foremost 'an assemblage of words...and reality, is first and foremost, an assemblage of images'. Unlike all the other philosophers we have looked at, Rancière writes 'first and foremost' as an art theorist (rather than as a metaphysician, or linguistic philosopher, or Lacanian), and perhaps that adds to his advantage too. His concept of the different 'distributions of the sensible' amongst distinct regimes of art (pre-eminently, the 'representational' and the 'aesthetic') is meticulous in keeping the war of words, the dissonance between types of word and types of image, close to hand. Indeed, the categories of narrative within classical aesthetics are subverted by cinema. In the context of *Film Fables*, consequently, Aristotle's *muthos* is understood as 'fable or fiction' rather than as myth, thereby multiplying the types of word or narrative with which we can theorize.[2] As Tom Conley puts it:

> The fable or narration belonging to Aristotelian poetics is undone by the art of the camera, but the camera cannot fail to let its gaze concatenate the many sensations and impressions it brings forward, thus also belonging to the narrative arts.[3]

The film's 'fable' is more than its script taken in opposition to its images, for the problem of 'the cinematographic fable' is exactly the problem of 'the relationship between cinema and the appearances it creates'. The art of cinema involves a fabulation of images, a narrative of images that may well (indeed, will) 'thwart' the textual narrative, interrupting it, contradicting it. There is a certain *way* in which 'the play of appearances' is put 'into images', a 'logic that puts the fable into images' that is different from the 'story', so-called, the plot or *fabula* (as Bordwell described it). A fable has a moral that both 'meets' the narrated story and thwarts it in a twofold approach: through another meaning and, more essentially, through being another *source* of meaning.[4] Films can tell stories cinematically that exceed both their scripts and their concepts. As Rancière states when discussing *They Live by Night* (Nicholas Ray, 1948), a woman's words may say one thing, but her 'loose and brushed hair' admit something else.[5] An actor's performance, even his or her appearance, is another writing of the work.

The nature of this proliferation of kinds of narrative will be doubly interesting for our analysis, firstly on account of what it carries over from Rancière's general aesthetics, and secondly for the very fact that it does carry his own project further. It would be going too far to say that Rancière ontologizes narrative (and thereby lends narration the philosophical respectability that Deleuze denies it), but he certainly does politicize it in Rancièrian terms. He does this by simultaneously making the film-aesthetic representative of something more than film (and more than epistemology), while also using it to illustrate his own type of political philosophy, a philosophy of dissensus and absolute equality.

In the collection of essays, *The Future of the Image*, Rancière sets out the basis of this dissent within the film-aesthetic, a disagreement between two regimes of art. The 'representative regime' is a system that coordinates 'the relations between what can be seen and what can be said, between the unfolding of schemas of intelligibility and the unfolding of material manifestations'. There is a strict regime of what counts as art, what makes a suitable subject for art, and what rules must be adhered to to render this subject into art. The 'aesthetic regime', by contrast, rejects this 'double identity of opposites', seeing both as 'an absolute power of *making* on the part of the artwork', as well as a site for this power of unconditioned production in '*absolute passivity*'. To cite Novalis (as Rancière is fond of doing) 'everything speaks' – not just those parts of reality deemed appropriately 'aesthetic'.[6] Art is autonomous and anything can be art – animals, trees, stones. There are even the unseen aesthetic adventures of matter both on the surface and beneath the subject of figuration:[7]

> Everything is now on the same level, the great and the small, important events and insignificant episodes, human beings and things. Everything is equal, equally representable. And this 'equally representable' spells the ruin of the representative system...
>
> Now there is poetry anywhere and everywhere – in the attitude of a bear, the flick of a fan, or the movement of a head of hair. There is poetry wherever some spectacle can symbolize the identity of what is thought and what is not thought, what is wanted and what is not wanted.[8]

On the other hand, however, this 'everything' that speaks is also absolutely passive, for it *now* needs an artist to *let* it speak, to let its activity act. And this is the paradox of the aesthetic regime, both in the arts in general and in film art in particular. The aesthetic regime posits the 'radical autonomy of art' from any rule external to art, but it therewith makes everything artful and so mundane. This very mundanity of the world beckons the power of the artist as the necessary centre through which the world can assume its artful mantle. We are left, as *Film Fables* puts it, with a bipolar 'pure creative activity thenceforward thought to be without rules or models, and the pure passivity of the expressive power inscribed on the very surface of things, independently of every desire to signify or create'.[9]

The aesthetic regime is all too evident in the seventh art, whose beginning lent itself most easily to this romanticism of the material image. Jean Epstein captured it with his adage that 'Cinema is true. A story is a lie'. Deleuze echoes it with the notion that narrative is generated by a composition of images, and not the other way around. Because cinema expands the human range of perception to see things we cannot normally see, it pierces into reality itself – the 'micro-movements' of matter. It can consequently reject Aristotle's preference for *muthos*, the coherence of plot, and give favour back to *opsis*, the 'spectacle's sensible effect'.[10]

There is a double movement here, however. Cinema is both the art that 'emerges after the Romantic de-figuration of stories, and the art that returns the work of de-figuration to classical imitation'. As such, it creates dissonance. A film's *mise-en-scène* can thwart the continuity of the narrative with its own 'aberrant movements', sometimes imposed by the characters themselves when they are both in alignment with the story's goals as well as perverting them. An actor's performance, for instance, can create what might best be described as moving *puncta* (to borrow an idea from Roland Barthes) that run counter to the narrative (think only of Glenn Close's nuanced portrayal of Alex in *Fatal Attraction*'s (1987) simple misogynistic tale).[11] As the pre-eminently modern art, cinema experiences 'more than any other art' the conflict between the two poetics of Aristotelian representation and the Romantic power of signs. And its art consists precisely in its 'attempts to combine them' at all costs.[12]

Yet, and here is a second, central dilemma, this new regime is *but one more fable*, one more reading of cinema using cinema's own storytelling. It is an example of 'making a fable with another' which is 'a constitutive fact of the cinema as experience, art, and idea of art'. This fable-making or 'fabulation' (to use Bergson's term) works with many stories beyond that provided by the screenplay: there is also the story made by the director who films the script, the story made by the audience who watch the film with 'a potpourri of mixed memories', and also the story made by the critics and film theorists who 'extract a work of pure plastic forms from the body of a commercial fiction'. Indeed, the writings of Deleuze on film are but one other fable, a 'dramaturgy' that constitutes 'an ontology of the cinema argued for with bits and pieces gleaned from the entire *corpus* of the cinematographic art'. And it is a fable constructed by extracting, 'after the fact, the original essence of the cinematographic art from the plots the art of cinema shares with the old art of telling stories'. Every theorist shares in this dramaturgy, which is 'consubstantial with cinema as an art and as an object of thought'. The fable that proclaims the antinarrative essence of cinema is, ironically, 'extracted from the stories narrated on its screens'.[13]

Rancière turns to the neo-realist films of Roberto Rossellini for his examples of these multiple scripts. Far from evidencing the impossibility of (re)action, as Deleuze says of them in *Cinema 2*, they superimpose 'onto the normal movement of narrative continuity another movement directed by a fable of *vocation*', such as Pina's love in *Rome, Open City* (1945), or Edmund's excessive reactions in *Germany Year Zero* (1948). Beyond the story there is the film fable, the latter being a 'counter-movement', a 'fleeing movement, added by the director to script'. Hence, Deleuze's reading of neo-realism relies too much on the scriptural narrative of impossible action, and so remains blind to a set of *filmed* movements, a superimposition by the film fable of cinematic movements onto the scriptural. The antinarrativists like Deleuze (and, we might add, Badiou and Frampton) who try to deduce a pure cinema, do so from the body of cinema's various storytelling methods, sometimes (ironically) even relying on the most obvious of these, the screenplay itself.[14]

In Chapter 4 we heard Rancière refute Deleuze's own deduction of the duality of time and movement with counter-examples of his own. Other Deleuzian distinctions are similarly critiqued.[15] The point made by Rancière throughout is that what appears to be exclusive to the time-image – pure sound and optical situations, for example – is actually the result of 'those operations whereby the cinematographic art thwarts its own powers'. Any apparent purity is a derivative effect produced by the multiple forms of fable-making enacted by cinema's complexity of movements. But Rancière also has a metaphilosophical critique (similar to the one I launched against Deleuze), that harks back to his notion of the thwarted fable. According to Deleuze, images are 'things of the world' such that cinema is given a metaphysical status, or rather, the world is given cinematic status – the world is filmic. But why is cinema special, Rancière then asks, if the world is *already* cinematic? After some investigation, he discovers that the answer concerns redemption. The protocinematic world of pure moving images (described in *Matter and Memory*) has been immobilized due to the imposition by our brains of a sensory-motor frame. The original world has been robbed of its proper temporal flux. Paradise can be regained, however, but only through montage and the subsequent time-image that restores the original flux. Deleuze's story of cinema, then, is a 'history of redemption'.[16]

Moreover, the part of this story that positions the time-image as the saviour of cinema relies both on a 'fictive rupture' (between movement and time) and on the double-edged sword of passivity–activity that we saw was the paradoxical hallmark of the aesthetic regime. If the world is already cinematic (pure aesthetic activity) why does it need the active film-maker (and the cinema theorist) to *show* that it is? The answer, of course, is because it is also absolutely passive – the world is both vocal *and* muted. In other words, Deleuze's auteurism thwarts his energetic materialism, and the movement-image, like the cine-world, is only '"in crisis" because the thinker needs it to be'. Hence, Rancière adds, Deleuze's need to 'paralyze' the films of Hitchcock, for instance, to 'isolate' their images and 'transform the *dramatic* progression of his cinema into moments of passivity'.[17] The image Deleuze wants from Hitchcock (as a mental-image maker) is created by the immobilization of something Deleuze doesn't recognize – the story-making process specific to cinema. But Deleuze's neglect is only a particular symptom of a problem belonging to the aesthetic regime in general.

Towards the end of *Film Fables* Rancière directs the implications of this dilemma towards film theory. The fable of cinema (and the regime of aesthetics) is that cinema is *supposedly* the pure material image that can speak for itself, yet this very (theoretical) statement is a performative contradiction (thwarted), for it implies an artist (and artistic power) to make this matter/cinema speak for itself. Cinema needs to be spoken for (or, as I have been saying throughout this study when faced with transcendent claims about film: if all cinema is like this, why are *some* films better than others, why do these films need to be *pointed* out?). Cinema has to be redeemed, *turned back* to its lost essence and primary vocation. The putative power of the 'naked image' must be restored by clothing it in words: 'the moral of the cinema is, much like its fables, thwarted'.

We've just seen Rancière target Deleuze in this respect, but he is even more trenchant in his critique of Jean-Luc Godard, for his film-document *Histoire(s) du cinema* (1988–98), and of Chris Marker, for his account of cinema in *The Last Bolshevik* (1992). For both, 'the director's visual demonstration ... has been anticipated and made redundant by the professor's explanation'.[18] The dilemma lies in cinema's images supposedly speaking 'for themselves' and yet always being given with words telling us what they say. Images must be *talking* images.

And what of Rancière's own words in all of this, what of *his* theoretical work on film, given his ongoing criticisms of other theorists? Has he succeeded in distinguishing between what he tells us 'about the film and what the film shows', between words and images? By the lights of his own theory, the answer has to be yes, because it consistently reflects the distinction he creates between the two regimes of art, representational and aesthetic, which cinema has as its (futile) purpose to unite. But cinema is not alone. Literature too can also embody this predicament, as can be seen in the work of Stéphane Mallarmé, who, for Rancière, is a figure embodying 'the positive contradiction of literature, whose work is to be read as setting up the battle between the tendency for incorporation and that for disincorporation which forms the contradiction'. Literature exists, to quote Hector Kollias, on 'an agonistic plane' for Rancière. Literary language (of a sort) is 'clamorous and conflictual', but its internal tensions are not signs of failure: no less than the inherently thwarted fable-making of cinema, these tensions reflect something beyond art. And in Rancière's case, that 'beyond' is the political.

Rancière's theory of literature, like his theory of film, implements his conception of politics. But this conception is unlike any classical political model aiming for a coordination of individual wills, for it rests instead 'on a fundamental dissensus'.[19] Dissent, disagreement, dissonance. The Rancièrian political emerges solely in the struggle between an established social order and its excluded element, a democracy of the 'part which has no part'. A genuine political transformation is only inaugurated when a previously ostracized group requires a transformation of the rules of political inclusion, given that the group was so radically excluded beforehand. Genuine politics is either a democracy of absolute equality, or nothing at all.[20] And art too concerns democratic transformations, conflicting distributions of the sensible, of words and images and their various usages. There is a politics, an agonistic politics, of aesthetics (and, equally, there is an aesthetics of politics too, for the included and excluded also involve the sensible and its distribution).

Such aesthetic conflict goes back to the Greeks. As Rancière says in his *Parole muette*, it recalls Plato's views on writing, and the

> 'democratic chattering of the letter', an assumption of the world being given in the form of impotent/omnipotent Platonic writing. Their function as opposites pits writing against writing: writing as verb bearing witness to a power of incarnation, present in the poem, the people, and the stone, against writing as letter without a body: available for any use and any speaker since it is separate from any body that would confirm its truth.[21]

Incarnation or disembodiment. Image or word. *Opsis* or *muthos*. These disjunctions are not inclusive (as in the Deleuzian '*sive*'), but they are nonetheless constitutive of their terms, which exist in perpetual conflict with their other.

Film, like all the arts, bears out Rancière's picture of the political as a plurality of discordant voices ranged against each other in absolute democratic equality. Is his film theory, then, simply one more illustrative use of the medium? Though Rancière doesn't give film an ontological bearing as Deleuze and Cavell do, nonetheless, his politicized treatment is in full accord with his own general philosophy, even when one allows for the fact that that philosophy concerns itself, entirely in its own way, with the multiple differences between kinds of showing and saying, *and so pertains extremely well to the problem of talking about film*. His theory of cinema's thwarted fables are in complete assent with his theory of political dissensions. In fact, even Rancière's methodology incorporates such dissent, for he employs a *differential* analysis in each chapter of *Film Fables*, be it between films in one director's output (Anthony Mann's *Winchester 73* (1950) versus *The Tin Star* (1957), Fritz Lang's *M* (1931) versus *While the City Sleeps* (1956)); or performances in an actor's career (in Godard's *Le Chinoise* (1967) Rancière remarks on 'Jean-Pierre Léaud, who still seems to be acting in *Masculine Feminine*, and Anne Wiazemsky, who's still speaking the Bresson of *Au hazard, Balthazar*').[22] Dissonance again. Consequently, film contributes little that is *new* to Ranciere's philosophy of art-politics: what he tells us about film is the same as what film shows us in his examples.

At the outset of *Film Fables* Rancière promised that his theory would not exhaust 'the field of possibilities of the art of cinema', and yet, at its conclusion, we are left with another theory of what film is that finds its grounding in something non-cinematic.[23] Indeed, Rancière is not averse to using words like 'illustrate' and 'illustration' in his analyses, this tendency coming to its apotheosis with the claim that, as a Romantic art, the principle of film 'had been worked out in the final chapter of Schelling's *System of Transcendental Idealism*, a good hundred years before the first public screenings'.[24] Added to this intellectualizing approach is the other mark of pre-emptive film-philosophy, auteurism – the power of each film being appropriated by its director alone in

Rancière's accounts ('Marker's ... Jenning's ... Rossellini's'). While Rancière gives more time to acting performance than Deleuze, it is ultimately a performance whose glory (or lack of it) reflects the director's (potential) power over the actor's skills (Lang's over Peter Lorre in *M* or, less successfully, over Robert Manners in *While the City Sleeps*) – the actor has little to do with it.[25]

Given Rancière's sensitivity to the dynamics between theory and its object, this can only be regarded as a missed opportunity. This is especially so given Rancière's democratizing impulses: his work on the historical relationship between philosophers and non-philosophers (the 'masses', the 'poor') has lead him to postulate a 'wild philosophy' created by autodidactic non-philosophers in epistemology and education theory. Yet, what underscores the writings of these autodidacts *as philosophical*, is always a resemblance with *extant* 'Philosophy', be it Plato's or Kant's.[26] A 'wild', *non-philosophical* philosophy is never posited, and, certainly, in *Film Fables* we have not seen one coming from cinema either.

Yet, we did not introduce Rancière's work on cinema merely in order to line-up one more philosophy that fails in its most noble aspirations to let film think for itself. Rather, Rancière can also be seen as a figure whose theory of film tempers any ontologization of film (even while still telling us finally what film *is*, like everyone else) by rendering the conflict between epistemology (narrative-fable) and ontology (image-fable) inherent to the way cinema works: film tells stories in various (conflicting) ways because there is no such thing as a pure image, nor any pure information behind, or within, the image.

In what follows, the metaphysics of filmic story-making, especially its temporal features, will come all the more to the fore, and from that will emerge our own first tentative outline of a cinematic thinking. Certain things make us think, and those things, so this argument goes, are ultimately types of time. Things happen on screen that give us pause for thought, but what must happen first is that the film pauses itself – its normal speeds – to make us think at all that something out of the ordinary is happening.

Thoughts taken out of context

Let's talk about coffee for a moment. When looking at *Star Trek*'s 'Wink of an Eye' episode, we noted how the Scalosians accelerated Captain Kirk by spiking his coffee, itself an everyday stimulant for those who need to 'get moving'. Interestingly, there is a history to the making and consuming of caffeine on screen that mostly serves to *slow us down*, and, with that, often leads us to think about why what is happening on screen is occurring the way it is. No doubt Godard's two-minute contemplation on the swirls of coffee in *Two or Three Things I Know About Her* (1967) is the most famous cinematic instance of *un café*. But also in *Umberto D.*, for example, we see the morning ritual of one character, Maria, including a 36-second shot of her grinding coffee beans that eventually takes on an almost sublime character. Or in *Dead Men Don't Wear Plaid* (1982), there is a seemingly interminable shot of Rigby (Steve Martin) pouring coffee grinds into a pot – the pouring itself lasting 50 seconds. The longer this pouring goes on, of course, the more comical it becomes, the time consumed clearly taking on new meanings with each added second (about the character, the situation, the film and even the audience). And as to drinking coffee, probably the most interesting coffee-shot of all is the four and a half second clip in Krzysztof Kieslowski's *Three Colours: Blue* (1993) of a sugar cube soaking up an espresso. In an essay on the philosopher Giorgio Agamben's relationship to film, Benjamin Noys describes the scene thus:

> Could we not also see this scene, after Agamben, as the recovery of a gesture as simple as dropping a sugar cube into coffee. The cube touches the surface of the coffee and in four and a half seconds the coffee soaks into the cube which is then dropped into the coffee. In this 'stoppage' the dynamic potential of the image is freed as we are forced, if only for four and a half seconds, to watch the coffee slowly soaking into the cube. In this way, it may be, the image of dropping sugar into coffee is de-created and our attention drawn to the image and the gesture as such.[27]

A prolonged shot like this forces us to think, because it is so out of the ordinary, so out of the usual context. In terms of the plight of the film's heroine, Julie (a woman who is taking a long time to learn how to mourn the death of her husband and child in a car crash), this shot can lead to questions such as 'why is this shot this long?', 'why is it here?' or 'what does it mean?'. What is most interesting from our point of view is that Kieslowski has himself provided a 'masterclass' on how the shot was made.[28] In the class he asks after his film's own 'obsession with closeups'. The answer is that it is trying to show how the heroine perceives the world, how she focuses on small things, 'on things which are close to her'. 'She is trying to limit her world', Kieslowski continues, 'to limit it to herself and her immediate environment', so that she can ignore 'other things'. We only care about a 'silly sugar cube' if 'we enter the world of the heroine'.

Both Noys and Kieslowski, then, start their hermeneutics of this film moment in terms of shots, of close-ups and gestures. But even before that comes its timing. Without time there would be no questions at all. The shot of the sugar cube soaking up coffee takes four and a half seconds. During Kieslowski's masterclass, he takes another actual espresso and times another sugar cube's absorption. It takes eight seconds, which, he says, is 'at least three seconds too long'. This is because 'a detail like this should last no longer than that'. Kieslowski uses his watch throughout to time the processes, both the one before him and the one on film. His care for timings, he adds, comes from him thinking about the audience 'all the time'. An audience can endure a four and a half second shot of a sugar cube, but 'eight and a half would be too long'. Any longer and the audience would lose their patience.

But perhaps Kieslowski should have more faith in the necessity of patience: *Julie* certainly doesn't mind the sugar cube taking its time to do its thing (just as she is taking her own time in mourning), so perhaps a sympathetic audience might be able to endure this extended duration too. Bergson would definitely think that it *must*:

> If I want to mix a glass of sugar and water, I must, willy nilly, wait until the sugar melts. This little fact is big with meaning. For here the time I have to wait is not that mathematical time which would apply equally well to the entire history of the material world, even if that history were spread out instantaneously in space. It coincides with my impatience, that is to say, with a certain portion of my own duration, which I cannot protract or contract as I like. It is no longer something *thought*, it is something *lived*. It is no longer a relation, it is an absolute. What else can this mean than that the glass of water, the sugar, and the process of the sugar's melting in the water are abstractions, and that the Whole within which they have been cut out by my senses and understanding progresses, it may be in the manner of a consciousness?[29]

Of course, we are impatient with the length that things take in reality when it seems *excessive*. So we must be patient. We have to wait. No longer just an intellectual relation, my affective relation to the dissolving sugar is an 'absolute', the absolute of my impatience. And if film speeds this process up, then that only shows its distorting effects all the more:

> Let me come back again to the sugar in my glass of water: why must I wait for it to melt? ... What is it that obliges me to wait, and to wait for a certain length of psychical duration which is forced upon me, over which I have no power? If succession, in so far as distinct from mere juxtaposition, has no real efficacy, if time is not a kind of force, why does the universe unfold its successive states with a velocity which, in regard to my consciousness, is a veritable absolute? Why with this particular velocity rather than any other? Why not with an infinite velocity? Why, in other words, is not everything given at once, as on the film of the cinematograph?[30]

This is always Bergson's temporal question, not why is there something rather than nothing? (an ontological query based on the false premise that nothingness precedes being), but, instead, why aren't things instantaneous? Why is there no 'always'? Why is the universe temporal? Why do we have to wait for the sugar to dissolve? These questions are paramount, and they are the first ones that come when there is *felt* time. Why is this pouring of coffee grinds taking so long? Why is this woman grinding beans so slowly? These are questions born of affect, or enforced patience, born from the need to slow down for certain things and speed up for others. The becoming of being again. Thinking for Bergson is always about time, about slowing down or speeding up, putting the usual direction of our thinking into reverse so that it can sympathize with the movement and 'very life' of other things. And thought also involves the painful affects that this recalibration of time causes us, which is as true of film as it is of life.[31]

Naturally, different affects emerge in different contexts. We laugh when Steve Martin pours his grinds for too long, but not at Julie's sugar cube. What each context involves is complex, involving technology, spectatorship, performance and more (which in Chapter 8 I will explain as intricate forms of time as well). Most importantly, what makes the moment stand out is its moment being *too long* against our expected norms. Not everything can be abnormal, however: the novel requires a background of non-novelty against which it can be figured. And another name for such a background is 'context'. New timings make one think, but always against a familiar context. If the context wasn't there, and wasn't behaving normally, then *this* other outstanding abnormality would go by unnoticed.

A 'normal context' for some, however, would seem to be a contradiction in terms. Contexts, under certain definitions, extend indefinitely. Take speech. It is usually thought that the meaning of any speech act gains its fullness when taken in the context of its utterance – the situation at the time of its utterance. But context is not a separate variable upon which the meaning 'within' the context is dependent: the meaning is a part of the context. Meaning does not reside *in* the environment, it emerges *as* it. The 'pragmatics' of communication *is* its semantics, only at another level. Bergson described this as the 'whole' in which the sugar, water and our affective relation to them must be embedded. Jacques Derrida, in like manner, taught that it is highly problematic to think that we can represent any context exhaustively, for that would involve artificially immobilizing its infinite expansion. And Gregory Bateson has described this same illimitation as the necessary ecology or unity of mind and nature.[32] What Bateson adds, though, which is crucial for us, is that we *must* be able to act *as if* this context were delimited if any new meaning is ever to stand out. There is no one objective and infinite context other than the infinity of subjective finite contexts, each of which are made finite, immobilized, by *their* specific point of view. There must be thresholds, even if only apparent ones.

However, these thresholds don't come transcendentally as Deleuze believes, but are created immanently. Any perspective entails being a view from somewhere, and so having a horizon of finitude. If something new is to stand out, to make us laugh or cry, then its novelty must emerge against a background of familiarity, of stability. But given that the background is, in principle, infinite and infinitely varied at every moment, this means that it must be somehow immobilized. We must ignore this background's real expanse, this Bergsonian 'whole'. *Matter and Memory* puts it clearer still: we have to 'obscure some of its aspects, to diminish it by the greater part of itself, so that the remainder, instead of being encased in its surroundings as a *thing*, should detach itself from them as a *picture*'.[33] And this process occurs mostly, though not entirely (according to Gregory Bateson), at a basic biological level.

Take learning. At the simplest biological level there is what Bateson calls, in his *Steps to an Ecology of Mind*, 'Zero Learning' (or 'specificity of response'). These are simple or complex acts that are not open to trial and error. They allow for no freedom and no acquisition of new meaning. This would be 'learning' in name only (hence 'zero'), for it is really an innate, 'hard-wired' disposition involving no change at all. Then there is what he calls 'Learning I', which allows for 'revision of choice within an unchanged set of alternatives'. This is the infamous Pavlovian conditioning, enabling changes in zero learning through habituation. But Learning I requires an assumption of an *unchanging* context, for otherwise this apparent change too would really be a preprogrammed zero learning. In other words, when the unfortunate Pavlovian dog learns that the bell signifies not just a sound but also the appearance of food, this is because the dog is able to filter out all the different contextual changes in the previous, myriad occasions during the conditioning period when repeatedly presented food after a bell-ring. Without being able to immobilize those shifting contexts into a static background, into one definite 'context', the dog would not have been able to learn. In due course, it must hear the ringing bell as something other than one in a series of slightly different bell-ringing situations; it must eventually hear it as a bell that, by association through memory, *newly* means 'food is coming'. The other tolls were the same, and so this bell-toll is new. The bell is heard *as* food because the bell-ringing contexts have been condensed into one situation, this immobilization of context being for Bateson 'a necessary premise for any theory which defines "learning" as change'.

'Learning II', therefore, would be a higher-level 'learning to learn': the ability, based on even greater powers of memory, to abstract from *one* set of repeated contexts to other *sets* of contexts, that is, to a metacontext. An illustration of Learning II would be the progression from learning that 'this bell means this *x*' to learning that *any* bell can mean *x*. From learning instances such as 'this friend betrayed me', and 'that friend betrayed me', I go on to generalize that 'friends are traitors'. I might then conjoin that learning with other genera such as 'effort is never rewarded' and 'managers are incompetent' to the further universal truth that 'life sucks'. Indeed, that is how we learn the characters we become, according to Bateson, how we acquire our temperament as optimists, pessimists, sentimental, anal or whatever else – through the generation of meta-emotions. But note how such learning entails creating immobile metacontexts: 'friend', 'effort', 'manager' and even 'life' must have their minute differentiating nuances homogenized away too. The contexts are made redundant and predictable through repetition in memory.[34] Or rather, homogenization just is this memory. It is memory, the resurrection of the past and so the immobilization of the full force of the changing present, the indefinite, inexhaustible context, that facilitates learning. Only the stereotypical goldfish is able to notice such nuances, and so sees the world anew each moment with surprise and wonder: 'blessed are the forgetful' says Nietzsche.[35]

In Batesonian terms, goldfish are Derridian, with spotless minds. If one isn't able to see a definite and discrete context, then one will misinterpret the message every time ('did she mean that?', 'was that a put-down?', 'was that a come on?'). Messages go astray, never reaching their proper address. Meaning regains its native, Derridian indeterminacy on account of an inability to be myopic, the inability to curtail dissemination. Yet, such excessive awareness may also be defined as an *intelligence* that forestalls the necessary framing actions in art. To quote from Mrs Talmann's speech to the artist Mr Neville (as they converse before a perspectival grid) in Peter Greenaway's *The Draughtsman's Contract* (1984):

> I have grown to believe that a really intelligent man makes an indifferent painter, for painting requires a certain blindness, a partial refusal to be aware of all the options. An intelligent man will know more about what he is drawing than he will see and in the space between knowing and seeing he will become... *constrained,* unable to pursue an idea strongly – fearing that the discerning, those who he is eager to please, will find him wanting if he does not put in not only what he knows but what they know as well.[36]

Contexts are frames – and goldfish are too intelligent for their own good. It takes a 'certain blindness', or memory, to make such a frame, that is, to isolate and filter out the shifting background noise (and so objectify that background as '*the* (back) *ground*') such that a figure stands out as unusual. What is unusual is always something specific to a fixed context; for example, an utterance like 'you're a fox' will be determined as a statement or a metaphor (or a 'put-down' or a 'come-on') by that context. Taking the idea of frame-context from Bateson, Joseph Anderson writes that watching a film too is a framed 'play' of make-believe. Indeed, not knowing the difference between the 'framed event (the fiction) and reality', he continues, would 'constitute insanity'.[37] Intelligence can equal insanity, depending on context.

This varying ability to enframe, that most of us nonetheless have to a relatively fixed degree, is neither voluntary nor intellectual, however, but part of our bodily, species being. Antonio Damasio calls such everyday, interactive objectifications of context, 'somatic markers'. These assist in our deliberations by 'highlighting' some options with a view either to retaining them or 'eliminating them rapidly from subsequent consideration'. As such, they 'reduce the need for sifting because they provide an automated detection of the scenario components which are more likely to be relevant'.[38] Here is film theorist William Connolly explaining Damasio's idea with a vivid illustration:

> A somatic marker operates below the threshold of reflection; it mixes culture and nature into perception, thinking, and judgment; and it folds gut feelings into these mixtures...Such markers might be triggered when you are invited to a sexually attractive friend's home at the end of a casual evening. Time is short, and you cannot address all the considerations relevant to the decision. You don't, perhaps, ask yourself in detail whether the event may carry future burdens with it, whether your partner would be disturbed upon learning about it, whether you are discontented in your current relationship, whether your future friendship with the colleague could be damaged, and so on. You respond to a series of implicit, affect-imbued judgments gathered from the past before deliberating briefly.[39]

The natural origin of our ability to fix context, therefore, does not preclude any role at all to culture: the two are mixed together in this operation. Bergson called this ability our 'attention to life', and it is social, psychological and biological in origin; indeed, in this respect we can all be said to suffer from some form of 'attention deficit disorder' (which Bergson, for one, believed art tries to remedy).

Making movies and art with time

At this point, dear reader, you may be asking yourself where this is all going. Where has the context of film and philosophy gone from this discussion of context and learning? What have Pavlovian dogs got to do with film? To place things back in (your) context, then, we can now say that *our* context or frame is one with two sides. Firstly, it is the repetitions, decelerations and accelerations *in* films 'out of context' that make us think, or, rather, *this multiplicity of times leads to thinking.* Secondly, it is *our* repetition *of* films in an increasingly homogenized context that creates the object we call 'the film'. Both the film and the thinking it implants in us (be it 'philosophical' or not) are products of time, of different speeds and immobilizations; and these timings concern us, the viewing contexts and the 'film', in interrelation. It is the nature of this interrelation, of the refractions between different times – my own, the screen's and the world's – that I will tackle through the rest of this book.

There is indeed something Pavlovian about film, not in Sergei Eisenstein's idea of a dialectical cinema that would train the audience's emotions, but through the way that our own viewing habits always co-engender the appropriate object to view along with them. This is not a relativistic idealism (that each man is the measure of every film), but simply to say that a multiplicity of films coexist within the different temporalities of any one collective film experience, many of which run at an overlapping speed (the 'nodal' points on which we all tend to agree – for example, on whether or not a certain film has an elephant in it). The 'film', seen again and again, in certain situations, is like a meal repeatedly presented when a bell tolls. Something new emerges: the film is seen at a different temporality, one belonging partly to it but also to the repetition imposed on it by reviewing and our own speeds of reception. The film as a specific kind of object emerges, slowed down to the viewing context applied, revealing new things about itself and us in that setting. Here, for example, is Susan Sontag expressing her admiration for Béla Tarr's *Sátántangó*: 'devastating, enthralling for every minute of its seven hours. I'd be glad to see it every year for the rest of my life'.[40] The association between her delight and her anticipated re-viewings is not incidental. No less than Žižek re-created Hitchcock's *Psycho* through watching it 20 times (and no doubt continues to re-create it in further viewings), or Bordwell discerned the director's technique (such as the serialism in Bresson's *Pickpocket*) only through 'close viewings', or Deleuze found Hitchcock's mental-images by immobilizing the story-making process specific to cinema, or (contrariwise) Cavell's reliance on his memories from a *single* viewing produced films that are unique to him, so Sontag has outlined the concentration she'll employ in the creation of her *Sátántangó*. Indeed, it will be through a concentration in time and of times that the film will be formed. But each of these theorists will also, of course, have thoughts engendered in them at the *same time*. Subject and object coevolve through these durations.

Alternatively, and for once taking the goldfish's perspective, here is Daniel Herwitz on a possible dispersal rather than concentration of the art-object: 'we come back to the film we saw a hundred times in the 1960s and see it with really new eyes. Did we miss what was in it the first time, are we noticing different features of it, or have our eyes simply changed, making it as new as the city of Rome after our 20 year absence?'.[41] Have our eyes changed or has the movie offered up new riches? Apt though his queries are, Herwitz is still putting the questions in terms of subject *or* object. The argument offered here, on the other hand, is that the richness, and thinking, in film is founded on the temporal relations *between* subject and object, relations that both differentiate subject and object from each other and make subject and object different each time through the force of time.

But these interrelations of times do not emerge via a representational *association* of ideas (one thought *of* a context leading to another thought *of* the film), but a *dissociation* operated by time itself. What Bergson calls the 'ideal genesis of the material object' and, along with it, the intellectualizing subject, are both formed through an immobilization or interruption of movement. According to Bergson, matter, or the object, and intellect, or subject, are both products of a process of immobilization of what we are really given, namely a '*moving continuity*'.[42] And he insists that the genesis of the object cannot be considered 'without making the genesis of the other' the subject. Both film and viewer are created as temporal phenomena and by temporal phenomena, dissociated from a 'whole' (or indefinite context) through its immobilization.

So, where David Rodowick has pleaded that we 'must stop corrupting the film experience *by immobilizing it* as static shots, textualizing the experience *by rendering it static*', we see this process of immobilization as inevitable; indeed, there would be no film without it.[43] Having objectified or paused the context – quite literally when studying freeze-frames – we are given pause for thought. And this pertains to film and theory no less than to films and viewers. The circular processes of theory–film infusion, that Branigan termed context 'framing' above, are processes of immobilization that have their own specific temporality that is neither objective nor subjective, realist nor relativist, epistemological nor ontological.

What does this position entail as regards those special emergent objects we call 'works of art'? Is there no *art* to film, then, other than what habitual spectatorship can train our minds to see in it? Can art come from anywhere? In spite of the relativistic tone struck here at times, the answer must still be no, because any perceptual phenomenon, short of a *ganzfield*, will offer more or less complexity between certain (Deleuzian) thresholds. One always sees a film within a frame that is itself composed of myriad other frames (as Branigan writes), some of which are less mutable than others. Short of artificially induced amnesia (or acquired autism), one cannot undo one's learning; nor can one unsee what has been seen previously, such that what is presented before one *now* appears more or less novel. But such novelty neither begins nor ends with the film object alone (and certainly not with its author) – for that is a product increasingly refined by the viewing process as such, the complexity of which involves both the subject and the subject's world. These other variables help create the frame or immobilized context (thresholds or standards) in and through which evaluations of artfulness can be and are mounted. All I am asserting, therefore, is that any frame, threshold or fixed context is an imposition of sorts, and it must be allowed that other frames, some of them bodily, some psychological, some cultural, can be created alongside the ones we do mostly recognize.

Here again, by contrast, is Stanley Cavell offering us a criterion for true art, both in film and in general: 'pride of place within the canon of serious films will be found occupied by those films that most clearly and most deeply discover the powers of the medium itself, those that give fullest significance to the possibilities and necessities of its physical basis'. One might agree that art is to be found in principle where the greatest relational effect between object and audience occurs via the 'medium itself'. But what if that medium, its 'physical basis' or technology, keeps on evolving through numerous modes of convergence, as is increasingly the case with cinema? Film's indefinite progress creates *new* possibilities, *ad infinitum*. Even further, what if the medium itself keeps mediating itself through new, varied contexts of viewing that bring the production and consumption of film into close alliance (new types of audience coevolving within fresh viewing contexts that together generate new theories of what the film experience involves)? There is no absolute 'view from nowhere' that can accumulate and essentialize the progressive achievements and experiences of film, no God or Hegelian Spirit, nor even a naturalized viewpoint based on optimal cognitive competence à la Bordwell. There are only the myriad occasions of temporal relation between film and audience.[44]

Cinema is multifaceted, comprising the traits of being an (art) object and a psychological performance in one process. It is, after all, a *moving* art-object, the objectivity of which *precisely being* the movements it embodies and exchanges with those who watch it. Hence, while *Sátántangó*, like every other film, can be seemingly immobilized by our repeated viewing (through which one version of its objecthood emerges), it too effects us *at the same time* through deceleration or, as with *Bourne*, acceleration. This 'same time', however, is the time co-engendered by film and viewer in relation, indeed it is the relation as such. Other relations are always possible (for those already slower than *Sátántangó* or already too fast for *Bourne*). The 'judgement of art' is also the *art* of 'judgement' (so-called), the art of 'seeing-as' that is frequently a 'feeling-as' below and above the thresholds of visibility.[45]

The necessity to repeat these platitudes, that 'cinema is temporal', that 'film is a moving-image', and so on, is itself an issue worthy of some reflection. Continually invoking the cliché that 'film is always what moves' can itself inure us to this very novelty, and what it might fully entail.[46] One consequence might be this: that film cannot be *one* object of reflection at all. Film doesn't exist outside of what we make of it and what it makes of us – a making that is both corporeal and cultural in nature. From what Mary Ann Doane calls the 'emergence of cinematic time' as *immeasurable* movement (that is, movement beyond any one objective measure), it follows that film can never stand still long enough to reflect on itself. If aesthetic modernism, after Godard, hoped to operate within the episteme of reflection (albeit through a radical gesture of opening up its own mode of production to that reflection, that is, to absolute self-reflection), then it must reckon with the challenge that such reflection will distort or refract what is mirrored in its forms of representation.[47] The attempt to heighten reflection and consciousness succumbs to the fact that such picturing always fails in its task and refracts its object.

Yet, and here is the crucial point, the product of such refraction, far from being the original pure image supplemented with a complete awareness of its own contingency and artifice, is instead *a new reality*. Branigan's paradox again. If modernism concerns itself with breaking classical conventions by representing them, denaturalizing them, then the 'post-modern' film, in a special sense of the term that belongs only *here* and on *this* view, embodies a productive refraction of that very act of representing representation. But such temporal tags as 'classical', 'modern' or 'post-modern' are themselves contextual rather than absolute, depending on the audience a film receives. It may be open to the radical impact of that film (if only because of being in a certain disposition, or being rarely exposed to film at all, whether it be 'officially' avant-garde or not) or it may be jaded with and inured to the effects of *any film*, be it classical, modern or post-modern. The impact of film is not located solely in the film, but in the multiple processes of film viewing. To say that cinema is temporal is not vacuous, but it can become commonplace unless it is said differently and in new ways all the time, for temporality, like film, comes in numerous forms.

Fabulating the film event

We've discussed the speeds that create the film and the thinking of the film. The more Rigby pours his coffee grinds in *Dead Men Don't Wear Plaid*, the more it makes us think and laugh, as it takes itself out of the usual context (or what *we* take and make, or immobilize, as its 'usual' context). This repetition-that-makes-one-think can itself be represented (or immobilized) in terms of intersubjectivity or 'Other Minds' (a common strategy in both cognitivist approaches and Stanley Cavell's notion that there is cinematic thought in the specific choice of images a film shows). After a few too many seconds pouring, we realize that the film is making a point and directing our attention to it (but not with a close-up); a few seconds more and it seems to be testing us as regards the limits of our patience and what it can get away with; a few seconds further again and the audacity of the scene becomes clearer as we resign ourselves to the will of the film to play with us. Note these attributions of mind: 'direct', 'test', 'play', 'will', and so on, whether they be credited directly to the film or by proxy of the film's makers. Another example. In *There's Something About Mary* (1998), one scene involves Pat (Matt Damon) visiting Mary (Cameron Diaz) at her apartment, where he also meets her friend Magda with her normally snappy, unfriendly dog, Puffer. Left alone with the dog in the lounge for a moment, Puffer lies blissfully in Pat's arms being stroked (Pat having earlier secretly tranquilized the dog in order to make it seem to like him and so endear him with Mary). But then Puffer stops moving altogether. We subsequently see Pat desperately trying to resurrect Puffer (before Mary and Magda return) through a series of improvized medical procedures: mouth-to-mouth resuscitation and cardiac massage, electroshock with live wires and, after the dog is set on fire following that, a final splash of soda water (that magically brings Puffer back to life).

Clearly, the comedy at one level comes from Pat trying to impress a prospective girlfriend and failing miserably, that is, killing her friend's dog. At another level, though, there is something much more complex going on. Here is a scene that focuses our attention on many layers of implied intersubjectivity. We can see clearly that the 'dog' is in fact a stuffed dummy, but only during its life or death crisis. The humour in the scene utilizing such a fake dog plays on and with our expected revulsion towards any act of cruelty to animals for mere entertainment (such as a film like this), *and the fact that the film-makers know this* (as signalled by the caution that 'no animals were harmed in the making of this film', ubiquitous in Western films today). But the film (makers) also play with *this* knowledge that *we* know that *they* know this, and *also* that *they* know that *we* know that *they* know this. We know, for example, that a film of this nature – with Hollywood A-list stars and a good-sized budget – can afford the best special effects and an animatronic dog much more convincing than the stuffed model actually employed. But that is the whole point. We know that they used an unconvincing fake dog *intentionally*. And the film-makers know that we know. And finally, we know that they know that we know. It is precisely this conspiracy of artifice-pretending-to-be-real that we are laughing at: not so much at the predicament of Pat alone, as at our own otherwise foolish credulity in Hollywood trickery, here exposed as laughable. That is, the joke is on all of us: we are laughing at cinema-viewing itself, at the whole immersion effect of watching film and how ridiculous it is that we fall for its illusions every time.[48]

There are great levels of mentality being projected here. But how does this happen, and how is it connected with movement? The cognitivist model of 'Other Minds', as we'll see, only explains the process part of the way. Indeed, we have to return to Bergson again for a more complete theory of projected mentality in his concept of 'fabulation', which is a theory of the origin of all make-believe that works at the level of *movement* specific to the question. Introduced in Bergson's final book *The Two Sources of Morality and Religion*, fabulation is the basis of fiction-making through which processes come alive for us as *Events*, not just in aesthetic make-believe, but at a very present and real (though primitive) level of our perception. Bergson argues that *perceived* movement is something we anthropomorphize at an unconscious level. As a study on the origins of religion, moreover, his theory of fabulation concerns the initially protoreligious effects of this creation of living, mindful events out of movements. The natural world, originally regarded as replete with animate processes (animatism), gradually has this vitality restricted to certain parts (as immaterial spirits in animism or gods in theism), with other parts being immobilized as a static, inert background.

Filmed fiction is an exemplary instance of fabulation because it exploits one of the main conditions necessary for such a 'willing suspension of disbelief', namely apparent motion. However, *pace* Joseph Anderson, the reality effect primarily concerns both what is moving and how it moves in the film before us, rather than any supposed *general* effects on the brain of an abstract seen movement. Bergson's fabulation does indeed, like Anderson, involve evolutionary psychology (how we perceive movement), yet it does not reduce the reality effect to the mechanics of biology. Its effects reside at the level of how we perceive movement in all its rich complexity. It is the moving-image, as we'll see, that entices us to transform a filmed fiction into a reality. There are other requirements, of course, for this transformation – story, acting, music and much else – but their first condition is movement.[49] Moreover, the reality given to movement is not abstract but *living*: it is as a living image, a projection of life onto cinematic movement, that the primary condition of seeing the film-image as *mindful* is fulfilled.

Though Deleuze adapts fabulation for his own political use (fabulating a 'people to come' with art), we shall keep to Bergson's original narratological context, given that his was the first use of the term in philosophy.[50] Deleuze's motives for his shift of meaning are obvious given his strong antinarrative stand – 'narration results from the sensory-motor schema, and not the other way round' – but he neglects the fact that fabulation is not representation but the process of creating representation.[51] Fabulation is also the process that can transform our conception of cinematic fabula or narrative from being a piece of information or proposition, to a process, or the process of many processes (and for which neither narrative nor psychological norms can provide a static foundation). On offer will be a picture of story-making as an ongoing process created by various other processes, each of them structured differently (cognitively, affectively, materially, culturally), though all together, as we'll see, having something else in common – the manifestation of an Event.

While the word 'fabulation' connotes a counterfeit operation, it is not wholly unnatural, nor unfounded: it is neither fictitious nor relative to individual whimsy. Its connection to and resolution of the 'paradox of fiction' – why do we feel real emotions for unreal (fictitious) people and the events that befall them? – pertains to very real perceptual processes. Fabulation is additionally important because of Bergson's own ambivalence towards it, for whilst calling its *effects* 'a counterfeit of experience', or 'systematically false experience', he also asks whether 'the errors into which this tendency led are not the distortions, at the time beneficial to the species, of a truth'.[52] In other words, what we have here may well be a faculty whose symbolic expression is distorting, but the source of which is illuminating. Indeed, we will see that the faculty that would so de-animate the world *as a whole* (as it moves from animatism to theism) needs only the shock of certain traumatic processes – disasters – to see *parts* of it again intentionally as events.

Indeed, fabulation concerns the primitive state of mind in all of us (so that when it comes to images, we surely have 'never been modern').[53] It is a 'virtual instinct' that underpins our rudimentary forms of religion (such as animatism and animism), as well as relating us to the world as such, by anthropomorphizing its processes and activities as events and actions. In fact, fabulation is the basis for creating other personalities, other spirits, in a phrase, 'Other Minds'. Yet, it would be imprecise to think of it as a species of imagination, still less a form of mimesis, simulation or pretence, for it is more primitive than all of these and lies at their source.[54] Though Bergson's discussion of fabulation concerns religion specifically, this faculty is at the origin of fiction and a good deal of our more creative representations of the world – he mentions children's play, writing, theatre and hero worship in quick succession.[55]

There are three fundamental kinds of religious fabulation in this account, animatism, animism and theism, each of which can also be seen as three forms of mediation, three forms of creating representation or 'seeing as'.[56] The second form is significant for marking the shift from animatism to animism, moving us from a vision of the entire universe as animate to one which divides the universe into that which is animated (with spirits) and that which is inanimate. A *selective* perception of life. What spurs this first dissociative fabulation is what Bergson regards as the ultimate disaster for the mind: *its representation of its own death.* The evolution of intelligence brings with it the foresight of death and, with that, an interference with our survival instinct.[57] Intelligence can thereby lead to a 'disturbance of life' and the 'intellectual representation which thus restores the balance to nature's advantage is of a *religious* order', concerning life and death. The traumatic representation of death (and its depressive effects on our animal will to live) must be eased by the formation of quasi-hallucinations, fictions, myths and ultimately the whole panoply of religious symbolism which, at source, is a supplement from nature to compensate for the effects of this shock to thought. Myth, understood in the broadest terms possible, is a refinement of a protoreligious faculty of mind to animate nature with intentions and actions.[58]

So, there is the shock generated by an intelligent representation (the vision of death), and there is the reply to that shock, which generates another representation, this time of a spiritual world that embodies the promise of survival post-mortem. Our intelligence goes beyond its original function by abstracting death from the particular (the seen death of certain others) to the general (everyone, including itself). In turning its reflective power onto itself, it interferes with its own infinite vision and purpose (to live), refracting it through this scene of deadly finitude such that a distorted view of the infinite is generated: the fantasy of *survival*. Death refracts or mediates life into an image *of* life or *sur-vival*, a kind of super-life or meta-life. This image *of* life is a spectre that comes in various forms: animatist force, animist spirit, theist person.

From force through spirit to person, we also see different refractions of life as it is lived: through our bodies. There is a notable progress from an experience of dispersed embodiment to a body that is all the more individuated, more integrated, as the *lived* body is superseded by its *visual* image. To quote:

> For contemporary science the body is essentially what it is to the touch; ... the visual image of it would in that case be a phenomenon whose variation we must constantly rectify by recourse to the tactile image ... But the immediate impression is nothing of the kind. An unwary mind will put the visual and the tactile image in the same category, will attribute to them the same reality, and will assume them to be relatively independent of one another. The 'primitive' man has only to stoop over a pool to see his body just as it really appears, detached from the tactile body.[59]

As we see, this spirit-life is facilitated in part by Bergson's own version of a mirror-stage, whereby we see our reflection in water – a false, whole (visual) image that we dissociate from an embodied (tactile) image. But what forces the dissociation is the traumatic idea of death, the image of our finitude. Where Lacan sees the visual image in terms of a false *spatial* continuity (ego identity), Bergson sees it as the false promise of *temporal* continuity (survival).

Fabulation, then, is a 'partial anthropomorphism', an intentionalization and vitalization of nature, beginning with diffused, impersonal forces, then crystallizing those forces into spirits localized in particular places (animism), before imparting ever more human personality to those spirits while at the same time detaching them from the world, until we have a full-blown monotheism with a divinity that transcends its creatures. A case in point is Bergson's depiction of fabulation in the crucial second phase, animism, with regard to a water spring. The meaningful action of giving water, for instance, was once a 'datum provided directly by the senses' with its 'own independent existence'. But then it became the 'spirit of the spring', localized firstly in a thing and then in a person. It is the 'persistence' (or repetition) of this activity of giving water that 'set it [the action] up as the animating spirit of the spring at which we drink, whilst the spring, detached from the function which it performs ... relapse[d] the more completely into the state of a thing pure and simple'.[60] Repetition created the object (and our thought of it) by dissociating a real movement into the discrete idea of its movement in the foreground and its static support (or substance) in the background. The *activity* of the spring – the *giving* of water – has been extracted as an idea (form or *morphé*) of movement, leaving the spring to 'relapse' into a state of inert materiality (*hylé*).

Throughout Bergson's explanation of fabulation, one cannot miss the connection with trauma. Such traumas are significant, not so much for what they are in themselves – 'earthquakes, floods, tornados' or 'aggression in nature', as well as illness, serious accident and, of course, death, 'the greatest accident of all' – as for our response to them, how we see them. Firstly, they are given an intentionality, for if the effect has an importance to us, if the effect has meaning for us (*our* death, *our* injury), then the cause must have the same level of significance (on the basis of a primitive logic of 'like coming from like').[61] Bergson cites the example of First World War soldiers being far more fearful of bullets than of shrapnel, despite the latter being so much more deadly. The reason for this, he argues, is that we fear that which is prima facie an intended effect, and while shrapnel may be more likely to hit us, it does so by relative accident compared to the (literal) *aim* of the rifleman. If the effect is to be our death, then we feel it should result from a malicious force rather than an indifferent one. And when there is *only* a force of nature at play (say in a lightning strike), then we animate that nature with malign will.

But what good does this do us? According to Bergson, we do it simply to have an effect ourselves, to have the possibility of effective resistance (at least in our imagination). That which is intended, that which is mindful and alive, can be influenced. And processes are sometimes translated into mindful events just by giving them a name. Writing of William James's account of his experience of the 1906 San Francisco earthquake, Bergson contends that the naming of an event makes it the event, that is, naming it individuates it, at least in part. An 'earthquake' itself is simply a disparate set of physical processes, but, with a name, we individuate the earthquake as the *cause* of these processes (rather than the set of them), and, thereby, are better able to see an 'intention pervading the act' that may be served or thwarted. The disturbances with which we have to deal, 'each of them entirely mechanical', combine into an 'Event' with an elemental personality, mind or interiority.[62] This 'image' of interiority 'lends to the Event a unity and an individuality which make of it a mischievous, maybe a malignant being'.[63] Indifferent processes become a living, breathing Event.[64]

Events, therefore, have a face, so to speak, but it is one *we* impose in order to master our fate through the ascribed identity or identification of the event. They are an example of what Žižek (who has analysed Bergson's idea in a discussion of freewill) would call the 'Big Other' that injects meaning into the meaningless.[65] Yet, it is not a question of self-deception or false consciousness for Bergson, but the perception of life and death. To take a cinematic example, the horror of a film like *Hostel* (2005) concerns what we regard as vital and other – in particular, another person's view of us – not regarding us as vital beings at all, but indifferently as things (an indifference Žižek would call the 'void of the Other'). Indeed, for Bergson the origin of the comical is only the flip-side of the origin of horror: where the comical concerns what is alive and of value *making itself* inert and worthless, horror relates to a subject *being made* worthless and inert *by another.*[66] What would be truly horrific (were we not to fabulate in the face of this trauma) is not the monster *as* monster (being evil and loving it), but the banality *to him or her* of being monstrous *to us* (as when one's death becomes a mere tourist attraction). The horror of *Hostel* (or *Two Thousand Maniacs* (1964) to a lesser degree) is where tourism meets murder: the psychopath is no longer sick but the new type of normal – one that wants to kill you for fun within an institution that makes what you regard as evil into a mere matter of procedure. Hence, the need of the victim to fabulate a deeper motive for the tormentor, be it social, psychological, biological or metaphysical ('evil').

In any case, fabulation serves to empower. Once named and personalized, the event or events can be effected, if only by magic. Discussing the nature of 'chance', 'luck' and accident', Bergson sees even in these names an anthropomorphization of processes that allows us a possible magical influence. When the gambler at a roulette wheel makes a swift gesture with his or her hand at the point where they want the ball to fall into the wheel, this gesture is 'a transfiguration of the will to win'. 'Chance' or 'Lady Luck' can be influenced, even physically. Bergson calls it a 'logic of the body, an extension of desire', as seen in the war dances of (so-called) primitives, performed in order to frustrate their enemies magically. Yet, these bodily comportments are in everyone – 'a sudden shock arouses the primitive man dormant within us all', Bergson claims.[67] Fabulation is, again, not only a naming and perceiving function, but also has an embodied dimension.

Fundamental to Bergson's approach is that such representations of mythic, supernatural forces always originate (even in magical thought) within a *real* trauma of accident, illness or observed death. They are encounters with what Žižek calls the Real. They stem from an 'out-of-the-way experience', excess novelty or 'sudden shock' that ruptures the veneer of our ordinary psychic life. In one example, Bergson writes from his own experience of a 'vague foreboding' of what would be known eventually as the Great War in Europe. This was an event much discussed and predicted during the 43 years after the end of the Franco-Prussian War in 1871. Bergson describes how, on the German declaration of war with France in August 1914, he suddenly felt an 'invisible *presence*', as what was once only an abstract idea gradually became real. As an idea, it had remained both 'probable and impossible', a 'contradictory idea', keeping an 'abstract character' until the very last moment, whereupon he had this strange 'feeling of admiration for the smoothness of the transition from the abstract to the concrete'.[68]

Here, finally, we come to the heart of fabulation, for its own source – in the traumas of illness, natural disaster, war and, pre-eminently, anticipated death – begins with disturbance, with interruption, and what is *felt* as a shock. And the felt trauma, ultimately the shock of the idea of death, is what allows us to *see as*, to see 'x *as* y': it creates a faculty (or virtual instinct) that can see anger in the dark clouds above, spirits in water springs, God's design in the workings of nature, and reality in fiction, including cinematic fiction. It is to refract the world through our own image rather than to reflect it 'in itself'. In this vein, Bergson discusses our primitive emotional reaction even to such meagre things as a domestic collision, such as when we accidentally bang our leg against a table. Naturally, we blame the table. He continues:

> Between the identification of the table with a person and the perception of the table as an inanimate object, there lies an intermediate representation which is neither that of a thing nor of a person; it is the image of the act accomplished by the striking or, better still, the image of the act of striking...The act of striking is an element of personality, but not yet a complete personality.[69]

Turning from the psychological function of fabulation to the aesthetic one, we see that the so-called 'willing suspension of disbelief' in fictitious events and our empathy for fictional characters are proliferations of this biologically determined faculty.[70] When fiction moves us, the result resembles what caused the origin of fabulation in the first place: an 'incipient hallucination'. At least at its source, then, fiction is a trauma-reaction in Bergson's view.

In addition, the aesthetic is in fact another form of perception for Bergson rather than something qualitatively different. To carve out events from the 'continuity of the real' is how fabulation is described in *The Two Sources*, but that is precisely how *all* perception is described in Bergson's *Matter and Memory*. Perception is closely related to fabulation: they both fragment (by selection) our experience of 'the real', although to some degree they are also both redeemable or 'defragmentable' (to borrow an unsightly word from computing), through art *and* through philosophy. Our senses can be partially re-educated by contagion from the less selective ways that artists and philosophers see the world. Only what makes fabulation specifically interesting is that without it, without the faculty of *seeing as*, we wouldn't have the art which redeems the fragmenting activity of all perception in general. The affect, or shock, to thought that generates fabulation, that refracts our vision of the real, also creates the very same reality *effects* (or 'illusions') that allow art to defragment the real (to some degree).

Paradoxical feelings: moved by movements

Remember that fabulation concerns fiction vis-à-vis the idea of Other Minds, going from an attribution of mind to all of nature, to an attribution of mind to just a part – namely the most human (monotheism here being read as a narcissistic mirror-image of human subjectivity). Significantly, the 'illusion or fiction of reality' in our experience of cinema has been linked to Other Minds in recent cognitivist approaches within film theory, in particular Gregory Currie's imagination theory of the cinematic illusion.[71] For Currie, however, imagination (rather than affect or shock) has the central role. It is, moreover, a representational model of the image that he works with (which is often the case in analytical approaches like his). For Bergson, by contrast, fabulation comes before representational imagination: at its source it is a felt or affective recognition of mindfulness in *all* of nature that is slowly restricted to an image of the self (that is, humanity and its anthropomorphic God). Moreover, Bergson's is not an empathy model of Other Minds like Currie's, as these tend to be *associationist* whilst Bergson's model is *dissociationist*. That is, our consciousness itself of the other mind (like all consciousness) is what *remains* of the fragmentation (through disturbance) of a prior, partial whole (the set of all images in *Matter and Memory*). It is a residual affect due to what was always only a *partial* individuality, an interpenetration: it is not built up by association or analogy between discrete individuals comparing their public behaviour (as in Currie's view) but what remains after dissociation.

Now let's bring this fabulation back to film. To begin with, there are the findings of the filmologist Albert Michotte, who showed experimentally that people tend to anthropomorphize even the simplest films of moving dots and squares with qualities like causality, life and intention.[72] Since it is the movement alone, he argued, that is actual on the screen (as opposed to the objects which are represented) it is *that* which 'liberates the object from the plane in which it is integrated' when the viewer identifies the filmic object with what it represents. Objects only appear on the screen, while the movement there *is a reality*.[73] It is movement that makes it live. A comical example of this can be seen in Ernest Pintoff's animated short, *The Critic* (1963), voiced by Mel Brooks. Film theorist James Monaco describes it as follows:

> *Abstract animated shapes perform on the screen as we hear the voice of Brooks, an old man, puzzle his way happily through the significance of this 'art'*:
> 'Vot da hell is dis?! Mus' be a cahtoon. Op... Mus' be boith. Dis looks like boith. I remembeh when I was a boy in Russia... biology.
> Op! It's born. Whatever it is, it's born... Look out! Too late. It's dead already... Vot's dis? Usher! Dis is cute. Dis is cute. Dis is nice. Vot da hell is it? Oh. I know vot it is. It's gobbage. Dat's vot it is! Two dollas I pay for a French movie, a foreign movie, and now I gotta see dis junk!'
> *The first shape is joined by a second, and Brooks interprets*:
> 'Yes. Its two... two *things* dat, dat, dat-they like each other. Sure. Lookit da sparks. Two things in love! Ya see how it got more like? – it envied the other thing so much. Could dis be the sex life of two *things?*'[74]

While talking about cartoons, we might even say that *all* films are animations. By saying this I mean that, in giving movement to still images, there is also the gift of life: animation is both giving movement and giving life. Indeed, following Metz and Burch, Richard Allen has argued that movement is vital in filmic projective illusion, or the reality effect.[75] Consider also the following passage from Colin Radford's classic essay on the paradox of fiction, or why we are moved by characters and events we know to be unreal, such as the fate of Anna Karenina. His own argument dismisses the reality effect as irrational, yet his study throws up many interesting points, one of which concerns film:

> A man has a genre painting. It shows a young man being slain in battle (but it is not an historical picture, that is, of the death of some particular real young man who was killed in a particular battle). He says that he finds the picture moving and we understand, even if we do not agree. But then he says that, when he looks at the picture, he feels pity, sorrow, etc., for the young man in the picture. Surely, this very odd response would be extremely puzzling? How can he feel sorry for the young man in the painting? But now suppose that the picture is a moving picture; i.e., a movie, and it tells a story. In this case we do say that we feel sorry for the young man in the film who is killed. But is there a difference between these two cases which not only explains but justifies our differing responses?[76]

Radford offers no answer, but I would suggest that what adds life to this projection, what makes it plausible, is the crucial addition of movement. Movement animates. Yet, we will see that not just any movement, nor a movement 'in general' will do; it is the *particularity* of different non-abstract, real movements that is operative for each specific context.

In one scene from James Cameron's *Titanic*, we witness the night-time events just before the ship collides with an iceberg in the North Atlantic. Lookouts, helmsmen and engineers do their best to turn the Titanic from its course. With them, we watch the final moments of the ship drawing closer to the iceberg, edging slightly to port, but nevertheless eventually hitting the obstacle. In attempting to apply some of my own filmological science to this investigation, I showed the collision scene from *Titanic* to a group of 31 first-level film-studies students, all of whom had seen the film before.[77] They were then asked the following question:

> On a scale of 1–10, to what extent would you agree with the following statement (1 equalling no agreement and 10 equalling full agreement)?:
>
> 'When watching the sequence – especially as the ship nears the iceberg – I felt myself hoping that it might miss, and/or felt myself willing it to turn in time to miss'.

Of the 31 responses returned, there were eight scores of 10, three scores of 9, eleven scores of 8 and nine scores of 7, averaging a score of 8.3. Something certainly has been demonstrated here, though exactly what remains to be established.

Disaster films are very good at this individuation of events, especially in their early parts before the havoc is unleashed: steam from the volcano in

Dante's Peak (1997), the portentous smoke or small flames in *The Towering Inferno* (1974), both work as signs of the danger to come, of an event that is looming, stalking the characters (almost like another character) as they go about their business, oblivious to the growing danger.[78] According to Bergson, by anthropomorphizing processes as an event we objectify them and give them a personality such that we can use our will and action against them. We think we can prevent some of their effects by imagining all that we might do, or (in a film) all that might occur or might be done to forestall the eventuality. Perhaps this is why we feel we can change or hope to change the course of the *Titanic*, despite our knowledge of its fate. It is not that the iceberg is made human, but *the collision* with the iceberg (an 'act of striking') is made into an event with intentionality – and what has intent can have that intent thwarted.[79]

Of course, the sinking of the *Titanic* did actually happen, which, perhaps, makes Cameron's *Titanic* a less than ideal choice (it might be easier to confuse fiction with fact when the fiction is based on fact). Yet, it still works well *because* it is a real event that we know has a past and yet which we feel is present. In fact, what is truly interesting is not whether any belief (in fiction as fact) is present or absent, rational or irrational at all, so much as the roots of that belief *when* it is there. Naturally, few people confuse art with reality and interrupt *Macbeth* on stage before the first murder. But there are degrees in which we have to resist such (bodily) impulses to intervene. Turning to Colin Radford again, we see another illuminating point at the end of his essay that echoes Bergson's description of the gambler's gesture at the roulette wheel:

> a tennis player who sees his shot going into the net will often give a little involuntary jump to lift it over. Because he knows that this can have no effect, it is tempting to say that the jump is purely expressive. But almost anyone who has played tennis will know that this is not true.[80]

Beliefs, if we must talk of them at all, come in degrees: we *do* try to push the ball into the roulette wheel, we *do* try to lift the tennis ball over the net, and we *do* try to move the ship out of the way of the iceberg. We don't move in any overt fashion, but the bodily need to do so is there, if only in degrees, as in our desire to move the *Titanic* by shifting in our seat or by pointing our shoulders in the direction it must go. And it is indeed a desire and logic of the *body*, as Bergson calls it, rather than a representational *belief*.[81] Narrative, far from being the representational dullard Deleuze wants to paint it as, comes tethered to bodily and affective structures, for our feelings carry story-making or fabulatory powers within them.[82] The reason that this is all the more obvious in the collision event from *Titanic*, as compared to 'suspense' scenes found in literary fiction (or other film moments), is precisely because it exploits our primitive connection to movement in such a sustained fashion, a connection that has become rarefied in the literary device (as used in literature *or* film).

Finally, then, the reality effect in fictional film lies not simply in the artifice of fabricating *fact*, but also in fabricating *time*, bringing to the image (constructed in the past) the 'illusion of the present tense'. But this illusion of the present, which James Agee used to describe Italian neo-realism in particular, can also be generalized. Hoping to alter the course of the *Titanic* doesn't come only from making its collision a living, mindful event, but also from making it present, reliving its present, and so reopening its future. We feel that we are seeing it happen *now*, and it is from this temporal state of actuality that our paradoxical 'beliefs and desires' also follow. One could argue that animating fiction is, by the same token, a present-making, for what is alive must also be present.

It was this power to animate further, seeing a film event as both happening and (possibly) not happening, as both real and unrealized or indefinite (film seeming both so real and so illusory), that confounded Joseph Anderson. Yet, this is exactly the sign of reality's own movement: film always *contends* its own putatively complete reality, no less than reality does (the paradox inherent in this statement is only another expression of the paradox of becoming, when something both is and is not itself). They are both incomplete, indefinite, on the move. It was the dissenting, duplicitous narrative that Rancière dubbed the thwarted film fable (though he might take exception to applying this to a film about a 'love affair upon a sinking ship'). Film thwarts its own 'reality' with contending movements. Regarding the famous scene in *M* between the child killer and the little girl at the shop window, he writes:

> the issue here is not one of narrative suspension, but of poetics, of Aristotle's requirement that the narrative must lead the criminal to the point where he'll be caught and unmasked runs into a new, and conflicting, requirement: the *aesthetic* requirement for suspending shots, for a counter-logic that at every turn interrupts the progression of the plot and the revelation of the secret. In these moments, we experience the power of time, the time of goals held in abeyance.[83]

This multifabling or counter-logic is facilitated by the primitive fabulations that enliven a moving image and allow a film scene enough reality that it can go elsewhere, against type and narrative norms. And fabulation is, in fact, a 'power of time', of a reactualized present. Strictly speaking, it does not concern narrative as script (or 'forking plots', counterfactuals and virtual history, to add a few other suggestions), but how narrative emerges through felt movement.[84]

Casino Royale (2006), for instance, plays on a younger Bond's struggle between his humanity (still being prone to falling in love and making mistakes) and his nascent inhumanity (being invulnerable to love and impervious to error). His identity and even the identity of the film series itself are put in question in this revamp of the franchise, through a new form of 'becoming-Bond'. The law of identity is stated twice in the dialogue – 'you were you' as his boss 'M' keeps saying – and the issue of Bond's name, his ego and of who the 'new' Bond is (as both actor, Daniel Craig, and character) keep this leitmotif going through the film. When we wonder what might happen in the Bond-world were Bond to find sustained happiness with his lover Vesper Lynd, we fabulate a new world within the one we are ostensibly given by *Casino Royale*'s plot. Another fable, in Rancière's terms. We see him live anew because of a whole panoply of reality effects (some of which will last longer than others), ranging from the metaphysics of movement and psychology of perception (*Casino Royale* also has the kinetic cinematography and editing of the *Bourne* series), to the culture of reception and aesthetics of performance (Bond is scripted and played with more 'realism' than ever before). Yet, we also know that this is just a film, within a very specific genre, and so Bond must not find happiness *if there is to be a Bond film at all*: we want Bond to be real, but not too much. Between this being Bond and not being Bond, we enjoy the vital process of growth and decay. The paradoxical feelings we have during this 'becoming-Bond' are Parmenidean in origin. We thwart our own desires and expectations. We want *Bond's* movement and yet we don't; or rather, our ambivalent desires are part and parcel of *the film's* duplicitous movement. And the film plays with this ambivalence throughout.

As all films do. There is no need for film to reveal its inner workings either to explain them away (as Anderson desires) or to expose their artificiality (as Godard does), because the double effect of real/unreal is present in every film. Bond *can* have a soul, and the ship *can* miss the iceberg, but only while an audience *actually* watches them (especially for the first time, before repetition dulls the novelty and our anticipation with knowledge).[85] Neither 'character' will escape, however, for the audience is hoping *and* moving (no matter how subtly) against another hope and another movement, of generic destiny.[86] This doubled movement is also a sign of reality, of its duplicity to 'itself' such that when film refers to this reality, when it is 'realistic', its realism works best when it is refracted, thwarted. Hence, the perpetual impasse between realism and anti-realism in film theory, between documentary and fantasy, can only be remobilized if we look again at its terms and how they mediate each other constantly, as refractions of reality. (This will be the task for my final chapter.)

One such term is 'the present'. Stanley Cavell asks, 'how can one be present at something that has happened, that is over?'; while Deleuze declares 'the present is not at all a natural given of the image'.[87] But aren't these qualms and denigrations due to an impoverished, unitary notion of the present?[88] We should note that Deleuze's own 'sonsigns' – harbingers of the supposedly *real* time-image – turn material sound into a living sign. Is not fabulation itself of this ilk, letting matter live? Think again of the swinging kitchen door in Tati's *Les Vacances de Monsieur Hulot*: it becomes a kind of person, a tired and bored presence coexisting with the waiters themselves, but not in the same moment as the waiters. This living sound is another present, another life, created alongside those others already perceptible in the film. No less than we saw in *Awakenings* and 'Wink of an Eye', there is no one speed at which the film can be seen nor one present in which the film itself moves. The present, like movement, is neither simple nor obvious, but plural and only ever glimpsed in a fleeting, felt image.

So what is fabulation doing? Is it an attribution of mind, an anthropomorphization, or is it a giving of life, or even a making present? It is all of these. Multiple presents are made, or better again: in fabulation, an intuition of the alien presence of others – their life and movement – is given a partial or distorted expression. A living, actual present is created in these 'efficient presences', as Bergson calls them. If it seems counter-intuitive to give fabulation such primacy, given its connotations of falsity and artifice, remember that fabulation is not an error for Bergson. Rather, it lies in the verisimilar expression of a genuine intuition. Qua what is expressed, fabulation creates static products no doubt (myths, superstitions, fictions, and so on). Qua process, that is, the movement of expression, however, fabulation is dynamic and creative, and what is dynamic for Bergson is never wholly wrong. It creates new lives (events) on the basis of the real lives (processes) to which we are normally blind. This is not a 'life of things' by proxy of social ritual, cultural biography, or phenomenology, but something more direct, closer to what W. J. T. Mitchell describes as imitations taking on 'lives of their own'.[89] When we talk of pictures 'drawing' us in, 'attracting' us, 'grabbing our attention', being 'animated' or 'live', there is something more behind the language we use than mere metaphorical fancy.[90]

In fabulation we are moved to move other movements further and make them others' movements, the movements *of* others (which sometimes they are). It is not so much the viewer imposing his or her time on film, but film *and* viewer exchanging times, refracting each other's movements. This is the contagion of movement-imaginations that underlies our representational imaginations. And every movement can be animated, only some – ones *in extremis* concerning death and disaster – are commonly vitalized by all of us into events (at least primitively). In a crisis, we all become artists. Ordinarily, however, we don't. So, the banality of movement and the platitude of recalling film to its temporal essence (which is only to say that it has no essence) must be set against the possibility of seeing something richer in movement than we normally do. Movement is real inasmuch as it is individual, there being no such thing as 'movement in general', according to Bergson, but only particular movements.[91] It is a 'radial' concept with no centre of radiation other than what we create by immobilization. Bergson's philosophy of consciousness concerns *non-subjective* consciousness, remember: perception is not an '*interior* and *subjective* vision'.[92] But by 'non-subjective' we should not infer that it is objective in any non-processual manner: if it is an object of any sort, then it is a changing one, a moving one.

W. J. T. Mitchell has also remarked on how the word 'image' is 'notoriously ambiguous', just as we have spoken of movement as a radial concept.[93] These are all cross-categorial concepts – 'Life' being another of them – that ground our argument, and that is why they cannot be *proven* empirically in a non-circular fashion. So it is important to note that it must be something other than an empirical hypothesis when we say that 'everything is movement', or that everything is 'Life', or 'image' (or 'machine' as Deleuze and Guattari do in *Anti-Oedipus*).[94] Rather, these 'everything is' expressions are attempts at forging new types of radiating, oozing thoughts. None will ever reduce all others to itself, but each one-off attempt at making such universal glue may itself evince a new movement – beyond any one propositional content – that will attract some readers with its suggestive novelty. Perhaps some words, like some films (or film scenes), in some contexts, may still offer the possibility of redeeming our ordinary perception, as Siegfried Kracauer once believed.

8

Refractions of Reality, or, What is Thinking Anyway?

> Finally, there can be no doubt that the one characteristic of 'reality' is that it lacks essence. That is not to say it has no essence, but merely lacks it. (The reality I speak of here is the same Hobbes described, but a little smaller.)[1]

Outline of an outline

Let's begin with the passage from *Matter and Memory* that has guided this study throughout:

> But, if we suppose centres of real, that is to say of spontaneous, activity, the rays which reach it, and which *interest* that activity, instead of passing through those centres, will appear to be reflected and thus to indicate the *outlines* of the object which emits them. There is nothing positive here, nothing added to the image, nothing new. The objects merely abandon something of their real action in order to manifest their virtual influence of the living being upon them. Perception therefore resembles those phenomena of reflexion which result from an *impeded refraction*.[2]

So what, finally, is film's own thinking? Or, what *will be called* its thinking if it is not a form of reflection? We can't answer that question just yet, but we can guess at the shape one possible answer might take. If one thinks of thought as a mirror of reality, as 'reflexion', then its shape is refractive, for reflexion is an 'impeded refraction', an interruption.[3] Reflection, as representational perception and thought, is a limit case of refraction that mediates its objects at the highest speed and shortest time (being just those parts of the object sent back to us that our theory wanted to see) and in the narrowest movement (or angle) of the present possible. Yet, it is a possibility or limit set by other, broader movements – cultural, psychological and biological. Film's own thinking belongs to these broader movements, to the broader, refractive presents of our bodies and affects, as I will elucidate in this chapter. The centre of freedom (or 'spontaneous activity') in the quotation from *Matter and Memory* above is 'Film' itself. Our representations of it, our perceptions, are reflections that are only 'outlines of the object'. But this reflection is simply our 'virtual influence' on the object, our possible action on it, because each point of view, each frame of reference, has different outlines reflected back to it.

This impeded refraction is also a moving resistance. What resists our frame of reference are all the refracted rays that are mediated through it. All the resistances, the impediments, the refractions of theory, *together*, make a more complete outline of film: a contour whose shape is somewhere between Edward Branigan's 'indefinite boundary' and Rick Altman's insubstantial 'pinhole' camera. This is not forwarded as one more philosophy *of* film, however, but what François Laruelle calls a 'non-philosophy' of film, that thinks according to the Real, which, in this context, entails a responsibility towards film's own 'intentions' (to echo Cavell), or to what film 'wants' (to use W. J. T. Mitchell's phrase). What film wants is shown indirectly through its resistance to extant philosophy and theory. We can never know what film is directly (there is no top-down definition of film, no ontology of film), but we can infer what it is not in the peculiarities of its recalcitrance to various theories of film (whatever philosophers try to posit as the meaning or being of film).

Others' reflected rays appear to me as refractions. But the refraction *proper* to me, my refraction, always appears to me as a reflection, as a veridical thought-perception. Another's reflection, another's frame of reference, is always moving, never standing still long enough to be veridical, to correspond to or re-present reality. My refraction, as a reflection to me, is an immobilizing stand, a standing-still that immobilizes my refraction as reflection, and so immobilizes the object as object. Other people have accents, I have a voice. Others are ghosts, I am real. As Bergson argues in *Duration and Simultaneity*, we stand still (to reflect) at the expense of disregarding others' proper immobilizations, others' reflections (which we see as just refractions, as missing the full account *of* the object because they are mediated by it). In form or shape at least, thought is the refraction of the object proper to me – *my* reflective outline of the object. I always see the world in my own image, in 'a realised contradiction', says Bergson.[4]

This partiality whereby others' thoughts, inasmuch as they remain other, are *seen as* merely refractive is what Bergson calls a 'half-relativism' in *Duration and Simultaneity*, one that assigns mutability to others while retaining a static vantage point from which to cast aspersions. But the system of refractions as a whole – which simply is this Bergsonian account – sees no difference between proper and improper, between first person and second person: they are all refractive. This is what he names a 'complete relativism'.[5] One might say that Bergson's project in *Duration and Simultaneity* was to relativize relativity. Yet, doing so lets him emerge with this complete relativity that actually reinstates a new absolute. For if each perspective takes its own frame of reference as an immobile absolute, then integrating these partisan immobilizations neutralizes their distortive effects. And so a new absolute is restored. This new absolute is fundamentally grounded on the recognition, or *affective acknowledgement*, of our selectivist tendency to centralize our own point of view by making everything else move relative to it, to be private Ptolemaicists. It is the new absolute of a complete relativism that integrates each of the partial frames of reference, or reflective outlines, within a system of refractions. In turn, this acknowledgement is also a process and never final: it is itself an integration, a mediation, and so another form of refraction – the 'system' is unsystematic, the 'whole' is open, and the absolute is an indefinite becoming. If post-modern relativism is 'ironic' in attitude because it does everything within a hyperknowing and reflexivity, then Bergson's complete relativism is the affective unknowing of such knowing.

In *Making Meaning,* David Bordwell writes that 'in order to study practice as such, we must pretend that all theories are correct, all methods are valid, and all critics right'.[6] Yet, the full implications of this expansive democracy are rarely acknowledged by him. In actual fact, Bordwell assumes that all theories are *equally wrong* relative to the twin truths of cognitive science and his poetics of film form. All other perspectives are mobile save for his, which transcends the others. His is a negative democracy, which is also a half relativism that masks an absolutism. A complete relativism is always reflexive, involving itself as well, with an immanent absolute concerning its own indefinite purchase.

A regress beckons here, of course, but it is not vicious: for if reality itself is mutable or 'lacks essence' (our opening hypothesis), then what starts out as merely a 'refractory' representation can become a given truth simply by virtue of our exposure to the concept *over time*. A true affirmation can thus have a 'retroactive' or 'retrograde' movement. Truth *becomes*, it grows (which is why thinking is something that *will be called* thinking).[7] A paradox becomes true by sedimentation or multiple refraction, whereby the early mediation has become so overlaid with other mediations (social, psychological, biological, physical) that the overall effect is one of opaque, thick truth – a 'hard-wiring' – rather than transparent *doxa*. The 'hyper' in hyperreality is not a surface excess of signs, but a deep layering and refractivity of signs through which the hype becomes real.

With regards to cinema, film's own thinking would reside in its freedom to refract our attempts to think it – a freedom that *we* only see as a shortfall of reflection, *a failure of proper thought*. Cinematic thought or philosophy, I'll contend, is never about reflection (through language, rationality, logic, inference to the best explanation, or consciousness), but about resistant refraction, a freedom that resists definitions of essence (even and especially about itself). The essential inessence of cinema – which Badiou referred to when he wrote that 'there is nothing' to constitute the essence of film – *also* marks (contra Badiou) the insufficiencies and unnecessities of thought. The system of refractions provides a differential morphology of any specific film. We are not lost in (half) relativism, but are thinking 'according to' the Real alongside the differential outlines of film. The more 'complex' a film (a status set between various thresholds, with a *ganzfield* as the human minimum), the more complex the outlines of resistance (or specificities of theoretical failure), the better our glimpse of the Real. Like the invisible monster in *Forbidden Planet* (1956) that is revealed in outline when a force field blocks its path, so the contours of film are illuminated when our theories pitch themselves against it.

In what follows I shall try to reveal various kinds of contour that indicate a resistance to, and refraction of, the reflective ambitions of theory. They are the dimensions of film that refuse to stand still and be 'classical', moving centrifugally from the psychological through the physical to the cultural, and coming in six categories: affective embodiment, new media technology, differential spectatorship, cinematic sound, acting realism and the screening of animals. We have touched on some of them already when discussing the film theories of Deleuze and Bordwell in particular, but now they can be placed in a context that explains why film's status as classical or 'movement-image' is always relational and never substantial. The first five demonstrate what indirect routes film must take to achieve its effects (whether or not that includes the illusion of reality); the last, however, shows how easily the reality effect in particular is spoilt by confusing reality with a substance. This relationality of film does not invoke mere (or 'half') relativism, but the new absolute of film's complete relationality – the 'growing truth' that we mentioned at the outset.

Affective embodiment

Still grappling with the unreality of film or 'film-as-surrogate-reality', Joseph Anderson takes solace in the fact that, while 'the tragedy in a movie's narrative is not real; the empathy and sorrow we feel are'. On this account at least, he comes close to the anti-representationalism of Deleuze, which has an affective-becoming underpinning any film's apparent mimetic qualities. Behind the 'I see' or 'I hear' there is an 'I feel'.[8] *Affect*. We've met with this notion already, however, and know that there are different theories of affect to choose from – for instance, Deleuze's or Grodal's (non-cognitivist or cognitivist). So which notion of affect should we put in play now? Let's return to caffeine for an answer, to the need for patience when awaiting the dissolution of sugar in coffee.[9] This slowing down is a required passivity that is marked by an affect, our own impatient resistance to this other temporality. Such a feeling, a pathos, is undeniably uncomfortable, a form of suffering as we integrate, or refract, our dominant *durée* with that of another (the etymology of 'patience' itself being 'suffering').[10] Just as the sugar-in-coffee is a material endosmosis – an exchange, a montage, a refraction – so is our affective engagement with that process. We dissolve into the film's duration just as it mixes itself with ours, emerging as an object for us as this happens. And so too for theory. *Its* impatience with film is also a refractive affect (that Laruelle will conceptualize as a '*mixte*').

In *Matter and Memory*, Bergson defines pain or suffering as a part trying to think the whole. Within any complex organism, the individual parts seem to have abrogated their right to move individually in favour of the movement of the whole they constitute. Yet, in an attack upon themselves (and thus also upon the whole), they still have the ability *to attempt to move as if they were the whole*, that is, to set things aright for themselves and by themselves. However, this attempt must always fail simply because it *is* only a local effort against a cause that is targeted against more than they are alone (that is, the whole): 'every pain is a *local* effort, and in its very isolation lies the cause of its impotence; because the organism, by reason of the solidarity of its parts, is able to move only as a whole'.[11] This description perfectly fits the relationship between theory and film: each of our theories is *a* part of film, immanent to it rather than representative of it – a part that is trying to think the whole of film, to tell us what it really is. Hence, the affect, hence, the vain effort. And it is indeed an effort. To reverse this tendency, this ontological desire, involves another painful effort as we overturn our normal habits of mind. That is why what Bergson calls 'philosophical intuition' and Laruelle calls thinking 'according to' or 'alongside' the Real (rather than *of* it) is such an effort, being a violent struggle to reverse the normal direction of thought back towards its object, to reintegrate our partial ideas into the whole.

There are a number of particular ways in which the materiality of our *durée*, our embodied affectivity, plays a vital role amongst the non-representationalist mediations within film experience. From Vivian Sobchack and Barbara Muriel Kennedy to Mark Hansen and William Connolly, the emphasis in much recent film scholarship has been on the way in which the meaning taken from (or information 'in') film alters with our various bodily situations, the affective body 'framing' things differently according to 'tactility, movement and the rhythmical'.[12] Hansen and Connolly in particular place Bergson at the centre of this tendency, Hansen writing of the 'Bergsonist foundation to all image technology' whereby images are created by selection, enframing or 'giving body' to digital data. The work of embodied cognitivists and 'extended mind' theorists was also prefigured in Bergson (Antonio Damasio's ideas, especially, closely track Bergson's theory of perception, though Damasio doesn't appear to know this).[13]

Mark Hansen, for instance, goes against new media theorist Friedrich Kittler's idea that the emerging 'digital convergence' does away with materiality (of both the body and the medium), by showing how it is precisely the affective body that does the work of embodying the reception of information from the digital image: 'the "image" has itself become a process and, as such, has become irreducibly bound up with the activity of the body'.[14] Digitization, of course, would seem to challenge Marshall McLuhan's idea that the 'medium is the message', and so confirm Kittler's view. Yet, Hansen's Bergsonian framework, on the contrary, makes the perceiver's body the new medium of digital information and thereby retains a central place for mediation, though without calling on McLuhan's representationalism.

However, even Hansen still talks of the digital and information as the 'raw data of reality' rather than go all the way with Bergson and Deleuze on the 'superiority of the analog'.[15] Like Anderson before him, Hansen retains a *place* in which the art-object can be isolated, albeit one that is 'virtual' now rather than 'actual'.[16] His focus on the body restricts its role to reception-consumption. Hansen goes awry chiefly when thinking of the body as 'a selective processor' in the creation of images (no less than more classical cognitivists like Bordwell and even Anderson do when they objectify *process* as *processor*). The digital image is said to be the 'entire process by which information is made perceivable through embodied experience'. But note the contradiction of the body *informing* information versus the body merely making information *perceptible*: the first is active constitution, the second is passive vis-à-vis the form of information.[17] By placing more emphasis on the latter, Hansen retains a substance dualism of body and data, even if within a more corporeal notion of the subject. Bergson's broader, temporal framework shows how information, or the artwork qua proposition, is itself created and consumed by means of refraction. Indeed, the real issue is not of old analogical media (celluloid) versus new digital media (MPEG), for 'the film' was never what was *on the film strip* in any case. Hence, it is not the body that processes 'information' (if we must use this term) as subject to object, but that 'inform-ation' is a dynamic relation, a process with only virtual poles of subject (body) and object (information as 'raw data') that emerge *subsequently* and *variously* under different forms of temporal refraction.

New mediations

William Connolly's work in 'neuropolitics' goes even further than Hansen in showing how 'multimedia techniques' provide a dynamic medium 'through which cultures and brains infuse each other', involving 'genetic endowment, image, movement, sound, rhythm, smell, touch, technique, trauma, exercise, thinking, and sensibility'.[18] Of course, there have always been attempts to accelerate the rate at which film experience might be destandardized. The 1960s avant-garde had already played with the analogue image by stretching its material limits – scratching the celluloid, puncturing it or even sticking moths to it (as in Stan Brakhage's *Mothlight* of 1963). These too were attempts to radicalize our film experience by renewal. There were cameraless films (that just used celluloid and light) and filmless films (with just light); there were experiments with screens – triangular screens, inflatable screens, multiple screens, domed screens, fragmented screens (completed by the audience) and floating screens; films were projected onto buildings or even onto dancers.

The digital cinema of the 1990s onwards, however, wished to supersede such experimentation with the still too cumbersome optical apparatus. It turned instead to creating new experiences constructed from looped images (from a finite archive), and multiple, moving desktop windows, utilizing 'spatial' over 'sequential' montage that presents action simultaneously from different, coexisting viewpoints. Film merged with hypertext so that clicking on parts of an image now helps create the narrative, as in Chris Hales's *Granddad* (2000), which has branching interactive stories that the audience chooses. Less radically, Mike Figgis's *Timecode* (2000) splits the screen into four parts and follows, in four uninterrupted shots, a series of overlapping stories made on digital video. The notion of a different film existing for each viewer has also been literalized by allowing stories to be interactively constructed by different audiences via the Internet (choice of perspective, character identification, and so on). In this respect, the exhibition of film has also converged with the possibilities offered by television broadcasting, showing stories from different perspectives on different TV channels, as in the Swedish TV production, *Noodles*, for instance, in 1996. Finally, more 'immersive' film-making has worked with properly embodied means to distend our experience by making the projection interact with our bodies. It could be that parts of the body, such as one's feet, or the whole body are required to run the film, be it directly (Jeffrey Shaw's *Reconfiguring the Cave* (1997), for example) or indirectly via motion sensing (Toni Dove's *Artificial Changelings* (1993–98)).

Each of these endeavours aim for a democratizing effect on the eye and/or the body of the viewer, though one wonders how far such freedom will go before the viewer gets bored with this increasingly one-sided activity. Of course, I do not wish to bite the hand that feeds me such wonderful examples; yet it is not my intention here to translate the idea that the film object emerges through refraction into an *imperative* for new film practices. That would be to miss the point: while each of the new media forms above are certainly exciting developments, they will themselves eventually become habitual forms such that even the use of the viewer's hand to run a film will become a transparent medium of reception (just as the eye, with repeated exposure, familiarized itself through interaction with the strange lights it first encountered in the 1890s).[19] That is why it can frequently seem that new media advocates go somewhat overboard when they regard it as the universal panacea for all art, theory and much else besides. Like Gene Youngblood's utopian vision through an expanded cinema, it almost sounds like salvation itself is being promised through new media practice. Here is

Suzanne Guerlac on media artist Luc Courchesne, whose optimism for his art seems boundless:

> This new media practice, which emphasizes features of immersivity, movement and interactivity, provides, according to Courchesne, the parameters of an 'expanded cinema', which Courchesne characterizes as 'the next mass medium', one that will supercede cinema, and that Courchesne refers back to 19th-century technologies of 'immergence' such as the panorama.[20]

The supersession of 'cinema', or analogue film per se, is not our topic. That the moving image is revealing itself to be unforeseeably plastic as it converges with other modes of sensation, communication and entertainment is. Expanding cinemas, the multiplication of the film experience, democratizing film, immersive cinema, synesthetic cinema – all of these still retain a moving image with an ability to be refracted through other media and yet maintain its identity, *just because its identity is movement in itself.*

Nevertheless, there continue to be biological thresholds, albeit ones whose restrictions can be tempered for a while. With respect to mainstream cinema, of the many complaints aimed at the use of CGI by Hollywood, what remains of most interest is less the fact that CGI habitually fails to imitate reality convincingly, but the instances when it tries to match an *unreality* that purports to be real.[21] In Chapter 2 I mentioned lens-flare as an instance of this, an artefact of optical film-making that is reproduced artificially in CGI films. It is one attempt to emulate the imperfections of the optical *in order to be real* – its flaring, its blurriness.[22] Indeed, the optical and the analogical are inherently limited (one can only zoom so fast, one can only go so high in a crane shot), and that shortfall from perfection, no matter how curtailed by effort, is also the index of its material power. It is the weightlessness of CGI – the ability to see anywhere in focus and move anywhere at speed – that fails to convince us because it offers no material resistance, no material freedom.[23]

One could, of course, attempt to program into the CGI image various forms of weight, finitude and imperfection (just as the computer in *The Matrix* attempted to program imperfections in order to placate its dreaming subjects). But, at any one time, these would be partial and haphazard, the merest outlines of reality's 'effects'. When new, these CGIs do indeed distract us from noticing the other, indefinite contextual effects which remain missing from the simulation. That is why they convince *only* when new, because they are only seen partially, the inexhaustible reserve of other random effects of the Real – when they can still resist emulation – thwarting the power of any new CGI once it has lost its fascination for us. This is matter's own resistance, its own freedom, and its own *durée.*

It is a commonplace to say that many films in the horror genre date poorly after a few years, even becoming laughable over time. Yet, it remains a telling truth, especially for those films that rely on the body and the organic for their horrific effects, for it is especially this gore that becomes comical later. Like CGI, horror dates poorly because it only works *when new*, when it has that most distracting effect of all, the effect-of-newness. The reason why the two convince so well initially is the same reason why they date and no longer persuade us in due course, because the new rarely works more than once. Their destiny is to become cartoon-like, in look and in tone. But just the same can be said about kinetic editing (such as in the *Bourne* series), and, as we will see below, our notions of acting realism (from melodrama through naturalism and Method acting to the new realisms), and even 'realism' itself: each of these is an effect of time that will eventually be refracted through new forms of time, namely from newness to pastness. Indeed, what has been said of digital CGI also pertains to the analogical: its special effects – opticals, miniatures, stunt-work, the whole realm of artifice playing for real – also succeed and then fail on account of temporal forces. Hence, Christian Metz was right to say that 'all cinema is a special effect', for any realism it possesses is an artefact that lasts at different rates and on different levels.[24]

This passing of the new need not always be a linear process either, for it can recoil on itself such that aspects of what was once out-moded can later be rediscovered as novel in unexpected ways. The earliest horror films, for instance, can take on new, frightening aspects as they reappear to more recent audiences as increasingly bizarre with age. It is not that Todd Browning's *Dracula* (1931) or F. W. Murnau's *Nosferatu* (1922), for instance, still scare us in ways that they intended (*their* special effects), but due to the unforeseen manner in which aspects of the *entire aesthetic world* they embody strike less-contemporary viewers as uncanny. What makes them disturbing is that their world or context is *so* unknown to us, literally 'un-canny' (in a non-Freudian sense): we can no longer filter out or immobilize their contexts because they are too unfamiliar to us, and it is these forgotten worlds that strike the unfamiliar viewer first, gaining the film new powers for as long as they remain novel.[25] Despite its power, however, this uncanniness cannot be called a reality *effect* for the new audience, because its visceral force stems from inadvertent processes, that is, the *real* changing ecologies surrounding the film – its own time contra the subsequent times of the audience.

The slippage between special effect and reality is not because the latter is inviolable, but precisely because reality is what continually violates *itself*, surpasses itself, so that *any* simulation of it can only ever win temporary reprieve from incredulity: there is nothing *in* reality standing still long enough to simulate for more than a passing period – that is part and parcel of the limited freedom and unpredictability of a reality in process. However, this 'passing period' of any one computer-generated image, or any other special effect, does not mark its failure but precisely the tenure of novelty during which it succeeds. It must be 'special' for a while, not forever. It succeeds while new, its novelty being what is most real about it. The only thing different about extra-filmic reality is that it has an inexhaustible supply and broader range of special effects (that surprise much more than just the eye), which is why it keeps tricking us with its unpredictability. Hagiographies of our digital or 'post-filmic' age are indeed correct as to the greater freedom to be found in CGI over the optical image, a freedom that moves cinema closer to painting than recording device.[26] But the new worlds that CGI creates are all the more convincing only in so far as they *differ* from a fixed image our own world, and not in so far as they *refer* back to it. Moreover, their greater freedom, their weightlessness, must ultimately prove a false freedom precisely because it is so pure, because it lacks the necessary resistance (or 'facticity', as Sartre would say) against which freedom can feel itself.

Differential spectatorship

No less than the film, the spectator has not been allowed to sit still either.[27] The rules of exhibition, standard for a while after the introduction of 'anamorphic' (widescreen) CinemaScope, have been moving increasingly further from the theatrical proscenium arch in recent years, with huge, curved screens coming into use that overflow our peripheral vision both laterally (in 'IMAX' cinemas) and vertically ('OMNIMAX'). But the mediations of consumption run much further than developments in exhibition. The most obvious 'distortions' to viewing frontloaded at the production end would include, to list just a few, digitization, the colourizing of black and white films, the re-editing of films for TV distribution, 'Directors' cuts', the use of 'pan and scan' home video, as well as the 'making of' documentaries on DVD that obviously effect our film understanding.

And then there are the more subtle nuances of reception proper. The use of black and white in *Schindler's List* (1993), for instance, gives it the feel of documentary, just as the camcorder presentation of *The Blair Witch* (1999) and *Cloverfield* gives both films the feel of a home-movie; and each of these, documentary and home-movie, are signifiers of realism.[28] The strategy employed in these cases marks them out as part of a larger 'visual culture' of consumption. Sometimes the mediations of new consumer technology can have unplanned retrospective effects too. When we see the painted face of Bengt Ekerot as 'Death' in Ingmar Bergman's *The Seventh Seal*, for instance, we naturally imagine that its 'theatrical' effect was intended rather than merely a by-product of the make-up available at the time. But will the make-up lines on Ewan McGregor's face, now unexpectedly visible on new high definition TV screens, make *Star Wars I: The Phantom Menace* (2001) gradually seem theatrical in years to come? In this quotation from a study of Spike Lee, we have one example of the myriad kinds of refraction present in just a simple instance of film-viewing:

> An Australian student once told me that she thought *Do the Right Thing* (1989) looked a bit like *Sesame Street*, and when I first saw the film I felt

> too as if it had been shot on a set, maybe because I have never seen it on the big screen, or maybe because its opening credit sequence shot on a sound stage colours the rest of the film.[29]

Australia alongside America, the 1970s alongside the 1980s, television alongside cinema (and so the small screen alongside the much larger one), cinema projection alongside VCR/DVD recording, the title sequence alongside the main body of the film, the studio set alongside location, as well as other filters in music video and colour schemes: fundamentally, these 'alongsides' are differentials, and they are *part of* the experience of the film, not outside of it.

Sound and false fidelity

One might have thought that the addition of sound to the silent film-image from 1925 onwards would have been a straightforward gesture towards realism, and yet even here the realities produced were and are most convincing in virtue of their inauthentic, or creative, relation between sound and vision. Michel Chion is one theorist who has listened to film sound more attentively than most. In particular, he has developed a concept he calls 'synchresis', which exposes the *unfaithful* unity between sound and image. Synchresis (a word formed by combining 'synchronism' and 'synthesis') is the psycho-physiological phenomenon in which different sensory modalities refract each other through coordination or covariance. What synchresis shows is that sound effects can be used to generate a reality effect in virtue of a *mismatch* between sound and image. Sounds are added to visual images irrespective of their true or false fidelity: all that counts is that they are 'in sync'. To quote:

> *Synchresis*... is the spontaneous and irresistible weld produced between a particular auditory phenomenon and visual phenomenon when they occur at the same time. This join results independently of any rational logic. Synchresis is responsible for our conviction that the sounds heard over the shots of the hands in the prologue of *Persona* are indeed the sounds of the hammer pounding nails into them. Synchresis is what makes dubbing, postsynchronization, and sound-effects mixing possible, and enables such a wide array of choice in these processes. For a single body and a single face on the screen, thanks to synchresis, there are dozens of allowable voices – just as, for a shot of a hammer, any one of a hundred sounds will do.... In *Mon Oncle* Tati drew on all kinds of noises for human footsteps, including ping-pong balls and glass objects.[30]

The synthesis occurs simply because of the synchronism – *Chronos* itself welding sound and image together. What is most notable is how film-makers exploit synchresis to *increase* the reality of certain implausible scenes. Various special visual effects, for instance, are made to seem 'more real' by adding an artificial sound, explosions being the most obvious case when lacklustre pyrotechnics are conjoined with thunderous noise. But how many of us have actually heard any of the kinds of different explosions depicted on-screen such that we can verify their 'soundness' (in every sense)? The same can be said for the sound of fighters' punches, or machine-gun fire, or spaceship rumble (which, of course, makes no sound at all in space). We can thus say that synchresis has a refractive function that also fabulates reality effects. Chion adds that it is not a purely conventional device, however, for not just any conjunction will work. Indeed, he states that synchresis 'very probably has an innate basis'. Hence, in addition to the conjunction between sound and visual image, another condition for a workable fabulation of reality is *refraction through ourselves* (that is, our own innate tendencies): some linkages work and others do not. Yet, the admission of the innate or hard-wired should not license any drift to essentialism: our bodies move very slowly compared to our minds (indeed, this difference in speed is the only essential thing that separates them), but they are never immobile.

Acting realism

When discussing *Casino Royale* earlier, we concluded that its equivocal reality (both being and not being Bond, or becoming-Bond) only exposed the ambivalence of all film towards the supposedly singular value of cinematic realism, given that reality itself is processual. The two final areas wherein to examine this denaturing of 'realism' – screen acting and animality – betray interesting connections in this matter. What has counted as a realistic acting performance, for instance, has continually shifted as its terms of reference have been mediated through different contexts in an alleged progress, as David Mayer puts it, from 'the "histrionic" and the "pose"... towards the verisimilar'.[31] After all, the non-acting in Italian neo-realist films like *Umberto D.*, for example, was once regarded as the high point of realism but today seems sentimental (though this may well have less to do with the performances themselves than other elements such as the music, which is often mawkish for contemporary tastes).

Moreover, it was only in the nineteenth century that realism began to invade all art forms and the word 'real' became a 'term of critical approval'.[32] As such, François Delsarte's codification of a 'gestural vocabulary' for the stage in the 1830s, for instance, seems overly 'theatrical' to us now, with its exceedingly posed movements of head, hands and arms. This gestural acting harked back to Henri Rousseau's idea of a universal preverbal language of gesture, later linked by psychologists to inner psychological states. Delsarte's theory also harboured the early eighteenth-century notion that any stance which deviated from the norm of a relaxed, upright and symmetrical body posture (the '*crux scenica*') could be read as a sign of character. This 'gestural acting', therefore, while not being realistic by our standards, could nonetheless be regarded at the time as a verisimilar performance. For what that theatre (and the early film performances it later inspired) then sought was an acting *Truth* rather than an acting realism, all art in that era being deemed a simulacrum in any case, so that reality could by necessity only appear *indirectly*.

The new 'realism' from the 1890s to the 1920s, by contrast, felt that the actor's behaviour must approach reality more immediately. Yet, such a 'direct realism', so to speak, had to face Denis Diderot's paradox for all acting, namely that 'one cannot act without feeling, yet if one feels one cannot act'. With the rise of naturalism in both D. W. Griffith's work on screen and Constantin Stanislavsky's on stage, this dilemma manifested itself in the desire for less theatrical acting on the one side, while also retaining emotional melodrama on the other.[33]

With the advent of the 'talkies', the influence of radio began to permeate film, with voice artists, trained in creating a sense of intimacy and recognizable 'types', starting to take over leading Hollywood roles. And this created another new realism through the sound of people just 'being themselves' rather than through the emotional images found in silent cinema (including Griffith). By the 1930s, these radio voices had invaded Hollywood, forming a standardization of speech around a regionless, middle-class model.[34] Subsequent, 'classical' Hollywood stars were mostly performers who specialized supposedly in being just themselves, or being 'natural' actors, playing variations of their own personality in every film. The truth of the ordinary. Yet, this ordinariness, to be sure, was a very technical achievement, especially of the voice.

Following Lee Strasberg's development in 1947 of the Method at the Actors' Studio in New York, the focus now turned to privileging emotion over such ordinary intimacy. But such emotion was now read according to Freud rather than any conventional moralism, as was the case with Griffith's emotivism. Strasberg put the emphasis on 'inner work', 'self' and 'private moment', grooming extremely sensitive and emotional (even neurotic) heroes, where weeping 'for real' became the new sign of acting greatness. Acting now involved using one's own self, one's own affective memories, to recreate the experiences needed for a role. Realism was transformed into a bare, unembellished even primitive intensity as actors seemingly *became* the characters they were playing.[35]

Yet, there remained an ambiguity within 'the' Method given the huge range of acting styles it inspired. Common ground may be discerned between Marlon Brando, James Dean, Rod Steiger, Dustin Hoffman, Al Pacino, Robert De Niro and Jack Nicholson, but it is much harder to categorize Montgomery Clift, Paul Newman, Jane Fonda, Faye Dunaway and Diane Keaton (there being noticeably more women in the second, maverick list than the first, which gathers 'neurotic' males exclusively).[36] Even the supposedly model Method acting of Marlon Brando did not always adhere to the formula of unadorned intensity, with his large use of accents and make-up and his broad portrayal of Mexicans, Indians, Orientals and Romans. None of this was a very 'Method' thing to do. Today, beyond the Method itself, we have numerous 'para-method' styles of acting in the work of contemporaries like Daniel Day-Lewis and Sean Penn, or the naturalism of Ken Loach's amateurs (which harks back to the Soviet school's use of 'types' being cast in order to play themselves), or the improvisational performances of Mike Leigh's professional actors. Acting realism comes in various guises, in other words, and seems to require periodic reformulation, from truth to naturalism, from ordinariness to intensity, in order to maintain its effect. Yet, the one sure thing about each new realism is that it affects us precisely when new, only in order to become passé subsequently, an obvious *style* refracted through time to emerge as an imitable artefact, an object (Brando's 'mumbling' or Pacino's 'shouting'). What was once a new movement must inevitably date with time, its novelty dissipating through the other, slower (or immobilized) movements around it, and therewith it becomes a thing.

Animal cinema

The addition after 1925 of sound to the cinematic image is renowned for having spelt the end of many Hollywood careers, John Gilbert's most famously, on account of their lack of voice skills. The voice in particular could be something that either reinforced the reality effect ('Garbo talks!') or ruined it. It is ironic then that Brando's gritty realism was often marked by the use and abuse of his voice – the affected mumbling being the perfect accompaniment to his far-off gaze. Such inarticulacy, the making of animal noises, remains in vogue to this day (see Philip Seymour Hoffman's work in *Happiness* (1998) especially) as if some kind of pre-verbal truth is heard when representational language is subverted by 'the inability to communicate'. Such animality in the human was particularly noted in Brando's first film performance in *A Streetcar Named Desire* (1951).[37] Brando was a new 'breed' of actor, yet one that eventually became a recognizable type (the Brando male), normally involving a highly physical, neurotic performance with a range of behavioural 'ticks'. Through his primitive grunting, but also through his body (a physically relaxed, self-touching body that scratched, ate, drank and interacted with props 'naturally'), his performance was regarded as that of the *truthful animal*.

Animals were there at the beginning of cinema, of course, in Muybridge's protofilmic attempts in the 1870s to capture animal movement, through to the early 'actualities' like the Edison Company's *Electrocuting an Elephant* (1903), the early surrealist work *Un Chien andalou* (1929), and even on into experimentalist film like Stan Brakhage's *Mothlight*. But the animal relationship with the animated image, the movie, has always been double-edged. Simply on account of the fact that the animal is not typically a performer, its presence on screen can often puncture the reality effect. Yes, of course, if a domestic animal is being treated normally, or a wild animal has been well-trained off-screen, then they appear to belong to the story. But cosy animal fables like this only serve to highlight the aberrant movements of those other animals which do shatter the illusion. The one true reason why actors should never work with animals or children (that is, humans who have yet to stop being animal) is that their lack of performance brings a rival, aleatory or thwarting movement onto the screen.[38] They are not actors, and so there is no method to them at all; nothing but the randomness of the Real.

Earlier, we cited Joseph Anderson's argument that the viewer's affects are real despite the affects on the screen being unreal. In fact, if the affects on the screen *were* real, then they would produce a very different effect in us. An animal's real on-screen pain, for instance, breaks the reality effect produced by fiction simply because it appears as a piece of the unmediated Real. If we recall the 'Puffer' episode from *There's Something about Mary*, we'll know what comedic potential lies in playing with the conventions concerning the treatment of animals in the pursuit of entertaining fictions. The presence of animal affects (or para-animal affects, as when a human baby is crying on-screen) acts like a moving *punctum*, shattering the fabulatory *studium* of all the other movements, contrived or not.[39] The animal's 'performance' only creates *puncta* that, in Rancière's phrase, thwart every other narrative function in the film. They are the animal fable that ruins the film's realism fable.

Béla Tarr's *Sátántangó* is a film with a lot of animals and animal movements. It begins with a slow tracking shot of cows walking across a farm yard, and throughout the film there are pivotal scenes with chickens, dogs, cats and horses at their visual core.[40] In one prolonged scene, however, there is a convincing portrayal of a child torturing a cat that many viewers find distressing to watch. This culminates in what appears to be the poisoning of the animal. If one does some research, however, it turns out that the cat was drugged, the poisoning simulated and the cruelty mostly only apparent. Yet, in places, the film does come very close to infringing modern standards of animal welfare in the film industry. Whatever the effect desired for the scene by the director, it usually results in distraction for many audiences. The use of real suffering in order to portray fictive suffering is fundamentally disturbing, despite the fact that social mores are also involved (it is always contestable why the killing of a fly is less worrying to most audiences than the killing of a cat).[41] But the film-makers should know this, and so should also be prepared for the feelings of repugnance that actually interfere with the viewing experience. While watching this scene from *Sátántangó* I no longer took part in the story, but was distracted by questions of reality and realism: did the makers really inflict torture? Is it a fake cat? Is it pretend poison? Are its limbs really being twisted? Did the film-makers have any animal welfare obligations? What were their motives for these scenes?[42] The de-realizing questions created by *There's Something about Mary* were clearly intended as part of the film, but in *Sátántangó* one cannot be so sure. And so the question of Other Minds – those of the makers as well as that of the animal – arises in a new, distorting fashion. The traumatic fiction on screen is lost in favour of fabulating fictions concerning what goes on *behind* the screen. That is why the graphic shooting and death of a giraffe in Chris Marker's documentary *Sans Soleil* (1983), by contrast, while disturbing to watch for many, nevertheless does *not* interrupt the effect of the film qua documentary – this a matter for the reality effect in *fiction* film only. The question is, though, why?

Between Robert Bresson's *Au Hasard Balthazar* (1966), where it is obvious that the animal cruelty is mostly simulated (especially the final shooting of the donkey), and Elem Klimov's *Come and See* (1985), where a cow clearly really is shot, lies a range of animal performers being exposed to pain, suffering and even death. Sometimes this is so that the animal can play the role it most often plays in art: that of allegory or metaphor. As John Berger writes in his essay, 'Why Look at Animals?', 'the first subject matter for painting was animal. Probably the first paint was animal blood. Prior to that, it is not unreasonable to suppose that the first metaphor was animal'. Perhaps it is only a matter of aesthetic credibility that certain films put animals under duress, for who could complain that a film reconstructing in fictive terms the massacre of thousands of Belarussians (*Come and See*) should baulk at actually killing a cow given the authenticity this adds to the *mise-en-scène* (or the artistic timidity were one to avoid it)?[43] And yet the overall effect, because the film *manipulates* real affect (by killing *for* effect), is one that ruptures the very reality desired. It creates a new reality as a side-effect – the one we fabulate concerning the making of the film, the values of its makers and the exploitation of its non-actors.[44] All Others' Minds.

The 'reduction' of human actors to suffering, starved or sexually penetrated animality in recent times – Daniel Day-Lewis in *My Left Foot* (1989), Christian Bale in *The Machinist* (2004) and *Rescue Dawn* (2006), Kerry Fox in *Intimacy* (2001) or Margo Stilley in *9 Songs* (2004), for instance – only brings this process full circle with performances that are endurance tests for the actors' bodies as much as they are tests of their skilful acting; the Real as actor as suffering animal. These 'realisms' too only serve to distract; the starved or bloated bodies of Christian Bale or Robert de Niro (in *Raging Bull* (1979)) becoming a spectacle overshadowing the rest of the *mise-en-scène* (at least while these bodily acts are novel). It is because Brando's animality, by contrast, was still and all a performance, that it achieved its pathos so much better. There was no purportedly direct exploitation (manipulation) of the Real to create reality, as if that were *the* way to reality. Instead, we are given a fabricated reality with all the resources of the unreal (performance) that thereby succeeds all the more in the mimicry of reality's own perpetual movement. Reality is not like itself either, but is what always mimics or coincides with itself only in part. Less is always more.

Realism is not a state but a movement because all perceptual reality is refractive, a 'realized contradiction' of self and world. So attempting to make it 'just so', to make a just so story with dying animals, always misses its mark. Sometimes this will be done intentionally for reasons of comedy, sometimes just to be sensational. But whereas the comedic (in *Something about Mary*) knows that we don't believe it could be just so, the sensationalist (in *Come and See*) thinks that we do. And that is why that reality breaks down at the very moment of its *imputed* credulity, for the truly moving thing about film is that it is its *own* varying reality (that creates a reality effect), not the picture of a supposed reality beyond it, 'just so' and 'out there'. The mimesis of film is of one movement by another, not of one state by another; and the miming movement is always *its own reality*, which is precisely what makes it effective. Both it, and its supposed 'object', participate in reality as parts to a whole – a whole which is itself open and indefinite.

That is why the reality effect is Pavlovian in essence: because cinema is itself animal. Its power to animate pertains to the conditionable animal in all of us, it has nothing to do with the animals (human and non-human, living and non-living) it *might* represent on screen (even with the immediacy of a 'snuff movie'). The supposed paradox of filmic reality is rather a constitutive duplicity that it shares with our equivocal reality as a whole, where everything must be partially glimpsed from varying, often elusive, perspectives. Whilst Alain Badiou rightly remarked that 'the principle of the art of cinema lies precisely in subtly showing that it is only cinema, that its images only testify to the real to the extent that they are *manifestly* images', we should not take this (as Badiou himself does) to imply that reality itself might be something qualitatively different from such images, that it *isn't* something in movement.[45] In what remains of this study, we shall look at how a philosophy that is truly *of* film, that comes *from* film, can help us think this reality-in-the-making in its own, immanent way.

A non-philosophy of cinema

According to François Laruelle, philosophy can never avoid making a 'circle with its object', for there is a necessarily circular form to explanation itself. Should one hope to discover something within a subject like film that is particularly philosophical, therefore, a transcendental stance, or prior model of philosophy, must be maintained in order to recognize it there in film. Any form of philosophical representation or reflection on the subject infects it with that philosophy's own nature. Indeed, all philosophical systems are transcendental in this sense. What philosophy calls the reality of the subject is always *its* concept *of* the subject. Hence, every philosophy is a *mixture* ('*mixte*') of that reality with a predefined interpretative schema, be it emotivist or cognitivist, materialist or idealist, ontological or epistemological. So long as we are philosophers, then, we cannot escape from the *petitio principii* of explanation.

Laruelle's own 'non-philosophy', however, makes no explanatory claims at all about the nature of any subject, or even the Real as such – it is instead a thought alongside the Real. The Real is simply *posited* as that which resists philosophy. Indeed, non-philosophy is defined as an immanent thought precisely because it does not try to think *of* the Real but is hypothesized as a part of it.[46] We must understand non-philosophy as both a practice and a metatheory, therefore. It is a practice because it is always applied to other subjects. It is a metatheory, however, because it applies itself to other philosophies too – a non-aesthetics for aesthetics, for instance, or a non-epistemology for epistemology.[47] A non-aesthetics or non-epistemology would utilize the failures of transcendental approaches to art or knowledge respectively in order to discern how the Real resists these philosophical onslaughts. Laruelle's position as regards the truth of each explanation, however, is agnostic: non-philosophy works by positing the equivalence (as regards the Real) of all philosophical positions. The autonomy of the Real leaves all philosophies relative. In a sense, non-philosophy is a metatheory that discerns the activity of the Real (in any field) through its resistance to explanation, a resistance exposed by the fall-back or recoil of *other* philosophies into their own explanatory circles. Their failures to penetrate exclusively into the heart of the matter without question begging are themselves enlightening. The epistemic failures suffered by philosophy, seen in the new, immanent light of the Real, becomes the raw material through which non-philosophy can succeed, *as Real.*

We have been pursuing a mix of Bergsonism and Laruellian thought for some time in this study as an antidote to the desire to provide necessary and sufficient accounts of what Film is. The non-philosophical Real of film has rebounded each and every philosophical attempt to explain it exhaustively. What is being offered here, then, is not one more philosophy of film, but instead a thinking alongside the Real, which, in this context, means a passivity towards film in *its* thoughtful resistance to extant philosophy. We can never know what film is directly (again, there is no top-down definition of film, no ontology of film), but, again, we can infer what it is *not* in the peculiarities of individual films' recalcitrance to various transcendent theories of film (whatever philosophers try to impose as the meaning or being of film through these films).

Such metatheorizations are not new. After all, in *Making Meaning* David Bordwell aimed for an 'analysis of the logic underlying the interpretive activity' – the irony being that the 'logic' he found in other theories (a hermeneutics of suspicion regarding 'implicit or symptomatic' meanings), actually reflected back on Bordwell's own stratagem of analysing an 'underlying' logic.[48] Bordwell's use of science, moreover, was supposed to immunize his own discourse from any circular application of such a logic (just as Edward Branigan's cognitivism kept his own Wittgensteinian relativism at bay), but could do so only by dogmatic assertion. William Connolly, however, comes closer to the effect that I hope to achieve. Comparing his own reading of Hitchcock's *Vertigo* with what he describes as the 'too complete and closed' interpretation of Slavoj Žižek, Connolly subsequently argues for a new 'reciprocal modesty' that must keep the text open:

> Interpretations presented as both authoritative and final close down experimentation with new possibilities of being and action before the experiments have a chance to get off the ground. An inordinate confidence in the explanatory sufficiency of a particular narrative often goes hand in hand with the tendency to mute the significance of technique in film and life.[49]

Of course, this statement also rebounds on itself by implying an authority, by pointing out the fluid contingency of everyone (else) from a place of rest and necessity. Yet, it would be all too facile and probably churlish for us, at this stage, to make the *tu quoque* argument once more, this time against Connolly. For Connolly's purpose is not primarily the epistemic one that would fall foul of such a relativism. His is not a question of knowledge so much as of attitude:

> It is not Žižek's interpretation, then, that I contest, but the aura of certainty and incorrigibility that surrounds it...Žižek gives no sign that he *acknowledges* the deep contestability of the most basic assumptions of Lacanian theory. I will argue that this *acknowledgment* forms a critical virtue of theory itself.[50]

Acknowledgement (so important, as we saw, for Cavell too) is a kind of action as much as a kind of knowledge. It is perhaps a performative knowledge, a practice, and the only way to escape the circularity of explanation, of knowledge as the representation of *how things are*, is through such a kind of emergent knowledge through practice. This active knowledge is not a representation but an affect, an attitude that imbues the willingness to constantly re-vision the object, and to re-view (again and again) how others view it too. The 'affect' mentioned above is the patience to look at all views, a re-viewing patience that will thereby fabulate the event of a new philosophy of film composed from the processes of other philosophies.

Such an ecumenical position is more than mere liberal-minded openness (that only succeeds in offending everybody equally), but the achievement of something positive. The relative failure of each theory is also a partial success, each one catching a glimpse of what it is trying to explain that, when mixed together, allows a new view to emerge. Deleuze *and* Bordwell *and* Cavell *and* Žižek... offer us a differential philosophy of film, a montage of theories that refract each other simply by their being copresented. Branigan's radiality, Deleuze's movement-image, Anderson's selective perception, Bordwell's empiricism, Badiou's empty essence of cinema, Žižek's traumatic Real, Cavell's acknowledgment, Perkins's suggestion, Rancière's thwarted fable, Laruelle's non-philosophy, Bergson's fabulation: all are partial glimpses but are never, and could never be, the whole. And there is something quite cinematic about this very process of stitching ideas together. In *Creative Evolution*, Bergson argues that both perception and intellect are cinematographic in form. We for our part might say that each theory of cinema is also a perceptual frame: only when projected together from the one, moving reel do we get an approximation to the reality of film.

This could also put us in mind of the founding phenomenon of the Soviet school of cinema, the 'Kuleshov Effect', which showed how crucial montage is to film experience. The Kuleshov Effect describes how subsequent images change the meaning of previous ones when they are cut together: the same image of an unexpressive face intercut with a laughing baby is interpreted as happy by one audience, but intercut with a dying soldier is interpreted as sad by another.[51] Such emergent effects are differential – *and so is a comparative philosophy such as this*: that is, it builds its effect by mixing the partial failures of others together. We edit others to create our own meaning (and one for the audience), and such refractive practice involves names (Bordwell, Badiou, Branigan, and so on) as well as themes (embodiment, spectatorship, performance, animality). What some disparage as 'associational thought' can be given a new methodological purpose, therefore, as 'montage thinking', for all thought is a *mixte* of some kind.[52]

Again, this is not simply a question of relative views. In *On the Genealogy of Morals*, Nietzsche insists that if our search for knowledge is possible then it must be multiperspectival: 'there is only a perspective seeing, only a perspective "knowing"; and the more affects we allow to speak about one thing, the more eyes, different eyes, we can use to observe one thing, the more complete will our "concept" of this thing, our "objectivity", be'.[53] Yet, it is not so much that *we* have 'more eyes' when perspectives are spliced together like this in montage thinking, but that we see further how the subject matter or Real (in our case, film) shapes our thinking, quite literally, in terms of the relationship of spurned overtures between theory and film. An immanent thought – one belonging to the subject *matter* as well as the subject – doesn't represent its object. It is not 'about' it, but is a part of it, and as such thinks alongside it. We should no longer think of thought as something representing passive things, but rather as something *that things do themselves alongside us*. In other words, an immanent thought thinks in a spatial configuration that is also a temporal co-genesis – this very metaphilosophical presentation *here* being born alongside a re-visioning (over time) of others' views and viewings, one that recontextualizes them in a view of our own making (in part), a meaning of our own making (in part). It can be called a 'Pavlovian' thinking in virtue of certain repetitions, accelerations and decelerations conditioning new thoughts in us and new objects before us out of our encounters with others, be they either films or views of films. We see others' images refracted through ours, adding our views into the mix of their own various *mixtes*.

What is thinking (again)?

And what, in all of this, has become of 'thinking' when it proceeds immanently according to the Real or mereologically as 'part to whole'? What is a non-philosophical thinking, be it in film or anywhere else? Laruelle himself doesn't say. He does say that it is ubiquitous, however. Whereas philosophy is 'intrinsically anti-democratic' and judgemental, non-philosophy denies nothing and affirms all: it seeks a 'democracy between philosophies, and between philosophy and the sciences, arts, ethics, etc'. It is also called a 'science of science'.[54] The principle of our post-Heideggerian age, on the other hand, has been to ask continually for true thought and real thinking. This is because, supposedly, the most thought-provoking thing in our thought-provoking time is that 'we are still not thinking'. From the position articulated here, however, the opposite is the case. Thinking is everywhere. For some, this will be unacceptable. For some, the true philosophical horror is not that we are not (yet) thinking, but that we have *always* been thinking. Given the view that philosophy must have an essence and so an exclusivity, then what is (philosophically) unthinkable is that thinking might be found all about us. As F. H. Bradley quaintly put it in his *Aphorisms*: 'it is not true that Mr. X never thinks. On the contrary, he is always thinking – about something else'.[55] The question, then, might not be what is thinking (singular)?, but what is it that makes thinking plural? – what is this 'something else' that makes thinking democratic rather than aristocratic?

I am not offering an essence of thinking here, of course: just an outline formed by thinking's resistance to any essentialist definitions of it. But what does that outline show – what is the 'it' that does this resisting? For one, it is that there is no 'it' at all, but *many kinds* of thinking, such as that shown by film when it resists us. One can't point to thinking in any current situation other than by sheer *fiat* – 'I hereby name this activity "thinking"'. Neither, surely, is it a matter of *what* we think or *that* we think or even *who* is thinking to the exclusion of all and everyone else; rather, it is *how* we think and *with what* we think and *why* we think, irrespective of whether this includes too much (wine, football, cinema) or too many ('idiots', animals, bodies). For instance, if thinking was restricted to the articulation of language, then it would essentially be the same as human speech (be it internal 'mentalese' or public behaviour). If it was restricted to information processing, then it would essentially be the same as the cognitivist view of perception and representation. The same goes for definitions in terms of complexity of response, which essentializes the question in terms of supposedly identifiable, extant and (normally) human behaviour. Even if thinking is given a privileged, special relationship with Being (rather than human being), then it would still be exhausted in the *ontology* of that relation. Or if it were seen in a creative encounter with an outside force, then it would be exhausted in the *concept* of that creativity.[56]

And so on. Each of these *exemplary* cases restricts the idea of thinking in a presumptive manner. What we have learnt through the course of this work about 'philosophies of film being philosophical' is also true, therefore, of philosophies of thinking: they presuppose what they wish to prove through the examples they choose. That is, if thinking is ever described in terms of any exemplary activity, then it is confined to the implementations of that activity – be it the examples on which the definition has been based, or those which have 'based' themselves on the definition (either an empiricist or a rationalist rendering will suffice). If, alternatively, we reject this move, then we are left with either a dogmatic assertion from one amongst the contending definitions and examples (that will always involve a question-begging presupposition that selects just the right examples to support the dogma), or an openly axiomatic choice from the same set. Either covert or overt question begging.

Philosophy, to return to what we said at the outset, is a subject perpetually in search of its content (once it has given up the dream of being a science with its own set of eternal truths).[57] It is a parasite or symbiant, inherently relational: the philosophical is the moment when 'another' discipline, like politics or literature, or another object, like film or wine, finds itself in a state of transformation, with its own identity crisis. Or rather, it is when such matters find subjects whose relationship with them is mutually transformative. It is the *relationship* between those subjects (its audience, its practitioners) and the subject matter that is philosophical. That, at least, is the optimal case whereby the philosophical status of wine, say, concerns what we mean by philosophy as much as what we mean by the experience of wine (that is, the meaning, concept or being of wine; or, in sum, just 'wine').[58] A relational philosophy, consequently, is a tautology. Philosophy becomes itself only when it stops trying to be one thing, when it gives up on the dream of eternal truths, and finds itself again in the philosophical (transformative) moments of non-philosophies.

We are doing philosophy, in other words, when our relations (with politics, with film, with wine) give rise to new philosophy, to new thinking, rather than simply offering reflective mirrors for ready-made philosophy or thought. Of course, this will not aid us in finding a definition of either thought or philosophy (in its mantle of 'real thinking') given that the *explanans* has been rendered in terms correlated with the *explanandum*. But that is precisely the point: the *correlation* is all that matters, for what is correlated is not one subject representing another (in a 'philosophy of *x*') as if both were standing still long enough to be defined so that the one can be a picture of the other. The correlation is the *novelty* that the two *co-engender* in each other, subject and object, so-called. No less than a film coevolves with its spectator (a single viewer or large audience) in each viewing event, so philosophy coevolves with its 'object' (or subject matter) in an event of novelty when both refract each other (a fabulated significance rendered by that subject from the processes of the subject matter). Philosophy is not *of* the new, it *is* the new – in its struggle, in its shock and its wonder. Which is not to define it at all in terms of 'the new' (as if we *knew* what that meant), but only to say that philosophy is perpetually indefinite and resists definition.

So, in coming back to the question, 'what is thinking?', perhaps we should stop begging for these questions of definition altogether. To offer a first alternative: what, instead, if thinking was never any definite or extant activity? What if thinking was simply whatever undoes any simple, extant definition? What if it were based on something baseless, namely novelty (but without any one definition of the novel) or movement (but without regard for 'movement in general')? We could then simply say that thinking is everywhere and anything (there is no exclusive locus for it, it is found at all loci). But with that, we would have a rather unhelpful and empty form of relativism. A second alternative, though, would be to add 'something else' to this half assertion: that our inability to exclude any locus for thinking is predicated on the openness of thinking from our point of view (what Bergson would call a complete relativism that reinstalls a new meta-absolute of openness), an openness that *sees* the multiplicity of definitions of thinking *together* as an increasingly detailed group of contours. This outline itself shows one thing only, not a complete content (*the* definition) but a further, perpetual movement machine (the indefinite). The plurality together gives us the outline of perpetual renewal: extant plurality equals *more* plurality to come. Not many truths equalling no truth, but the endless becoming of truth.

Such openness to the new is not *reflective* knowledge (be it even a metarepresentation or higher order logic) but an acknowledgment made visible through action and affect. Such modesty is hard to come by (as William Connolly found when reading Žižek). When, for example, the American film producer in Godard's *Contempt* (1963), Jeremy Prokosch, reads the following Socratic wisdom from his little red book, one suspects that we are about to hear a thwarted fable: 'to know that one does not know, is the gift of a superior spirit. Not to know and to think that one does know, is a mistake. To know that this is a mistake, keeps one from making it'. Prokosch (played wonderfully by Jack Palance) seems to embody William Goldman's rule that 'nobody knows anything' in Hollywood with appropriate epistemic modesty. But it is soon clear that this modesty is false, not only because of his simultaneous display of arrogance during and after this scene, but because of the impossibility of such a statement as this left on its own. Indeed, Prokosch immediately concludes his speech by showing his book and adding 'I have the knowledge here', putting into words what his performance was already telling us visually – that 'superiority' doesn't come from second-hand truisms.

The knowledge of 'unknowing' is a kind of affect and action (rather than the representation of unknowing that we saw in Žižek's 'traversing the fantasy'). Hence, we do not know or define what the new is because the new *can only* be felt – that is why it is new, why it is a 'shock to the system'. The new is an affective moment of a peculiar sort (for not every affect is new); it is the new emotion, what Bergson calls a 'creative emotion' that at one and the same time also engenders new thoughts. Such an affect is opposed to neither reason nor representation, but overcomes the duality of rationalism and emotivism. In *The Two Sources of Morality and Religion*, for instance, Bergson looks at the non-philosophical origin of ethics:

> alongside of the emotion which is a result of the representation and which is added to it, there is the emotion which precedes the image, which virtually contains it, and is to a certain extent its cause…an emotion capable of crystallising into representations and even into an ethical doctrine.[59]

Out of such affectivity comes new doctrine. Yet, the affectivity in question here is not any supposedly dumb feeling, but precisely the affective thinking *in* time (which is all that Bergson means by 'intuition') that precedes its spatialization into doctrine:

> Antecedent to the new morality, and also the new metaphysics, there is the emotion…neither has its metaphysics enforced moral practice, nor the moral practice induced a disposition to its metaphysics. Metaphysics and morality express here the self-same thing.[60]

Remember that affects are not opposed to concepts – indeed, our affective temperament, according to Gregory Bateson, is a learnt one, a form of knowledge involving meta-emotions. Recall also that inverting our thinking about anything (including thinking itself) is not easy but painful (in Bergson's view). Such pain is not with respect to its content but its form as a part, not representational or reflective but mereological – a relation of part to whole. Intuition takes a violent effort, a huge and difficult struggle against common sense: it is the effort to *bend thought backwards towards its object*. The part tries to part-icipate all the more in the world, to expand itself, to return itself to the object, to think as things think themselves. So the 'self-same thing' that is being co-expressed is neither propositional content awaiting form, nor formless affect awaiting its concept, but the 'creative emotion' or intuition that is contentful because creative or new, and new because affective – the affect of the new.

Is this *finally*, then, the definition of thinking in film that we've been waiting for? Real, that is philosophical, thinking equals 'the affect of the new'? Or should one call it the 'shock' of the new, or 'wonder' at the new, or the 'pain' of the new? Without wishing to abuse the reader's patience any longer, we must still note that these formulae are all, in Branigan's phrase, 'vacuous', and doubtlessly circular in Laruelle's view too. Acknowledged. As a consequence, they are only quasi-definitions or pseudo-formulae, for they point to what cannot be defined. Still, they do so with word combinations that try to *suggest* a meaning and affect in the reader by only providing a glimpse. That is why they do not form a complete picture but an outline, created through the combination of terms, mixture of ideas or refraction of concepts that a reader may fabulate in his or her own mind (or not). It is a type of Kuleshov effect with no guaranteed result, only the suggestion of one 'brought from below' (*suggerere*), a 'script outline' for the viewer's movement-imagination to complete.[61] A definition aspires to represent the whole, in part or in full, but an outline can only present the whole in part, to show it in part, when that whole is itself never complete.

Bergson gives some quasi-definitions of his own for this partiality: 'thinking in duration' (*penser en durée*), the 'inversion' of the 'habitual direction of the work of thought' (*invertir la direction habituelle du travail de la pensée*), 'thought and the moving' (*la pensée et le mouvant*). If one asks after 'the moving', to wit, 'the moving *what?*', the answer will be the moving *anything*, including the *moving image*, so long as that 'thing' is genuinely moving for you, that it transforms you. It is not the thing that counts (which is itself a complexity of other movements condensed into an immobile by your perception), but how it moves (you) – the movement as transformative relation between subject and object.[62] Everything is indeed a refractive movement, but in any one situation we must acknowledge the impeded refraction facing back at us as our reflection, our image, our truth. The play here on 'movement' – qua passage *and* affect – is not intended to boil movement and novelty down to affectivity on the subject-side, for the play itself is *another* movement between the false dichotomy of objective passage and subjective affect. That is, it must not be reduced to a one-sided current definition, which is why these are pseudo-formulae or indefinite, 'dynamic' definitions.[63]

Finally, if the suspicion again arises that 'novelty' or 'movement' are being described in circular terms here (a 'genuine movement' being a 'transformation' that genuinely moves us) then this definitional circularity must be displaced through action. Bergson gives the example of actually swimming in order to break the definitional circle that knowledge of swimming is a prerequisite of learning to swim; that is, an actual movement must be enacted to show that something new – beyond present knowing *and* being – is possible. Or as Rancière puts it in *The Ignorant Schoolmaster*, 'the circle of emancipation must be *begun*'.[64] Only *this* enactment and showing acknowledges its own new knowledge. Is not something similar happening when film moves us to think its thoughts by 'inverting' our normal ways of thinking? It breaks our definitions of what is and is not 'thinking' by retrospectively creating new possibilities in the wake of its own actuality. Cinema then co-engenders a new notion of philosophy, a philosophy that may well be unrecognizable to all those who take pride in calling themselves 'philosopher'. To many, this would be the unphilosophical in person.

Conclusion: Code Unknown – A Bastard Theory for a Bastard Art

I think you're right...
He thinks you're talking a load of shit.
Swings and roundabouts innit?[1]

In praise of being unphilosophical

It is in his *Essays on the Blurring of Art and Life* that Allan Kaprow writes of the process of 'un-arting' or the taking of 'art out of art', which he describes as that 'act or thought whose identity as art must forever remain unknown'. Art's identity comes through not being self-identical. What will be the great dramatic work of tomorrow, for instance? This work, according to Bergson, is 'not yet possible', but it '*will have been possible*' in the future anterior where such things exist.[2] Such things are unforeseeable, unrecognizable. The becoming of being again. Can't we say the same for philosophy? To dephilosophize or unphilosophize, to embrace the insult of being 'unphilosophical' as one's own, because the alternative of being recognized as 'proper' comes at the cost of also being a cliché. This is not to romanticize a reflex negation of *all* philosophy following Wittgenstein or Rorty, but the necessary change of orientation that is the only way to enact a new philosophy. According to Alain Badiou, there are no events in philosophy, not real ones anyway – but there are. Just as a political event redefines what we mean by the political (a view he shares with Jacques Rancière), so too a philosophical event will redraw the map of non-philosophy and philosophy.[3] Socratic unknowing, or the methodological agnosticism practised in Laruelle's non-philosophy, is not about weaving exotic mysteries just for the sake of failing, for the sheer lack of it, but to create something new in the name of what *could* become 'philosophy'.[4] If philosophy has always appeared most clearly when tackling insoluble problems (and hence 'mysteries'), it is not for reasons of representation, but because philosophy itself *is* the gap between part and whole, the *mere*-ological glimpse of an indefinite whole, as when a part tries to think the whole. This gap is not at all empty but filled with affect – the pain of inverted thinking, as Bergson put it.

Cinema thinks, but in a non-philosophical way. Or rather, cinema unphilosophizes what philosophy – and thinking – thought it was. And it does this by resisting what philosophy thinks film and so also it itself are when philosophy *applies* itself to film and *illustrates* itself through films. Just as we cannot say what Life *is*, other than the biological process that undoes any attempt at saying what it is (and the *élan vital* is the principle of this unknowing or 'uncanniness'), so we can also hypothesize an *'élan cinématique'*, the force of which undoes any attempt at saying what film is – world-view, concept creator, cultural product, unconscious identification, information process... The *élan cinématique* offers us no content but only a (dynamic) form, a dia-gram, resisting any complete explanation.[5] Deleuze, of course, had already written that thought can only be born when an outside encounters the unthought within the thinking brain.[6] Yet, he then went on to fill in that formula with a definition of philosophical thought – as concept creation – that retrieved a privileged and impenetrable position for philosophy (and so also another for non-philosophy). But philosophy and its non-philosophies are only place-holders; they are provisional, temporal entities. At any one moment, though, a philosophy of film will fabulate both (the event of) film and of itself from the processes of viewing films and other film theories. (Even the theory of 'fabulation' is itself only another name for a movement *as seen* in the processes of fiction-making.)

A 'process metaphysics' of film highlights nothing more than film's own boundlessness and resistance to theory, especially ontological theory. Admittedly, this idea could be applied to every art (indeed, strictly speaking, it must apply to every 'thing' too), but film is of significance for being that art which *ostensibly* resists definition like few others, just because 'it' is so hybrid (part theatrical, part literary, part photographic, part musical, a group-manufactured commercial art-product). Film is hybridity itself, or, in Bergsonian terms, creativity in the raw: which is only to say that the very messiness of film – which is fast approaching even further levels of divergent mess through new forms of media and spectatorship – merges with the same messiness of reality.

Is that it then? Not an answer to the question posed at the outset but a resetting of what that question should have meant, namely, a suggestive outline (formed via the differentials of cinematic resistance to theory) that the reader must complete by refraction through his or her own imagination? As regards answering with *one* philosophy of filmic thinking, yes, that's all folks.[7] But as regards the practice of further cinema theory, perhaps there could be more. Perhaps there can be a 'science' to this unknowing in Laruelle's sense of a democracy of thought or 'science of science'.

Filmology: from unknowing to pluriknowing

Certainly, I don't believe that any one theoretical approach can exhaust the potential of film: the effects of film-meaning are stratified in physical, psychological and social realms each one of which can be addressed, in part, by numerous descriptions stemming from diverse conceptual stances. Indeed, one might argue that there is no such thing as film per se but only and ever particular films, and that the singular empirical reality of each – as silent or 'talkie', as black and white or colour, as mainstream or avant-garde, as French or German, as pre-War or post-War, on this film stock or that, and so on – may *sometimes* warrant an emphasis on one approach over others, without at the same time reducing those others to zero.

But this is only another way of saying that a pluralist science of film is desirable (or that 'Film' is an indefinite concept). And more *can* be said about that, for there was a moment when such a science did exist. It was during the post-war Filmology movement in France and before the hegemony of the semiological approach from the mid-1950s onwards. This was an extensive school of thought, with books, conventions and a journal produced under its patronage. Ironically, in his book *Language and Film*, Christian Metz himself characterized this filmological era as a pluralist and eclectic movement, a brief interlude of uncertainties between the generalistic approach of pre-war theory and the synthetic one of structuralist semiology.[8] Though it gradually became a narrower, more empiricist project in the 1950s (even prefiguring Metz's search for the underlying codes of film), it initially took a pluralist view of film research, analysing both what it called 'filmic facts' and 'cinematic facts' (or cognition *and* culture, broadly speaking) and insisting on the need to study them through psychology, phenomenology, sociology, anthropology, linguistics, pedagogy and aesthetics.[9] One of its chief exponents, Étienne Souriau, set out seven levels of reality relevant to film: the afilmic (or world), the profilmic (the reality photographed), the filmographic (the film as material object, celluloid), the filmophanic (the film as projected on screen), the diegetic (the film's world), as well as creatorial and spectatorial realities.[10] Each reality was to be given its due and its own scientific methodology. Indeed, the founder of Filmology, Gilbert Cohen-Séat, was initially inspired by Bergson to pursue the study of 'elements and different groups of facts, each of which, without bringing us to a desired conclusion, points to a direction in which it will be found'.[11]

As a movement, however, Filmology was deemed a failure because it never achieved a 'true synthesis' or systemization of all the various facts it accumulated (which even included research into how dogs watched films). It was criticized by Marxist theorists, such as Maurice Caveing, for not employing any method other than 'a quasi-undefined enumeration of constantly changing materials'. Rather than being a true, dialectical science, filmology was 'all enumeration and addition'. Xavier Tilliette compared it to the story of the blind men examining an elephant who conclude separately that it must be a snake (for the nose), spear (tusk), wall (belly), tree (leg) or fan (tail). Yet, the defence from filmologists was that 'one cannot make [cinema] an object of study unless one first takes it as a whole, indistinctly, in all the reality of its own existence'.[12] As another member of the movement, Marc Soriano, wrote: 'Filmology is oriented in so many directions because its object is so vast'.[13] For our own part we would say that those blind men glimpsed more than those who do see an 'elephant in the room' – they only went wrong in reaching (hasty) conclusions about what it was that they were feeling. And given that there is no transcendent view of film – so that we are *all* partially blind – it is best to stay with the facts, chaotic though they may be.

The alternative to Filmology – indeed the alternative that was historically realized and which we have been studying throughout – has been a 'hierarchy of hermetic discourses', some favouring the cognitive (Bordwell), some the psychoanalytic (Žižek), some the naturalistic (Deleuze), some the phenomenological (Cavell). All have taken just one or two of Souriau's seven levels of cinematic reality (the filmophanic being most prevalent). Christian Metz himself focused only on the diegetic level, interpreting the six others through it according to a linguistic paradigm. Yet, we don't have to stay within the hermetic. Might it not be possible to reignite the original pluralism of Filmology, which Edward Lowry described as a 'free forum where all ideas related to a methodical study of film were welcome and sought out'? All that unites those who are interested in film is its name and its varying object, an object of divergence. Not simply unknowing, then, but unknowing in action – a minimalist view of science such as this (the ongoing disunity of enquiry) could offer a banner broad enough for all.[14] This would be an eclecticism without dilettantism, for there is no lack of commitment in thinking that every position warrants commitment.[15]

Beyond coprology

Conversely, might not philosophy also learn from such pluralism? Indeed, don't we practise it in any case, unacknowledged? Why, after all, do philosophers, more than any other theorists, always disagree with each other? Why has no one philosophy ever been hegemonic (when not within the favour of a state's Christian or Marxist violence)? To put it in other words, why isn't philosophy ever like (normal) science? We could give an answer in direct epistemological terms: philosophy just hasn't learnt enough yet. Or we could offer the more indirect, ontological answer: philosophy is destined to err because it can never relate itself to Being appropriately. Yet, the ontological response assumes a knowledge of Being just as the epistemological response assumes the Being that will be known when philosophy finally gets its act together as a science (perhaps through logic or cognitivism). The circle of being and knowing again.

But what of the time of this circularity? Might the *agon* of philosophy be neither because one theory is right and the other wrong, but simply because time exists? Time is real. Hence, no theory can be acceptable, no stasis or status quo ever accepted – not because we can't desire it, but because desire is temporal like everything else, because things would stop otherwise. Alain Badiou is fond of reciting the end of Beckett's *Unnameable* with respect to the paradox of eventful action (pursuing an action whose justification *must be* a self-fulfilling prophecy): 'You must go on, I can't go on, I will go on'.[16] With respect to philosophers, however, the only certainty is that they do always go on.

A part *must not* be the whole, even though it tries to be. Indeed, though 'normal science' never stands still for long either, what makes philosophy different is that its nominated problems are whichever ones refuse and refute unanimity at any one time.[17] Out of this conflict of times we glimpse the shape that every thought has as its form; and this form is nothing less than the complexity of its own movements, which include its resistances. These resistances give us a glimpse of thinking, its form as movement against our movements. And, finally, this also gives every philosophy, including the philosophy of film, a nascent shape, created in the interference between contrary movements.

I said at the beginning that Derrida was 'nearly right' when he proposed that the death of philosophy is the one remaining question that might found a community of philosophers.[18] And nearly being right, or approaching the truth, is the best we can wish for, because it is not a death or absence that is ever in question, nor its opposite in a singular presence (philosophy as the a priori, as logic, cognition, concept, or whatever else): rather, it is the ongoing regeneration and reformulation of that which it 'will have been possible' to call philosophy. That future anterior is co-engendered through the refraction between philosophies and their provisional non-philosophies. What Rick Altman writes of cinema – that it is 'constituted by a continuing interchange, neither beginning nor ending at any specific point' – must also be true of philosophical thought.[19] Philosophy is the continual interchange or refraction between itself and its other. What matters, therefore, is not trying to establish once and for all which theory is right and which 'a load of shit', but only whether or not to continue on the swings and roundabouts of thinking.

Notes

Preface

1. MacNeice 1979 (*Snow*, 1935).
2. Light 2003, p. 1.
3. See Badiou 2005b.
4. Kaprow 2003a, p. 7. David Bordwell traces this essentialism back to Kant and the neo-Kantians, who thought each art would have an aesthetic essence, with the avant-gardist artist being the one 'to safeguard the purity of each medium' (Bordwell 1997, p. 28).
5. Bazin 1967, p. 14; Kracauer 1960; Youngblood 1970; Cavell 1979, pp. 4, 164; McGinn 2005, p. 3. See also Nancy 2001, p. 20: 'all in one, film is ubiquitous, it can take in everything, from one far end of the earth to the other'; he also writes here that 'film is also present in everyone's experience'.
6. McGinn 2005, pp. 4–5.
7. McGinn 2005, pp. 132, 136.
8. McGinn 2005, p. 201.
9. See, most famously, Jean-Louis Baudry's essay 'The Apparatus: Metapsychological Approaches to the Impression of Reality in Cinema' (Baudry 1992, p. 693): 'Plato's prisoner is the victim of an illusion of reality, that is, of precisely what is known as a hallucination, if one is awake, as a dream; he is the prey of an impression, of an impression of reality.'
10. Horkheimer and Adorno 1969, p. 107.
11. See Herwitz 2008, p. 4: 'It is like supplying the words for a man who is stumbling upon a great idea without quite being able to articulate it, in whose genius the idea appears intuitively, in the form of a radiant image which needs to be analytically unpacked.'
12. Herwitz 2008, p. 125.
13. Frampton 2006, pp. 12, 189; Goodenough 2005, p. 30.
14. Merleau-Ponty 1964, pp. 59, 54; Lyotard 1991, p. 176.
15. Laruelle 2006.
16. Mitchell 2005, p. 5.
17. Watson 1984, pp. 17, 18–19.
18. Badiou 2004a, p. 79; Rancière 2006, p. 4; Ingarden 1989, p. 321. This is not an uncommon view, as David Bordwell points out: 'What sort of art was cinema? Some observers held it to be a synthesis of older arts' (Bordwell 1997, p. 29).
19. Bazin 1967, p. 21; Keane 2007, pp. 2, 151. Here, on the other hand, is Anne Friedberg taking the pessimistic line on convergence: 'As new technologies trouble the futures of cinematic projection and reception, "film" as a discrete object becomes more and more of an endangered species.' (Friedberg 2000, p. 448). But even here it is the material basis of 'film' as film-reel, as celluloid, rather than optical medium, that is in crisis.
20. This use of 'virtual' and 'actual' is from their original Bergsonian sense, not the Deleuzian one that reverses their values; see Mullarkey 2005.
21. Throughout this study I will specify any film mentioned by the year it went on general release and/or its director. The latter, however, is in no way an

endorsement of *auteur* theory – the idea that the director is the master of the film's value (if it has any) – but simply in conformity with the current convention. I would be just as happy if films were conventionally specified by the name of their 'best boy' instead.

22. See Noël Carroll's (2000) essay 'Moving and Moving': '"Structural film"...was represented, perhaps most illustriously, by Michael Snow, Hollis Frampton, and Ernie Gehr. Structural filmmakers – like the minimalist postmodern choreographers – attempted to pare down whatever seemed extraneous in their work in order to discover the nature of film. They sought to shrink their repertoire of devices to just those that would foreground the essential elements of the medium. If a film like *Wavelength* – a zoom shot, sometimes interrupted, of a loft – contained anecdotal or narrative material, it was only there in order to be parodied and, ultimately, to be bypassed in favor of the real star of the show: cinema as personified by the play of pure cinematic devices, such as the zoom shot, which itself was predicated upon engaging the audience in a rarefied act of apperception regarding the conditions of the cinematic experience.'
23. 'Nonart is whatever has not yet been accepted as art but has caught the artist's attention with that possibility in mind.' Non-art, Kaprow says, 'exists only fleetingly...Indeed, the moment any such example is offered publicly, it automatically becomes a type of art' (Kaprow 2003b, p. 98).
24. Kaprow 2003b, pp. 111, 146. See also Zepke forthcoming.
25. Derrida 1978, p. 79; 1994, p. 373.
26. See Hardcastle 2006 and Frankfurt 2005.
27. Cited in Bordwell 1985, p. 48.
28. In one of Alain Badiou's most recent Paris seminars (for October 2007, as transcribed by Daniel Fischer), he confessed (not for the first time) to wanting to make a film on the life of Plato, with Brad Pitt in the lead role: 'Dans le film que j'ai l'intention de consacrer à la Vie de Platon, je pense, après avoir apprécié sa performance dans *L'assassinat de Jesse James*, que Brad Pitt serait excellent dans le rôle de Platon. DiCaprio serait très bien dans celui d'Alcibiade, mais je ne vois pas bien encore quel comédien pourrait interpréter celui d'Aristote.' One suspects that he must be joking, but the matter is undecidable.

Introduction: Nobody Knows Anything!

1. Jeremy Prokosch (Jack Palance) in Jean-Luc Godard's *Contempt* (1963).
2. Homer Simpson in *The Simpsons*, 'Sweets and Sour Marge', Episode 277 (Season 13). First aired: Sunday 20 January 2002.
3. Perniola 2004, p. 34.
4. Deleuze 1986, p. 152; Rancière 2006, p. 51; Cavell 1979, pp. 65, 66, 67; Deleuze 1986, p. 203; Žižek 1991, p. 105. See also Žižek 1991, p. 106: 'the birds, far from functioning as a "symbol" whose "signification" can be detected, on the contrary *block*, *mask*, by their massive presence, the film's "signification", their function being to make us *forget*...with what, in the end, we are dealing: the triangle of a mother, her son, and the woman he loves.'
5. Connolly 2002, p. 13.
6. Frampton 2006, p. 12; Goodenough 2005, p. 30.
7. We'll later see Stanley Cavell make the point that if 'the only films you care about are carefully chosen masterpieces' then one doesn't really care about film as such (Cavell 1979, pp. 6, 15).

8. See Deleuze 1986; 1989; and Shaviro 1993.
9. I am making no distinction between the 'transcendent' and the 'transcendental' (as Kantians claim should be made), for the latter is simply the Platonization of one type of logic, making a certain kind of conceptual (and spatial) thought normative.
10. See Mullarkey 2006, pp. 127–8.
11. Noël Carroll also asks whether film theory 'should be catholic about the methodological frameworks it explores' rather than essentialist (Carroll 2003, p. 361); nonetheless, as we'll eventually see, this doesn't stop him forwarding a form of methodological purity and aesthetic essence of his own in film theory, one based on cognitivism.
12. And, of course, 'Film Theory' itself (which I'm here contrasting with 'Film Studies' with only some slight exaggeration) has always been interdisciplinary: indeed, this has arguably been the source of its perpetual anxiety – its *lack* of any separate identity (ironically, something it shares with 'pure' philosophy). See Friedberg 2000, p. 448: 'As the field of "film studies" has been redefining itself, both revising its internal historical accounts and opening up its field to the emerging multiplicities of "cultural studies" and "visual studies", much of this work has been coincident with the campaign for the academic legitimacy of film studies as a republic separate from its former disciplinary overlords.' (Friedberg is using 'film studies' where I would say 'film theory'.)
13. Wollen 1980, p. 21.
14. Jancovich 2002, p. 154.
15. Tania Modleski cited in Cherry 2002, p. 170.
16. Miller 2001, p. 309.
17. See Bergson 1988; Badiou 2004a; Rancière 2006; and Agamben 2000.
18. Bordwell and Carroll 1996, p. xvi.
19. As we will see, Deleuze's so-called 'irrational' cut, for instance (part of the time-image), has come to be used for wholly rational, expressive ends in much commercial (or movement-image) cinema.
20. See Lowry 1985.
21. Frampton 2006, p. 12; see Mullarkey 2006, pp. 125–56.
22. Jarvie 1987, p. 34.

1 Illustrating Manuscripts

1. Rowlands 2003, p. 111.
2. The same could be said for the murderer's 'point-of-view' shots on the men fishing in Ray Lawrence's *Jindabyne* (2006), which turn out to be something else entirely. See Chapter 6 n. 10.
3. Chiesa 2007, p. 18.
4. See Falzon 2002, pp. 13–14.
5. See Abrams 2007; Conard 2007.
6. See, for instance, Litch 2002, p. 1: 'a work of fiction can sometimes function like an argument'.
7. Strictly speaking, Anderton is not one of the predictors – this is done by the pre-cogs, three humans with the psychic ability to foresee certain future events – but, nonetheless, he heads up the team that interprets the pre-cogs' visions as predictions of future criminal acts. As one of the characters puts it: 'the oracle isn't where the power is anyway. The power's always been with

the priests.' There is a nice analysis of the paradox of predictions interfering with themselves reflexively in Žižek 2006, pp. 201–2, 207–8 that compares the film with Dick's original story.

8. Though it is argued that *Jaws* (1975) was the first high-concept film, it is really from the 1980s onwards that this form of film came to the fore. That film-philosophy itself emerged on the heels of this development is probably no coincidence.
9. Alain Badiou configures the proposition of *The Matrix* thus: '*The Matrix* deals with the question: what is a subject who struggles to escape the slavery of semblance, which is in turn the subjectivated form of biological slavery?' (Badiou 2008). He even finds that, at a more general level again, this film shares the very same problem with two other science-fiction films released in 1999 (*eXistenZ* and *Cube*): 'the fundamental problem of cognition: what is it that, from within our own capacity to know, testifies that it is indeed the real that is at stake in our cognition?'.
10. J.G. Ballard and Kurt Vonnegut would be two of those exceptions. Though one might also mention Jules Verne or H.G. Wells as important literary figures in their own right, this is more for their decisive contributions to the genre in which they wrote rather than any to the literary form as such that might come near to that of peers like Emile Zola and James Joyce, respectively. In film science fiction itself, after some dominance of the genre by thinly veiled anti-science and anti-communist allegories in the post-war era (*It Came from Outer Space* (1953) or *Them!* (1954), for example), more seriousness was injected into the genre by French film-makers like François Truffaut (*Fahrenheit 451* (1966)), Jean-Luc Godard (*Alphaville* (1965)) and Alain Resnais (*Je t'aime, je t'aime* (1968)). This more mature attitude rebounded on the US scene in the late 1960s and early 1970s in subsequent films such as *Planet of the Apes* (1968), *2001: A Space Odyssey* and *THX-1138* (1971), paving the way for the high-concept films of the 1980s onwards.
11. Rowlands 2003, pp. vii, ix, 207.
12. Rowlands 2003, pp. 187–8.
13. Rowlands 2003, p. 111.
14. Rowlands 2003, p. 256.
15. Litch 2002, p. 2.
16. Litch 2002, p. 117.
17. Litch 2002, p. 44. She notes (p. 203 n. 9) that *Memento* also communicates its ideas more through its structure rather than plot and dialogue.
18. Litch 2002, p. 46.
19. Falzon 2002, pp. 4–5, 6, 19.
20. Falzon 2002, p. 38.
21. Falzon 2002, p. 6.
22. In this volume, only the first film in the trilogy is examined, a testament to the fact that this one alone has spawned a good number of other studies by philosophers. There was a sequel, *More Matrix and Philosophy* (2005), which covered the later films, *The Matrix Reloaded* (2003) and *The Matrix Revolutions* (2003). See also Faller 2004, Couch 2003, Gerrold 2003 and Lawrence 2004.
23. See Knight and McKnight 2002; Freeland 2002, pp. 213–15.
24. Of course, illustrations, qua diagrams or pictures, may be able to do something some might call philosophy or thinking through their own intrinsic properties (see Mullarkey 2006, pp. 157–186). But when such pictures are treated, not for their own pictoriality, but as illustrative of something else, then, in this mode

at least, they do not philosophize anew but simply repeat old ideas. However, a recent work by Thomas Wartenberg (2007) makes an interesting attempt to by-pass the dichotomy of 'illustrating' versus 'doing' philosophy by thinking of illustration as a doing. Wartenberg (p.44) achieves this, however, only by calling 'philosophy' any expression that sufficiently refers to certain nominated 'philosophical' topics (in certain nominated articles, books, and so on). Consequently, films that illustrate can 'do' philosophy as well because such reference without creativity is what most traditionally nominated philosophy texts do in any case. In other words, Wartenberg has allowed film enter the philosophical club simply by lowering the entry requirement to the little that film can do, that is, repetition is enough. Yet, though textual philosophy must also be allowed its own, albeit rare, moments of philosophical creativity (which is to say, those moments when it is quintessentially philosophical simply because it is not repeating extant 'philosophy'), where are we to find the equivalent moments in cinema? Textual philosophy can both repeat and create, for Wartenberg, and still be philosophical in both modes. But while cinema is allowed to repeat others (philosophical texts), when is it allowed to create for itself, that is, to be cinematically philosophical? In Wartenberg's account, cinema can think only when it is doing the least thing that words can do; but where does that leave the other, more prized notion of thinking, if not in the hands of non-cinematic philosophy alone? On the view of the present study, however, given philosophy's inessentialist essence (where, contra Wartenberg, creativity really does count), then neither books and essays in journals that simply repeat prior views (with different but familiar words), nor films deemed illustrative of similarly prior views, are philosophical. My argument against reducing film to text throughout this book, therefore, is two-fold: it concerns both specific textual philosophical positions being the pre-text to read films in the light of their prior written wisdom (and so ignoring the possibility of films creating their own, new, philosophies, by whatever means available to them); and, at the same time, philosophy per se (new or old) only being recognized in a film's textual elements (plot and dialogue). Indeed, it is because film's audio-visual nature is not allowed its own philosophical creativity, that film is reduced to prior, that is, textual, forms of philosophy. In this sense, every text is a pre-text.

25. See Smith 1995; Litch 2002, p. 2.

2 Bordwell and Other Cogitators

1. Bordwell 1997, p. 31.
2. Bordwell 1997, pp. 30, 69–70, 31, 43, 44, 2–3, 4.
3. Bordwell 1985, pp. xi, xiii, 30. We should note that Bordwell forcefully rejects the overly abstract theories of classical information processing (with its sender, receiver, code, message, context, noise, channel, etc.), and lays stress instead on concrete information/cue processes that push the spectator toward making various sorts of inferences from what he or she sees on-screen. Even with this more embodied approach, however, there is still a distinction in his account between the isolable content of the film (*syuzhet*) and what we do to it (how our brain processes it into the *fabula*). It is this duality that we have in mind when using the term information with respect to Bordwell and his representationalism. See pp. 49, 50: The *fabula* is the 'pattern which perceivers of narratives create through assumptions and inferences. It is the developing result of picking up

narrative cues, applying schema, framing and testing hypotheses'. The *syuzhet* 'is the actual arrangement and presentation of the fabula in the film'. It is the 'architectonics of the film's presentation of the fabula'. Bordwell separates out style as an additional dimension that interacts with *syuzhet* and beyond the arrangement of story (actions, scenes, plot turning points).

4. Bordwell 1997, p. 150.
5. See Caughie 2007, pp. 418. Even non-cognitivists agree that, in place of theory, academics are now 'developing "mixed genres" of writing which merge textual analysis with historical or ethnographic research' (see Jenkins 2000, p. 177).
6. Bordwell 1997, pp. 4, 6; Bordwell 1989a, p. 274.
7. Bordwell 1990, p. 109; Bordwell 1985, p. 76; Bordwell 1989a, p. 266.
8. Bordwell 2006, p. 119: 'What has changed, in both the most conservative registers and the most adventurous ones, is not the stylistic system of classical filmmaking but rather certain technical devices functioning within that system. The new devices very often serve the traditional purposes. And the change hasn't been radical.'
9. Bordwell 1985, pp. 228, 80, 39, 151.
10. This was written in collaboration with his partner Kristin Thompson in Bordwell and Thompson 1992, pp. 436–42.
11. See also Catherine Belsey's analysis of the Brechtian elements of *Tout va bien* in Belsey 1992, pp. 125–46.
12. Bordwell and Thompson 1992, p. 438.
13. Bordwell and Thompson 1992, p. 439.
14. Bordwell and Thompson 1992, p. 441.
15. Bordwell 1985, p. 332. But see Frampton 2006, p. 110: 'there might be many "camera/figure orientations" in a difficult Godard film, but it is a little simplistic to see these technical aspects as reflexive "themes"'; and 'when writers cannot make dramatic sense of a stylistic moment, they often chuck it in the excess bin of "reflexivity"'.
16. Bordwell 1985, p. 54; Frampton 2006, p. 108: 'Following Bordwell we might just get analyses of stylistically innovative films as simply *deformed* or *abnormal*'.
17. Frampton 2006, p. 104. Frampton rightly regards Bordwell's peculiar category of 'parametric cinema' cited here – where art films sustain their transgressions in a finely patterned order (the work of Bresson being most indicative) – as a 'sub-genre of art-cinema'.
18. Bordwell 1985, pp. 206, 212; see Frampton 2006, p. 109: 'we may "understand" these kinds of films better – understand their structures and modes – but this is a limited and limiting kind of "understanding". Bordwell's clarifying ambitions dull these films'.
19. Bordwell 1996a, p. 29.
20. Bordwell and Carroll 1996a, p. xiii.
21. Bordwell claims that his 'Poetics' (as he calls it) is not a theory like Marxism or psychoanalysis, but a 'conceptual framework' (Bordwell 1989a, p. 273), as it doesn't provide a hermeneutics, only a poetics of interpretation. He also states in this text that even to criticize him entails using his own concepts: 'criticising this book's conclusions will entail using its own concepts. The interpreter can probe the preceding chapters for implicit meanings, expose what is repressed, project new semantic fields onto nodal passages, trace out a journey of values or an Oedipal allegory, pun on my terms, deflate my rhetorical pretensions, and so on'. Of course, this would imply that Bordwell's poetics is irrefutable and so, by its own lights, non-scientific.

22. See Bordwell 1996a; Bordwell 1989a, pp. 96, 104, 217, 219, 221 222. He adds as well that it was mostly an 'aggressive rhetorical stance' that maintained 'theory's institutional authority'.
23. Bordwell 1989b, p. 11; Bordwell 1997, pp. 8–9.
24. Bordwell 1997, pp. 10, 144.
25. Bordwell 1989b, p. 19.
26. Bordwell 1989b, pp. 18, 22.
27. Bordwell 1989a, p. 248; Bordwell 1985, p. 231.
28. At times there is even a neoconservative tone to Bordwell's rejection of Theory. He cites as an 'excellent study' (Bordwell 1996a, p. 33 n. 53) Gross and Levitt's *Higher Superstition: The Academic Left and its Quarrels with Science*, a well-known weapon in the armoury of right-thinking positivists during the science wars of the 1990s, which themselves replayed themes from the culture wars of the 1980s between the Liberal Left and neoconservative right wings of academia. Žižek also places the post-Theory debate within the context of the science wars (Žižek 2001d, p. 2). And Murray Smith explicitly links Sokal and the science wars to film theory's excessive continentalism, and its lack of interest in truth, verification, honesty, clarity, etc (as if these terms were neutral predefined values); see Smith 1997.
29. Bordwell 1985, p. 33; Bordwell 1989b, p. 12.; Bordwell 1985, p. 31.
30. Bordwell 1989a, pp. 79–82; Nowell-Smith 2000, p. 14.
31. See also Perkins 1990, p. 5 for another criticism of Bordwell's notion of 'cue': 'A cue is not a cue until it is picked up, but if we retreat to speaking of potential cues we are then talking of everything that the film contains'.
32. Bordwell 1985, p. 62. In Philosophy of Mind this is known as the 'homunculus fallacy'.
33. Perkins 1990, p. 2. In other words, aesthetics is not reducible to ideology.
34. Perkins 1990, p. 4.
35. Perkins 1990, p. 6. He gives the example of how fly swatting in one scene from *Caught* can mean something romantic.
36. Perkins 1990, pp. 1–2.
37. Bordwell 1989b, pp. 263, 16, 14. See also p. 15: 'cognitivism assumes that empirical science may help solve traditional philosophical problems'.
38. Bordwell 1989b, p. 17 (the second sentence in this quote was added in Bordwell's on-line version of this article); Bordwell 1989a, pp. 208, 209, 38. By contrast, bad theorists use 'inductive or pseudoinductive arguments which back up a claim' – and enthymemes – 'deductive or pseudoinductive arguments' (Bordwell 1989a, p. 36).
39. Bordwell 1990, p. 108; Bordwell 1997, p. 113. Sometimes the particularism of specific analyses can reach extremes even for Bordwell, such as with Raymond Bellour's famous article 'The Obvious and the Code' that devotes itself to examining a simple segment of just 12 shots from *The Big Sleep* (see Bellour 1986). Here we might conjecture that an empirical method that plunges so deeply into one supposedly exemplary example does so partly in order to evade having to tackle other less compatible examples.
40. See McGowan and Kunkle, p. xxi: 'For Lacan, as for Freud, psychoanalysis is a project of interpretation that has nothing to do with empirical research'.
41. See Bordwell 1998, p. 1.
42. Bordwell 1997, p. 269. In *Narration in the Fiction Film* Bordwell uses the phrase 'in our culture' a good deal (Bordwell 1985, pp. 32, 34, 35, 38) when establishing his universals.
43. Bordwell 1996b, pp. 91, 92, 93.

44. Bordwell 1997, p. 269; Bordwell 1989a, pp. 248, 208.
45. Bordwell 1996b, pp. 105, 94; Bordwell 1997, pp. 152, 155. A reason for its popularity with film-makers is that it solves the problem of ensuring that the audience's attention is directed where the film-makers want it to be at any one time.
46. Bordwell 1989b, p. 18.
47. Bordwell 1985, p. 32; see Bordwell 1997, p. 164: 'Our capacity to shift visual attention' is 'transcultural'.
48. See Bordwell 2005a, pp. 264–5.
49. Bordwell denies having a 'theory-neutral' sense of comprehension. But he does forward a sense based on an 'intuitive theory about stories and human action that cultures share' (Bordwell 2005a, p. 262). As regards Žižek's argument, the nuances Bordwell introduces here smack of hair-splitting, for they are mostly irrelevant.
50. Žižek 2000, p. 39. Rancière 2006 (pp. 9, 98) also talks of Flaubert's 'frames', micro-narrations framed like film-shots, in what he also calls 'literary cinematographism'. See Bordwell 2005a, pp. 298–9 n. 59 for Bordwell's rebuttal of Žižek, which does not impact on the general point against Bordwell's conflationism. Hence, we only go *part* of the way with Žižek's culturalism: it is not via textual culture that differences can be spotted within the universal, but also via embodiment, that is, even biology is different, its universality being itself mobile and non-cognitive, and *for perfectly biological reasons*.
51. Bordwell 1985, p. 31.
52. Varela et al. 1991, pp. 139–40 (cited in Connolly 2002, p. 92). See also Tikka 2006, pp. 141–3.
53. Bordwell 1985, p. 31; Bordwell 1990, p. 107; Bordwell and Carroll 1996a, p. xvi; Bordwell 1989b, p. 24; see also Bordwell 1985, pp. 46–7: 'every fiction film ... asks us to tune our sensory capacities to certain informational wavelengths and then translate given data into a story'.
54. Here is Bordwell's formal definition (Bordwell 1985, p. 53): 'In the fiction film, narrative is *the process whereby the film's syuzhet and style interact in the course of cueing and channeling the spectator's construction of the fabula*'. As Frampton puts it (2006, p. 114): 'Theories of narration ultimately separate form and content'.
55. Bordwell 1985, pp. 54, 283, 136; Perkins 1990, p. 3. Frampton 2006, pp. 103, 4: 'he believes that cinema is always attempting communication'; or 'for Bordwell (and his structuralism) images are only there to tell us something'. Of course, Bordwell doesn't think of this proposition as a hidden or repressed *meaning*.
56. See Deleuze 2000, p. 371: 'In the same way, Sandra's car in Visconti's film [*Vaghe stelle dell'Orsa* (1965)] is embedded in the past, and we see it at the same time as she travels through space in the present. It has nothing to do with a flashback or with memory, because memory is only that which was once present, whereas the character in the image is literally embedded in the past, or emerges from the past.'
57. Bordwell 1985, p. 79.
58. Frampton 2006, p. 111.
59. Bordwell 1989a, p. 268; Bordwell 1985, p. 166 (here he is talking about Lubitsch's *Lady Windamere's Fan*, 1925).
60. See also Bordwell 1985, p. 74: 'The film absolutely controls the order, frequency, and duration of the presentation of the events. You cannot skip a dull spot or linger over a rich one, jump back to an earlier passage or start at the end of the film and work your way forward.'
61. Cited in Bordwell 1985, p. 283.
62. Bordwell follows the 'searchlight' rather than 'bucket' metaphor of mind.

63. Frampton 2006, pp. 108, 106. See also p. 106: 'Bordwell, for all his intentions, is still ultimately *separating* style and plot, and even asks whether a filmgoer can see film style on its own, separate to the story.'
64. See Frampton 2006, p. 112: 'Narration only concerns plot events and structure, and not all film is dedicated to storytelling, or *storyshowing*. Narration is a *process*, and to stretch this concept of process into "being" in order to cover every element of the film (images, characters, edit shifts) is to virtually cut all ties with its original literary meaning, and thus delete any original usefulness. It also carries a limiting resonance of this literary usage: it denotes "story construction" and a story-bound entity, rather than the fluid mixture of story and pure, autonomous sound-image-art that we find in the most interesting cinema. Narration is direction of the drama, not the creation of film-worlds, and consequently theories of film narration are overly "dramatic" and "literary" in their concerns.'
65. See Anderson 1998, p. 123.
66. Branigan 1986, p. 49.
67. Branigan 1986, p. 50.
68. See Mullarkey 1999 and 2005.
69. See Bergson 1988, p. 37.
70. Bordwell 1985, p. 219. He is referring to Resnais's *La Guerre est fini* (1966) here.
71. Cavell 1979, p. 129. See, for example, this instance of Bordwell's bias: 'In my terms here, the critic ascribes expressive qualities to certain referential and explicit meanings'. An example he provides is when one critic describes a facial wound as a Lacanian lack (Bordwell 1989a, pp. 264, 217). Yet, who could ever sensibly say that a facial *wound* is itself a theory-free description?
72. See Cutting 2007, p. 9, putting the view bluntly: the *'Hollywood style'* that Bordwell portrays has evolved in the way it has because 'it must mesh with the human visual system'. Yet, Cutting will also admit (p. 22) that there are no hard and fast rules of editing so much as 'axioms'.
73. See Douglass 1999, p. 216: 'The "key-hole effect" of the very tight shot maximises awareness of this limitation, which does not disappear as the shot widens – rather, it becomes simply less occlusive, leaving us less *consciously* aware of our dependence upon the camera's movement to disclose what lies out of frame. As [William] Wees says, the peculiar thing is how desensitised audiences are to film's distortions: "The situation has become so thoroughly institutionalised that the dominant cinema, its audiences, and most critics who write about it happily accept perspectivist norms".' Conversely, it is now said that Imax is *not* good for narrative (faces are too large, cuts must be limited, there cannot be too much movement, close-ups are too grainy, and the overall effect is nauseating). But the same was said of CinemaScope at first – no doubt we'll get over it.
74. Bordwell himself points to Jacques Tati's amazing ability in *Playtime* (1968) to present six hours of *fabula* and *syuzhet* time in just 45 minutes of screen time, *even though he uses continuity cuts throughout*. See Bordwell 1985, p. 82.
75. As Edward Branigan writes, whenever we are 'perceiving fictionally', mistakes in continuity can be overlooked because we inhabit an imaginative diegetic world built upon our acquired bodily knowledge of the 'real world'. We would simply add that that knowledge and world is itself not static. See Branigan 2005, pp. 176–7.
76. Bordwell 1985, p. 164, my emphasis.
77. Bordwell 1985, pp. 157, 158: 'Spatial configurations are motivated by realism (a newspaper office must contain desks, typewriters, phones) and, chiefly, by compositional necessity.'

78. Bordwell 1985, p. 328.
79. See Wuss 2002.
80. Bordwell 1985, p. 207.
81. Rancière 2006, p. 13.
82. Cited in Maltby 1996, p. 434.
83. See Frampton 2006, pp. 110–11: 'Ellipses may be modernist, but what does that tell us about their appearance in a film such as Steven Soderbergh's *The Limey.*' Frampton wants to focus on how the film's ellipse 'thinks a relationship to the characters'.
84. Metz 1977, p. 665.
85. Žižek 2001d, pp. 21, 18. Žižek also argues that it is erroneous to think that an abstract 'depth of field' has persisted across classical cinema. But note the illogic of the logic of non-abstract, singular examples – how are they *all of* 'cross-cutting', for instance? Is Žižek getting his generalization for free, or is this a (wilful) performative contradiction? Bordwell exploits this weakness in his reply to Žižek in Bordwell 2005a, pp. 298–9 n. 59.
86. See Deleuze 1986, p. 160; see Bordwell 1985, p. 166 where he admits that Hollywood classicism is not exactly the same as Italian 1930s classicism, or Polish 1950s classicism (for instance, less happy endings): 'But most of classical narrations *principles* and *functions* can be considered congruent with those outlined here'.
87. Bordwell 1996b, pp. 95, 92.
88. And Bordwell knows this, as when he states that expectations are also transtextual, founded on other films and genres (Bordwell 1985, p. 44). So why does he demote this value when it comes to specifics like reading a character? Why does he reduce it to the face? As Frampton argues: 'there seems to be little or no mention of the *experience* of these films, and the possible ways a filmgoer might *see* a film using, for example, the knowledge they have about the genre of "parametric narration"' (Frampton 2006, p. 110).
89. See Bordwell 1997, pp. 96, 99, 106. A good example of the cultural variant of Bordwell's classicism is Noël Burch's early socio-political explanation of the emergence of the 'Institutional Mode of Representation'.
90. Bergson 1972, p. 1092.
91. See Merrin 2003.
92. This adoption has not always been uncritical, however: some analytic film philosophy is at times confident enough to question the probity of the cognitivist approach. See Allen and Murray 1999, p. 3.
93. McGowan and Kunkle 2004, p. xii n. 1.
94. With the exception of Noël Carroll, who does still work on creating ontologies for film.
95. Carroll 1988, p. 149.
96. Carroll 1999, p. 21. It has been said that cognitivists oppose their 'rational' filmgoer's activity to that of the 'irrational' mental activity of the continental subject (see Frampton 2006, p. 150). If 'irrational' here means 'emotional', then this is surely an overstatement as regards analytical philosophy and even cognitivist film theory. Bordwell, however, admits that he is ignoring affectivity in his approach, which he believes he can separate off from the information a film conveys. See Bordwell 1985, p. 30: 'a perceptual-cognitive account...does not address affective features of film viewing', and 'I am assuming that a spectator's comprehension of the film's narrative is theoretically separable from his or her emotional responses'.

97. We are using 'emotion' and 'affectivity' interchangeably here.
98. Plantinga and Smith 1999, p. 6: 'the cognitive philosopher emphasises the thinking part of an emotion, with thinking consisting of the emoter's evaluation or judgment about the object of the emotion'. In other words 'thinking' means representing the object.
99. See, for example, Tan 1996, p. 197: 'As is customary in theories of the cognition of discourse, we are assuming that the viewer's comprehension of the film narrative begins with the formation of the text base, a propositional representation of the discourse. This text base is the first result of following with understanding the filmic action, which is relatively close to the directly observable surface structure of the film.'
100. See Grodal 2000.
101. Grodal 1999, pp. 133, 144.

3 Žižek and the Cinema of Perversion

1. Žižek 1991, p. 105.
2. Bordwell 1989a, pp. 272, 257.
3. Bordwell 1989a, pp. 251, 13.
4. Bordwell 2005b.
5. Žižek 2006, pp. 209, 170, 224.
6. Žižek 2006, pp. 216–17.
7. Bordwell 1989a, p. 264: 'A sensuous criticism needs rich models of perceiving, and the best ones currently available emphasize that perceiving is structural and categorial.'
8. For example, Bordwell simply ignores the fact that Žižek has good reasons for denying the 'subject–object split'. For Bordwell, the split is a 'good thing' lest we lose our 'personal identity, veridical perception, and inner states of pain and memories' (Bordwell 2005a, p. 264). The irony that such so-called desirables as 'personal identity' have not been heavily critiqued by Lacanians seems lost on him.
9. Bordwell finds Žižek's arguments 'commonplace', 'banal', 'possibly unintelligible', 'imprecise', 'idiosyncratic', 'rhetorical' or even simply absent; Bordwell 2005a, pp. 260–4, 298–9 n. 59.
10. Žižek 2001c, p. 65, my emphasis; see Bordwell 1985, p. 29. Hence, the accusation that he has only internalized the representational phenomenon (rather than explained it), and that he has ignored the role of the viewer proper in favour of the non-conscious activities of his or her brain.
11. See Bordwell 2005a, p. 299 n. 59 where Bordwell concludes that, on account of various hostages to fortune in Žižek's arguments, 'he agrees with me even when he says he doesn't'.
12. Shaviro 1993, p. ix.
13. Cavell 1996, p. 91; see Boothby 2001.
14. McGowan and Kunkle 2004, p. xii; Freeland 1996, p. 198. Moreover, it is a particular Freudian priesthood that is perennially invoked – Freud, Lacan and sometimes Julia Kristeva. But what about Adler, Reich, Horney or Klein? See Freeland 1996, pp. 199–200.
15. See Eysenck 1985. The concept of the unconscious has alternative psychological origins too in the work of Jean Charcot, Pierre Janet and numerous other models that were current at the end of the nineteenth century: See Ellenberger 1970. (Which is still not yet to mention its literary origins in Robert Louis Stevenson, Bram Stoker et al.)

16. Cited in Eitzen 1999, p. 86.
17. Thornham 1997, p. 33. The Lacanian approach was introduced into film theory by figures such as Metz and Baudry, and it was soon echoed and amplified across the English Channel in the writings for the journal *Screen* by Stephen Heath and others.
18. Lacan himself restates the problem by making woman's non-existence (at least symbolically, given that language operates 'in the name of the father') an explicit theme. In their turn, post-Lacanian feminists, from Irigaray to Butler, have remedied this problem with different heterodoxies, most often by postulating other grounds for language, from a feminine symbolic to performative communication.
19. Baudry 1992, pp. 706–7.
20. As Freeland asserts: 'in broader ways that go beyond psychoanalysis, in all these theories (Mulvey's, Creed's, and Williams's) the focus is also psychodynamic – that is, there is some presumed general or universal psychological theory that grounds their analysis' (Freeland 1996, p. 198). See for instance the following: 'In my view, the black thing on the horse's mouth which frightens Hans makes more sense if linked to the mother's black underwear, which no doubt included garters/suspender belt' (Creed 1993 p. 95).
21. This section's title alludes to Hal Foster's *The Return of the Real: Art and Theory at the End of the Century* (1996), a book that, in its own sphere of art theory, plays out the same return to Lacanian motifs, especially the idea of trauma as precursor to the ingress of the Real, as found in Žižekian film theory.
22. Silverman 1988, p. 35.
23. Žižek 1991, p. viii.
24. McGowan and Kunkle 2004, p. xiii. The essays in this collection are said by the editors to take Žižek's work 'as their point of departure'.
25. Žižekians have argued that contemporary films (1990s onwards) are also much more open to such analyses given their proximity to the Real: 'the encounter with the kernel of the Real' – this is what 'much film today' concerns. The contemporary scene offers us a 'series of films that enact trauma, jouissance, fantasy, and desire in unprecedented ways' (McGowan and Kunkle 2004, p. xxiii).
26. Žižek 2001a, p. 33, my italics. See also Myers 2003, pp. 15–17.
27. McGowan and Kunkle 2004, p. xvii.
28. Žižek 2001d, p. 148.
29. Žižek 2002, p. 254.
30. Žižek 2001b, p. 21. See also Ronen 2000, p. 129: 'unlike the ethics of deconstructive aporia which poses a moment of fracture or split as part of the process of symbolization itself, Lacanian psychoanalysis poses a distance between the Real and its symbolization and, as noted by Žižek, a well-acknowledged interpreter of psychoanalysis, the moment of fracture is caused by the surplus of the Real over every symbolization. This surplus is what I believe philosophy misses when it only refers to whatever symbolization can contain. To acknowledge this surplus means that we come to terms with a kernel resisting symbolic integration and know that it is in this kernel, which meaningfulness cannot inhere, that shows interpretation as involving more than comprehension...The symptom, that impossible presence of the Real in the symbolic structure is both a presence and an absence and is therefore what cannot be dissolved through interpretation. The place of the symptom in the analysand's discourse is the same as the place of the 'object a' in language'.

31. Žižek 2000, p. 43; 2002, pp. 259, 262, 264.
32. Žižek 2002, p. 246.
33. Žižek 2001a, p. 40; 2000, p. 29; see Žižek 2001c, pp. 61–3. In fact, metaphysics is perhaps the ultimate conspiracy theory on this view. It is interesting that the title of Žižek's recent text, *The Parallax View*, comes from a 1974 film typical of its era, a paranoid thriller reflecting the anti-establishment politics of the mid-1970s as also found in *The Conversation* (1974), *All the Presidents Men* (1976), *Marathon Man* (1976) and *Three Days of the Condor* (1975).
34. Žižek 2001c, p. 84: 'Reduced to its elementary skeleton, perversion can be seen as a defence against the Real of death and sexuality, against the threat of mortality as well as the contingent imposition of sexual difference.'
35. Žižek 2001a, p. 49; 1991, p. 86; 2001d, p. 176.
36. Žižek 2001d, p. 34.
37. Žižek 2001c, p. 60.
38. See Žižek 2000, pp. 23, 46 n. 23. See also p. 46 n. 28: 'a phallic dimension to the twin personae of Little Man and Giant in the Mr Ed Room in "Twin Peaks": the two anamorphically distorted versions of "normal size" man, one too short, the other too large, like a penis in erection and non-erection.'
39. Žižek 2001a, p. 13 (this is said in regard to a message returning to its sender in such a true form that it repulses him, that is, when Rupert discovers that Brandon and Philip have lived out his Nietzschean teaching by committing murder).
40. Žižek 2000, p. 17.
41. Žižek 2001a, pp. 146, 32. Žižek states that Wilhelm Reich was no longer a psychoanalyst once he began bodily massages to relieve neurotic tensions.
42. Žižek 2001a, p. 54. See also: 'in pronouncing a word, the subject contracts his being outside himself; he "coagulates" the core of his being in an external sign. In the (verbal) sign, I – as it were – find myself outside myself, I posit my unity outside myself, in a signifier which represents me' (*The Indivisible Remainder: An Essay on Schelling and Related Matters* cited in Myers 2003, p. 42).
43. Žižek 2001d, p. 160.
44. Žižek 2006, pp. 207, 208. See Žižek 2003, pp. 111–47 ('Science: Cognitivism with Freud') which pre-empts some of the cognitivist material published later in *The Parallax View*.
45. Žižek 2006, p. 215. Žižek says he is here following the representationalism of Thomas Metzinger.
46. Žižek 2001d, p. 15.
47. Lacan 1994, p. 250; McGowan and Kunkle 2004, pp. xxii, xxiv, xxvii; Žižek 2000, p. 43.
48. See Myers 2003, pp. 16–17. W.J.T. Mitchell comments on this dogmatism as follows: 'there are two Žižeks for me: the good Žižek, who is an anarchist, a magnificent if sometimes perverse interpreter and speculative theorist... Then there is the bad Žižek, who is a fundamentalist, a paranoiac, a Leninist, and (that terrible temptation) a moralist' (Mitchell 2005, p. 71).
49. Interestingly, Žižek defends himself against charges of charlatanism (as when he openly created a spurious argument concerning 'the double frame' in *The Fright of Real Tears*) by showing how it was done *consciously*. His acts of academic fraud (especially regarding his 'cut and paste' method of republishing old writings as new) are not symptoms or actings out, but conscious and intended. See Žižek 2007a.

50. See Myers 2003, pp. 108–9.
51. Žižek 2000, p. 41, my italics.
52. Žižek 2002, p. 247; Lacan has always said 'there's no such thing as a metalanguage' (Lacan 1999, pp. 118–19).
53. See also Žižek 2007b, p. 188 on Freudianism supplementing cognitive science in terms of its own inherent contradictions (between reductive materialism and non-reductive materialism, between antimaterialism and new mysterianism – Colin McGinn's view): 'if psychoanalysis is to survive and retain its key status, one has to find a place for it within the brain sciences themselves, from their inherent blanks and impossibilities'. See also Žižek 2007b p. 187 on quantum physics: 'quantum physics confronts us with the gap between Real and reality at its most radical: what we get in it is the mathematical Real of formulas which cannot be translated into ontologically consistent reality'.
54. See Balmary 1982; Miller 1986; Masson 1985; Esterson 1998 argues against Masson that both the fantasy theory *and* the seduction theory were foisted on analysands, that is, they were constructions of Freud's changing theories.
55. It is doubly ironic, then, that the myth of *Oedipus Rex* that Freud so heavily leans on actually begins with his parents' mutilation and abandonment of him as a child. That Freud only picks up the story when the adult Oedipus kills his father Laius clearly facilitates Freud's own fantasy of childhood desire rather than a realist interpretation of childhood abuse. I mention this to underline how films can be read again in the light of non-Freudian and non-fantasy theory. One such example is in the work of William Paul. Contra the interpretations of Barbara Creed or Carol Clover, he argues that a good deal of post-1960s horror is focused on the child (be it girl *or* boy), and that some films from this genre even engage in an apologetics for 'child abuse' (Paul 1994, p. 282).
56. Žižek 2000, p. 42.
57. Deleuze and Guattari 1984, p. 58.
58. Žižek 2000, pp. 29, 30, 31, 34. See also Žižek 2001d, p. 115, where 'incest' is glossed as 'honouring one's father'!
59. Žižek 2005, p.175. It should be noted that Žižek has a theory of imbecility or stupidity at work here which takes it beyond being merely a term of abuse, as we'll see.
60. Žižek 2001a, p. 195; 2002, p. 240. See McGowan and Kunkle 2004, pp. xxi, xxii: 'conceiving reception as intrinsic to the filmic text itself removes the analysis of film from the realm of the social sciences and returns it to the domain of interpretation – its proper province'; or we must focus on interpreting 'the filmic text (and find the spectator inherent within – rather than external to – this text)'.
61. Bordwell 2005a, p. 269.
62. Kennedy 2000, p. 5; Cavell 1979, p. 122, 39.
63. Jarvie 1987, p. 34.

4 Deleuze's Kinematic Philosophy

1. Deleuze 1980, pp. 205–6.
2. Deleuze 1989, p. 280.
3. Deleuze 2000, pp. 366, 367; 1989, p. 36. Another shared problem would be the opposition between 'extreme moralism' and morality, which 'weaves a whole set of relations of great value between philosophy and the cinema' (Deleuze 1986, p. 116).

4. Deleuze 1989, p. 209.
5. Martin 1993, p. 172; Deleuze 1989, p. 161; Mengue 1994, p. 284. Of course, there is another direction that the sin of mere application could take, when a philosopher translates another's theory (of film) into his philosophy, something Noël Burch comes close to accusing Deleuze of in an interview (see Myer 2004, p. 75, where Burch talks of Deleuze translating his *Theory of Film Practice* into philosophy).
6. Deleuze 1995, p. 58. We will see later that the affective and perceptual are only two aspects of cinematic imagery in the *Cinema* books.
7. Deleuze and Guattari 1994, pp. 8, 24, 167, 191–2, 199, 218, 208. Cinema is referred to in the main text on pp. 2, 163, 186 – that is, rarely.
8. Bogue 2003, p. 23 (my italics); Deleuze and Guattari 1994, p. 171.
9. Deleuze 1980, p. 209. Nor can there be a synthesis of the *Cinema* books according to Ropars-Wuilleumier (1994, p. 255).
10. Deleuze and Guattari 1994, pp. 197, 198; Deleuze 1986, p. 185.
11. Deleuze 1986, p. xiv.
12. Deleuze 1986, pp. 116, x, 18; 1989, pp. 286 n. 8, 48, 101.
13. Deleuze 1989, pp. 137, 139, 145, 146, 140.
14. Deleuze 1986, p. 200; 1989, pp. 168, 174.
15. Deleuze 1986, p. 97.
16. See Deleuze 1986 pp. 130ff.
17. See Deleuze 1986, pp. 76ff; 39, 40, 81, 58–9, 99.
18. See Deleuze 1986, pp. 41, 47, 125, 130; 1989, p. xii.
19. Deleuze 1995, p. 46; 1986, p. xiv.
20. See *Phaedrus* 265d–266a; Deleuze 1986, p. 25.
21. Deleuze 2000, p. 368.
22. Deleuze 2000, p. 369; 1989 p. 205; 1995, p. 58; 1986, p. 151.
23. Deleuze 2000, p. 366; 1995, pp. 149, 58; 1986, p. 181.
24. Deleuze 1989, p. 37; Deleuze and Guattari 1984, pp. 66, 67.
25. To quote Steven Shaviro (1993), p. 69: 'to build a model is to proclaim a necessity. It is very well for the Freudians to claim that sexual difference is socially constructed and not naturally given; nothing is really changed, since for them this social construction is as inevitable as any natural necessity might have been'.
26. Deleuze and Guattari 1988, pp. 28, 38.
27. As Shaviro 1993, p. 259, puts it: 'In the tradition of dialectical thought, from Hegel and Marx through Kojève to Sartre and Lacan, negativity is the motor of change'.
28. Deleuze and Guattari 1984, p. 25. Desire is not strengthened by needs, rather, the needs are derived from desire. We create the object we 'lack'. Likewise, the unconscious itself is a positive creation – a production for Deleuze – whereas for Freud it is formed through absence, a negative created by repression. See Deleuze and Guattari 1984, p. 27. See also p. 26: 'If desire produces, its product is real. If desire is productive, it can be productive only in the real world and can produce only reality.'
29. Shaviro 1993, p. 17.
30. Deleuze 1989, p. 29; 2000, p. 368; Ropars-Wuilleumier 1994, p. 256; Deleuze 1989, pp. 160, 57.
31. Deleuze and Guattari 1994, pp. 209–11.
32. Deleuze 1989, p. 125; Flaxman 2000, p. 54 n. 144. According to Flaxman, the old notion of 'suture' now becomes the sensory-motor complex of the movement-image in Deleuze's hands.

33. Deleuze 1989, pp. 156, 165, 278.
34. Deleuze 1986, pp. 7, 46; 1989, pp. xi, 271.
35. Deleuze 1986, pp. 60, 61.
36. See Blassnigg 2006, p. 108; and Pisters 2006, p. 128, for a reading of this Deleuzian phrase in terms of 'mirror-neurons'.
37. Bergson 1988, pp. 22, 35.
38. Deleuze 1986, p. ix.
39. If we were also to invoke Deleuze's Spinozism here, then there must be more than just two basic types of image but an infinite number (just as there are an infinite number of attributes from Spinoza, not just the two that are known to us of thought and extension). Were that the case, then the discovery of new cinema images (see Martin-Jones 2008) might also have metaphysical implications for Deleuzians.
40. Deleuze 1986, p. 11.
41. Deleuze 1986, pp. 12–17. As I will explore in Chapter 6, this thread between the particular and a whole is also experienced in the endurance and patience required of us when watching *new* films, that is, films that change us while we watch them, in order that we can watch more of them.
42. Deleuze 1986, p. 23.
43. Deleuze 1986, pp. 29–30, 62, 63.
44. Each of these biases is itself expressed by a different type of film image: the perception-image as such (images that act on a central image), along with action-images (reaction of that centre to those images) and affection-images (the gap between that action and reaction, internal or undischarged reaction), as well as even further subdivisions (the impulse-image coming in between action and affect as a kind of virtual action, of potential acts more than actual ones).
45. Deleuze 1986, pp. 72, 74. Deleuze offers the example of 'the obsessive framings' of Eric Rohmer's *The Marquis of O* (1976) as expressing this objective phenomenology, or semi-subjectivity. He also invokes Pasolini's linguistic model of free indirect discourse to explain it.
46. See Deleuze 1995, p. 59: 'Narrative in cinema is like the imaginary: it's a very indirect product of motion and time, rather than the other way around. Cinema always narrates what the images' movements and times make it narrate'. With the time-image, we get 'becomings rather than stories'.
47. Deleuze 1986, pp. 155, 141ff.
48. Deleuze 1986, pp. 87–90, 96–97. Deleuze offers the example of Eisenstein.
49. The affection-image, for instance, extracts the face, but also carries with that its own peculiar form of 'space-time – a scrap of vision, sky, countryside or background', as can be seen in Robert Bresson's *The Trial of Joan of Arc* (1962) or in the tactile spaces of his *Pickpocket*. See Deleuze 1986, pp. 108, 109.
50. Deleuze 1986, pp. 200, 205; 1989, p. 34.
51. Deleuze 1986, pp. 205, 208–9, 210–211, 212; 1995, p. 60.
52. Deleuze and Guattari 1994, pp. 204, 214.
53. Martin Schwab (2000, p. 134 n) argues that there is a strong shift in theoretical orientation between the two *Cinema* books, *Cinema 2* largely ignoring the image-ontology set up in *Cinema 1*.
54. Deleuze 1986, p. 205.
55. See Deleuze 1989, p. 20.
56. Deleuze 1986, p. 69: 'a sign appears to be a particular image which represents a type of image, sometimes from the point of view of its composition, sometimes from the point of view of its genesis of formation (or even its extinction).'

57. Deleuze 1989, pp. 67, 18. Other new signs enter into relation with a set of different types of time-image: readable and thinkable images or 'chronosigns' (points of the present and sheets of the past), 'crystal-images' (where actual and virtual are held together), 'lectosigns' (readable images) and 'noosigns' (signs which can only be thought); see Deleuze 1995, p. 53. With the lectosigns of modern cinema, for example, sounds now constitute an 'autonomous sonic continuum', to use Ronald Bogues's phrase, while images constitute a separate visual continuum, the two being put into relation with one another through their *mutual differences* – their asynchrony rather than synchrony (see Bogue 2003, pp. 7–8).
58. See Bogue 2006, pp. 212–13 on this power of the false, or 'fabulation', that is not fictive.
59. Deleuze 1989, pp. 143, 172, 173, 202, 20, 193, 203, 276. With 'in a plurality of ways of being present in the world', Deleuze is citing Gilbert Simondon (see Simondon 1964, pp. 233–4).
60. Deleuze 1989, pp. 69, 79, 273. Though Deleuze says that there were earlier indications in Welles, Ozu and Tati.
61. See Bergson 2007c, pp. 106–48.
62. Deleuze 1989, p. 81.
63. Indeed, Deleuze characteristically favours all the pathologies or failings of memory and recognition – déjà vu, dream-images, fantasies, visions of the dying – as the proper cinematic avatars of real time; see Deleuze 1989, pp. 39, 55. These pathologies are also Bergson's favourite entrées into time.
64. This argument comes directly from *Difference and Repetition*: there Deleuze talks of the paradox of the present as the need for a time in which to constitute/synthesize time (past, present and future). So '*there must be another time in which the first synthesis of time can occur*'. That other time of passage is the past or 'past in general' (Deleuze 1994, p. 79).
65. Deleuze 1989, p. 98.
66. Deleuze 1989, pp. 106, 109, 105, 101. This was the scriptwriter Alain Robbe-Grillet's influence on the film more than Resnais's (according to Deleuze) – and in this Robbe-Grillet showed his Augustinian heritage.
67. These others are that between between the limpid and the opaque, and the seed and the environment; see Deleuze 1989, p. 74. Ronald Bogue (2003, p. 26) reminds us that Deleuze alters Bergson to see 'movement as the expression of *durée*' (rather than the same as it). And Deleuze's notion of expression is Neoplatonic and Spinozist.
68. Deleuze 1989, pp. 248–9.
69. Deleuze 1989, p. 109.
70. Chateau 2005, p. 7.
71. Michel Georges-Michel 1914, cited in Douglass 1999, p. 218.
72. Bergson 2007a, pp. 305–6, my italics. It continues: 'The process then consists in extracting from all the movements peculiar to all the figures an impersonal movement abstract and simple, *movement in general*, so to speak: we put this into the apparatus, and we reconstitute the individuality of each particular movement by combining this nameless movement with the personal attitudes'.
73. 'Metacinema' is how François Zourabichvili puts it (Zourabichvili 2000, p. 142).
74. Douglass 1999, p. 224; Bogue 2003, p. 3.
75. Deleuze 1986 pp. 2, 3; 1995, p. 46; Douglass 1999, p. 221. Though Douglass goes on, rather less critically, 'still, Deleuze's use of his concepts of memory and

time in film are thought-provoking, and he makes us believe that perhaps he understood Bergson better than the philosopher understood himself'. We will see, however, that Bergson's theory of film is no less thought-provoking, and not because of anyone else's superior insights.

76. See Deleuze 1989, p. 11; 1995, p. 52. 'Time is the number of motion (change) in respect of before and after'; Aristotle, *Physics* 219b2.
77. Only in Deleuze 1989, pp. 271, 277 is there talk of 'measure of movement'. Yet, Deleuze claims that Kant's reversal does invoke 'aberrant movement' in order to subordinate it to time – Deleuze 1989, p. 39.
78. Deleuze 1986, p. 8.
79. Deleuze 1986, pp. 60, 81; 1989, p. 33; Bogue 2003, p. 34. Bergson 1988, p. 9: 'by "image" we mean a certain existence which is more than that which the idealist calls a representation, but less than that which the realist calls a thing – an existence placed halfway between the "thing" and the "representation"'.
80. It also allows Deleuze to avoid too much exegetical accuracy, which he openly admitted to doing whenever possible.
81. In terms of modern, electronic screen technology, Bergson's critique would turn to screen refresh rates instead of frame projection rates. But the emphasis would still be on the apparent movement of the cinema images being parasitic upon real physical movement existing elsewhere (ultimately, of whatever generates the power for an electrical device in this case).
82. See Bergson 1946, p. 77; Deleuze 1995, p. 42. This use of 'things' comes closer to Bergson. Deleuze's other description of *Matter and Memory* is even more accurate: 'a marriage...of pure spiritualism and radical materialism' (Deleuze 1995, p. 48).
83. According to Dorothea Olkowski, even where Deleuze acknowledges his abuses of Bergson with respect to the ontology of the image, a reconciliation can be arranged (which is also to say that Deleuze's advance on Bergson was less than he might have thought). See Olkowski 2008: 'As Deleuze comments in his notes, "this notion of the plane of immanence and the characteristics which we give it, seem to be a long way from Bergson", but Deleuze is trying to make the plane of matter into, not just an instantaneous section, but an instantaneous section of becoming, where becoming is still understood as instantaneous succession. This is, Deleuze asserts, a view of cinema totally different from that which Bergson describes. Is it? Has the addition of time to the instantaneous section resulted in something totally different from the view of cinema that Bergson critiques? To differentiate the universe that evolves from the universe that merely changes place, Bergson theorizes the existence of luminous images, movements between images, and intervals which define zones of indetermination and choice. The set theoretical plane of immanence proposed by Deleuze still operates in accordance with the structures defined by modern science. Sets must be axiomatized; rules govern their behavior; entities are externally related according to these rules. What, after all is a tendency? "A perfect definition applies only to a *completed reality*; now, vital properties are never entirely realized, though always on the way to becoming so; they are not so much *states as tendencies*. And a tendency achieves all that it aims at only if it is not thwarted by another tendency." May we not posit that the return is exactly what Bergson cautions against in his critique of cinematographic knowledge and in *Duration and Simultaneity*? The immobilization of affection, which is the immobilization of pleasure and pain, and the immobilization of evolution which is the immobilization of life,

for which is substituted external relations, blocs of becoming and ultimately, extinction?'

84. Deleuze 1989, p. 41.
85. Deleuze 1989, pp. 128, 214, 181.
86. A good example of a sceptic is Smith 2001.
87. Deleuze 1989, pp. 213, 13. Indeed Ozu is their 'inventor'. See Deleuze 1995, p. 49, where Deleuze says that his 'history of images' is not 'developmental'; 'all images combine the same elements, the same signs, differently'.
88. Deleuze 1986, p. 70. See also Deleuze 1989, p. 22: 'The movement-image has not disappeared, but now exists only as the first dimension of an image that never stops growing in dimensions'.
89. Deleuze 1989, pp. 179, 2, 279, 40; 1986, pp. 215, 206, 110, 127.
90. Bordwell 1997, p. 117.
91. Deleuze 1986, p. 208. Indeed, all the stereotypes of the art-house film of the 1960s and 1970s are here: slow-moving action with aimless plots lacking narrative structure; undividuated characters with no point of identification for audiences; apparently improvised dialogue, often recorded on a dirty soundtrack, and so on.
92. See also O'Neill 1998: 'What is *Titanic* if not a highly conventional film which gives us a time-image?'
93. Hence, when Gregory Flaxman writes that John Wayne simply does what a man's 'gotta do' in *The Searchers* (Flaxman 2000, p. 101), a good deal of the subtlety of the film is lost. Ironically, Flaxman is very good at pointing out the conventionality of Bordwell's cognitivist schemata (p. 49 n), but then misses the larger point that if these schemata are acquired by convention and habit, they cannot have a Deleuzian sensory-motor essence either (see also p. 96).
94. His hesitancy of movement, especially at the climactic scene at the doorway as the restituted family celebrate before him, but not with him (a scene reversed by Cronenberg's finale in *A History of Violence* (2005)), is indicative here of the complexity of movement in this film, which cannot be deemed on the same level as Ford's earlier action-images such as in *Stagecoach* (1939).
95. Rancière 2006, pp. 113, 112.
96. Just as Godard was pivotal to Bordwell's cine-dualism, so too is he for Deleuze's: see Bellour's essay cited in O'Neill 1998.
97. Deleuze 1989, p. 21.
98. *If* the time-image and movement-image are relational, that is, their function stems from when and where they are vis-à-vis an audience, expectation, mode of exhibition, and so on (and not from content – rational or irrational cuts), *then* one could imagine the two cinema books being written in reverse – all of the content of time-images being attributed to the movement-image (and vice versa), with no further alteration.
99. See Martin-Jones 2008, p. 46: 'Popular Indian cinema's plane of organisation is decidedly less linear in its reterritorialisation of the plane of consistency than the movement-image, especially in its Hollywood action-image form. Instead, it reterritorialises as a non-Aristotelian narrative of sequential episodes, a masala-image. For this reason it often appears closer to the time-image in places, even though it also bears a close affinity to the movement-image. It is characterised by a dual movement, a movement of world on the one hand, and a sensory-motor movement of characters on the other.'

100. Deleuze 2000, pp. 253, 367, 369, 370. See also p. 370: 'Every [truly creative piece of] work, even a short one, implies a significant undertaking or a long internal duration'; 'in creative works there is a multiplication of emotion, a liberation of emotion, and even the invention of new emotions. This distinguishes creative works from the prefabricated emotions of commerce.'
101. Following the ideas of Louis Althusser, Marxist–Structuralist studies debated the locus of power in cinema – was it in the text, its production or its consumption? If it was in its production, a top-down economic approach was needed; if it was in its consumption, a bottom-up cultural approach was required. For some, it was the *productive* (economic) axis that dominated the political ideology of film. Here is Jean-Louis Comolli and Jean Narboni: '*Every film is political*, inasmuch as it is determined by the ideology which produces it (or within which it is produced, which stems from the same thing)...This includes every stage in the process of production: subjects, styles, forms, meanings, narrative traditions; all underline the general ideological discourse' (Comolli and Narboni 1992, pp. 684, 685). As Douglass writes (1999, p. 217): 'Comolli, especially, argued that the apparatus itself embodied a capitalistic ideology, not the "scientific character" to which it pretended'.
102. Deleuze 1989, p. 164
103. Deleuze 1995, p. 53. And, of course, auteurism, which localizes the work of art in an individual artist, makes that work normally more comparable with the single-authored works of philosophers (in terms of influence, conception and method). I say normally because some – like Deleuze's own with Guattari – fail to comply with the norm.
104. Deleuze 1986, p. x; see Deleuze 1989, pp. 53, 93, 232. For a host of other post-production influences on a film beyond the directorial, see Perkins 1972, pp. 166ff.
105. Deleuze 1986, pp. 206, 184, 103, 78.
106. It is arguable that Deleuze also selected the best work in film studies amongst his contemporaries to appropriate as his own. See O'Neill 1998. It is left unclear by O'Neill how much of this was a creative selection (Deleuze does always cite his sources) or an excessive dependency signalling a lack of originality. But see again Myer 2004 for Noël Burch's view on this.
107. Even when Deleuzians like Steve Shaviro do put Deleuze and Fassbinder together (in a work like Fassbinder's *Querelle*, 1982) it is with reference to the work on bodily affect in *Capitalism and Schizophrenia* rather than time in the *Cinema* volumes.
108. Gregory Flaxman has denied any excess theoreticism on Deleuze's part (see Flaxman 2000, p. 9: 'Deleuze is much more the avatar of the end of grand theories: for him, the specificity of cinematographic images invariably elude the rigid determinations of any overarching schematism') but this seems to be denying the obvious, at least with respect to his engagement with cinema (which clearly does have an 'overarching schematism').
109. See also Mullarkey 2006, pp. 36–41 on the problem of norms in Deleuze.
110. Deleuze 1994, p. xxi.
111. See Bogue 2003, p. 1.
112. See Deleuze 1986, pp. 29–40. Such generalism is less true of Deleuze's courses on film at Vincennes, however, where he makes sustained analyses of many specific film scenes. These courses are now documented as audio files at the Institut National de l'Audiovisuel in France. My thanks to Elie During for this information.
113. Rancière 2006, p. 5.
114. Deleuze 1995, p. 64.

5 Cavell, Badiou and Other Ontologists

1. Cavell 1979, p. xix.
2. Cavell 1979, p. 162.
3. As Rothman and Keane put it (2000, p. 18): 'to embrace theory as a higher authority than our experience of movies, as the field of film study has done, is to divorce the study of film from the philosophical perspective of self-reflection apart from which we cannot know what movies mean, or *what they really are*' (my emphasis). Of course, to allege that film studies has placed theory over practice/experience is going too far.
4. See for example, Cavell 1979, pp. 88, 91–3, 120–1.
5. See Rothman and Keane 2000, p. 40. See also Rothman and Keane, p. 21: 'all of Cavell's work is engaged in extending Wittgenstein's and Austin's efforts to transform analytical philosophy radically from within'.
6. Cavell 1996, p. 92.
7. See Rothman and Keane, p. 261: 'The view of philosophy articulated in *Must We Mean What We Say?* underlies, and underwrites, *The World Viewed*, too'. Or 'in the pages of *The World Viewed*, film and philosophy are happily married, but the kinds of remarks about philosophy everywhere to be found in *Must We Mean What We Say?* are all completely absent'.
8. Goodenough 2005, p. 30.
9. Cavell 1996, p. 89.
10. Cavell 1979, pp. 6, 15, 9.
11. Cavell 1979, p. 7. Cavell sides with Ingmar Bergman in the view that making movies is more like building a cathedral, with the director being, at best, like the master builder (Cavell 1979, p. 8).
12. Cavell 2005, p. 169; Rothman and Keane 2000, pp. 18, 264. Rothman and Keane also analyse this method of *The World Viewed* in terms of Cavell's later use of Emerson's concepts of intuition and tuition. In his book *Disowning Knowledge* (Cavell 1987, p. 3), Cavell defines an intuition with the following example: 'An intuition, say that God is expressed in the world, does not require, or tolerate, evidence but rather, let us say, understanding of a particular sort'. Rothman and Keane adumbrate this as follows (2000, p. 25): '*The World Viewed* incorporates insightful remarks – remarks that in each case follow out the complete tuition for the given intuition'.
13. See Critchley 1997, pp. 138ff.
14. Cavell 1979, pp. ix, 10, 12, 16–17. Given that memory helps to create a film too, it could be said that some films make for better memories than perceptions, so that looking again at an old favourite film may not always be such a good thing.
15. Oddly, however, Rothman and Keane reject the mnemonic approach, saying that 'we are well aware that no serious book about film can be written from memory now' (2000, p. 10), and that there is now no need for this method given the ease of access to DVDs and VCRs. Yet, it is clear that Cavell was not making a virtue out of a necessity, for the technological impediment of the time would still have been no obstacle to a more orthodox academic study of film (private viewing facilities have always been available to scholars). The use of memory is a crucial method rather than a 'make-do' one.
16. Cavell 1979, pp. 74, xvi. Sometimes, Cavell's realism is less focused on the ordinary mystery of our experience of (or presence to) film, and comes close to an approximation of Husserl's definition of objective reality as infinite

Abschattungen: 'the incompleteness, or outsideness, or contingency of the angle of viewing, the fact that each is merely one among endless possibilities' (Cavell 1979, p. 203).

17. Indeed, in a later edition of *The World Viewed*, Cavell sees cartoons participating in this filmic realism, even though they are pure constructions rather than a recording medium. Cavell tackles the charge that, by his theory's lights, cartoons are not films because they are not photographic records, and concludes with the view that animation *can* fit within his paradigm by categorizing cartoons as a series of 'animated world projections' (see Cavell 1979, pp. 167–73). There is still a world, only it is an animated one.
18. Cavell 1979, pp. 43, 213, 211, 166.
19. Cavell says (1979, p. 73) that he has no desire to retrace lines of thought leading either to montage or continuity as the essence of film. Isolated possibilities of art do not have their significance shown in a 'given discovery'. This notion of 'significance', as a relevance *ex post facto*, will be a crucial part of Cavell's understanding of the film medium as such, as we will see.
20. See Cavell 1979, p. 103, or p. 24: 'A painting *is* a world, a photograph is *of* the world'. Contra Noël Carroll's view that Cavell is a Bazinian, Rothman and Keane say (2000, p. 61) that all Cavell argues is that 'a photograph does not bear the relationship to *anything* that a recording bears to the sound it reproduces'.
21. Cavell 1979, pp. 183, 193, 184, 197, 191, 201, 184, 198.
22. Cavell 1979, p. xvi.
23. See Cavell 1979, p. xxiii: 'I of course want the sense of *Weltanschauung* in my title, and though I felt it arise naturally in the way I was thinking about film, I was helped to it by my awareness of Heidegger's'.
24. Cavell 1979, p. 102.
25. Cavell 1979, pp. 39, 19.
26. Cavell 1979, pp. 31, 32, 204.
27. Cavell 1979, p. 134. I have both repeated and embellished upon some of Cavell's list of significances for this scene.
28. Cavell 1979, pp. 204, 187, 104–7, 61–2.
29. Cavell says that automatisms are only successful if they are integrated into a work with 'conviction' (1979, pp. 141–2).
30. Cavell 1979, p. 72.
31. Cavell 1979, pp. 65, 66, 67, 209.
32. See Rothman and Keane 2000, p. 27: 'In *Pursuits of Happiness* and *Contesting Tears*, Cavell's intuition that Hollywood movies have inherited the philosophical concerns of American transcendentalism, conjoined with his intuition that he has inherited these concerns too, leads to the astonishing further intuition that his own philosophical procedures are underwritten by the ways American movies think about society, human relationships, and their own condition as films'.
33. Cavell 1979, p. 71.
34. See Cavell 1979, pp. 67–8.
35. Cavell 1979, p. 131. Cavell even cites Hitchcock as one director parodying this awareness, thus locating him in the same position as Deleuze does with the thinking-image, the last and most reflective of the movement-images.
36. See Rothman and Keane 2000, p. 23. Of course, Greenberg did not directly address film himself.
37. Cavell 1979, pp. 127ff.

38. Cavell 1979, pp. 215ff, 219.
39. Rothman and Keane 2000, p. 52; Cavell 1979, p. 39
40. Cavell 1979, p. 122. See also p. 31: Film developed as 'narrative' because 'someone "saw the possibilities" of the medium – cutting and editing and taking shots at different distances from the subject'.
41. Cavell 2005, p. 189.
42. Cavell 2005, p. 186.
43. Cavell 1979, pp. 146, 202; Cavell 2005, pp. 182, 181. See also Cavell 2005, pp. 181–2: 'You remind me of a little private concept of mine – 'the nothing shot'. Sometimes just rhetorically it makes a break in the narrative at certain times. In another Frank Capra film, *It Happened One Night* (1934), with the pair Clark Gable and Claudette Colbert, we find them walking together down a road away from us, an empty road, and that's a shot that over and over I came back to in my mind. I had nothing to say about it. I knew that it punctuated a moment in the film; it was the end of something and the beginning of something. It could have been months, maybe years, until I just stopped and asked myself, in the right mood, what is it about a couple together at dawn walking down a road together away from us? Where are they coming from (what is dawning), and going to; why are they – are they – silent? They direct brief words to each other, but what are they thinking about? And suddenly every word seemed to mean something and at that stage I could hardly keep up with thoughts that I was having about it. I then wrote a brief essay about simply that shot, simply that shot, which seemed to me to raise every issue in the whole film'.
44. Cavell 1979, p. 147.
45. Cavell 1979, p. 239 n. 40. It is also the problem at the centre of *The Claim of Reason*. Cavell discusses this in *Contesting Tears* (1996, p. 94): 'It is some such question that Nietzsche took as the issue of what he called nihilism, a matter in which he had taken decisive instruction from Ralph Waldo Emerson. I persist, as indicated, in calling the issue by its, or its ancestor's, older name of skepticism; as I persist in thinking that to lose knowledge of the human possibility of skepticism means to lose knowledge of the human, something whose possibility I envision in *The Claim of Reason*, extending a problematic of Wittgenstein's under the title of soul-blindness'.
46. See Cavell 1969, p. 270: 'The issue is one of placing the words and experiences with which philosophers have always begun in alignment with human beings in particular circumstances who can be imagined to be having those experiences and saying and meaning those words. This is all that "ordinary" in the phrase "ordinary language philosophy" means, or ought to mean' (cited in Rothman and Keane 2000, p. 272). See also Rothman and Keane 2000, p. 276: 'To be an audience for modern philosophy, one must test the philosopher's words against one's own experience, must ask oneself with absolute veracity whether these are words one could honestly say and mean in this context. To be an audience for philosophy, one must perform philosophy. And to perform philosophy, one must discover an audience for philosophy within oneself. In Cavell's understanding, these have always been conditions of philosophy; the modernist situation only makes these conditions evident'.
47. To gain an insight into how Cavell has been read more recently within film studies, the reader should consult the essays in *Film International*, Issue 22, Vol. 4, No. 4 (2006), especially Brouwers and Paulus 2006 and Bird 2006.
48. Goodenough 2005, pp. 32, 33, 34.

49. Goodenough 2005, pp. 13, 21. Goodenough is here echoing Stephen Mulhall.
50. Goodenough 2005, pp. 23, 24, 80, 25.
51. Mulhall 2001, p. 6. Mulhall's is a very faithful implementation of Cavell's ideas nonetheless, looking at the four films in terms of their genre, their intertextual references (as part of the same franchise), their modernism (being about film per se as well), their director's other works (especially Fincher's *Se7en* (1995) versus his *Alien 3* (1992)), and so on. But it also carries across the weaknesses of Cavell, especially as regards an a priori of the ordinary passing itself off as film being philosophical, as well as remaining largely within an auteurist paradigm (contra Cavell).
52. Critchley 2005, p. 139.
53. It is notable that in Cavell's forward to the 1979 expanded edition of *The World Viewed* (p. xv), when discussing *Days of Heaven*, he says that he does not wish 'to hide the knowledge' that Malick was a Heidegger translator.
54. Frampton 2006, p. 12.
55. Frampton 2006, p. 6.
56. See Frampton 2006, pp. 8, 10, 121, 123, 129, 140.
57. Frampton 2006, p. 5. See also p. 83: 'Each film is unique then, with its own film-ind steering the film-world'. Indeed, Frampton says that we can now help Cavell conceptualize the way film shows a world, something he seemed 'unable' to do!
58. Frampton 2006, p. 9.
59. Frampton 2006, p. 73: 'It is called "filmind" because, simply, it is not a human mind. It is another kind of mind, its own mind, a new mind...The meaning of mind has been changed towards its expression in film'.
60. Frampton 2006, pp. 89, 92, 76, 74. It is specifically a 'rhetorical extension' of Deleuze's notion of 'spiritual automaton' in *Cinema 2*.
61. Frampton 2006, pp. 3, 197. See also pp. 200–1: 'film as nonphilosophy (or pre-philosophy, as Deleuze would argue), becomes the "Eros" to philosophy's "Logos"...Film is a new metaphysic, a post-metaphysic, in that it can provide a direct thinking of such abstract concepts as being, knowing, substance, cause, identity, time, space'.
62. Frampton 2006, pp. 93, 10, 162, 10, 203, 171.
63. For example (Frampton 2006, p. 141) Michael Haneke's *Funny Games* is described as follows: 'it is a certain smoothness that pervades the film's thinking...The calmness of the film is also the calmness of Peter making his sandwich while Paul shoots the boy', 'we are held to these events and are unable to change our perspective'. Where does this calmness arise – in the film or in Frampton?
64. Frampton 2006, pp. 2, 75.
65. Frampton 2006, p. 12.
66. It was originally published in *L'Art du cinema* (No. 4), pp. 1–5.
67. See Mullarkey 2006, Chapter 3.
68. Badiou 2004a, p. 79.
69. Badiou 2004a, pp. 82, 86, 84.
70. Badiou 2004a, p. 83.
71. Badiou 2004a, p. 78.
72. Badiou 2004a, p. 86.
73. Badiou 2004a, p. 84.
74. Badiou 2008.
75. On this centrality of the letter in Badiou, see Mullarkey 2006, pp. 172–3 and Clemens 2003, pp. 73–102.

6 Extended Cognitions and the Speeds of Cinema

1. *Eternal Sunshine of the Spotless Mind* (2004).
2. Anderson 1998, pp. 1, 166.
3. See Anderson 1998, pp. 51–2 where he says that discussing a film involves our higher brain functions, but that seeing it involves the brain's more basic systems – the 'perceptual basis' that gives film its reality effect. We would agree, so long as the 'perceptual basis' for seeing 'realism' in the acting of Marlon Brando, for example (crucial to the reality effect for certain audiences), includes more than simply a part of the brain. A brain is necessary to see him move, of course, but insufficient to see the way that he moved that made such an impact on audiences when *A Streetcar Named Desire* was released in 1951, or the decline of that impact thereafter. The 'how' of movement is vital, and it is neither cultural nor biological alone.
4. Anderson 1998, p. 47. In Chapter 7 I will look at the paradox of fiction in depth.
5. Anderson 1998, pp. 3, 10, 17, 18, 19, 28.
6. Anderson 1998, pp. 40, 43, 42, 50, 137, 147, 89, 49.
7. See Robbins 2000, p. 37: 'In essence, Gibson had gone as far as Bergson's vision of perception as the display of an array of possible action'. See, for example from the first chapter of *Matter and Memory* ('Of the Selection of Images for Representation'), pp. 30–1: 'In other words, the brain appears to us to be an instrument of analysis in regard to the movement received, and an instrument of selection in regard to the movement executed. But, in the one case as in the other, its office is limited to the transmission and division of movement. And no more in the higher centres of the cortex than in the spinal cord do the nervous elements work with a view to knowledge: they do but indicate a number of possible actions at once, or organize one of them. That is to say that the nervous system is in no sense an apparatus which may serve to fabricate, or even to prepare, representations. Its function is to receive stimulation, to provide motor apparatus, and to present the largest possible number of these apparatuses to a given stimulus'.
8. Anderson 1998, pp. 22, 29; 2007, p. 3. See also Anderson 2007, p. 131: 'Information, then, consists of patterns of actual relationships between objects in the world. It is not something added, deduced, or inferred from raw data. The information contained in patterns of light'. Here, information is *in* light, rather than the relationship *with* light. But the confusion may also come from Gibson himself who can also talk of affordance as something perceived *in* the environment as well as a relationship *with* it.
9. See Grodal 2007, p. 162 n. 1.
10. See Anderson 1998, pp. 104, 107. Contra Anderson's specularization of the camera, one might cite the supposed 'point of view' shots in *Jindabyne* of the men fishing, or throughout *Cache*, operating precisely because what might have been points of view (of the murderer or the blackmailer) *are not* point of view shots at all. The camera is not a view here.
11. Anderson 1998, pp. 13, 30, 53. On p. 32, computation is understood as 'cells being excited or inhibited, reaching threshold or not reaching threshold, firing or not firing' – still evincing a discrete and digital either/or logic which has less to do with the analogic of a brain-world ecological continuity.

12. Anderson 1998, p. 14, 44. For more on this 'error problem' facing materialist accounts of misrepresentation (Dretske's and Fodor's in particular), see Mullarkey 1999, pp. 131–3.
13. At one point, Anderson (1998, p. 48) does put this duplicity down to the brain flipping between two incompatible sets of information, as with the face/vase example popular with Wittgensteinians. But the perspectivism of seeing aspects that comes with this is overlooked in favour of bivalent logic.
14. Branigan 2005, p. 115.
15. Branigan 2005, pp. 101, 121, 119, 216, 220. One might think that Branigan overstates the case here, but I don't. Admittedly, few theorists openly state that their theory is a purely objective one, yet there is a certain disingenuousness in this gesture. Having provided a theory of *what film is* (even albeit in 'essence'), I have yet to hear one theorist add that this is only his or her subjective opinion.
16. Branigan 2005, pp. 193–5.
17. The figure of containment is particularly prevalent in these image schema. Johnson's research has shown what hold the image of containment has on our thought, both in terms of how we think of our body, the world and abstract reasoning; see Mark Johnson 1987, pp. 20–40. In particular he states that (p. 22) 'whether in one, two, or three dimensions, the physical in-out orientation involves separation, differentiation, and enclosure, which implies restriction and limitation'. He also lists five 'entailments' of containment: protection from/resistance to external forces; limitation; fixity of location; accessibility/inaccessibility to view; and transitivity.
18. The whole list comprises: the real edge of the screen, the illusory border of an image, the gestalt of the image, the shape of the object(s) seen in outline in the image, the overall composition of the image, the totality of the two-dimensional area of the image, the physical surroundings of the image in its exhibition space, the implicit rationale for seeing the image, the view given of a fictive action within the diegesis, the situation or context, the scene, the narrative structure, the narration, the psychic state undergirding the spectators' emotions, and the world-knowledge presupposed by the story and/or the viewer (see Branigan 2005, pp. 103–13).
19. See Branigan 2005, pp. 117, 118.
20. Branigan 2005, p. 149.
21. Branigan 2005, pp. 168–9, 177, 202.
22. Branigan 2005, p. 166.
23. See Branigan 2005, pp. 286–7 n. 61 where Branigan shows that he is aware of the problem of family resemblances, and even points to resemblance itself being a family resemblance term. He resists defining 'family' a priori: indeed, his diagram of radial meaning (p. 122) allows for discontinuities due to cultural difference rather than any smooth 'continuous transitions'.
24. Branigan, p. 148. See also p. 123: 'Can a single, unified theory of film be constructed? Could there be, for example, a single, unified theory of "frame lines"? Perhaps a film theory, like a polysemous word, can only be constructed of dispersed but linked "pieces", each with a *distinct* logical structure'.
25. Kemper 2007, pp. 147–8: 'If the various film theories remain only different language games, then, Branigan argues, they all possess a blind spot, in that they fail to acknowledge the embodied nature of their conceptual and linguistic structures...Thus, while his book recognizes the existence of many film theories, Branigan only sanctions or legitimizes those aware of, rooted in, and

self-consciously working with the embodied nature of our language-games and cognitive activity'.

26. See Branigan 2005, p. 219: '*the uses of* language through which our thought and our body project signs onto the world'.
27. Branigan 2005, p. 224. See also p. 198: 'what a thing "is" depends on *which relations* are being selected as the most important when one is looking at or thinking about the thing'.
28. Branigan 2005, pp. 217, 327 n. 81.
29. See Altman 1992, p. 9: 'current theaters tend toward what we might call zero degree performance (standardized spaces, automatic projection, a program limited to the feature film)'.
30. See Conley 2000; Herzog 2001; Lessard 2008.
31. Altman 1992, p. 4.
32. Altman 1992, pp. 2–4. Altman lists a dozen attributes of the cinema event through the course of his essay: multiplicity, three-dimensionality, materiality, heterogeneity, intersection, performance, multidiscursivity, instability, mediation, choice, diffusion and interchange.
33. See Book V of Badiou 2006, pp. 375ff, which amends the simple dualism of event and non-event in *Being and Event* with the four forms of change: modifications, facts, weak singularities and strong singularities (or events).
34. Badiou 2005a, p. 179: 'The site is only ever a *condition of being* for the event'.
35. Badiou 2000, p. 64. For more on these issues in Badiou, see Mullarkey 2006, pp. 100ff.
36. Deleuze 1989, p. 255.
37. Deleuze 1990, p. 178.
38. Deleuze 1995, p. 141. There is a reading of Deleuze's *eventum tantum* that takes it to be the one and only 'univocal' event of which all other events are simulacra (see Badiou 1997): however, this ignores *what* is univocal in the *eventum tantum*, namely difference. The formula in *A Thousand Plateaus*, that monism equals pluralism, conveys the fact that the only thing that is always the same is that nothing is the same, that there is only difference.
39. Deleuze 1994, p. 79.
40. Deleuze 1990, p. 63.
41. As regards form, the last illusory encounter of Ana and Otto is shot as if both were not in the same room, or were in the same room but at different times.
42. The opening and closing shot of Otto's reflection in Ana's eye is both very Sartrean and Lacanian. The themes of loving mothers, mourning sons and missing fathers come all too readily to mind (Otto enters into the Symbolic in his father's car when he is instructed on how nothing lasts forever below the Arctic Circle). Likewise, for the missed encounter with death and the impossibility of a sexual relationship.
43. Rancière 2006, p. 77.
44. I measure these two films' popularity in box-office grosses, adjusted and unadjusted respectively for inflation.
45. I'm alluding here to Daniel Frampton's idea that Béla Tarr's *Damnation* is 'a thinking of stasis and movement' (Frampton 2006, p. 140).
46. Deleuze and Guattari 1988, pp. 280–1, my italics after 'continues'.
47. Deleuze and Guattari 1988, pp. 281, 282. This notion of an absolute, virtual threshold harks back to Deleuze's transcendental empiricism in *Difference and Repetition*, when he proposes to reinstate a doctrine of the faculties – of thought,

of memory and of sensibility – each with their own exclusive transcendental object (see Deleuze 1994, pp. 140ff).

48. See Bergson 1946, p. 303 n. 6. See Mullarkey 1999, Chapters 2 and 8 for more on this.
49. Bergson 2007a, p. 195, my italics.
50. Perhaps Deleuze had in mind the definition of the machine from *Anti-Oedipus*, as that which also interrupts flow and, as such, cannot now be thought to think through pure movement.
51. By 'apparatus', remember, Bergson means the projector rather than the camera (though he uses the term *'appareil'* throughout, it actually comes closer to Jean-Louis Baudry's notion of *'dispositif'*); hence, issues concerning the difference between digital and analogical (optical) capture are not relevant. Optical projection is no different to other forms of projection, electronic or digital, inasmuch as they all depend on renewing (refreshing) a static image (or image-component such as a 'pixel') using movement from elsewhere, e.g. a moving electron beam (directed by 'steering coils') for television, or the electrical charge that controls the on-off rate of each pixel in a TFT screen (such charge being itself traceable to kinetic energy such as the turbines in an electricity supply station).
52. Yet, they can be heard as a strange buzzing noise when later they visit the *Enterprise* itself.
53. The men of Scalos are all infertile, and all she wants to do is envelop Kirk (for interpenetration to take place).
54. We might note that the serialism in standard TV series like *Star Trek*, not to mention more prolonged examples in British soaps, North American daytime dramas and South American telenovelas, are all very different, and, contra Rancière, do produce events over their time spans. Like all serialism in the arts, they are an acquired cognitive skill in pattern recognition. This is one reason for avoiding the use of Godard's *Slow Motion* (1980) for this part of the argument, for its perfect suitability might imply that only 'the best' in the visual arts can teach us these things in exemplary fashion.
55. Deleuze and Parnet 1987, p. 2. In season three of the 'new' *Dr Who* series (2007), there is an episode, entitled 'Blink', that is entirely based on this Deleuzian adage: the 'weeping angels' can only move when those before them blink their eyes.
56. See Pepperell 2006, p. 187: 'Change Blindness is a remarkable phenomenon, discovered by [Kevin] O'Regan and colleagues, in which quite large changes between images will usually not be perceived if there is a brief interruption, like a blank or a flash, between one image and the next. O'Regan claims that we do not hold a detailed representation of the visual world in our brain, but continually access the real detail "out there" through active engagement with the world'. This isn't the same as the pathology of akinetopsia, but rather our own built-in normalized glimpse of it.
57. Conversely, there are subjects with 'form imperception', who are only able to identify objects in motion, but have great difficulty doing so when they are at rest. Living Heracliteans. See Anderson 1998, p. 61.
58. Corliss 2007.
59. It must be admitted, however, that peer pressure may have an impact on how one *reports* one's impression of film pacing when seen in a group. See Lowry 1985, pp. 83–4 on Etienne Souriau's experiment on 'rhythm and unanimity'. Likewise, even the anticipation of one's own impatience and endurance before watching a long film can help make its time go quicker than first imagined. Such

temporal mediations by the viewer of filmic time are not to be underestimated either.

60. Deleuze 2000, p. 366.
61. However, inasmuch as film affects us through its own durations, speeds and rhythms infecting ours, then any verbal description *of these elements* will break down those temporal qualities into those of the sentences describing them, into a representational, second-hand discourse with its own *durée*, thereby refracting what could only be experienced bodily and first hand into something else again.
62. There is, of course, a clarity of a different sort – perspicuity – that belongs more to the body than the intellect.
63. See Salt 1974 and 1992.
64. See Deleuze 1986, pp. 206–7; see also Deleuze 2000, p. 369: 'Right now many forces are trying to deny any distinction between the commercial and the creative. The more that we deny this distinction, the more we consider ourselves clever, understanding, and "in the know". In fact, we are only betraying one of the demands of capitalism: rapid turnover. When advertisers explain that advertisements are the poetry of the modern world, they shamelessly forget that no real art tries to create or exhibit a product in order to correspond to the public's expectations. Advertising can shock or try to shock because it responds to an alleged expectation. The opposite of this is art produced from the unexpected, the unrecognized, the unrecognizable. There is no commercial art: that's nonsense.'
65. Despite being conscious of a preceding relationship and choosing to go around once more, they are still destined to repeat even this choice in an eternal return.
66. Altman 1992, pp. 4, 11.

7 Fabulation, Process and Event

1. Rancière 2006, p. 31; I have rearranged Rancière's indirect question into a direct one.
2. Rancière 2006, pp. 135, 146, 158. And the fable itself, for Rancière, will not simply be an arrangement of actions to prepare adventure for the characters and 'intrigue and denouement' for the audience, as he claims it was for Aristotle (p.1).
3. Conley 2005, p. 97.
4. Rancière 2006, pp. 41–2; see also p. 64 on Fritz Lang's 'art' of putting appearances into images, or p. 76 on Arthur Mann's 'way', as when he must fashion a certain kind of hero from the material provided by a different kind of star actor (James Stewart in *Winchester 73* (1950)); see also p. 73 on 'where the moral of the fable and the logic of the narration meet'.
5. Rancière 2006, p. 101.
6. Rancière 2007, pp. 117, 119.
7. Rancière 2006, p. 8: The aesthetic age is where 'anything and everything in the world is available to art'. See also Kollias 2007, p. 85.
8. Rancière 2007, pp. 120, 122.
9. Rancière 2006, p. 8.
10. Rancière 2006, p. 2.
11. One can formulate the point thus: a brilliant performance (in the broadest sense) from an otherwise miscast actor has the potential to thwart the film's script with a fable of its own.

12. Rancière 2006, pp. 11, 16, 161.
13. Rancière 2006, pp. 5, 6.
14. Rancière 2006, pp. 13, 14; see also p. 15: 'all these great figures of whose fables and forms would easily be deducible from its essence do no more than offer up the best examples of the film-fable, split and thwarted: *mise-en-scène* of a *mise-en-scène*'.
15. See Rancière 2006, p. 98 on *They Live by Night*: 'Keeping herself constantly busy is her way of being fully present to, but also fully absent from, her father and her uncle's world. Keechie's absent presence cuts right through Deleuze's very neat opposition between the functionality of the action-image and the expressive power of the affection-image'.
16. Rancière 2006, pp. 12, 109, 110, 111.
17. Rancière 2006, pp. 119, 116, my italics.
18. Rancière 2006, pp. 185, 186, 168, 167.
19. Kollias 2007, pp. 92, 86–7, 88.
20. See May 2008 for more on the politics of absolute equality in Rancière.
21. Rancière 1998, p. 72, cited in Kollias 2007, p. 86.
22. Rancière 2006, p. 151.
23. Rancière 2006, p. 15.
24. Rancière 2006, pp. 126, 175, 166. See also p. 103: 'such is the Romantic law of beauty, exemplarily illustrated in this film'.
25. Rancière 2006, pp. 48, 53.
26. See Rancière 2004; 1991; and Gauny 1983.
27. Noys 2004.
28. This is found on the DVD version of *Three Colours: Blue*.
29. Bergson 2007a, pp. 6–7.
30. Bergson 2007a, pp. 216–17.
31. See Mullarkey 2007b, pp. ix–xxxii.
32. See Bateson 1972, p. 292; Derrida 1982.
33. Bergson 1988, p. 36.
34. See Bateson 1972, pp. 130–1, 406, 414ff.
35. This is the quote from Nietzsche's *Beyond Good and Evil* that Mary cites in *Eternal Sunshine of the Spotless Mind*. Naturally, I refer only to the Western stereotype of the goldfish and not to real goldfish, whose temporalities are probably invisible to us (even under close observation).
36. For more on the need for (partial) blindness when constructing meaning, see my *Post-Continental Philosophy* (2006), pp. 157–61.
37. Anderson 1998, pp. 126, 156.
38. Damasio 1994, p. 175.
39. Connolly 2002, p. 35.
40. This commendation is on the DVD sleeve.
41. Herwitz 2008, p. 50.
42. Bergson 1988, p. 260.
43. Rodowick 2001, pp. 80–1.
44. Cavell 1979, p. 219. Perhaps some will argue that the art and reflexivity of film lies in montage, of manipulating shots, and so it is the literal shot, dissociated from the editing process, which provides the undistorted and immutable object for reflection. But can one speak here of the 'literal shot' at all? When was any film-shot not also an art and artificial well before the editing process? This is more than just saying that there is also artfulness in the *mise-en-scène*, for it also

concerns the technology of film making, of film stock, of film exhibition, of luminescence, and so on.

45. See Herwitz 2008, p. 49: 'One person's sex is another's sleep. The judge is the one who can deliver exemplary subtlety within a community of interpretation, a practice, a way of hearing that bonds people together and creates intimacy between one listener and another. It is what Ted Cohen calls the role of intimacy in art, a role extending to the judge, whose judgements, rather than true or being trued by the joint verdict, deliver a way of seeing-as which a community responds to, learns from, takes the linguistic message of, and also enjoys reading.'
46. See, for instance, McGinn 2005, p. 11: 'perhaps without movement movies would not strongly engage us, but movement by itself is not enough to account for the hold that movies have over the mind'. McGinn's demotion of the power of movement comes from an attitude that takes motion primarily as geometric displacement rather than a qualitative change of state. In addition, when he does take movement to be primary, it is on account of its representational form: see p. 62: '(So the title "moving pictures" for cinema is not quite accurate – it is not the fact that the pictures themselves move that is so important, but that they can convey a sense of movement in what they are pictures of.) In any case, movie images are active, animated, sprightly – they get around.' But as we'll soon see, the power of cinema is due more to a direct, immanent contagion of movement, not what appears to move.
47. See Cannon 1996, p. 283.
48. See McGinn 2005, p. 89, for a different but kindred thought: 'the uncanny ability of the screen to simulate life – not just inorganic movement – is likewise an ironic achievement. It seems to me that irony is at the heart of the movie-watching experience – the irony of a medium with one kind of nature is so successfully conveying a reality whose nature is very different. The feeling of mismatch, of incongruity, is almost comical. Think of an old silent film, black-and-white, no voices, too fast, probably "unrealistic": isn't it ironic that it manages to tell us so much about the real world of noisy, colored, speaking, slow-moving people? It ought not to be able to do this, and yet it pulls the trick off. And isn't this irony part of its charm? It is as if one is constantly suppressing a smile by watching a film – a smile of appreciation at the ingenious irony of it all.'
49. These others – acting, music, and so on, – also being, as I will outline in Chapter 8, forms of movement themselves.
50. As when Deleuze says that 'we should take up again the Bergsonian notion of fabulation and give it a political sense', meaning by this the creation through the 'minor' arts of a missing people or audience. See Bogue 2006, p. 222 n. 1. See also Deleuze 1995, p. 174 and Rodowick 1997, pp. 156–62. See also Deleuze and Guattari 1994, pp. 171ff on 'creative fabulation' as a *vision*.
51. Deleuze 1989, p. 272. See also p. 26: 'The first difficulty concerns narration: this is not an evident given in cinematographical images in general, even ones which are historically established ... On the contrary, it seems to us that narration is only a consequence of the visible images themselves and their direct combinations – it is never a given. So-called classical narration derives directly from the organic composition of movement-images or from their specification as perception-images, affection-images and action-images, according to laws of sensory-motor schema.'
52. Bergson 1977, p. 110. Likewise, the original fabulation of taboos is not absurd (p. 128).

53. See Mitchell 2005, pp. 8, 106 for the following statements endorsing Bergson's position: 'I believe that magical attitudes toward images are just as powerful in the modern world as they were in the so-called ages of faith'; 'the double consciousness about images is a deep and abiding feature of human responses to representation'; 'when it comes to images, as Bruno Latour would put it, we have never been modern and probably never will be modern'.
54. Bergson 1977, pp. 110, 107. Bergson 1977, p. 195: fabulation is another faculty, not a variation on a general theme.
55. Bergson 1977, p. 108: that said, all these other forms of representation come back to fabulation in its religious origins. Bergson's investigation foreshadows a type of structural anthropology: by studying the *structure* of myths and myth-making without prejudice, that is, by taking their content seriously, Bergson hopes to see what function they perform. He is thus critical of Levy-Bruhl's idea that primitive mentality is unique to primitives: the human mind works the same throughout the population, but on different material (Bergson 1977, pp. 103, 104, 108–9). There is the same 'psychological origin of superstition' for all.
56. One could argue that there is also a fourth, pantheistic fabulation that sees God operating immanently within the world. The basis for this would be Bergson's own final philosophy of God, which is a mix of Christianity and Spinozism. See Mullarkey 2007a. In other words, Bergson's theory of universal duration can be read as fabulative.
57. Bergson 1977, p. 204: man is 'alone in knowing that he must die'.
58. Bergson 1977, pp. 129, 125.
59. Bergson 1977, p. 133.
60. Bergson 1977, pp. 152, 176, 180. No longer ourselves being animists, we now think of this spirit as an 'an abstract idea [of giving water] ... extracted from things by an intellectual effort', whereas it was originally thought that this spirit *was* that action. It might be truer to say that with the 'spirit of the spring' we already have the beginnings of that extraction, and that *our* conception of this spirit now as merely one abstract idea amongst others, far from being an innocent description of a tenet of animism, is actually a furtherance of this extractive process (partly effected by our language of 'substance' and 'attributes').
61. Bergson 1977, pp. 153, 146, 138, 145.
62. Bergson 1977, pp. 156, 169, 175. '*Evénement*' is capitalized by Bergson throughout these passages.
63. Bergson 1977, pp. 157, 158. Bergson 1977, pp. 158–60: 'events', for example 'accidents', are carved out of 'the continuity of the real' by anthropomorphization.
64. Ronald Bogue (2006, p. 206) argues that 'the shock of the event induces awe, elation, and a spontaneous natural attribution of intention and personhood to the Earthquake', but misses Bergson's point that it is the shock of the *processes* that pushes us to construct them into an Event.
65. See Žižek 2006, p. 202. See also 2001c, p. 67.
66. See Bergson 1911.
67. Bergson 1977, pp. 141, 167, 176.
68. Bergson 1977, pp. 144, 160.
69. Bergson 1977, p. 125. See also Kracauer 1992, p. 252: 'actually, the urge to raise hats and chairs to the status of full-fledged actors has never been completely atrophied (since the early days of cinema). From the malicious escalators, the unruly Murphy beds, the mad automobiles in silent comedy, to the cruiser *Potemkin*, the oil Derek in *Louisiana Story* and the dilapidated kitchen in *Umberto D.*, a long

procession of unforgettable objects has passed across the screen – objects which stand out as protagonists and all but overshadow the rest of the cast.' The 'Basil Fawlty' aspect to Bergson's example of the unruly table is also evident. What is interesting in this regard is that John Cleese reports that the famous scene in *Fawlty Towers*, when Basil whips his car with a tree branch for breaking down on him once again, needed to be filmed a number of times with different sizes of branch, the larger sizes losing the comical effect in place of something more sadistic and horrific. See DVD *Fawlty Towers: Series 1 and 2* (2 Entertain Video (BBC), 2001), interview with John Cleese.

70. Bergson 1977, p. 196.
71. See Currie 1995.
72. See Michotte 1963.
73. Lowry 1985, pp. 129, 165. This quote comes from an early, though related, experiment. Note that Bergson would agree that the movement is real, but that it originates in the projector.
74. Monaco 1981, p. 309.
75. Allen 1997, p. 108, 112.
76. Radford 1975, p. 79 n. 3.
77. See Lowry 1985, pp. 83–4 on the experiment on 'rhythm and unanimity' conducted by filmologist Etienne Souriau on 14 students' impressions of film pacing, the results of which were published in 1953.
78. This personification of deadly disaster (be it simply by the merest accident) is brought to an extreme in the *Final Destination* movies (2000, 2003).
79. Naturally, there are various other ways to describe what is going on by reference to the vague notion of 'suspended disbelief' as it may be operating in such cases as these. To begin with the most obvious concerning *Titanic*, it could be that we simply *identify* with the characters and their desires. Yet, it is odd that most of the on-screen characters (especially those in close-up and point of view shots) during this sequence are unsympathetic, being the overconfident, arrogant representatives of a Victorian culture that was doomed because it put too much faith in machinery and not enough in nature (the simple moral of Cameron's tale). Moreover, the work we mentioned earlier by Murray Smith on optical alignment and affective allegiance complicates that traditional response, given that we are not allied with the characters we are optically aligned with in this scene (see Smith 1995). Another alternative account for the peculiar illusion of reality in this scene might be that the narrative tone here is one of suspense, either by proxy of the characters' situation or even directly, as in Susan Smith's notion of 'direct suspense' (see Smith 2000). Yet, suspense works through not *fully* knowing the outcome of events, and we certainly do know the outcome of the *Titanic*'s story (that's why our response to it is intriguing). Nor is this a matter of anxiety in the face of an unsure future, or even a probable one: this is an affect created despite the future being absolutely certain, and unless one is to invoke exotica such as alternative universes where the film (and/or history itself) has a happier ending, the fact remains that the *Titanic* will sink because, as one character tells us knowingly, it's 'made of iron'. Douglas Pye's notion of foreboding when rewatching a film won't fit either because it lacks a full analysis of the temporal differences between repeating the past (re-watching) and seeing a *present* (even if only in fantasy), which is the key to my own final answer to the paradox. Finally, the music too contributes in its own way to creating suspense, but, again, cannot alone generate the sense of actuality we feel when watching the scene.

I won't go on any more, for we could engage with a host of other explanations concerning the reality effect in fiction (both filmic and general), some aggrandizing, like Nelson Goodman's notion of world-making (which bears considerable comparison to Bergson's fabulation) or Baudry's Freudian analogy of the dream-like impression of reality in cinema; some more prosaic, such as Kendall Walton's concept of mimesis as make-believe (see Walton 1990). But each of these other explanations, while relevant, always omit an account of the genesis of the faculty of (aesthetic) representation. Oddly enough, the same criticism can be turned to classical explanations of the paradox of fiction, such as the theory of catharsis, for while this provides a description of the emotional function of art (the 'how' issue), it too omits an explanation of the source of our sensitivity to art, that is, why we are able to 'see as'.

80. Radford 1975, p. 78.
81. See Williams 2002, p. 166: 'The somewhat defensive postures indicate anticipation – arms are crossed, while several people hold their ears, suggesting the importance of sound in cueing terror'.
82. As Patrick Hogan writes (2003, p. 250): 'stories are connected with, indeed, formed out of emotions and emotion ideas. [But] ... emotions and emotion ideas are connected with, indeed, formed out of stories as well'.
83. Rancière 2006, pp. 49–50.
84. See Branigan 2002, pp. 105–14.
85. That said, however, such unknowing anticipation is only *gradually* dulled by repetition and knowledge (all else being equal), which is why scenes we have experienced before can still repeatedly move us, especially when we re-view a scene in a *new* context. Here is further proof that this is not an affair concerning epistemological representation directly. See Smith 1999 on a scene that 'never fails to move' (though he puts much emphasis on the other means for directly affecting an audience other than movement, namely music).
86. Narrative could be said to be enjoyable in general because it *suspends* us between expectations that are both fulfilled and thwarted with each new event (or as Bergson says of the event, between the probable and impossible).
87. Cavell 1979, p. 211; Deleuze 2000, p. 372. See also, Deleuze 1989, p. 271: the empirical form of time given in the movement-image might tempt us to think that 'the cinematographic image is necessarily in the present'. But this is 'disastrous for any understanding of cinema' (and formed through over-hasty reflection on the movement-image).
88. See Mullarkey 2005.
89. 'To look at the peculiar tendency of images to absorb and be absorbed by human subjects in processes that look suspiciously like those of living things. We have an incorrigible tendency to lapse into vitalistic and animistic ways of speaking when we talk about images. It's not just a question of their producing "imitations of life" (as the saying goes), but that the imitations seem to take on "lives of their own"' (Mitchell 2005, p. 2). See also p. 53: 'rather than allow the biology textbooks to dictate what it means to think of a picture as a living thing, we might be better advised to start from our own ordinary ways of talking about pictures as if they were animated'. Nonetheless, even Mitchell doesn't go all the way, saying (p. 11) that he doesn't 'really believe that images want things', but is focused on why 'human beings (including myself) insist on talking and behaving as if they did believe it'. For the variants of what fabulation is *not* describing, see Appadurai 1988 or Scott 2002.

90. Mitchell 2005, pp. 53, 36.
91. Recall that cinematic projection, for Bergson, consists in 'extracting from all the movements peculiar to all the figures an impersonal movement abstract and simple, *movement in general.*' (Bergson 2007a, pp. 305–6).
92. Bergson 1988, p. 25. One might imagine a neurological correlate for fabulation in the concept of mirror neurons. But, without denying this correlate's existence, it might remain pertinent to question its interpretation and whether the concept of a *mirror* neuron has explained mimesis or simply miniaturized it in another form of representation. Of course, we must be careful about mimesis: Taussig 1993 argues that it has never simply been about the reproduction of the same but is also about creating difference. It is not mere copying or realistic representation. See also Santoro 1993 on mimesis as an imitation of style rather than substance.
93. See Mitchell 2005, pp. 2, 11 n. 15 citing Michael Thompson (1995) on life as a 'logical category that does not admit of an empirical, positive definition'.
94. Deleuze and Guattari 1984, p. 2.

8 Refractions of Reality, or, What is Thinking Anyway?

1. Allen 1966, p. 29.
2. Bergson 1988, p. 37, my emphases.
3. The term 'refraction' appears throughout Bergson's work 31 times in the original French, in fact, most famously in the last sentence of *The Two Sources* that describes the 'refractory planet' whereupon gods are made. As Jean-Louis Vieillard-Baron notes, 'il use fréquemment d'images empruntées à la géométrié, comme la rotation ou la projection, ou à l'optique comme la réflexion et la réfraction; et, on ne comprend rien à sa pensée si l'on prend ces images en un sens vague et banal' (Vieillard-Baron 1993, p. 23).
4. The 'I' here, according to structuralism, is only the intersection of various codes. But then we might say that I am the refractive medium through which the world (nature, nurture and film) is encoded or refracted – a medium itself composed of other media.
5. See Bergson 1999, pp. 1–29 and Mullarkey 1999, pp. 112–17.
6. Bordwell 1989a, p. xii.
7. See the opening introduction of Bergson 1946, pp. 11–29 on the 'true growth of truth'.
8. Anderson 1998, p. 166; Kennedy 2000, p. 77 citing Deleuze and Guattari 1988, p. 32. The passage continues: 'The wolf, as the instantaneous apprehension of a multiplicity in a given region, is not a representative, a substitute, but an I feel. I feel myself becoming a wolf... it is not a question of representation: don't think for a minute that it has to do with believing oneself a wolf, representing oneself as a wolf. The wolf, wolves, are intensities, speeds, temperatures, non-decomposable variable distances. A swarming, a wolfing'.
9. It is a curious fact that one of the favourite examples in analytical philosophy of the event is that of spilling coffee accidentally (in order to expose the differences between *intentional* actions and mere events) as seen in Donald Davidson's work (see 'Agency' in Davidson 1980, pp. 43–61). My thanks to James Williams for reminding me of this. For my own analysis of Davidson on events, see Mullarkey 2006, pp. 115–17.

10. The suffering here is relative, of course, and paltry compared to our bodily, animal suffering. Yet, the two are not unconnected, which is precisely Bergson's point: it is simply a matter of distance.
11. Bergson 1988, p. 56.
12. Kennedy 2000, p. 43. See also Sobchack 1992, p. 305: 'As our embodiments differ and our situations change, so the film's activity of sign production and its meaning change for us in our differently situated activity of looking, in our different intentions towards it'.
13. Hansen 2004, pp. 10, 13; see Connolly 2002, p. 33.
14. Hansen 2004, pp. 1–2, 10. W.J.T. Mitchell (2005, p. 313 n. 4) agrees with Hansen in going against the digital hype, citing new media theorist Lev Manovich and Brian Massumi in this regard, though he also takes exception to Manovich's alternative notion of 'the programmable'.
15. See Massumi 2002, pp. 133–43 on the 'excess of the analog over the digital' (p. 143).
16. Hansen does support Massumi's primacy of the analogical vis-à-vis movement as affect, but not his 'movement-vision', which, ironically, Hansen feels is still not haptic enough, being too incorporeally virtual (see Hansen 2004, pp. 227–30). Yet, the same can be said of the digital as such before its bodily enframing. The digital is analogical at its finest grain level.
17. See Hansen 2004, p. 10 and p. 22: as 'media lose their material specificity, the body takes on a more prominent function as a selective processor of information'. In his Forward to Hansen's text (Lenoir 2004, p. xvi), Tim Lenoir disavows the (disembodied) Shannon-Weaver theory of information for both of them – a common gesture in such studies – but the incorporeal representational aspect is clearly still here.
18. Connolly 2002, pp. xiii, 13.
19. Either that or such body-work will be abandoned as an excessively laborious form of interaction: there are biological thresholds to be observed when balancing activity with passivity in film viewing.
20. Guerlac 2007, unpublished paper.
21. Another possibility, that a film might create an entirely non-mimetic computer-generated world, as in *Tron* (1982), involves neither failure nor success, having only its own standards to live up to, which it does by necessity.
22. See, for instance, *Monster House* (2006) for perfect reproductions of an unfocused background in shallow depths of field.
23. Some subjects are obviously more suited to CGI than others, such as toys (in *Toy Story* (1995) for instance), given their manufactured nature that lends itself to further mechanical reproduction. Other subjects that we are just less familiar with are also prime candidates, for example fish (*Finding Nemo* (2003) for the background animals, not the anthropomorphic 'leads'), insects (*A Bug's Life* (1998), again for the background animals), unseen animals (*Jurassic Park* (1993)), impossible animals (monsters from every movie), and hybrids (*Spiderman* (2002)), as well as exotic landscapes and fauna of all kinds (especially from aerial perspectives, see *Happy Feet* (2006) or *Lord of the Rings* (2001–03)). But these are simply things we are (normally) not familiar with perceptually, and so instances whose resistance and randomness are unknown to us (fish are doubtless more complex when taken out of the fishbowl). Subjects that don't lend themselves so well to the process include human faces, which have always been impossible for CGI to render convincingly (as evidenced in *Final*

Fantasy: The Spirits Within (2001) or *Hulk* (2003)) or domestic animals that we are familiar with, like cats and dogs (see the wolf in *The Brothers Grimm* (2005)). When it comes to motion capture CGI (as used in *Beowulf* (2007) and *The Polar Express* (2004)), or even more so in rotoscoped filming (*A Scanner Darkly* (2006)), we enter into the area of a photorealism (or movement realism) wholly parasitic on the hypostatized idea of the Real, and so whose victories are pyrrhic.

24. Christian Metz cited in Cubitt 2004, p. 1. Of course, Metz also uses the notion of special effect in the peculiar context of his still semiological notion of 'trucage' that we are not endorsing here: see Metz 1977, pp. 657–75. But see also McGinn 2005, p. 147: 'in a way, all film consists of special effects...Cinema is a special effect'.
25. This revitalized horror can be exploited anew, of course, by films that reference these uncanny aspects in their 'retro' lighting, cinematography, editing or make-up, as is evident in Werner Herzog's *Nosferatu* (1979) or Francis Ford Coppola's *Bram Stoker's Dracula* (1992), for example. The irony is that these rebirths of older forms date even more quickly than their referents because their excess self-consciousness eventually appears merely as 'camp'. It was the *seriousness* of the original's bizarre form that makes them uncanny.
26. See Frampton 2006 and Stewart 2007.
27. It is beyond the scope of this study to tackle the huge array of sociological audience research, but it has clearly shown how the reception of the image is heavily mediated by age group, gender, nationality, socio-economic group, as well as group dynamics in the viewing situation. An excellent example of this work is Jackie Stacey's *Star Gazing: Hollywood Cinema and Female Spectatorship* (1994).
28. Hartman 1997, p. 75.
29. Jayamanne 2001, p. 235.
30. Chion 1994, pp. 63–4. A wonderful example of conscious synchresis comes in Spielberg's *Indiana Jones and the Last Crusade* (1989) when the librarian's use of his date-punch is perfectly mixed to the sound of Jones's repeated, heavy hammering on the library's marble floor (out of sight and much to the former's astonished misapprehension).
31. See Mayer 1999, p. 11.
32. Mayer 1999, p. 12.
33. See Baron 1999, p. 43. Griffith's naturalism required the use of smaller gestures for the larger screen, mostly played out in the frontal plane due to the camera's poor depth of field. See Mayer 1999, pp. 22–3.
34. See Altman 1992, p. 14.
35. See Naremore 1988, pp. 202–3; Carnicke 1999, p. 81.
36. See Naremore 1988, p. 197.
37. Naremore 1988, p. 201; Blanche duBois describes Stanley (Brando's character) as 'like an animal. He has an animal's habits'.
38. See Burt 2002 and Ridout 2006, pp. 96–128.
39. Obviously my appropriation of Barthes's photographic concepts distorts them, given his cinephobia.
40. Tarr's *Werckmeister Harmonies* (2001) has a stuffed whale as its focus.
41. Though it is doubtless that each of us have different economies of moral regard (most humans are more fastidious about watching, and hearing, fellow mammals suffer than insects, with our own species being so well regarded that we label the *total* lack of respect for humans a 'psychopathology'), the fact remains that

we all care about *something* if we have cares at all (i.e. we are alive) no matter what that thing may be. That we should suffer at the spectacle of suffering can be explained either through transcendent representation (mirror neurons), which only palms off the problem through miniaturization, or the immanent contagion of movement (fabulation): to see suffering is to partake in it, pain itself (as Bergson says), being a participatory affect par excellence, when a part tries to become a whole.

42. This last question often reveals an interesting duplicity in itself: in order to narrate a moral of animal welfare (cruelty is bad), some cruelty is often inflicted on animals in film. Bresson's *Au Hasard Balthazar* is a good case in point, realizing its pious ambition through some (though not great) cruelty to the donkey. The *Free Willy* films (1993, 1995, 1997) are even more obvious, using a captive killer whale to tell a story about freeing a captive killer whale.
43. Berger 1991, p. 7. It should be noted that both animals and children can be exploited in an even more obvious, though reversed fashion – by playing on sentimental feelings for their beauty and 'cuteness'.
44. Roman Ingarden makes a related point in *The Ontology of the Work of Art* (Ingarden 1989, p. 319): 'In a film play, a hero of the story presented was supposed to undergo a surgical operation. In order to achieve the greatest possible impression upon the spectator, an actual operation on a sick person was filmed. But, as it happened, the surgeons encountered great difficulties in the course of the operation. An unforeseen complication, a strong and dangerous hemorrhage, occurred and for a time appeared to greatly endanger the patient, so that it was all the physicians could do to save the patient's life. This all took place with such "realism" and it was believed that the film would make a strong, perturbing impression on the spectators, and would thereby achieve a great aesthetic success. But while the actual effect was indeed great, it was of an entirely different kind than had been expected. The spectators simply protested. They were so deeply disturbed by experiencing a human being in real danger of death that they no longer wanted to look at the film. What happened? There came a moment when the unexpected consternation coming clearly to expression in the behavior of the physicians and the grisly details of the operation translated the spectators into the attitude of real, serious belief in the reality of what was happening. They could no longer regard the processes being shown them as a mere artistic presentation, and with that there disappeared not only the purely aesthetic effect, but also all desire to witness such a great turn of human fortune.' While I think Ingarden has described a genuine phenomenon of spectatorship here, what I find really interesting is not so much which *punctum* of reality – the *real* misfortune of a human, cat or fly, which is always a culturally relative concern – but the audience's observation of an abuse of a putative reality in the name of creating realism, as if reality itself was static enough to be so captured.
45. Badiou 2008.
46. He also describes it as an 'experience': 'an experience of the Real that escapes auto-position, that is not a circle of the Real and of thought…a Real that is *immanent (to) itself rather than to a form of thought,* to a "logic"' (Laruelle 1996, pp. 3–5, 6).
47. See Laruelle 1996, p. 253; Kieffer 2003; Schmid 2003. Laruelle himself would take exception to thinking that his non-philosophy is a metatheory (see Laruelle 2003, p. 184). Philosophy for him is already metaphilosophical, which is why it is inadequate. I, however, take the opposite view, given that I do not think it is

possible to immunize non-philosophy from becoming philosophy *over time* – any avant-garde is inevitably naturalized when replaced by a new non-philosophy. There is an alternative approach where non-philosophy would be understood as metaphilosophy in the etymological sense, that is, the perpetual self-overcoming of *philosophia* through movement. In its movement, there is still an inside and an outside to philosophy such that a reflection on philosophy (metaphilosophy) can be non-philosophical, but only *momentarily*. It is this momentary glimpse that I study here.

48. Bordwell 1989a, p. 42.
49. Connolly 2002, p. 16.
50. Connolly 2002, p. 204 n. 17, both emphases mine.
51. An example of this in cinema is the last close-up of Greta Garbo in Rouben Mamoulian's *Queen Christina* (1933), whose look from the ship back to her homeland has been interpreted as great acting, though Garbo herself was simply asked by Mamoulian to look out blankly. It is the intercuts that create the meaning on her face. We recall from our preface that Merleau-Ponty likened the Kuleshov Effect to a gestalt, an emergent whole greater than the sum of its parts.
52. See Bordwell 1996a, p. 23, where he argues that both subject-position and culturalist theory prefer verbal association over proper 'inductive, deductive, and abductive reasoning' (or 'inference to the best explanation'). See also Bordwell 1989a, p. 252 on the use of puns encouraging an associative play of meaning in film theory influenced by French philosophy. Clearly, though, any inductive reasoning that appears to someone as *unlikely* will then appear associationist to them. Any association which seems probable appears inductive.
53. Nietzsche 1989, p. 119.
54. Laruelle 1996, p. 54. See del Bufalo 2003, p. 42: Non-philosophy is a *'science première'* because, estranged from philosophy, it is 'the essence (of) the science of science'.
55. Heidegger 1968, p. 4; Bradley 1993, no. 79.
56. The allusion here, of course, is to Deleuze: 'To think is to create – there is no other creation – but to create is first of all to engender "thinking" in thought' (Deleuze 1994, p. 147). In *What is Philosophy?*, Deleuze (and Guattari) will delineate the scope of creation in a threefold manner – in philosophy (creation of concepts), art (creation of affects) and science (creation of functions).
57. Of course, some may never give up on that Platonic dream. And even where that dream has been renewed, as in the work on Badiou, one must ask whether its renewed *expression* also adds to its content such that the truth too is also in process. See Mullarkey 2006, pp. 129–34.
58. Regarding film, such relationality should not be taken as a species of relational aesthetics, which remains too much within a social domain for a metaphysical thesis such as this: see Bourriaud 2002.
59. Bergson 1977, p. 47. It is noteworthy that often *our* most thoughtful films (or film-scenes) do not make one think immediately, but remain as a disturbance or agitation that may later become a thought.
60. Bergson 1977, p. 49. At a number of specific points in Bergson 1977, pp. 46, 64, Bergson specifically calls this creative emotion, 'intuition'. The idea of creative emotion can also be a means of reconciling Bordwell and Žižek. For the latter, Freud subtracted affect from representation, that is, the Real of desire from the Symbolic. Although Žižek follows Lacan by accommodating *jouissance* as

an encounter with the void or Real, he only does so by rendering *jouissance* representational, for, as we saw, he cannot immunize his own discourse from being one more arbitrary symbolization without also assuming a transcendental position (Big Other) of his own. Cognitivists like Bordwell, on the other hand, try to accommodate affect, but only by cognitivizing it, that is, by rendering it representational immediately. It is ironic, then, that Bordwell regards Žižek as an emotivist while Žižek regards Bordwell as representationalist. However, if all symbolizations, including Bordwell's and Žižek's *own discourses*, are partially right because each is a part or level of the Real, then there is no need for either to renounce the other *completely*. Bergson's theory of affect (creative emotion) is also a theory of levels, of how representation is harboured *within* affect. It may well be that Žižek and Bordwell are not irreconcilable *tout court*, but simply operate at different levels.

61. What Victor Perkins recommended for film reading then (that it can only suggest to another how a film might be re-viewed *with time*), I am extending to the philosophy and thought of film.
62. Bergson 1946, p. 34, 190. In this respect the 'thing' does not exist as a substance at all – there is only 'the moving (of movements)', or if you prefer, the substantialization of movement: there is movement, but no thing beneath the movements that is not itself a becoming (Bergson 2007b, p. 38).
63. The concept of indefinites or 'dynamic definitions' are throughout Bergson: see Bergson 2007a, pp. 89, 90, 111–12; 1946, p. 211; 1977, p. 296.
64. See Bergson 2007a, pp. 124–5; Rancière 1991, p. 16.

Conclusion: Code Unknown – A Bastard Theory for a Bastard Art

1. PC Danny Butterman (Nick Frost) in *Hot Fuzz* (2007).
2. Kaprow 2003b, p. xxix; Bergson 1946, p. 100.
3. See Mullarkey 2006 for discussion of one such event in 1988, especially pp. 1–11.
4. Laruelle, however, retrieves a Gnosticism for his own position on account of thinking that the boundary between non-philosophy and philosophy is static rather than dynamic.
5. See Bergson 1977, pp. 112, 113, 114, 116. It is not that the term 'biological process' already carries an identifier for Life (which would explain what it is exactly), for it merely marks out a set of processes that have an indefinite kinship ('a family resemblance') with regard to how they strike us as movements we can fabulate.
6. See Deleuze 1989, p. 168: 'Maurice Blanchot was able to give the fundamental question of what makes us think, what forces us to think, back to Artaud: what forces us to think is "the inpower [*impouvoir*] of thought", the figure of nothingness, the inexistence of a whole which could be thought. What Blanchot diagnoses everywhere in literature is particularly clear in cinema: on the one hand the presence of an unthinkable in thought, which would be both its source and barrier; on the other hand the presence to infinity of another thinker in the thinker'. See also Deleuze 1989, pp. 156, 165, 278.
7. Or as Rancière quotes J.S. Van de Weyer on Joseph Jacotot, 'the ignorant schoolmaster': 'I must teach you that I have nothing to teach you' (Rancière 1991, p. 15). The ideas in this book are only 'suggestions', in Bergson's sense, to be passed between contagious imaginations (see Heidsieck 1957, pp. 90, 175). The

imagination in question here is as much the fabulatory imagining of movements as it is the representational imagination of ideas that it underlies.

8. Metz 1974, pp. 21–2, cited in Lowry 1985, p. 3.
9. Though the separability of these two realms – 'filmic facts' and 'cinematic facts' – was later disputed (Lowry 1985, p. 74).
10. See Lowry 1985, pp. 84–5. See also Souriau 1953.
11. Cohen-Séat 1946, p. 64, cited in Lowry 1985, p. 44. With respect to science, properly speaking, there is no science (*la science*) for Bergson, but only sciences (*les sciences*), 'not one science but several sciences of nature' (*Mélanges*, pp. 493–4). A consequence of this is that any fundamental unity found in nature (and the sciences) will be a human artefact, a 'factitious unity' or 'abstract unity' imposed on nature externally by the intellect through the projection of (or refraction with) its own unity. This term 'factitious' is of great significance here, for though it connotes a fabrication, it is not wholly unnatural, nor unfounded: it is not fictitious or purely relative to individual whimsy (see Bergson 2007, pp. 210ff). In fact, the unity of the sciences is something we fabulate.
12. Lowry 1985, pp. 68–9, 58, 69, 59.
13. Cited in Lowry 1985, p. 56. See also the idea that film is a total process that is 'irreducible to strict boundaries' (Lowry 1985, p. 50)
14. Lowry 1985, p. 157. An *ongoing* disunity (or continuous heterogeneity), rather than false synthesis, would be the ambition. For an alternative view of synthesis, see Bacon 2005. In addition, the emphasis on theoretic failure as nonetheless succeeding on account of reality's own non-self-identity may well put one in mind of Adorno's negative dialectic and its notion of irreconcilability. The difference, of course, is that the temporality of Adorno's movement is dialectical and thereby still fosters a nostalgia for eventual unity or *convergence*. See Osborne 1991, p. 39. Adorno also saw little value in cinema: as part of the culture industry, it could not counter social alienation, as true art must. See Horkheimer and Adorno 1969, pp. 126–7: 'The sound film, far surpassing the theater illusion, leaves no room for imagination or action on the part of the audience, who is to respond within the structure of the film yet deviate from its precise detail, without losing the thread of the story; hence the film forces its victims to equate it directly with reality... Sustained thought is out of the question, if the spectator is not to miss the relentless rush of the facts'. See also Waldman 1977, pp. 39–60.
15. As we noted in the Introduction, Noël Carroll makes the same point that film theory 'should be catholic about the methodological frameworks it explores' rather than essentialist or pure (Carroll 2003, p. 361). As he says, 'insofar as theorists approach film from many different angles, from different levels of abstraction and generality, they will have to avail themselves of multidisciplinary frameworks. Some questions about film may send the researcher toward economics, while others require a look into perceptual psychology. In other instances, sociology, political science, anthropology, communications theory, linguistics, artificial intelligence, biology, or narrative theory may provide the initial research tools which the film theorist requires in order to begin to evolve theories of this or that aspect of film' (p. 360). Yet, at the same time as this pluralism, Carroll still commits himself to placing cognitivist theory at its core, because, again, it is not a theory but 'a stance toward film research', one that 'advocates the exploration of hypotheses about film reception in terms of the cognitive and perceptual processes of spectators, rather than in terms of the unconscious processes and syndromes favored by the Theory' (p. 370). Carroll's

pluralism, and anti-essentialism, masks another form of methodological purity and aesthetic essence – all the other approaches must be refracted through the prism of cognition.

16. See Badiou 2004b, p. 133.
17. The philosophical moment, writes Bergson, begins in denial, in an assertion of impossibility before being able to assert anything positive and see the impossible *become* possible. Even its initial failure is also a partial success as positive temporality: the opposed movements that resist each other, because that's just what time is. See Bergson 1946, p. 110.
18. Derrida 1978, p. 79.
19. Altman 1992, p. 4. Bordwell decries this idea of 'interchange' as simply 'restating the humanist's truism that everything is connected to everything else. But it has the institutional advantage of validating a huge variety of research projects' (Bordwell 1996a, p. 12). Two things we can say: that truisms are simply those truths that need to be restated in new terms if their force is to be kept alive; and that Bordwell can turn to the rhetoric of ad hominem argument just as easily as his adversaries.

Bibliography

Abrams, Jerold J. (ed.), *The Philosophy of Stanley Kubrick*, The University Press of Kentucky, 2007.

Agamben, Giorgio, 'Notes on Gesture', in Giorgio Agamben (ed.), *Means Without End: Notes on Politics*, tr. Vincenzo Binetti and Cesare Casarino, University of Minnesota Press, 2000.

Allen, Richard, *Projecting Illusion: Film Spectatorship and the Impression of Reality*, University Press, 1997.

Allen, Richard and Murray Smith, 'Introduction', in Richard Allen and Murray Smith (eds), *Film Theory and Philosophy*, Oxford University Press, 1999, pp. 1–35.

Allen, Woody, *Getting Even*, Random House, 1966.

Altman, Rick, 'General Introduction: Cinema as Event', in Rick Altman (ed.), *Sound Theory/Sound Practice*, Routledge, 1992, pp. 1–14.

Anderson, Joseph D., *The Reality of Illusion: An Ecological Approach to Cognitive Film Theory*, Southern Illinois University Press, 1998.

——'Preliminary Considerations', in Joseph D. Anderson and Barbara Fisher Anderson (eds), *Moving Image Theory: Ecological Considerations*, S. Illinois UP, 2007.

Anderson, Joseph D. and Barbara Fisher Anderson (eds), *Moving Image Theory: Ecological Considerations*, S. Illinois UP, 2007.

Appadurai, Arjun, *The Social Life of Things: Commodities in Cultural Perspective*, Cambridge University Press, 1988.

Bacon, Henry, 'Synthesizing Approaches in Film Theory', pp. 1–14, available at www.avila.edu/journal/bacon1.pdf.

Badiou, Alain, *Deleuze: The Clamor of Being*, tr. Louise Burchill, Minnesota Press, 2000.

——*Handbook of Inaesthetics*, tr. Alberto Toscano, Stanford University Press, 2004a.

——*Theoretical Writings*, ed. and tr. Ray Brassier and Alberto Toscano, Continuum, 2004b.

——*Being and Event*, tr. Oliver Feltham, Continuum, 2005a.

——*Le Siècle*, Seuil, 2005b.

——*Logiques des mondes*, Seuil, 2006.

——'Dialectics of the Fable: Philosophical Myths and Cinema', tr. Alberto Toscano, *Science Fiction Film and Television*, vol. 1, no. 1 (2008), pp. 15–23.

Balmary, Marie, *Psychoanalyzing Psychoanalysis: Freud and the Hidden Faults of the Father*, Johns Hopkins University Press, 1982.

Baron, Cynthia, 'Crafting Film Performances: Acting in the Hollywood Studio Era', in Alan Lovell and Peter Kramer (eds), *Screen Acting*, Routledge, 1999, pp. 31–45.

Bateson, Gregory, *Steps to an Ecology of Mind: Collected Essays in Anthropology, Psychiatry, Evolution and Epistemology*, Ballantine Books, 1972.

Baudry, Jean-Louis, 'The Apparatus: Metapsychological Approaches to the Impression of Reality in Cinema', in Gerald Mast, Marshall Cohen and Leo Baudry (eds), *Film Theory and Criticism. Introductory Readings*, 4th edn, Oxford University Press, 1992, pp. 690–707.

Bazin, André, *What is Cinema?* vol. 1, University of California Press, 1967.

Bellour, Raymond, 'The Obvious and the Code', in Philip Rosen (ed.), *Narrative, Apparatus, Ideology: A Film Theory Reader*, Columbia University Press, 1986, pp. 93–101.

Belsey, Catherine, *Critical Practice*, Routledge, 1992.

Berger, John, *About Looking*, Vintage International, 1991.

Bergson, Henri, *Laughter: An Essay on the Meaning of the Comic*, tr. Cloudesley Brereton and Fred Rothwell, Macmillan, 1911.

——*The Creative Mind: An Introduction to Metaphysics*, tr. Mabelle L. Andison, Philosophical Library, 1946.

——*Mélanges*, Presses Universitaires de France, 1972.

——*The Two Sources of Morality and Religion*, tr. by R. Ashley Audra and Cloudesley Brereton, Notre Dame Press, 1977.

——*Matter and Memory*, tr. Nancy Margaret Paul and W. Scott Palmer, Zone Books, 1988.

——*Duration and Simultaneity*, tr. Leon Jacobson, Clinamen Press, 1999.

——*Creative Evolution*, tr. Arthur Mitchell, Palgrave Macmillan, 2007a.

——*An Introduction to Metaphysics*, tr. T.E. Hulme, Palgrave Macmillan, 2007b.

——*Mind-Energy*, tr. H. Wildon Carr, ed. Keith Ansell Pearson and Michael Kolkman, Palgrave Macmillan, 2007c.

Bird, Morgan, 'Insurmountable in their Wake: Paradox and Ideology in Cavell's Title Reading of *La Grande Illusion*', *Film International*, Volume 4, Issue 4 (2006), pp. 43–7.

Blassnigg, Martha, 'Clairvoyance, Cinema, and Consciousness', in Robert Pepperell and Michael Punt (eds), *Screen Consciousness: Cinema, Mind and World*, Rodopi, 2006, pp. 105–22.

Bogue, Ronald, *Deleuze on Cinema*, Routledge, 2003.

——'Fabulation, Narration, and the People to Come', in Constantin Boundas (ed.), *Deleuze and Philosophy*, Edinburgh University Press, 2006, pp. 202–23.

Boothby, Richard, *Freud as Philosopher: Metapsychology After Lacan*, Routledge, 2001

Bordwell, David, *Narration in the Fiction Film*, Methuen, 1985.

——*Making Meaning: Inference and Rhetoric in the Interpretation of Cinema*, Harvard University Press, 1989a.

——'A Case for Cognitivism', *Iris*, vol. 9 (1989b), pp. 11–40; available at http://www.davidbordwell.net/articles/Bordwell_Iris_no9_spring1989_11.pdf

——'A Case for Cognitivism: Further Reflections', *Iris*, vol. 11 (1990), pp. 107–11; available at http://www.davidbordwell.net/articles/Bordwell_Iris_no11_summer1990_107.pdf

——'Contemporary Film Studies and the Vicissitudes of Grand Theory', in David Bordwell and Noël Carroll (eds), *Post-Theory: Reconstructing Film Studies*, University of Wisconsin Press, 1996a, pp. 3–36.

——'Convention, Construction, and Cinematic Vision', in David Bordwell and Noël Carroll (eds), *Post-Theory: Reconstructing Film Studies*, University of Wisconsin Press, 1996b, pp. 87–107.

——*On the History of Film Style*, Harvard University Press, 1997.

——'Preaching Pluralism: Pluralism, Truth, and Scholarly Inquiry in Film Studies', *Cinema Journal*, vol. 37, no. 2 (1998), pp. 84–90.

——*Figures Traced in Light: On Cinematic Staging*, University of California Press, 2005a.

——'Slavoj Žižek: Say Anything' (2005b); available at http://www.davidbordwell.net/essays/zizek.php

——*The Way Hollywood Tells It: Story and Style in Modern Movies*, University of California Press, 2006.
Bordwell, David and Noël Carroll, 'Introduction', in David Bordwell and Noël Carroll (eds), *Post-Theory: Reconstructing Film Studies*, University of Wisconsin Press, 1996a, pp. xiii–xvii.
——(eds), *Post-Theory: Reconstructing Film Studies*, University of Wisconsin Press, 1996.
Bordwell, David and Kristin Thompson, *Film Art: An Introduction*, 4th edn, McGraw-Hill, 1992.
Bourriaud, Nicolas, *Relational Aesthetics*, La presses du réel, 2002.
Bradley, F.H., *The Presuppositions of Critical History and Aphorisms*, Thoemmes Press, 1993.
Branigan, Edward, 'Diegesis and Authorship in Film', *Iris*, vol. 7, no. 3, pp. 37–54.
——'Nearly True: Forking Plots, Forking Interpretations: A Response to David Bordwell's "Film Futures"', *SubStance*, issue 97, vol. 31, no. 1 (2002), pp. 105–14.
——*Projecting A Camera: Language-Games in Film Theory*, Routledge, 2005.
Brouwers, Anke and Tom Paulus, 'The Mortgage the Merrier: Hollywood Comedies of Remarriage in the Age of Domesticity', *Film International*, issue 22, vol. 4, no. 4 (2006), pp. 21–34.
Buckland, Warren, *The Cognitive Semiotics of Film*, Cambridge University Press, 2000.
del Bufalo, Erik, *Deleuze et Laruelle: de la Schizo-analyse à la non-philosophie*, Kimé, 2003.
Burt, Jonathan, *Animals in Film*, Reaktion Books, 2002.
Cannon, Steve, 'Not a Mere Question of Form; The Hybrid Realism of Godard's *Vivre sa vie*', *French Cultural Studies*, vol. 7 (1996), pp. 283–94.
Carnicke, Sharon Marie, 'Lee Strasberg's Paradox of the Actor', in Alan Lovell and Peter Kramer (eds), *Screen Acting*, Routledge, 1999, pp. 75–87.
Carroll, Noël, *Philosophical Problems of Classical Film Theory*, Princeton University Press, 1988.
——'Film, Emotion, and Genre,' in Carl Plantinga and Greg M. Smith (eds), *Passionate Views: Film Cognition, and Emotion*, The Johns Hopkins University Press, 1999, pp. 21–47.
——'Moving and Moving', *Millennium Film Journal*, no. 35/36 (Fall 2000); available at http://www.mfj-online.org/journalPages/MFJ35/MovingandMoving.htm
——*Engaging the Moving Image*, Yale University Press, 2003.
Caughie, John, 'Authors and Auteurs: The Uses of Theory', in James Donald and Michael Renov, *Handbook of Film Studies*, Sage, 2007, pp. 408–23.
Cavell, Stanley, *Must We Mean What We Say: A Book of Essays*, Scribner, 1969.
——*The World Viewed: Reflections on the Ontology of Film*, Harvard University Press, 1979.
——*Disowning Knowledge in Six Plays of Shakespeare*, Cambridge University Press, 1987.
——*Contesting Tears: The Hollywood Melodrama of the Unknown Woman*, University of Chicago Press, 1996.
——'What Becomes of Thinking on Film', in Rupert Read and Jerry Goodenough (eds), *Film as Philosophy: Essays on Cinema after Wittgenstein and Cavell*, Palgrave Macmillan, 2005, pp. 167–209.
Chateau, Dominique, *Cinéma et philosophie*, Armand Colin, 2005.
Cherry, Brigid, 'Refusing to Look: Female Viewers of the Horror Film', in Mark Jancovich (ed.), *Horror Film Reader*, Routledge, 2002, pp. 169–78.

Chiesa, Lorenzo, 'What is the Gift of Grace? On Dogville', *Film-Philosophy*, vol. 11, no. 3 (2007), pp. 1–22; available at http:/www.film-philosophy.com/2007v11n3/chiesa.pdf

Chion, Michel, *Audio-Vision*, tr. Claudia Gorbman, Columbia University Press, 1994.

Clemens, Justin, 'Letters as the Condition of Conditions for Alain Badiou', *Communication & Cognition*, vol. 36, nos 1–2 (2003), pp. 73–102.

Cohen-Séat, Gilbert, *Essai sur les principes d'une philosophie du cinéma*, 1st edn, Presses Universitaires de France, 1946.

Comolli, Jean-Luc and Jean Narboni, 'Cinema/Ideology/Criticism', in Gerald Mast et al. (eds), *Film Theory and Criticism*, Oxford University Press, 1992, pp. 682–9.

Conard, Mark T. (ed.), *The Philosophy of Martin Scorsese*, University Press of Kentucky, 2007.

Conley, Tom, 'The Film Event: From Interval to Interstice', in Gregory Flaxman (ed.), *The Brain is the Screen: Deleuze and the Philosophy of Cinema*, University of Minnesota Press, 2000, pp. 303–25.

Conley, Tom, 'Cinema and its Discontents: Jacques Rancière and Film Theory', *SubStance*, issue 108, vol. 34, no. 3, (2005), pp. 96–106.

Connolly, William, *Neuropolitics: Thinking, Culture, Speed*, University of Minnesota Press, 2002.

Corliss, Richard, '*The Bourne Ultimatum*: A Macho Fantasy', *Time Magazine*, 2 August 2007, available at http://www.time.com/time/arts/article/0,8599,1649187,00.html

Couch, Steve, *Matrix Revelations: A Thinking Fan's Guide to the Matrix Trilogy*, Damaris Publishing, 2003.

Creed, Barbara, *The Monstrous-Feminine: Film, Feminism, Psychoanalysis*, Routledge, 1993.

Critchley, Simon, *Very Little…Almost Nothing: Death, Philosophy, Literature*, Routledge, 1997.

——'Calm: On Terence Malik's *Thin Red Line*', in Rupert Read and Jerry Goodenough (eds), *Film as Philosophy: Essays on Cinema after Wittgenstein and Cavell*, Palgrave Macmillan, 2005, pp. 133–48.

Cubitt, Sean, *The Cinematic Effect*, MIT Press, 2004.

Currie, Gregory, *Image and Mind: Film, Philosophy and Cognitive Science*, Cambridge University Press, 1995.

Cutting, James E., 'Perceiving Scenes in Film and in the World', in Joseph Anderson and Barbara Fisher Anderson, *Moving Image Theory: Ecological Considerations*, S. Illinois UP, 2007, pp. 9–27.

Damasio, Antonio, R., *Descartes' Error: Emotion, Reason, and the Human Brain*, Avon, 1994.

Daney, Serge, 'The Tracking Shot in *Kapo*', tr. Laurent Kretzschmar, *Senses of Cinema* (2004); available at http://www.sensesofcinema.com/contents/04/30/kapo_daney.html

Davidson, Donald, 'Agency' in his *Essays on Actions and Events*, Clarendon, 1980, pp. 43–61.

Deleuze, Gilles, 'Intellectuals & Power: A Conversation between Michel Foucault and Gilles Deleuze', in Donald F. Bouchard (ed.), *Language, Counter-Memory, Practice: Selected Essays and Interviews by Michel Foucault*, Cornell University Press, 1980, pp. 205–18.

——*Cinema 1: The Movement-Image*, tr. Hugh Tomlinson and Barbara Habberjam, Athlone Press, 1986.

——*Cinema 2: The Time-Image*, tr. Hugh Tomlinson and Robert Galeta, Athlone Press, 1989.

——*The Logic of Sense*, tr. Mark Lester with Charles Stivale, ed. Constantin V. Boundas, Columbia University Press, 1990.
——*Difference and Repetition*, tr. Paul Patton, Athlone Press, 1994.
——*Negotiations: 1972–1990*, tr. Martin Joughin, Columbia University Press, 1995.
——'The Brain is the Screen: An Interview with Gilles Deleuze', in Gregory Flaxman (ed.), *The Brain is the Screen: Deleuze and the Philosophy of Cinema*, University of Minnesota Press, 2000, pp. 365–73.
Deleuze, Gilles and Félix Guattari, *The Anti-Oedipus*, tr. Robert Hurley, Mark Seem and Helen R. Lane, Athlone, 1984.
——*A Thousand Plateaus*, tr. Brian Massumi, Athlone Press, 1988.
——*What is Philosophy?* tr. Hugh Tomlinson and Graham Burchill, Verso, 1994.
Deleuze, Gilles and Claire Parnet, *Dialogues*, tr. Hugh Tomlinson and Barbara Habberjam, Athlone Press, 1987.
Derrida, Jacques, 'Violence and Metaphysics', in Jacques Derrida, *Writing and Difference*, tr., with an introduction and notes, Alan Bass, Routledge, 1978, pp. 79–153.
——'Signature, Event, Context', in Jacques Derrida, *Margins of Philosophy*, tr. Alan Bass, Harvester Press, 1982, pp. 307–30.
——'Deconstruction and the Other', in Paul Moser and Dwayne Mulder (eds), *Contemporary Approaches to Philosophy*, Macmillan, 1994.
Douglass, Paul, 'Bergson and Cinema: Friends or Foes?', in *The New Bergson*, ed. John Mullarkey, Manchester University Press, 1999, pp. 209–27.
Eitzen, Dirk, 'The Emotional Basis of Film Comedy', in Carl Plantinga and Greg Smith (eds), *Passionate Views: Film Cognition, and Emotion*, The Johns Hopkins University Press, 1999, pp. 84–99.
Ellenberger, Henri F., *The Discovery of the Unconscious: The History and Evolution of Dynamic Psychiatry*, New York: Basic Books, 1970.
Esterson, Allen, 'Jeffrey Masson and Freud's Seduction Theory: A New Fable Based on Old Myths', *History of the Human Sciences*, vol. 11, no. 1, February 1998, pp. 1–21.
Eysenck, Hans, *Decline and Fall of the Freudian Empire*, Penguin, 1985.
Faller, Stephen, *Beyond the Matrix: Revolutions and Revelations*, Chalice Press, 2004.
Falzon, Christopher, *Philosophy Goes to the Movies*, Routledge, 2002.
Flaxman, Gregory (ed.), *The Brain is the Screen: Deleuze and the Philosophy of Cinema*, University of Minnesota Press, 2000.
Foster, Hal, *The Return of the Real: Art and Theory at the End of the Century*, MIT, 1996.
Frampton, Daniel, *Filmosophy*, Wallflower Press, 2006.
Frankfurt, Harry G., *On Bullshit*, Princeton University Press, 2005.
Freeland, Cynthia, 'Feminist Frameworks for Horror Films', in David Bordwell and Noël Carroll (eds), *Post-Theory: Reconstructing Film Studies*, University of Wisconsin Press, 1996, pp. 195–218.
——'Penetrating Keanu: New Holes, but the Same Old Shit', in William Irwin (ed.), *The Matrix and Philosophy: Welcome to the Desert of the Real*, Open Court Publishing, 2002, pp. 205–15.
Friedberg, Anne, 'The End of Cinema: Multi-media and Technological Change', in Christine Gledhill and Linda Williams (eds), *Re-Inventing Film Studies*, Arnold Publishing, 2000, pp. 438–52.
Gauny, Gabriel, *Le Philosophe plébéien, textes presentés et rassemblés par Jacques Rancière*, La Découverte/Maspero, 1983.
Georges-Michel, Michel, 'Henri Bergson nous parle du cinema', *Le Journal*, 20 February 1914.
Gerrold, David, *Taking the Red Pill: Science, Philosophy and Religion in 'The Matrix'*, Summersdale Publishers, 2003.

Goodenough, Jerry, 'Introduction I: A Philosopher Goes to the Cinema', in Rupert Read and Jerry Goodenough (eds), *Film as Philosophy: Essays on Cinema after Wittgenstein and Cavell*, Palgrave Macmillan, 2005.

Grodal, Torben, 'Emotions, Cognitions, and Narrative Patterns in Film', in Carl Plantinga and Greg Smith (eds), *Passionate Views: Film, Cognition, and Emotion*, John Hopkins University Press, 1999, pp. 127–45.

——*Moving Pictures: A New Theory of Film Genres, Feelings and Cognition*, Clarendon Press, 2000.

——'Film Lighting and Mood', in Joseph Anderson and Barbara Fisher Anderson (eds), *Moving Image Theory: Ecological Considerations*, S. Illinois UP, 2007, pp. 152–63.

Gross, Paul R. and N. Levitt, *Higher Superstition: The Academic Left and its Quarrels with Science*, Johns Hopkins University Press, 1994.

Guerlac, Suzanne, 'A Leap in the Dark,' paper given at conference 'Creative Evolution: Histories of Reception', Kyoto, Japan, October 19, 2007.

Hansen, Mark, *New Philosophy for New Media*, MIT, 2004.

Hardcastle, Gary L. and George A. Reisch (eds), *Bullshit and Philosophy*, Open Court Publishing, 2006.

Hartman, Geoffrey, 'The Cinema Animal', in Yosefa Loshitzky (ed.), *Spielberg's Holocaust: Critical Perspectives on Schindler's List*, Indiana University Press, 1997.

Heidegger, Martin, *What is Called Thinking?*, tr. J. Glenn Gray and F. Wieck, with an introduction by J. Glenn Gray, Harper and Row, 1968.

Heidsieck, François, *Henri Bergson et la notion d'Espace*, Le Circle du Livre, 1957.

Herwitz, Daniel, *Key Concepts in Aesthetics*, Continuum, 2008.

Herzog, Amy, 'Affectivity, Becoming, and the Cinematic Event: Gilles Deleuze and the Futures of Feminist Film Theory', in Anu Koivunen and Susanna Paasonen (eds), *Affective Encounters: Rethinking Embodiment in Feminist Media Studies*, University of Turku, 2001, pp. 83–8; available at http://media.utu.fi/affective/herzog.pdf

Hogan, Patrick Colm, *The Mind and its Stories: Narrative Universals and Human Emotion*, Cambridge University Press, 2003.

Horkheimer, Max and Theodor Adorno, *Dialectic of Enlightenment*, Herder and Herder, 1969.

Ingarden, Roman, *The Ontology of the Work of Art: The Musical Work, The Picture, The Architectural Work, The Film*, tr. Raymond Meyer with John T. Goldthwait, Ohio University Press, 1989.

Irwin, William, *The Matrix and Philosophy: Welcome to the Desert of the Real*, Open Court Publishing, 2002.

——*More Matrix and Philosophy*, Open Court Publishing, 2005.

Jancovich, Mark, 'General Introduction', in Mark Jancovich (ed.), *Horror Film Reader*, Routledge, 2002, pp. 1–19.

Jarvie, I.C., *Philosophy of the Film: Epistemology, Ontology, Aesthetics*, Routledge & Kegan Paul, 1987.

Jayamanne, Laleen, '"Forty Acres and a Mule Filmworks" – DO THE RIGHT THING – "A Spike Lee joint": Blocking and Unblocking the Block', in Patricia Pisters (ed.), *Micropolitics of Media Culture: Reading the Rhizomes of Deleuze and Guattari*, Amsterdam University Press, 2001, pp. 235–49.

Jenkins, Henry, 'Reception Theory and Audience Research: The Mystery of the Vampire's Kiss', in Christine Gledhill and Linda Williams (eds), *Reinventing Film Studies*, Edward Arnold, 2000, pp. 165–82.

Johnson, Mark, *The Body in the Mind: The Bodily Basis of Meaning, Imagination, and Reason*, The University of Chicago Press, 1987.

Kaprow, Allan, 'Afterthoughts in 2002', in Geoffrey Hendricks (ed.), *Critical Mass: Happenings, Fluxus, Performance, Intermedia, and Rutgers University, 1958–1972*, Rutgers University Press, 2003a, p. 7.

——*Essays on the Blurring of Art and Life*, expanded edition, University of California Press, 2003b.

Keane, Stephen, *Cinetech: Film, Convergence and New Media*, Palgrave, 2007.

Kemper, Tomas, 'Review of Projecting a Camera', *International Journal of Communication*, vol. 1 (2007), pp. 143–8.

Kennedy, Barbara, *Deleuze and Cinema: The Aesthetics of Sensation*, Edinburgh University Press, 2000.

Kieffer, Gilbert, 'Le postulat premier de la non-esthétique future' paper given at 'Non-philosophy Now' conference, Middlesex, November 2003; available at http://www.onphi.net/texte-le-postulat-premier-de-la-non-esthetique-future.-35.html

Knight, Deborah and George McKnight, 'Real Genre and Virtual Philosophy', in William Irwin (ed.), *The Matrix and Philosophy: Welcome to the Desert of the Real*, Open Court Publishing, 2002, pp. 188–201.

Kollias, Hector, 'Taking Sides: Jacques Rancière and Agonistic Literature', *Paragraph*, vol. 30, no. 2 (2007), pp. 82–97.

Kracauer, Siegfried, *Theory of Film: The Redemption of Physical Reality*, Oxford University Press, 1960.

——'The Establishment of Physical Existence', in Gerald Mast et al. (ed.), *Film Theory and Criticism*, Oxford University Press, 1992, pp. 249–59.

Lacan, Jacques, *The Four Fundamental Concepts of Psycho-analysis*, tr. Alan Sheridan, Penguin, 1994.

——*Encore: The Seminar of Jacques Lacan Book XX*, tr. Bruce Fink, Norton, 1999.

Laruelle, François, *Principes de la Non-Philosophie*, Presses Universitaires de France, 1996.

——'What Can Non-Philosophy Do?' tr. Ray Brassier, *Angelaki*, vol. 8, no. 2 (2003), pp. 173–89.

——La lettre de François Laruelle du 30 Mai 2006, 'Les effets-Levinas'; available at http://www.onphi.org/lettre-laruelle----effets-levinas-12.html

Lawrence, Matt, *Like a Splinter in Your Mind: The Philosophy Behind the 'Matrix' Trilogy*, Wiley Blackwell, 2004.

Lenoir, Tim, 'Affect as Interface: Confronting the "Digital Facial Image"', Forward to Mark Hansen, *New Philosophy for New Media*, MIT, 2004, pp. xiii–xxviii.

Lessard, Bruno, '"It's the End of the World!": The Paradox of Event and Body in Hitchcock's *The Birds*', *Film-Philosophy*, forthcoming.

Light, Andrew, *Reel Arguments: Film, Philosophy, and Social Criticism*, Westview Press, 2003.

Litch, Mary, *Philosophy through Film*, Routledge, 2002.

Lowry, Edward, *The Filmology Movement and Film Study in France*, UMI Research Press, 1985.

Lyotard, Jean-François, 'Acinema', in Jean-François Lyotard, *The Lyotard Reader*, ed. Andrew Benjamin, Wiley-Blackwell, 1991, pp. 169–80.

MacNeice, Louis, *Collected Poems*, Faber and Faber, 1979.

Maltby, Richard, '"A Brief Romantic Interlude": Dick and Jane Go to 3 1/2 Seconds of the Classical Hollywood Cinema', in David Bordwell and Noël Carroll (eds), *Post-Theory: Reconstructing Film Studies*, University of Wisconsin Press, 1996, pp. 434–59.

Marks, Laura U., *The Skin of Film: Intercultural Cinema, Embodiment, and The Senses*, Duke University Press, 2000.

Martin, Jean-Clet, *Variations: La Philosophie de Gilles Deleuze*, Payot & Rivages, 1993.
Martin-Jones, David, 'Towards Another "–Image": Deleuze, Narrative Time, and Popular Indian Cinema', *Deleuze Studies*, vol. 1, no. 2 (2008), pp. 25–48.
Masson, Jeffrey, *The Assault on Truth: Freud's Suppression of the Seduction Theory*, Penguin, 1985.
Massumi, Brian, *Parables for the Virtual: Movement, Affect, Sensation*, Duke University Press, 2002.
Mast, Gerald, Leo Braudy, and Marshall Cohen (eds), *Film Theory and Criticism*, Oxford University Press, 1992.
May, Todd, *The Political Thought of Jacques Rancière: Creating Equality*, Penn State Press, 2008.
Mayer, David, 'Acting in Silent Film: Which Legacy of the Theatre?', in Alan Lovell and Peter Krämer (eds), *Screen Acting*, Routledge, 1999, pp. 10–30.
McGinn, Colin, *The Power of Movies: How Screen and Mind Interact*, Pantheon books, 2005.
McGowan, Todd and Sheila Kunkle (eds), *Lacan and Contemporary Film*, Other Press, 2004.
Mengue, Philippe, *Gilles Deleuze ou le système du multiple*, Kimé, 1994.
Merleau-Ponty, Maurice, 'The Film and the New Psychology', in Maurice Merleau-Ponty, *Sense and Nonsense*, tr. Hubert L. Dreyfus and Patricia Allen Dreyfus, Northwestern University Press, 1964, pp. 48–59.
Merrin, William, 'Did You Ever Eat Tasty Wheat? Baudrillard and *The Matrix*', *Scope: Online Journal of Film Studies* (June 2003); available at http://www.scope.nottingham.ac.uk/article.php?issue=may2003&id=257&section=article
Metz, Christian, *Language and Film*, tr. Donna Umiker-Sebeok, Moutin, 1974.
——'Trucage and the Film,' *Critical Inquiry*, vol. 4 (1977): pp. 657—75.
Michotte, Albert, *The Perception of Causality*, tr. J.R. Miles and E. Miles, Methuen, 1963.
Miller, Alice, *Thou Shalt not be Aware: Society's Betrayal of the Child*, tr. H. and H. Hannum, Meridian, 1986.
Miller, Toby, 'Cinema Studies Doesn't Matter; Or, I know What You Did Last Semester', in Matthew Tinkcom and Amy Villarejo (eds), *Keyframes: Popular Cinema and Cultural Studies*, Routledge, 2001, pp. 303–11.
Mitchell, W.J.T., *What Do Pictures Want?*, University of Chicago Press, 2005.
Monaco, James, *How to Read A Film*, Oxford University Press, 1981.
Mulhall, Stephen, *On Film*, Routledge, 2001.
Mullarkey, John, *Bergson and Philosophy*, Edinburgh, 1999.
——'Forget the Virtual', *Continental Philosophy Review*, vol. 37 (2005), pp. 469–93.
——*Post-Continental Philosophy*, Continuum, 2006.
——'Life, Movement, and the Fabulation of the Event', in *Theory, Culture & Society*, vol. 24, no. 6 (2007a), pp. 53–70.
——'The Very Life of Things: Reversing Thought and Thinking Objects in Bergsonian Metaphysics', introduction to *Henri Bergson: An Introduction to Metaphysics* (Bergson Centennial Series), ed. John Mullarkey and Michael Kolkman, Palgrave Macmillan, 2007b, pp. ix–xxxiv.
——'Film as Philosophy: A Mission Impossible?', in Temenuga Trifonova (ed.), *European Film Theory*, Routledge, 2008a, pp. 65–79.
——'Gilles Deleuze', in Felicity Coleman (ed.), *Philosophers on Film*, Acumen, 2008b.
Myer, Clive, 'Playing with Toys by the Wayside: An Interview with Noël Burch', *Journal of Media Practice*, vol. 5, no. 2 (2004), pp. 71–80.

Myers, Tony, *Slavoj Žižek*, Routledge, 2003.
Nancy, Jean-Luc, *Kiarostami Abbas: The Evidence of Film*, Yves Gevaert, 2001.
Naremore, James, *Acting in the Cinema*, University of California Press, 1988.
Nietzsche, Friedrich, *On the Genealogy of Morals and Ecce Homo*, tr. Walter Kaufmann/R. J. Hollingdale, Vintage, 1989.
Nowell-Smith, Geoffrey, 'How Films Mean, Or, from Aesthetics to Semiotics and Half-way Back Again,' in Christine Gledhill and Linda Williams (eds), *Reinventing Film Studies*, New York, Arnold, 2000, pp. 8–17.
Noys, Benjamin, 'Gestural Cinema?: Giorgio Agamben on Film', *Film-Philosophy*, vol. 8 (2004); available at http://www.film-philosophy.com/vol8–2004/n22noys
Olkowski, Dorothea, 'Deleuze and the Limits of Mathematical Time', *Deleuze Studies*, vol. 1, no. 2 (2008), pp. 1–17.
O'Neill, Edward R., 'Apprehending Deleuze Apprehending Cinema', *Film-Philosophy* vol. 2, (1998); available at http://www.film-philosophy.com/vol2–1998/n2oneill
Osborne, Peter, 'Adorno and the Metaphysics of Modernism: The Problem of a "Postmodern" Art', in Andrew Benjamin (ed.), *The Problems of Modernity: Adorno and Benjamin*, Routledge, 1991.
Paul, William, *Laughing Screaming: Modern Hollywood Horror and Comedy*, Columbia University Press, 1994.
Pepperell, Robert, 'Where's the Screen? The Paradoxical Relationship between Mind and World', in Robert Pepperell and Michael Punt (eds), *Screen Consciousness: Cinema, Mind and World*, Rodopi, 2006, pp. 181–97.
Pepperell, Robert and Michael Punt (eds), *Screen Consciousness: Cinema, Mind and World*, Rodopi, 2006.
Perkins, Victor, *Film as Film: Understanding And Judging Movies*, Penguin Books, 1972.
——'Must we Say what we Mean? Film Criticism and Interpretation', *Movie*, vols 34–5 (1990), pp. 1–6.
Perniola, Mario, *Art and Its Shadow*, tr. Massimo Verdicchio, Continuum, 2004.
Pisters, Patricia, 'The Spiritual Dimension of the Brain as Screen: Zigzagging from Cosmos to Earth (and Back)', in Robert Pepperell and Michael Punt (eds), *Screen Consciousness: Cinema, Mind and World*, Rodopi, 2006, pp. 123–37.
Plantinga, Carl, and Greg M. Smith (eds), 'Introduction', in their *Passionate Views: Film Cognition, and Emotion*, The Johns Hopkins University Press, 1999, pp. 1–17.
Plato, *Phaedrus and The Seventh and Eighth Letters*, tr. with introductions by Walter Hamilton, Penguin, 1973.
Radford, Colin, 'Why Are We Moved by the Fate of Anna Karenina?' *Proceedings of the Aristotelian Society*, supp. vol. XLIX (1975), pp. 67–80.
Rancière, Jacques, *The Ignorant Schoolmaster: Five Lessons in Intellectual Emancipation*, Stanford University Press, 1991.
——*La parole muette: Essai sur les contradictions de la littérature*, Hachette littératures, 1998.
——*The Philosopher and His Poor*, ed. and tr. Andrew Parke, Corinne Oster and John Drury, Duke University Press, 2004.
——*Film Fables (Talking Images)*, tr. Emiliano Battista, Berg, 2006.
——*The Future of the Image*, tr. Gregory Elliott, Verso, 2007.
Ridout, Nicholas, *Stage Fright, Animals, and Other Theatrical Problems*, Cambridge University Press, 2006.
Robbins, S.E., 'Bergson, Perception and Gibson', *Journal of Consciousness Studies*, vol. 7, no. 5 (2000), pp. 23–45.
Rodowick, D.N., *Gilles Deleuze's Time Machine*, Duke University Press, 1997.

Rodowick, D.N., *Reading the Figural, or, Philosophy after the New Media*, Duke University Press, 2001.
Ronen, Ruth, 'The Real as Limit to Interpretation', *Semiotica*, vol. 132, no. 1/2 (2000), pp. 121–35.
Ropars-Wuilleumier, Marie-Claire, 'The Cinema, Reader of Gilles Deleuze', tr. Dana Polan, in Dorothea Olkowski and Constantin V. Boundas (eds), *Gilles Deleuze and the Theater of Philosophy*, Routledge, 1994, pp. 255–60.
Rothman, William and Marian Keane, *Reading Cavell's The World Viewed: A Philosophical Perspective on Film*, Wayne, 2000.
Rowlands, Mark, *The Philosopher at the End of the Universe*, Ebury Press, 2003.
Rupert Read and Jerry Goodenough (eds), *Film as Philosophy: Essays on Cinema after Wittgenstein and Cavell*, Palgrave Macmillan, 2005.
Salt, Barry, 'The Statistical Style Analysis of Motion Pictures', *Film Quarterly*, vol. 28, no. 1 (1974), pp. 13–22.
——*Film Style and Technology: History and Analysis*, Starword, 1992.
Santoro, Liberato, 'Aristotle's Concept of Mimesis', in his *The Tortoise and the Lyre: Aesthetic Reconstructions*, Irish Academic Press, 1993.
Schmid, Anne-Francoise, 'The Hypothesis of a Non-Epistemology', paper given at 'Non-philosophy Now' conference, Middlesex, November 2003; available at http://www.onphi.net/texte-the-hypothesis-of-a-non-epistemology-50.html
Schwab, Martin, 'Escape from the Image: Deleuze's Image-Ontology', in Gregory Flaxman (ed.), *The Brain is the Screen: Deleuze and the Philosophy of Cinema*, University of Minnesota Press, 2000, pp. 109–40.
Scott, Charles E. *The Lives of Things*, Indiana University Press, 2002.
Shaviro, Steven, *The Cinematic Body*, University of Minnesota Press, 1993.
Silverman, Kaja, *The Acoustic Mirror: The Female Voice in Psychoanalysis and Cinema*, Indiana University Press, 1988.
Simondon, Gilbert, *L'individu et sa genese physico-biologique*, Presses Universitaires de France, 1964.
Smith, Jeff, 'Movie Music as Moving Music: Emotion, Cognition, and the Film Score', in Carl Plantinga and Greg M. Smith (eds), *Passionate Views: Film Cognition, and Emotion*, The Johns Hopkins University Press, 1999, pp. 147–67.
Smith, Murray, *Engaging Characters: Fiction, Emotion and the Cinema*, Oxford University Press, 1995.
——'Film Theory meets Analytic Philosophy; or, Film Studies and L'Affaire Sokal', *Institute for Cognitive Studies in Film and Video Electronic Newsletter – Special Edition*, vol. 3 no. 1 (November 1997).
Smith, Richard, 'The Philosopher with Two Brains: Review of "Gilles Deleuze: A Reason to Believe in this World"', *Discourse: Journal for Theoretical Studies in Media and Culture*, vol. 20, no. 3 (Fall 1998); also in *Film-Philosophy*, vol. 5, no. 34 (November 2001).
Smith, Susan, *Hitchcock: Suspense, Humour and Tone*, British Film Institute, 2000.
Sobchack, Vivian, *The Address of the Eye: A Phenomenology of Film Experience*, Princeton University Press, 1992.
Souriau, Étienne (ed.), *L'univers filmique*, Flammarion, 1953.
Stacey, Jackie, *Star Gazing: Hollywood Cinema and Female Spectatorship*, Routledge, 1994.
Stewart, Garret, *Framed Time: Toward a Postfilmic Cinema*, The University of Chicago Press, 2007.
Tan, Ed S., *Emotion and the Structure of Narrative Film: Film as an Emotion Machine*, tr. Barbara Fastin, Lawrence Erlbaum, 1996.

Taussig, Michael, *Mimesis and Alterity*, Routledge, 1993.

Thompson, Michael, 'The Representation of Life', in Rosalind Hursthouse, Gavin Lawrence and Warren Quinn (eds), *Virtues and Reasons: Essays in Honor of Philippa Foot*, Clarendon Press, 1995, pp. 248–96.

Thornham, Sue, *Passionate Detachments: An Introduction to Feminist Film Theory*, Arnold, 1997.

Tikka, Pia, 'Cinema as Externalisation of Consciousness', in Robert Pepperell and Michael Punt (eds), *Screen Consciousness: Cinema, Mind and World*, Rodopi, 2006, pp. 139–62.

Varela, Francisco J., Evan Thompson and Eleanor Rosch, *The Embodied Mind: Cognitive Science and Human Experience*, MIT Press, 1991.

Vieillard-Baron, Jean-Louis, *Bergson*, Presses Universitaires de France, 1993.

Waldman, Diane, 'Critical Theory and Film: Adorno and "The Culture Industry" Revisited', *New German Critique*, no. 12 (1977), pp. 39–60.

Walton, Kendall, *Mimesis as Make-Believe: On the Foundations of the Representational Arts*, Harvard University Press, 1990.

Wartenberg, Thomas, *Thinking Through Cinema: Film as Philosophy*, Routledge, 2007.

Watson, Stephen, 'Criticism and the Closure of "Modernism"', *SubStance*, vol. 13, no. 1, issue 42 (1984), pp. 15–30.

Williams, Linda, 'Learning to Scream', in Mark Jancovich (ed.), *Horror Film Reader*, Routledge, 2002, pp. 161–9.

Wollen, Peter, 'Cinema and Technology: An Historical Overview', in Teresa De Lauretis and Stephen Heath (eds), *The Cinema Apparatus*, Macmillan, 1980.

Wuss, Peter, 'Analyzing the Reality Effect in Dogma Films', *The Journal of Moving Image Studies*, vol. 1 (2002); available at http://www.avila.edu/journal/spring02/dogma.pdf

Youngblood, Gene, *Expanded Cinema*, introduction by R. Buckminster Fuller, P. Dutton & Co., 1970.

Zepke, Stephen, 'Becoming a Citizen of the World: Deleuze between Allan Kaprow and Adrian Piper', in Laura Cull (ed.), *Deleuze and Performance*, Edinburgh University Press, forthcoming.

Žižek, Slavoj, *Looking Awry: An Introduction to Jacques Lacan through Popular Culture*, MIT Press, 1991.

——*The Art of the Ridiculous Sublime: On David Lynch's 'Lost Highway'*, University of Washington Press, 2000.

——*Enjoy Your Symptom! Jacques Lacan in Hollywood and Out*, 2nd edn, Routledge, 2001a.

——*Everything You always Wanted to Know about Lacan but were Afraid to Ask Hitchcock*, 2nd edn, Routledge, 2001b.

——*Did Somebody Say Totalitarianism? Four Interventions in the (Mis)use of a Notion*, Verso, 2001c.

——*The Fright of Real Tears: Krzysztof Kieslowski between Theory and Post-Theory*, BFI Publishing, 2001d.

——'The Matrix: Or, the Two Sides of Perversion', in William Irwin (ed.), *The Matrix and Philosophy: Welcome to the Desert of the Real*, Open Court Publishing, 2002, pp. 240–66.

——*Organs without Bodies: On Deleuze and Consequences*, Routledge, 2003.

——*The Metastases of Enjoyment: Six Essays on Women and Causality*, Verso, 2005.

——*The Parallax View*, MIT Press, 2006.

Žižek, Slavoj, 'Afterword: With Defenders Like These, Who Needs Attackers?', in Paul Bowman and Richard Stamp (eds), *The Truth of Žižek*, Continuum, 2007a, pp. 197–255.

——'Science of Appearances, Politics of the Real', in Damian Sutton, Susan Brind and Ray McKenzie (eds), *The State of the Real: Aesthetics in the Digital Age*, I. B. Taurus, 2007b, pp. 181–98.

Zourabichvili, François, 'The Eye of Montage: Dziga Vertov and Bergsonian Materialism', tr. Melissa McMahon, in Gregory Flaxman (ed.), *The Brain is the Screen: Deleuze and the Philosophy of Cinema*, University of Minnesota Press, 2000, pp. 141–9.

Index